MCGILL-QUEEN'S RURAL, WILDLAND, AND RESOURCE STUDIES SERIES
Series editors: Colin A.M. Duncan, James Murton, and R.W. Sandwell

The Rural, Wildland, and Resource Studies Series includes monographs, thematically unified edited collections, and rare out-of-print classics. It is inspired by Canadian Papers in Rural History, Donald H. Akenson's influential occasional papers series, and seeks to catalyze reconsideration of communities and places lying beyond city limits, outside centres of urban political and cultural power, and located at past and present sites of resource procurement and environmental change. Scholarly and popular interest in the environment, climate change, food, and a seemingly deepening divide between city and country, is drawing non-urban places back into the mainstream. The series seeks to present the best environmentally contextualized research on topics such as agriculture, cottage living, fishing, the gathering of wild foods, mining, power generation, and rural commerce, within and beyond Canada's borders.

THE
SUBJUGATION
of CANADIAN
WILDLIFE

THE
SUBJUGATION
of CANADIAN
WILDLIFE

*Failures of Principle
and Policy*

MAX FORAN

McGill-Queen's University Press
Montreal & Kingston • London • Chicago

ISBN 978-0-7735-5316-3 (cloth)
ISBN 978-0-7735-5427-6 (ePDF)
ISBN 978-0-7735-5428-3 (ePUB)

Legal deposit second quarter 2018
Bibliothèque nationale du Québec

Printed in Canada on acid-free paper that is 100% ancient forest free (100% post-consumer recycled), processed chlorine free

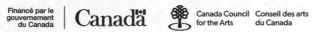

We acknowledge the support of the Canada Council for the Arts, which last year invested $153 million to bring the arts to Canadians throughout the country.

Nous remercions le Conseil des arts du Canada de son soutien. L'an dernier, le Conseil a investi 153 millions de dollars pour mettre de l'art dans la vie des Canadiennes et des Canadiens de tout le pays.

Library and Archives Canada Cataloguing in Publication

Foran, Max, author
    The subjugation of Canadian wildlife : failures of principle and policy / Max Foran.

(McGill-Queen's rural, wildland, and resource studies series ; 9)
Includes bibliographical references and index.
Issued in print and electronic formats.
ISBN 978-0-7735-5316-3 (cloth).–ISBN 978-0-7735-5427-6 (ePDF).–
ISBN 978-0-7735-5428-3 (ePUB)

    1. Wildlife conservation–Government policy–Canada. 2. Wildlife management–Government policy–Canada. I. Title. II. Series: McGill-Queen's rural, wildland, and resource studies series ; 9

QL84.24.F57 2018   333.95'4160971   C2017-908012-1
                                                  C2017-908013-X

This book was designed and typeset by Peggy & Co. Design Inc. in 11/15 Minion.

To Heather,
my inspiration and late soulmate,
who wrote every word with me

And to little Oliver, the ferret,
who inhabited my world but lived in his own

Contents

Preface

This book tells a story about Canadian wildlife and how a deep-seated belief system of anthropocentric principles informs the way animals are "captured" and, ultimately, subjugated and undervalued by government management regimes. It demonstrates the negative impact on wildlife that I believe will continue to be perpetuated in management policies and practices that put human interest front and centre.

All policies and practices, regardless of intent and no matter how diverse, complex, thoughtful, and focused, represent the vision and goals of their framers. When these policies and practices are acted out by governments with respect to nonhuman entities, they represent human perceptions about proper ends. Questions can and should be asked about these perceptions: what are their rationales, how valid are they, and to what degree do they benefit their nonhuman recipients?

The Subjugation of Canadian Wildlife addresses these questions as they pertain to a range of government policies and practices that impact Canadian wildlife. Through an analysis of specific federal and provincial wildlife policies and management practices, it challenges the dominant belief system, which holds that humans stand outside nature and are unique moral beings who owe animals nothing beyond "humane treatment," understood as an avoidance of cruelty and the right to a quick death. It takes strong issue with the belief that wildlife can be thought of as a renewable human resource, one whose "yield" can be managed on the level of species and territory, rather than being perceived as individuals. In reflecting the dominant belief system about animals in thought and practice, official Canadian wildlife management is not keeping pace with species and habitat loss.

Although the focus of this study is on Canadian wildlife and policy, the Canadian case is a telling part of the larger phenomenon of global biodiversity freefall. The loss of ecological integrity and biotic communities, due to ongoing anthropogenic causes, poses an undeniable challenge to the health of our planet. Just as certain species are indicators of general ecological stability in a specific biotic community, so can overall wildlife richness and diversity act as visible indicators of biodiversity degradation worldwide. The current global emphasis on sustainability and stewardship purports to recognize these relationships. However, if the Canadian experience is any indication, the global emphasis on sustainability will inevitably default to socio-economic considerations. To preserve wildlife, we must find a new way of thinking about the animals with whom we share the natural world.

THE SUBJUGATION of CANADIAN WILDLIFE

Introduction:
The Trajectory
of a Belief System

People must change their beliefs before they change their habits.

TOM REGAN

In October 2016 the World Wildlife Fund and partners issued a comprehensive report documenting a 58 per cent reduction in global vertebrate wildlife numbers between 1970 and 2012.[1] The report attributed this alarming trend to anthropogenic causes and included a variety of responses to address environmental and ecological degradation. The report did not, however, suggest that human-centred priorities should be abandoned. Instead, it recommended that they be more disciplined and purposeful in achieving sustainable goals. The advisability of a change in societal values was mentioned, but the basic assumptions about the human relationship with animals were not discussed. This is unfortunate, for the plight of wildlife and biodiversity demands a new way of thinking about the human-nonhuman relationship. Or in short, a new belief system.

The belief system about animals, although multi-layered, is essentially a series of rationalizations, or as Welsh philosopher Mark Rowlands has observed, "Humans are animals that believe the stories they tell about themselves."[2] These "stories" were evident in the hunter-gatherer cultures, were ingrained more firmly in biblical texts, and became truths in the Ancient Greek and Roman periods, when humans claimed superiority over animals on the basis of language, reason, self-awareness, and divine providence. This tale of power and superiority also holds that moral behaviour is an exclusive human faculty. Based on this view, nonhumans lack the capacity to discern between right and wrong, giving them no claim to moral status or to the ethical consideration humans extend to each other. There is no intrinsic wrongness, for example, when a human being kills a mourning dove or a deer. The only ethical duties owed to nonhumans reside in a very limited recognition of sentience as requiring the avoidance of cruelty. Although certain species clearly demonstrate intelligence, reasoning faculties, the capacity to negotiate complex social interactions, and even the possession of communicative powers and higher-order feelings like empathy and a sense of justice, the belief system stands steadfast against more ethical alignments. The notion of assigning moral worth to nonhuman beings, particularly those in the wild, demands a paradigmatic shift in the way humans think about themselves in relation to their fellow creatures. So, despite significant social, educational, scientific, psychological, and technological advances over the past two millennia, the belief system about animals has remained remarkably consistent. The price of change is just too high. When set against these longstanding and indelible assumptions about how humans should relate to animals, the implications of anthropocentric bias in Canadian wildlife policymaking and its management regimes become more transparent and understandable.

Historically, humans have always wrestled with the moral qualms associated with their power over animals. And their solutions have habitually involved rationalizations and ameliorations within the existing power structure. The hunter-gatherers who date from around 80,000 BCE provide the earliest, albeit contested, insights into the human-nonhuman relationship. A common interpretation suggests that hunter-gatherers, in following their natural inclinations, lived in a harmonious relationship with nature.[3] In these cyclical rhythms of being, the lives and ways of animals were vital components. For example, animism – the association of wild animals with the spirit world – was crucial to their construction of meaning.[4] British social anthropologist Tim Ingold believes that the hunter-gatherers treated the land as well as its animals and plants "with due consideration and respect, doing all one can to minimise damage and disturbance."[5] He also suggests that the hunter-prey relationship was one of trust. Similarly, anthropologist Erica Hill contends that the prehistoric Indigenous peoples along the coasts of Chukotka and Alaska conceptualized animals as other-than-human persons and as agents in myth and ritual. She notes that prey animals were perceived as social equals capable of deciding whether to favour humans by allowing themselves to be taken.[6]

Others argue that this interpretation overlooks the human propensity to rationalize. Although religious historian Karl Meuli acknowledges the traditional rituals of respect, they were also accompanied by "feelings of hesitation and bad conscience."[7] Anthropologist Brian Molyneaux, who refers to the "metaphorical status" accorded to animals by hunting and gathering groups, sees their accompanying rituals as attempts to compensate for the inner conflict occasioned by killing a creature who shared their environments.[8] Canadian political philosopher Rod Preece refers to "exculpatory explanations," and animal rights activist Norm Phelps notes the "volunteers for death theory."[9] Either way, the respectful relationship between hunter-gatherer groups and the creatures they hunted resulted in the extinction of fifty species of large mammals in North America, including mammoths, mastodons, horses, giant ground sloths, American camels, lions, and the saber-tooth cat.[10]

The attention paid to early Greek philosophy in defining the belief system about animals tends to undermine the equally formative role of the domestication process, which began between 15,000 and 20,000 years ago and which has been described as the driving force behind the survival and advancement of human civilization.[11] Through the domestication of animals, there emerged a human-oriented view of the world and, more significantly, a sense of human uniqueness. The domestication process was also a rationalized arrangement that separated domesticated animals from their wild brethren.[12] As property, domesticated animals had no autonomy and were forced to furnish labour and to forfeit their lives for food and other uses. At the same time, they were provided with food, shelter, and protection. As Aristotle observed, "All tame animals are better off when they are ruled by man; for then they are preserved."[13] Early animal welfare activist Porphyry, in referencing the status quo, defined the emerging belief system occasioned by domestication in the third century before Christ: "We shall also, after a manner, live the life of brutes, if we reject the use of which they are capable of affording."[14] The long association of domesticated animals with human property ownership contributed markedly to the rigidity of the belief system.

The intellectual underpinnings of the human-nonhuman relationship were defined roughly between the years 350 BCE and 450 CE, or more specifically by Aristotelian and Stoic philosophy and by early Christianity. Before then, animals filled important roles that spoke of domination but not domination by natural right. They permeated lifestyles in early civilizations on several levels.[15] In addition to their common roles as pets, food, labour, and entertainment, they met other human needs. They filled important symbolic functions. Serpents were influential cult objects and served as intermediaries with the supernatural. Sacrificial animals linked humans to the divine and represented covenants with the gods. Divination involving live animals and the entrails of sacrificial offerings enhanced medicinal curative and prophetic powers.[16]

Although all of the above were present in Ancient Greece, a blossoming of thought between 800 and 400 BCE manifested itself in a quest to define human uniqueness and to rise above the beasts. Although many thinkers speculated on the various qualities that set man above other beings, no one presented a systematic account as to why.[17] This task fell to Aristotle (385–322 BCE), a brilliant and prolific workaholic whose writings have earned him a place among Western civilization's greatest thinkers. Aristotle outlined the first systematic argument against animals by privileging the faculty of reason, attributing it to humans only, and linking it to other qualities like belief, concepts, and a sense of justice. He offered no equivocation in the following statement: "We may infer that, after the birth of animals, plants exist for their sake, and that the other animals exist for the sake of man, the tame for use and food, the wild, if not all at least the greater part of them, for food, and for the provision of clothing and various instruments. Now if nature makes nothing incomplete, and nothing in vain, the inference must be that she has made all animals for the sake of man."[18] Aristotle felt that the unique end of man was the happiness of virtue, which was predicated on rationality and achievable through language when men came together in the polis or in political and social organization. Lacking reason and speech, animals were excluded from the polis and denied the virtue and the justice that came with it. Or as he put it, "And it is a characteristic of man that he alone has any sense of good and evil, of just and unjust, and the like, and the association of living beings who have this sense makes a family and a state."[19] Aristotle's disallowance of reason to animals and their exclusion from happiness, justice, belief systems, or kinship with humans established the first draft of a blueprint for the human-nonhuman relationship that endures today in Western thought and practice. It was the first example of raising the bar according to arbitrary rules and standards that no nonhuman could reach. It was not to be the last.

Aristotle's claims about animals failing the test of reason and about all the positive benefits it bestowed on humans were reinforced by Stoicism – essentially a system of ethics involving a life in accordance with nature and guided by virtue – which began around 300 BCE and lasted in various forms for about 500 years. Stoic thought about animals echoed Aristotle's. For example, Seneca (4 BCE–65 CE) said, "Certainly the good cannot in any way occur in a dumb animal; it [the good] belongs to a better and more fortunate nature. There is no good except where there is room for reason."[20] The Stoics, however, went further than Aristotle by claiming that humans had no duties toward animals and could treat them any way they wished.[21] Epictetus (55–135 CE), arguably the most prominent exponent of Stoic philosophy, proclaimed that animals owe humans service but that humankind owes them nothing.[22] The Stoic Roman emperor Marcus Aurelius (121–180 CE) laid it out in more detail when he said: "As to the animals which have no reason and generally all things and objects, do thou, since thou hast reason and they have none, make use of them with a generous and liberal spirit."[23] That moral worth and reason are linked and that both can be attributed only to humans are the most significant assumptions in the belief system about animals.

Although Aristotle and the Stoics are rarely mentioned today outside the halls of academia, their thoughts about humanity's exclusive claim to reason and moral worth remain entrenched in the belief system about animals. Certainly, this is so in Canada, as attested in 1978 by a future chief justice of the Canadian Supreme Court during a court case involving animal cruelty:

The animal is inferior to man and takes its place within a hierarchy which is the hierarchy of the animals, and above all is a part of nature with all its "racial and natural" selections. The animal is sub-ordinate to nature and to man. It will often be in the interests of man to kill and mutilate wild or domestic animals, to subjugate them and, to this end, to tame them with all the painful consequences this may entail for them and, if they are too old or too numerous or abandoned, to kill them. This is why, in setting standards for the behaviour of men towards animals, we have taken into account our privileged position in nature and have been obliged to take into account at the outset the purpose sought.[24]

No Stoic could have said it better.

The rise of Christianity, described as possibly the most anthropocentric religion the world has seen, further consolidated the belief system.[25] Epitomized by spokesmen like Paul (5–67 CE) and Augustine (354–430 CE), early Christianity marginalized animals by allotting them a lowly place in the chain of being and none whatsoever in divine providence. Both rationalized the Scriptures to drive a stronger wedge between man and the beasts. Paul, an ultra-conservative zealot and misogynist who saw humans as the offspring of God and who used Stoic terms and metaphors to enrich his divinely revealed messages, was no friend of animals. He rationalized Deuteronomy 4:25 to conclude that God had no regard for oxen and that therefore man owed them nothing.[26] Similarly, the influential Augustine of Hippo used the Gadarene swine miracle – the account of Jesus exorcising demons from a demented man and placing them into swine, who subsequently committed suicide – to conclude that the moral qualities governing human behaviour do not apply to animals.[27] In linking reason to an immortal soul, Augustine announced a Christian dualism that asserted the ascendancy of the spiritual over the material in a hierarchy that placed humans closer to God. Denied the immortal soul breathed into humans by the Creator, animals occupied a subservient place in Augustine's fervour-driven embellishment.[28] "Irrational animals," he wrote, "that fly, swim, walk, or creep, … are dissociated from us by their want of reason, and are therefore by the just appointment of the Creator subjected to us to kill or keep alive for our own uses."[29] So, as God was being elevated as a figure welcoming to those who did what Christianity urged, animals were excluded entirely from the club. Through Paul and Augustine, Christianity reinforced the Stoics by invoking an omnipotent being who endorsed human exclusiveness. Or as the Second Vatican Council affirmed in 1965, "Human beings are the only creatures on earth that God has wanted for their own sake."[30]

The place of wild animals in Greco-Roman philosophy was of less significance than that of domestic animals. Consensus held that the tame were superior to the wild.[31] With regard to the gentler animals, who could not survive against the cunning, speed, and strength of wild creatures and instead sought out the guardianship of men, the Roman poet Lucretius wrote, "For anxiously they fled the savage beasts, and peace they sought."[32] The place of wild animals in early Christian thought was on the margins. One common theme related to humankind's fallen nature.[33] Having disobeyed God, Adam and Eve had debased humankind and, in so doing, had turned nature and its animals away from a state of bliss and toward one of savagery, which only ascetic men of God could transcend through their own sanctification. Thus, we have apocryphal stories of early saints eliciting friendship and duty from wild animals by virtue of their sanctity. Otters warmed St Cuthbert's chilled feet, a lion guarded St Jerome's donkey, a lioness brought a ram's skin to St Macarius in thanks for curing her sick cubs, a blackbird laid her eggs in St Kevin's hand, which remained immobile until they were hatched.[34] And so on.[35]

Early Christian writers drew parallels between wild animals and humans through strong doses of anthropomorphism and fanciful observations. For example, Theophilus of Antioch (d. 181 CE) believed that flightless birds were weighed down by sin.[36] Basil of Caesarea's (330–379 CE) comments on wild animals stressed their lack of virtue. For instance, he noted that since the not-so-wise owl sees well in the night but not in the day, the owl has a keen sense of vanity but no understanding of the true light. Furthermore, greed is reflected in birds with sharp talons, and duplicity is apparent in octopi who change colour.[37] In his *Etymologiae*, Isidore of Seville (560–636 CE) drew on earlier writers to make wild statements: elephants send their young to islands to escape dragons, beavers castrate themselves and offer their testicles to hunters as a gift for being spared, and female bears birth shapeless offspring to which they give form with their tongues.[38] In short, although wild animals did figure in early Christian thought and texts, they did so primarily through myth, ritual, and observation, rather than through knowledge or understanding, and they did so from the Christian perspective, always implying differences – fundamental, God-ordained differences.

The widespread ignorance about the nature of wild creatures evinces a jarring disconnect in the historic structuring of our relationship with animals. Domestic animals who served humans were portrayed as innocent, whereas the wolf who preyed upon domestic animals was innately evil, a deliberate murderer, if you will. Another example is the long list of birds and other wild creatures who were labelled as evil or verminous and could therefore be killed with impunity. In mediaeval literature, peasants were often portrayed as animals. Even here, wildlife came out second-best. The plodding, productive peasants were likened to the reliable, working domestic animals; if they were rebellious, they were likened to savage and dangerous wild beasts.[39]

Outside philosophical discourse and Christian theology, animals through time retained importance in everyday lives. According to intellectual historian Boria Sax, "If we look at the mediaeval books of hours, which record everyday life in the middle ages among all social classes, it is hard to find a single picture in which animals are absent. These animals are extremely varied in their roles and significance ... Animals penetrate every aspect of life and thought from religion to industry in highly visible ways."[40] The lavishly illustrated bestiaries, the medieval animal trials, and the enduring influence of the folkloric animal familiars who served as intermediaries with the spirit world are cases in point.[41]

The human exclusiveness that flowed from the dovetailing of Aristotelian-Stoic philosophy with Christianity was further reinforced centuries later in very different ways by philosopher and theologian Thomas Aquinas (1225–1274) and by scientist and rationalist philosopher René Descartes (1596–1650). One argued that humans received truths directly from God; the other claimed that humans transcended the material world.

Aquinas, whose works have been described as "the culmination of a legacy that began in Scripture," mirrored Augustine in asserting human dominance under God: "The highest creatures [humans] are under God and are governed by Him, so lower creatures should be under the higher and be governed by them. But of all creatures intelligent creatures are the highest. Therefore the plan of divine providence requires that other creatures should be governed by rational creatures."[42] However, Aquinas went further by asserting that since God transcended any understanding through reason, humans required divine revelation in order to be saved. His implication for animals, with their lack of language, is quite clear: "Now because those who receive a revelation from God ought in the order of divine enactment to instruct others, there needed to be further communicated to them the grace of speech."[43] Yet Aquinas, inadvertently perhaps, allowed animals an indirect concession. Because he was forced to explain scriptural revelations that proclaimed God's regard for animals, Aquinas acknowledged that cruelty to animals was not in line with God's wishes: "Wherever in Holy Scripture there are found prohibitions of cruelty to dumb animals," he wrote, "the object of such prohibition is ... to turn man's mind away from practising cruelty on his fellow men, lest from practising cruelties on dumb animals one should go on further to do the like to men."[44] Commonly referred to as the "indirect duties" argument, the belief that being kind to animals made humans better humans was taken up by other later prominent thinkers like John Locke, Immanuel Kant, and Peter Carruthers, as well as by the Canada Revenue Agency in 2006 when it stated, "The courts have decided that charitable purposes to promote the welfare of animals meet the public benefit test by providing an intangible moral benefit to humanity in general."[45]

Animals reached an all-time historical low in the writings of René Descartes (1596–1650), a Jesuit-educated Frenchman who developed a naturalist account of the world that included an immaterial mind directly related to the human brain and a mechanistic physiology and theory governed by the laws of matter.[46] Descartes's dualism separated humans from the corporeal world of nature.[47] In short, he argued that humans transcended the material body (and nature) via consciousness, reason, language, and the blend of mind and immortal soul. Lacking the above, corporeal animals were in effect mere machines, somewhat above man-made machines perhaps, but machines nonetheless. Or in Descartes's words, "It rather shows that they have no reason at all, and that it is nature which acts in them according to the disposition of their organs, just as a clock, which is only composed of wheels and weights, is able to tell the hours and measure the time more correctly than we can do with all our wisdom."[48] Fellow rationalist philosopher Nicolas Malebranche, in paraphrasing Descartes, said the same thing more succinctly: "Animals eat without pleasure, cry without pain, grow without knowing it; they desire nothing, fear nothing, know nothing."[49]

Descartes's contention that a crying dog was no different from a whining gear that required oil provided a justification for painful experiments on conscious animals.[50] For example, he wrote of testing the function of cardiac arteries by opening the chest of a live rabbit and removing the ribs to expose and then dissect the heart. On another occasion, he verified blood pressure by inserting his finger into the heart of a live dog.[51] Descartes's belief that only entities with rational minds experienced sensations like hunger, thirst, and pain defies any understanding. His view of animals as machines represented a philosophical low point in terms of the human-nonhuman relationship and doubtless was an influential force in legitimatizing vivisection and painful animal experimentation practices. Furthermore, Descartes's belief that humans were not part of the natural world complemented Catholic theology. It too was carried through subsequent centuries as a scientific norm and was to have tremendous implications in modern wildlife policymaking.

The first and arguably the only modification to the dominant belief system occurred in the late seventeenth and the eighteenth centuries and was due to new streams of thought and to changes in popular sentiment. Among the liberating forces were the rise of empiricism, or the belief that the origin of all knowledge is sense experience; the scientific revolution, with its transformative ethic about material truth; and the growing attention to the social contract and to an ideal state based on versions of natural law. At the popular level, an increasing public opposition to blood sports and the visible urban presence of overt cruelty to horses and dogs defined a new attitudinal trajectory. One result was a heightened awareness that one's sentience or feelings were worth considering, not just those of humans but also those of species who were part of human lifestyles. Or in French philosopher Jean-Jacques Rousseau's (1712–1778) words, "It appears, in fact, that if I am bound to do no injury to my fellow-creatures, this is less because they are rational than because they are sentient beings: and this quality, being common both to men and beasts, ought to entitle the latter at least to the privilege of not being wantonly ill-treated by the former."[52]

By this time, too, more practical, or brave, thinkers were saying what Aristotle likely believed but could never bring himself to say outright. Animals were capable of reason, nowhere near the level of humans but enough to demonstrate that they could and did think.[53] One early proponent was Scottish philosopher David Hume (1711–1776), a man who is described as the most important philosopher ever to write in English and whose work is a precursor of contemporary cognitive science. Although other individuals had made similar claims centuries earlier, it was Hume who affirmed that morality had all to do with emotion and nothing to do with reason: "Moral good and evil are certainly distinguished by our sentiments, not by reason."[54] He included animals in this sympathy-based moral spectrum: "'Tis true, there is no human, and indeed no sensible, creature, whose happiness or misery does not, in some measure, affect us … [as] this concern extends itself beyond our own species."[55] Hume's position was carried through by other philosophers until the nineteenth century, when it was developed by English philosopher and social reformer Jeremy Bentham (1748–1832) as a major school of thought known as utilitarianism. Arguing that the most appropriate action was always the one that maximized utility, or the absence of pain, Bentham encapsulated his thoughts on animals in a memorable footnote: "What else is it that should trace the insuperable line? Is it the faculty of reason, or, perhaps, the faculty of discourse? But a full-grown horse or dog is beyond comparison a more rational, as well as a more conversable animal, than an infant of a day, or a week, or even a month, old. But suppose the case were otherwise, what would it avail? The question is not, Can they *reason*? nor, Can they *talk*? but, Can they *suffer*?"[56]

The fusion of utilitarianism and the indirect duties argument to define the proper moral status of animals rounded out a philosophic discourse about animals that had begun with the humanism of the ancient Greeks. Within their entrenched status as inferior, irrational beings, animals were granted moral consideration on very limited terms. A narrow concept of sentience predicated this consideration on the absence of pain, and the indirect duties argument linked humane treatment of animals with individual and civic virtue. Supported by a growing Christian emphasis on God's concern for all his creatures, the classic animal welfare position was consolidated in anti-cruelty legislation in the early nineteenth century in Britain and a few decades later in the United States. It continues to dominate the belief system in Canada and official wildlife policymaking.

In many ways, the modern period has not been kind to animals. The growing technological capacity of humans to control and manipulate physical environments led to a massive assault on the habitats of all nonhuman living beings. The rise of speciesism, or human entitlement to animal exploitation, has entrenched the dominant belief system in spite of organized opposition, changes in public sensitivity toward animals, and most significant, the serious and sustained research on animal mental capabilities.

On the surface, the seminal work of biologist Charles Darwin (1809–1882) reinforced the importance of nonhumans by linking them with humans in an evolutionary continuum. His theories introduced a new and complex debate about the origins of humans and their place in the realm of species continuity. His theories were also not new. Pre-Socratic philosopher Empedocles (c. 490–430 BCE) and many other historical figures had uttered similar sentiments.[57] Darwin's uniqueness lay in his ideas about natural selection, or in arguing that instincts and behaviour were not the results of inherited abilities but were the consequences of the reproductive success of individuals already possessing these useful traits. By contending that animals share reason and consciousness with humans and that human morality is an elaboration of social instincts that other animals share, Darwin laid the scientific foundation for the "difference in degree" argument as a basis for distinguishing between humans and animals. In short, he stood Creationism on its head and put humans back into nature.[58] Further, in making it clear that animals and humans were more similar than different, Darwin raised the question of the existence of conscious states in animals.[59] Darwin's ideas about humans, animals, and their evolutionary ties to each other and the natural world possessed the potential to undermine the belief system. Thus, they were hotly contested by religious figures, laypersons, scientists, and a whole array of intellectual thought. The issue as it unfolded was not about the primacy of human reason, which was not undermined by the evolutionary principle. At stake were Darwin's contentions about the existence of the animal mind.

Despite Darwinian conclusions about species continuity, the idea that animals were capable of conscious thoughts and feelings was anathema to modern scientific thought. For the next hundred years, the pre-eminence of behaviourist psychology, supported in part by early ethologists and the doctrine of logical positivism, firmly rejected the notion of animal consciousness based on the absence of definitive proof. The assumption that subjective experiences – those belonging to the thinking subject alone – were essentially unknowable without the reporting mechanism of language was compatible with cultural norms, or more fundamentally, the abiding belief system about animals.

Early evidence of this anti-mentalist argument for animals came in the hostile reaction to the work of George Romanes (1848–1894), a Canadian-born psychologist and Darwin protégé. Convinced that he could combine his own private subjective thinking with objective observations to draw comparable conclusions about animal thought, Romanes elevated what he called "ejective anthropomorphism" to a scientific method.[60] In his book *Mental Evolution in Animals* (1884), Romanes attributed over two dozen human emotional states to animals based on inference from action and contended that this method was the "only instrument of analysis we possess."[61]

Predictably, Romanes's ideas did not sit well with mainstream scientific and popular opinion. They still do not, as witnessed by the ongoing derisive use of the term "anthropomorphism" to ridicule those who attribute "human" qualities to animals. To John Watson (1878–1958), a leading spokesperson in behavioural psychology, Romanes's interpretation of animal thought was untenable to the point of absurdity,[62] a position shared by another pioneer in experimental psychology, Edwin Boring (1886–1968), who in 1929 called Romanes's anecdotal method "a term of opprobrium in animal psychology."[63]

The most significant counter to Romanes, however, came from a contemporary who actually held him in high esteem and who agreed with him in many ways. Conwy Lloyd Morgan (1852–1936) was an English psychologist who, in trying to add some discipline to Romanes's attempts to explain animal behaviour, wrote what has been described as "possibly the most important single sentence in the history of the study of animal behavior."[64] A derivative of the parsimony principle, his approach to animal psychology, known as Morgan's canon, stated, "In no case may we interpret an action as the outcome of the exercise of a higher psychical faculty, if it can be interpreted as the outcome of the exercise of one which stands lower in the psychological scale."[65] In other words, one should not attribute complex mental behaviour to animals when a simpler instinctual or conditioned-response explanation is feasible.

Morgan's reductionist canon became the standard by which mental states in animals were rejected.[66] On this interpretation, animal capabilities could be assessed solely through learned behaviours because animals were unable to convey their feelings meaningfully to humans via language. In the absence of definitive proof, it was scientifically valid to assume that animals had no concept of self, no awareness of mortality, no notion of justice, no capacity for empathy, or none of the higher-order feelings that humans shared. In the first half of the twentieth century, under the influence of these beliefs and the emerging doctrines of logical positivism – which denied metaphysics and argued instead that "for a statement of fact to be genuine, some possible observations must be relevant to the determination of its truth and falsehood" – the right to exploit "unthinking, uncaring" animals in experimental laboratories, factory farms, and wherever they could be of service to humans became a comfortable cultural norm.[67] Or, put more simply, the justification for modern speciesism.

In the second half of the twentieth century, the rise of the cognitive sciences and the stirrings of the animal rights movement paved the way for modifications in the way people thought about animals. Much of the scientific community and, to a lesser degree, public opinion conceded to some animals the faculty of reason, albeit limited, and the capacity for volition involving individual choice and will. However, it was the decline of behaviourism that helped to shift the debate about the mental capacities of animals to the question of higher-order consciousness. Proponents argued that the parsimony principle itself was anthropomorphic and that degrees of animal consciousness could be inferred from scientific observation involving experiments on animal behaviour in the wild and further documented through brain research. As ethologist Nicholas Thompson noted in 1994, "Attributing mental states to animals is no more controversial than attributing those same states to human beings."[68]

A leading pioneer in legitimatizing claims for consciousness in animals was Donald Griffin (1915–2003), a cognitive ethologist who in the early

1970s refuted behaviourist notions and presented a compelling research-based argument in support of the presence of mental images and their practical applications in animals. In linking animal communication to human language, Griffin contended that "the employment of diversified communication systems by animals becomes evidence that they have mental experiences and communicate with conscious intent."[69] Griffin was further convinced that the "capability of conscious awareness under some conditions may well be so essential that it is the *sine qua non* of animal life, even for the smallest and simplest animals that have any central nervous system at all."[70] He also speculated on the possibility of reflective consciousness in animals.

Ongoing research in neuroscience and social neuroscience is demonstrating parallels in animals that reach into higher-order consciousness. Neuroscientist Jaak Panksepp contends, "Despite historical resistance, the existence of diverse emotional-affective networks in animal brains is empirically definitive."[71] For example, science has shown that the capacity for subjective experience is enabled by integrative structures in the mid-brain and is universal among vertebrates.[72] Another prominent neuroscientist, Antonio Damasio, sees animals as having a core consciousness that enables a sense of self, independent of reason and language.[73] Neurons, the brain's building blocks, are similar across species. Spindle neurons, for example, which are linked to emotion, vocalization control, and even facial expressions, and which were once considered unique to humans, have been found in the cerebral cortex of humpback whales.[74] Mirror neurons, which allow humans to recognize the actions and intentions of others, have been discovered in two regions of the brain in macaques.[75] The notion that the prefrontal cortex is not the only area of the brain responsible for conscious self-awareness received further support when a group of prominent scientists signed the Cambridge Declaration on Consciousness (2012), which affirms that "the neural substrates of emotions do not appear to be confined to cortical structures" and that "the weight of evidence indicates that humans are not unique in possessing the neurological substrates that generate consciousness. Non-human animals, including all mammals and birds, and many other creatures, including octopuses, also possess these neurological substrates."[76]

Field research is also leading scientists to draw conclusions about higher states of consciousness in animals. For example, baboons engage in deliberate acts of deception, magpies exhibit grief, and dolphins will band together to keep an injured fellow afloat.[77] Evolutionary biologist and ecologist Marc Bekoff believes that morality is an evolved trait shared by humans and nonhumans and that the cerebral cortex in nonhuman mammals "is linked with social organization, empathy, intuition about the feelings of others, as well as rapid, gut reactions."[78] Bekoff's research shows how different species of animals, including coyotes, elephants, and macaques, possess complex social behaviours that include a sense of justice, cooperation, empathy, and a readiness to aid their companions in distress.[79] Similarly, Dutch primatologist and ethologist Frans de Waal, whose research focuses on the social behaviour of primates, has demonstrated their facility for conflict resolution, cooperation, fairness, food sharing, an awareness of the permanence of death, and the capacity for empathy.[80] The presence of affective states like boredom and pleasure are acknowledged in some animals, and preliminary research is suggesting that some insects possess ganglion structures that are similar to the midbrain in mammals and enable the capacity for subjective experiences.[81] Bees, for example, are not only capable of learned behaviour but also possess the ability to pass it on to their fellows. Recent research has discovered that octopi, squid, and cuttlefish are able to adapt more quickly and flexibly to environmental changes by constantly editing or changing their RNA and bypassing the slower genetic mutations or changes to their DNA.[82] And there is always the unknown, as well as even the question of our right or need to know. For example, what impelled a group of seventeen wild turkeys on a Massachusetts street to circle a dead cat in almost ritualistic fashion?[83]

The consciousness debate is pivotal because of its link to moral worth or ethical treatment. Both are denied to animals on the grounds that they lack the mental ability to behave morally. And although research is increasingly demonstrating that certain species are moral beings, this evidence is not convincing nor sufficiently apparent to undermine the belief system. Many continue to deny animal consciousness on the grounds that, lacking language, animals can never demonstrate a truly conscious mental state. Others dismiss animal consciousness and its moral implications simply because it can never match that of humans.[84] Cognitive scientist Daniel Dennett denies consciousness in animals because "it is necessary to have a certain set of informational organization which is swiftly achieved in one species, ours, and in no other."[85]

Part of the reason has to do with the fact that animal capacities continue to be measured in human terms. Griffin, for example, debunked the idea that, to exist at all, animal consciousness must be identical to human, calling it a truly anthropomorphic deceit in assuming a single species monopoly of a crucial quality.[86] Similarly, American philosopher Thomas Nagel – in his classic article "What Is It Like to Be a Bat?" (1974) – gave a clear defence of consciousness in animals.[87] Although he recognized that an animal's subjective experience was beyond human scientific conclusiveness and essentially unknowable, Nagel was also convinced that these experiences existed and were "fully comparable in richness of detail to our own."[88] In hammering behaviourist doctrine and status quo thinking, Nagel stated the basic animal-consciousness position clearly: "To deny the reality or logical significance of what we can never describe or understand is the crudest form of cognitive dissonance."[89]

Other critics of the human-nonhuman relationship were not concerned about whether animals possessed sufficient higher-order consciousness levels to warrant moral worth but rather contested the legitimacy of assigning moral worth solely on the above criteria. To take the first of three examples, in 1975 Australian philosopher Peter Singer argued that sentience alone warrants moral consideration. He equated pleasure and pain with interests or preference satisfaction. These interests apply to both humans and sentient nonhumans, or in Singer's words, "The interests of every being affected by an action are to be taken into account and given the same weight as the like interests of every other being."[90] Since humans accept the principle of equality as a sound moral basis for relations with their own species, there is no sound reason why it should not be extended to members of other species. Second, writing in 1995, British philosopher Colin McGinn focused on subjective experience, the lowest level of consciousness, and argued that it is sufficient to warrant moral standing. He contended that if we are able to recognize animals as selves, interacting with their environments through their own subjective experiences, we can then empathize with them as moral beings. His case for moral standing in animals and their unequivocal claims of ethical treatment was quite clear: "This implies that no moral dividing-line can be erected around the idea that animals merely experience while we have a self that undergoes experience."[91] Finally, to American philosopher Tom Regan, writing in 1983, the central issue lies in a being's inherent value. Regan contended that any being who consciously negotiates and experiences his or her environment and life course is the subject of a life that matters to that being, a life with inherent value and therefore moral worth. Since most sentient mammals are able to satisfy their preferences by acting independently, intentionally, and emotionally, they too are subjects of a life and deserve moral consideration equal to that afforded humans.[92]

Not surprisingly, the positions of Singer, McGinn, Regan, and those who presented similar arguments are hotly contested. Both Singer and Regan "appeal to the notion that some beings have qualitatively different and ultimately more valuable experience for purposes of resolving conflicts between beings who have moral standing."[93] McGinn's association of any subjective experience with moral worth requires more elaboration. But that is not the point. The importance of Singer, Regan, McGinn, and other animal advocacy thinkers lies in their challenge to an entrenched belief system built around power relationships based on human superiority. In the traditional belief system, animals are regarded as inferior to humans because of cognitive deficiencies and are thus both powerless and devoid of inherent moral worth. Singer, McGinn, and Regan, among others, shifted the prime determinant in the human-nonhuman relationship from power to respect. Singer did so by giving equal consideration to interests based on utilitarian principles, McGinn by refusing to privilege human consciousness, and Regan by extending the inherent value of life to animals, thus helping to provide an intellectual basis not only for treating all sentient creatures with the same respect that humans expect from each other but also for suggesting that a creature's claim to ethical treatment has nothing to do with levels of cognition or higher-order consciousness and everything to do with complementary, self-directed life courses.

Singer, Regan, McGinn, and others argue for the rights of animals as opposed to the accepted animal welfare position, which focuses on animal cruelty, neglect, and inhumane practices.[94] Animal rights proponents want to end all instrumental use of animals and to apply the same ethical treatment humans expect from each other to animals as well. Thus far, the success of the animal rights movement has been limited. It is still subject to ridicule, the first stage that any new social movement must endure before discussion and ultimate adoption. Moreover, given that the animal rights proponents are asking for a different belief system, they are facing a daunting task.

These scientific and philosophical developments in the second half of the twentieth century and into the new millennium were accompanied by an increasing awareness of animal issues at mainstream levels. Many activist groups now work to improve the lot of animals. A survey of websites will show hundreds of organizations actively engaged worldwide in support of animal concerns. The vast majority of these bodies operate from the classic welfare position, condemning cruelty and working to secure better treatment of animals. Only a small minority take the animal rights position and advocate a different belief system altogether. But many people have developed a heightened sensitivity toward animals generally, especially companion animals, which have entered personal value systems at a high level. Some positive outcomes are visible. Animals in circus acts are frowned upon, and publicized instances of cruelty are condemned by popular outrage.

It would be wrong however to assume that these challenges to the belief system about animals belong to the modern era. Opposing voices have always been present, many making the same sorts of arguments that are used today. Pythagoras (570–485 BCE), whose school of naturalist philosophy lasted for centuries, argued for kinship based on the interchangeability of human and animal souls. "Animals are akin to us," he wrote, "sharing our life and our basic constituents and composition, linked in a kind of brotherhood."[95] Empedocles (c. 490–430 BCE) believed that the end of a bygone age of friendship between humans and animals was caused by humans when they killed and ate animals.[96] He also reached into an ecological continuum when he said, "There is no birth in mortal things, and no end in ruinous death. There is only mingling and interchange of parts, and it is this we call 'nature.'"[97] Theophrastus (c. 372–287 BCE) was Aristotle's colleague and best friend. Yet he did not think animals existed for the sake of humans. He envisaged a kinship based on shared origins and nature that entitled animals to justice as moral beings.[98]

Plutarch (c. 46–120 CE) articulated an animal rights position in the first century after Christ by advocating justice for animals and by separating morality from reason.[99] In emphasizing the capacity of animals to exhibit emotion, desire, social awareness, and even hostility, Plutarch made the first claim that associated moral worth in animals with their sentience. Sextus Empiricus (160–210 CE) was a Skeptic who challenged the veracity of human knowledge and argued that "the so-called 'non-rational'" animals were not inferior to humans in the acuteness of their senses nor in their capacity to discern between truth and falsehood.[100] Porphyry (234–305 CE) granted reason and justice to animals and believed that communication by language was not unique to humans.[101]

Francis of Assisi (1181–1226) offered the simplicity of coexistence and a Christian alternative to Aquinas's rigid human-centred theology.[102] Michel de Montaigne (1533–1592) lashed out at human pride and ignorance for building barriers of separation between humans and nonhumans.[103] Tom Tryon (1634–1703) used the word "rights" as it applied to animals as early as 1688.[104] Francis Hutcheson (1694–1746) argued that moral value for animals had nothing to do with their lack of moral sense or cognitive capacities but rather lay in human appreciation of their experiences.[105] Humphrey Primatt (1736–1779), in focusing on pain, championed the animal anti-cruelty cause by writing one of the most powerful defences of animals ever written, and he was a fitting example of the early modern Christian influence, using the indirect duties position to gain more humane treatment of animals.[106] In 1894 Henry Salt (1851–1939) wrote the first book that considered animal rights as separate from animal welfare.[107]

But despite modern scientific and philosophical thought and historical voices of animal advocacy, the belief system has stood firm in exalting reason and human exclusiveness and in linking them to moral standing. Even when compassion is acknowledged as being fundamental to moral values and behaviour, it is not extended to animals, who are seen as warranting consideration not as fellow beings capable of their own subjective experiences but as property and things whose sentience is acknowledged only as regards their capacity to feel pain or their right to a quick death – a right often dishonoured, as witnessed by the legal sale of diabolical instruments of death like leg-hold and glue traps. That these fundamental assumptions are based on subjective determinations about degrees of reason and consciousness and even more so on conclusions about God's priorities is irrelevant. On the surface, this might seem surprising given human advancements and enlightenment over the centuries. The tight grip of Christian authoritarianism is weaker, secular values are broader, the number of scholars challenging the belief system has increased, and most importantly, a wider awareness of the value of inclusiveness has become part of many nations' public fabric. But, as Canadian philosophers Sue Donaldson and Will Kymlicka have noted, "Defenders of human superiority will continue to engage in increasingly contorted mental gymnastics to defend the privileging of human beings."[108] Thus, at the basic level of human need and utility, the place of animals remains exploitive. Demand for animal products has increased exponentially, a demand that involves pain, misery, and death for billions of animals annually. Tens of thousands of animals are put near or above their pain thresholds every year in Canadian testing facilities.[109] Canadian law allows the legal killing of wild animals, and in at least one province, hunting is seen as a human right.

Generally, and particularly at all three levels of government – legislative, executive, and judicial – the fixed place of animals in the human belief system presumes their inferiority and ongoing instrumental use regardless of any scientific evidence to the contrary. Despite a growing awareness of animal issues and the close ties between wildlife and biodiversity health, a very human-centred view of the world generally pervades the political and bureaucratic halls of power where decisions are made and policies set. Politicians, being elected by majority public opinion, represent the dominant belief system in its most unabridged form. In the body public, the animal belief system accommodates an empathetic element. Not so in the politics of government. Elections are not fought on wildlife issues; wildlife are not even mentioned in campaign platforms. With rare exceptions, those who sit in the House of Commons, Senate, and the various legislatures exhibit minimal interest in the welfare of the wild creatures who eke out their lives in the constituencies of these government officials, and when they do take note of wildlife, their views are often hostile. The absence of a critical mass demanding change means that in the legislatures of Ottawa, Edmonton, Toronto, and all the other halls of political power in Canada, the plight of wildlife remains enmeshed in the dominant belief system. Under bureaucratic management regimes, more so than in the public eye, wild creatures are things whose individual claims to life are virtually nonexistent.

In short, most humans and their governments believe they are immutably different from animals and like it that way. We are a long way from philosopher Steve Sapontzis's hope that "the evolution of our concept of animals will merge with the evolution of our concept of humanity, and we will come to recognize that together we all form one living, morally significant and worthy community of interests on this planet."[110] The issue at stake here is why and how this perceived gulf between humans and nonhumans should absolve the former almost entirely from moral and ethical obligations to other sentient living beings. The following discussion explores the implications of this belief system as they apply to wildlife and wildlife policymaking in Canada.

PART ONE:
MANAGING WILDLIFE
UNDER THE BELIEF SYSTEM

Wildlife Policies

Wildlife preservation is a catastrophic heart-breaking disaster.
JOHN LIVINGSTON

Wildlife are the essence of interwoven existence. They are our brethren, linked to us in an evolutionary unfolding, and exist as autonomous beings on a planet to which no one has exclusive claim. Wildlife are ecological engines contributing immeasurably to the vital cycles and balances that sustain all life. From soil aeration to nutrient cycling, water purification, pollination, seed germination, and seed dispersal, wild creatures contribute to biotic communities in ways humans have lost or never had. Aesthetically, wildlife surpass any human creation. They present palettes of colour, beauty, and intricacy of form, harmonies of sound, and wondrous balletic, artistic, and athletic displays by being who they are. Entrances to their worlds are invitations to mystery, excitement, apprehension, and above all, the wondrous diversity of life. They complement the wilderness that demarks the place where humans hesitate to go and embody it in ways that define the timelessness of existence. Above all, they live independently in their own worlds and in their own ways, and to use Canadian naturalist John Livingston's wise words, "therein is comfort."[1]

As the discussion in this book's introduction has shown, the belief system that established the human-nonhuman relationship was mostly about domestic animals. The limits of human moral responsibility were defined and accepted as animal welfare and, in the main, pertained primarily to domesticated animals. In general, wild animals were not the primary focus in the 2,500-year process that defined the Western belief system about animals. Not living among humans, wildlife did not form the interactive relationships endured (and sometimes enjoyed) by domesticated animals. Their presence in everyday lives was less common and not subject to the ritualized familiarity that bound domestic animals to their masters. Whether despised and feared, commercialized and hunted, or symbolized and mythologized, wild animals remained outliers for centuries. Most knowledge about them was local, often grounded in hearsay and individual experiences, and made livelier by story, lore, and legend. Alien and beyond direct human control, wild animals occupied a lesser place in the human-nonhuman relationship than their domesticated fellows.

It is also true that humankind's achievements are in inverse proportion to the health of every other living thing on the planet, whether furred, feathered, scaled, or otherwise. Canada is no exception. Some species face extinction. Many more are threatened or sensitive. The pattern is not uniformly dismal, but the trend for most species is downward. The threats are varied and numerous. They include climate change, development pressures, agricultural expansion, urbanization, harmful public uses, invasive species, and pollution. All of the above impact wildlife habitat. Individually, they put certain species at risk. Collectively, they present an insurmountable barrier for wildlife to overcome. All are directly attributable to human self-interest.

Compared to other temperate zone countries, Canada is rich in wildlife diversity and abundance.[2] Its forests, plains, foothills, mountains, tundra, coastal seas, rivers, deltas, lakes, coulees, wetlands, marshes, and bogs are home to 244 mammal species, 505 bird species, 227 species of freshwater fish, 77 species of turtles and other reptiles, 57 species of amphibians, and 48,000 known species of invertebrates.[3] Unlike almost all other countries similarly favoured, Canada has a strong economy and a mature rule of law, or in other words, the financial capability and the institutional stability to be a global model for wildlife protection. Thus far, experience has shown otherwise. Many countries see Canada as a laggard rather than a leader. According to English psychologist Richard Ryder, Canadian governments and the media are unsympathetic, even hostile, to animal advocacy issues.[4] A 2003 background paper on wildlife conservation in Canada concluded,

"While the language of 'wildlife' has captured the popular imagination, it has failed to become the language of public policy."[5] It is with government approval that Canadian wildlife are shot, trapped, poisoned, displaced, evicted, and systematically killed regularly, consistently, and with little indication of change.

WILDLIFE MANAGEMENT IN CANADA

Wildlife's integration into the modern Canadian belief system about animals occurred primarily under the influence of the conservation movement in the first half of the twentieth century, when speciesism began defining the new human order. Regardless of changing attitudes toward wild animals over the past forty years, wildlife management has remained virtually unchanged. The classification of wildlife as a resource translated into a management system that recognized species, not individuals. Today, even as research has demonstrated heightened cognitive and mental states in many species, the modern management paradigm and the belief system that underpins it ignore the autonomous nature of wild beings, their life-negotiating skills, sophisticated social engagements, interactive communication levels, and behavioural complexities, as well as the abundant qualities they share with humans. It assumes the irrelevance of individual lives, assesses the worth of species based on human priorities, dictates a lot of death on rationalized grounds, and exhibits a paranoia about any threat posed by wild animals to humans.

The dominant historical narrative about wildlife in Canada attempts to explain how they were integrated into human perceptions, values, lifestyles, and policies. Some of these narratives recognize that wildlife were mute victims of human priorities. George Colpitts, for example, affirms the human-centred implications of classifying wildlife as a resource.[6] Donald Wetherell, in his study on the history of wildlife in prairie Canada, pays wildlife their due as sentient individual beings and dwells on attitudinal change by acknowledging growing awareness about animals' cognition and their emotional states.[7] In the main, however, Canadian wildlife historians have not been overly concerned with the moral and ethical implications of self-awareness or consciousness in sentient nonhumans. Furthermore, early environmental studies rarely focused on wildlife specifically, let alone in terms of their existence as living beings. In short, although the issues relevant to human interactions with wildlife have been discussed and debated, the belief system that underpins them has been an unstated given.

The following discussion is written from a different viewpoint and argues that the disrespect endemic in wildlife policies foreordains an ongoing downward trajectory despite remedial interventions and public advocacy. Whether as a resource to be exploited or as a sustainable component of an ecosystem, wildlife are victims in management regimes already constrained by a wide variety of anthropogenic disturbances. Since wild creatures receive minimal ethical consideration and since human incursions into their domains are ongoing and relentless, the management outcomes are predictable. The human intention to manage wildlife professionally and sustainably is not in dispute in this discussion. The point is solely to indicate how the belief system works against wild animals as living beings by treating them as things in management regimes that are supposed to value and protect them as living beings. As biologist Paul Paquet has so aptly observed, management *of* wildlife is not the same as management *for* wildlife.[8]

Modern wildlife management has its roots in the early-twentieth-century conservation movement and its later refinement as ecology in the second half of the century.[9] Conservation stressed careful management of natural resources, whereas ecology focused on the interactions that sustained the biotic community. They evolved in North America in reaction to the visible environmental ill effects of human expansion in industry, agriculture, logging, and mining. Although preservationists like John Muir (1838–1914) recognized the economic underpinnings of the conservationist movement and their threat to the natural world, the new resource-management paradigm, based on sustainability, wise use, efficiency, subjective judgments, and scientific guidance, defined the new order. In this conservationist environment, wildlife were not seen primarily as integral components of the natural world. Rather, they were objects of study to be managed as renewable resources for recreational and commercial purposes. But as geographer Dean Bavington has shown, wildlife, being living components in natural environments, embody too many unknowns to be managed either along predictable, prescribed lines or subject to the uncertainties inherent in adaptive management.[10]

Although it is commonly accepted that wildlife management has become more refined over the past half-century with an emphasis on ecology and the whole biotic community, principles inherent in the original conservationist mentality still prevail. It is assumed that humans are not part of the natural world, and it is taken for granted that wild living beings are a renewable resource to be managed in the human interest and that wildlife have no self-conscious states. The enduring legacies of pioneer Canadian conservationist Jack Miner and his more influential American contemporary Aldo Leopold are two outstanding individual examples of how beliefs about wildlife forged in the early conservationist movement still underpin wildlife management philosophy.

Jack Miner

Jack Miner (1865–1944) was born to a poor Ohio family that relocated to marginal agricultural land in Kingsville, Ontario, in 1878.[11] The discovery of commercial clay deposits on the 100-acre property ensured a level of prosperity for the family through the establishment of a brick and tile business, while inadvertently providing the basis for Jack Miner's bird sanctuary. Miner had a fascination with migratory ducks and geese, and when he discovered that they returned to the same water bodies each year, he transformed one of his clay pits into a pond to attract them. Four years later, in 1908, he had hundreds of birds. The number grew into thousands when he established more ponds. In 1909 Miner began banding his birds to gain knowledge of migratory patterns, and during his lifetime he banded over 50,000 ducks and 40,000 geese. By 1913 his ponds had become a sanctuary, being described by the Canadian Commission of Conservation as the "most spectacular demonstration of protection that you could see on the continent of North America."[12]

Miner was a charismatic figure who willingly and ably communicated his messages about conservation to thousands who read his books, saw him on film, and listened to his speeches and radio broadcasts. With his homespun wisdom and folksy style, Miner became a household name at a level rarely matched by any celebrity. Likened to both Francis of Assisi and Aristotle, Miner counted admirers among the rich, famous, and powerful, as well as the millions who affectionately referred to him as Uncle Jack.[13] According to one writer, Miner spoke "to more people than any other individual" between 1910 and 1940.[14] The recipient of numerous awards from private institutions and government, Miner was described by the chair of the World Wildlife Fund as "an outstanding champion of conservation issues and a leader in the raising of awareness of wildlife conservation."[15] His legacy is continued today through the Jack Miner Bird Sanctuary and the Jack Miner Bird Foundation.

Three elements of the early conservation movement were embodied in Jack Miner. First, he held the conviction that humankind's God-given right was to mould, guard, and protect nature. Second, he was an avid hunter who slaughtered the geese he purported to revere, including a percentage of the founding flocks he attracted to his original pond. In fact, one critic noted that between 1915 and 1925, Miner's sanctuary caused the deaths of more geese than it saved.[16] Third, Jack Miner ascribed to the "good animal versus bad animal" syndrome. He hated the animals who preyed upon his geese and gentle birds, calling them cannibals and murderers. He shot them, trapped them, hung them by the leg to be eaten by others, and took satisfaction in annihilating other bigger predators with the rifle he knew how to use so well. Miner's beliefs about humans standing outside nature, the positive place of hunters, and the management of predators within human comfort zones, all hallmarks of the early conservation movement, are beliefs that still influence modern wildlife management practices.

Aldo Leopold

There can be no doubt that Aldo Leopold (1887–1948) was a pivotal transformative agent in the North American conservation movement. By integrating ethics and science with an empathy for the land, Leopold helped to change the way professionals thought about the biotic community. Described as an "American Isaiah" and a man whose role was "instrumental in shaping modern game conservation, a force that united hunters, conservationists and landowners with the idea and intent of stewardship," Leopold was a crucial agent in bringing an ecological and ethical viewpoint to managing the land. Nearly seventy years after his death, his name and philosophy are identified with proper scientific conservation practice.[17] Or as he put it himself, "I must ask you to think of land and everything on it (soil, water, forests, birds, mammals, wildflowers, crops, livestock, farmers) not as separate things, but as parts – organs – of a body. That body I call the land (or if we want a fancy term, the biota)."[18] Yet, although his words echoed with the visionary zeal of a true change agent, Leopold's ideas about wild animals, or more specifically, high-profile wild animals, remained mired in early conservationist thought.

Born to a well-to-do family, Leopold received a privileged education and graduated with a master's degree in forestry from Yale Forest School in 1909.[19] He was employed in the federal forestry service in several capacities, during which time he became interested in wildlife, or more specifically, game animals. He left the forestry service in the mid-1920s, and between 1928 and 1932 he travelled through the north-central states, conducting several game surveys with funding from the Sporting Arms and Ammunition Manufacturers' Institute. His appraisal of the environmental factors that affect game species and the subsequent publication of his widely influential book *Game Management* (1933) made him the national authority on a new approach to wildlife conservation, one that linked the production and management of game with habitat carrying capacity. In 1933 he joined the Department of Agricultural Economics at the University of Wisconsin, where he held the United States' first chair in game management. He remained in this position until his untimely death from a heart attack in 1948 while fighting a fire near his farm.

Leopold articulated the harmony of the biotic community in his eloquent essays published in *A Sand County Almanac and Sketches Here and There* (1949). By integrating ethics and science with an empathy for the land, Leopold helped to change the way professionals thought about the biotic community. His land ethic has become the bible for humankind's belief in managing the land holistically along ethical and scientific lines. Encapsulated in two now-famous sentences, Leopold's ethic proclaims, "A thing is right when it tends to preserve the integrity, stability and beauty of the biotic community. It is wrong when it tends otherwise."[20] On the surface, his management philosophy was simple: "Conservation is a pipe-dream as long as *Homo sapiens* is cast in the role of conqueror, and his land in the role of slave and servant. Conservation becomes possible only when man assumes the role of citizen in a community of which soils and waters, plants and animals are fellow members, each dependent on the others, and each entitled to his place in the sun."[21] In his life story, we see the driven majesty of a man who saw the land in ethical terms but whose view of wildlife was more fractured and ambivalent.

Leopold believed that game animals were a crop to be managed like any other agro-resource.[22] In his words, "Game Management is the art of making land produce sustained annual crops of wild game for recreational use" and, more revealingly, the test of whether or not man is civilized.[23] He was also a lifelong, unrepentant hunter who purchased his Sand County farm primarily as a hunting preserve.[24] He once told a wildlife society that the future of hunting was contingent on the public's capacity to see the land as a community of belonging, without which, as he put it, "We cannot produce much to shoot."[25] Not surprisingly, given this mindset, Leopold reached into rationalizations to justify the inclusion of hunting in his land ethic. Aside from believing that hunting was instinctual, an aesthetic re-enactment of the past, and a testament to human civilization, Leopold argued that hunters were necessary components of the food chain in an era when space had become constricted and artificialized.[26]

Like Jack Miner, this man of contradictions who once referred to "a sense of kinship with fellow-creatures; a wish to live and let live," but who also lauded the fox hunt as one of the purest of sports, articulated the cognitive dissonance typical of hunters generally.[27] For example, after waxing sadly on the loneliness of a marsh where cranes no longer came, Leopold described the death throes of a duck he had shot, who "hit the snowy ice with a thud and lay there, belly up, red legs kicking."[28] Then, after grieving with a goose who had lost his mate, he could happily record after a successful hunt that "all the geese we could eat lay kicking on the [sand] bar."[29] As philosopher Peter List kindly notes, Leopold never really reconciled his ethical position about hunting as a sport with his role as a protector of animals.[30] Or as anthropologist Matt Cartmill wryly observes, most humans (Leopold included) "prize consistency less highly than sausage."[31]

With his notions about population control, carrying capacity, and desirous wildlife as a crop to be managed, Leopold epitomized the two elements of the belief system. He held the species-specific view, which implies a lack of conscious mental states in animals. He also adhered to the doctrine of human uniqueness and, like the early conservationists, believed that humans needed to preserve the natural world by managing its components. The validity of hunting in wildlife management was well served by Leopold's notion of game as a renewal crop in a balanced biotic community and by his separation of the living beings he loved from the things he killed. ·

Undeniably, Leopold wanted to use research and the methods of science to renew a natural environment under threat by human expansion and exploitation, as well as to encourage a new social concept of conservation. His convictions about the responsibility of humans to control nature and about their capacity to restore and maintain environmental harmony through manipulation and management paved the way for formal wildlife management policies. Yet, although the question of Leopold's commitment to the sanctity of land in its totality is not in dispute, his ideas about the human relationship with wild animals were far less visionary.

FOUNDATIONS OF WILDLIFE POLICIES IN CANADA

Three themes illustrate wildlife's marginalized place in official policy-making under the dominant belief system. The first is a by-product of wildlife's absence from the Canadian Constitution. The second is the anthropocentrism that underlies their official classification as a species-specific resource. The third concerns wildlife management itself and the human-based priorities that drive it.

Wildlife and Jurisdictional Fragmentation

Canada and wildlife have had a long and uneasy relationship. For centuries, wild animals were opportunistically used by early settlers and colonial "sportsmen," as well as commercially exploited in the fur trade and fishing industries. They entered the national narrative as nonentities with the formation of the Canadian nation-state under the British North America Act (1867). In fact, it is possible that the Fathers of Confederation viewed wildlife as a temporary obstacle to agriculture and other human interests.[32] That wildlife were not even mentioned in the act said volumes about the place of wild animals in the matters of state.[33] Under section 109, they were subsumed as part of the land and, as things and public property, fell largely under provincial and, more latterly, Aboriginal self-governing jurisdictions.[34]

The allocation of authority over wildlife primarily to the provinces has resulted in a weakening of federal power, a more limited vision, and a patchwork of conflicting provincial regulations and policies. Provinces prepare, enact, and administer their own wildlife legislation. Regulations involving rehabilitation of wildlife, hunting, and intrusive activities in protected areas vary widely between provinces. For example, the recovery measures for species at risk differ widely in scope and integrity. Injured or orphaned black bears can be rehabilitated by accredited groups in Ontario but not in Alberta. Grizzlies can be hunted in British Columbia but not in Alberta. Hunters can shoot polar bears in Nunavut but not in Manitoba. The federal government has jurisdiction over migratory birds but not raptors, and its influence over nonavian species is limited to federal lands and, even then, with some qualifications.[35] Trapping is allowed in some national parks. Although the federal government has constitutional power over fish, other marine creatures, and their habitats, provincial and sometimes local or regional powers apply to coastal foreshores. Pollution is under federal purview when it occurs at sea but under provincial purview if it emanates from land uses. Shared jurisdictional responsibility over inland waters is exercised in matters of pollution control, infrastructure development, and interprovincial and boundary waters. However, the fact that control over wildlife resides primarily in the provinces has led to differentiated policies and to the adoption of inefficient cooperative federalism as the best, and likely the only, way to support the totality of wildlife.[36]

The provinces and territories, the primary agencies that decide the fate of wildlife, do so through legislation, regulations, policies, and specific management plans. Federal responsibility for wildlife is vested in Environment Canada (currently, Environment and Climate Change Canada), Fisheries and Oceans Canada, and Parks Canada. The Canadian Wildlife Service, established in 1947, is a directorate of Environment

Canada and, in addition to enforcing the federal Wildlife Act (1973), focuses on migratory birds, species at risk, and habitat. The Canadian Wildlife Service also cooperates with the provinces and other jurisdictions with respect to the development and implementation of conservation partnership programs, protection and recovery planning for species at risk, and the monitoring of wetlands and habitat.[37] At the provincial level, wildlife are managed by specific ministries usually associated with natural resources or the environment. The administration of wildlife within that ministry varies between provinces, and it is difficult to establish any comparative importance attached to wildlife partly because specific allocations in wildlife budgets are not transparent. In terms of wildlife generally, the provincial governments focus primarily on revenue-raising animals through hunting and tourism and tend to ignore arthropods, amphibians, most nonmigratory birds, and many mammals like skunks, raccoons, foxes, squirrels, and porcupines, except when they impinge on human economic interest or psychological comfort zones. For example, coyotes, wolves, and beavers are still subject to bounty programs in some provinces.

The lack of federal constitutional power over wildlife and biotic communities is best exemplified in two national initiatives. Both the Canadian Biodiversity Strategy (1995) and the Species at Risk Act (2002) are undermined by jurisdictional issues. The voluntary compliance by the provinces, the blurring of responsibility guidelines, the lack of consistent consultative protocols, and different regimes over species management across fourteen jurisdictions make it very difficult to achieve goals quickly, meaningfully, and in the best interests of wildlife. The special position occupied by Indigenous peoples within these frameworks is a further exacerbating factor.

INDIGENOUS PEOPLES

Jurisdictional issues involving Indigenous peoples stand in the way of consistent wildlife policymaking and management. Contemporary Aboriginal groups have deep connections to wildlife because of their continuing links to the fur trade, a quasi-subsistence way of life, especially in isolated arctic regions, and the hunting and trapping privileges granted by governments through historic treaty rights. Generally, First Nations with treaty rights can hunt, fish, and trap for food in all seasons of the year on unoccupied Crown land and on private land with the permission of the owner. In the Canadian North, the First Nations groups and the Inuit, under separate governance, agreements, and licences, are allowed to hunt wildlife, including vulnerable species like polar bears and whales. Indigenous people thus claim a separate status when it comes to wildlife. In 2010, for example, BC First Nations claimed a Charter right to kill bald eagles.[38] Commercial trapping is permitted in Wapusk National Park, just south of Churchill, Manitoba, to accommodate First Nations and Inuit.[39] Consultation with Aboriginal jurisdictions is required before certain species are listed under the Species at Risk Act. The differentiation of wildlife policies based on treaty and hunting rights and more loosely on hunter-gatherer traditions is a crucial element of wildlife management.

In many ways, wildlife protection policies and First Nations are complementary. Aboriginal traditional knowledge recognizes the intimate knowledge of the land and its wildlife held by Aboriginal peoples in Canada. It is a mandatory component in government dialogue respecting at-risk species; it is the concern of a subcommittee of the Committee on the Status of Endangered Wildlife in Canada; and it is incorporated into the decision-making process there and elsewhere. The National Aboriginal Council on Species at Risk is composed of representatives of Indigenous peoples in Canada and offers advice and recommendations to the Canadian Endangered Species Conservation Council. The federal government's Aboriginal Fund for Species at Risk provides funds to Indigenous organizations and communities across Canada in order to enhance the conservation and recovery of species at risk.

Arguably, First Nations make their greatest positive contribution to wildlife, albeit indirectly, through their efforts to preserve their lifestyles by securing protection of ancestral lands from industrial and other development. Examples include the Broadback River Valley in Quebec, the Peel River watershed in the Yukon, and the North French watershed in Ontario.[40] In 2016 Indigenous peoples made a significant contribution to biodiversity and wildlife in Canada and to global environmental health when, after twenty years of intense negotiations, they were successful in securing an agreement with the BC government preventing logging in 85 per cent, or 3.1 million hectares, of the Great Bear Rainforest.[41] Due to their historic presence, their support from prominent conservation organizations, and their own emergence as a potent political force, Aboriginal peoples comprise one of the few coalitions able to stand up to threats posed by modern resource development. With regard to specific wildlife, they are also active in protecting vulnerable habitats of the grizzly bear, the boreal woodland caribou, and the beluga whale.

Although Native groups have always defended their treaty and natural rights to hunt and fish, they were victimized for much of the twentieth century. The Anglo-Saxon hunting fraternity blamed Indigenous people for wasteful hunting practices that were detrimental to game. Both the federal and provincial governments viewed the Native presence as inimical to wildlife management. The pendulum shifted in the last quarter of the twentieth century when Aboriginal land claims and rights to self-government were recognized and when a comprehensive land claims policy was adopted in 1973. To date, twenty-nine comprehensive land claim and/or self-government agreements, predominantly in the North and covering over 40 per cent of Canada's land mass, have been ratified and brought into effect, with many more at the negotiating table. These constitutionally protected agreements transferred extensive powers to First Nations and Inuit groups over wildlife and – in practice, if not in fact – have effectively distanced the federal government from a pivotal role in directing the future of wildlife in much of the country. Politics and differing cultural viewpoints make this worrying. For instance, the Inuit need the polar bear as an economic lifeline. Given the implications of climate change, a "threatened" listing under the Species at Risk Act is advisable. This has not transpired, primarily because hunting would then be disallowed, something the Inuit do not want since they believe that the bears are in no danger whatsoever.

In that they argue for a need to protect a traditional and symbolic subsistence lifestyle based on hunter-gatherer traditions, Aboriginal people in Canada have a point, up to a point. In isolated areas, especially in the North, arguments have been made for a different belief system, one rooted in need, tradition, and a less anthropocentric way of life than in mainstream Canada. In his reflections, Canadian Swampy-Cree elder Louis Bird contends that hunting constitutes an agreement by animals to give their lives to humans for food in return for respect.[42] Anthropologist

George Wenzel, perhaps the foremost authority on Inuit culture, takes this view. To the Inuit on the east coast of Baffin Island, the polar bear is aware of the hunter's intent and becomes complicit if the proper respect is exhibited.[43] IKANAWTIKET, an initiative of the Maritime Aboriginal Peoples Council, took the same tone in 2011 in a powerful and impassioned indictment of the human-centred and anti-ecological agendas inherent in the implementation of the Species at Risk Act.[44] However, in the main and despite the above, Aboriginal perceptions of animals are aligned with the dominant belief system, particularly in cities or on reserves that are close to major urban centres. Additionally, their long association with the fur trade served to weaken the sort of symbolic respect for wild animals often claimed by First Nations groups. In fact, it has been argued that these symbolic attachments to wildlife and the notion of the Native peoples as natural conservationists emerged only in the post-European contact era.[45] Nevertheless, the federal Department of Indian Affairs bought into the idea and, for practical and political reasons, has continued to sustain it. Canadian governments continue to bolster wildlife trapping by First Nations and Métis people on cultural grounds.[46] Referring to the trapping industry and the cruelty it embodies, John Livingston has noted, "It is in the interests of both governments and the fashion trade that trapping be perceived by the native people themselves as an integral part of their social heritage."[47]

It is true that, historically, Indigenous peoples have suffered from exposure to Europeans via the fur trade, whaling, and the injustices associated with the reserve system and that their pace of economic advancement has fallen well below that of the Canadian norm. Partly in an attempt to make amends for wrong deeds and partly to enable Indigenous peoples to maintain a quasi-traditional lifestyle in economically deprived areas, the federal government has granted extensive control of wildlife management to Indigenous peoples in the North. Is it too naive to expect that these Native groups will manifest the respect for wildlife that they claim is implicit in their cultures?

Within a labyrinthine array of interrelated and separate jurisdictional arrangements, wildlife lack any consistent protection. The federal government is at arm's length from the provinces and the territories. Due to their large-scale ineffectiveness, the Species at Risk Act and the Canadian Biodiversity Strategy (to be discussed) are the two most outstanding examples of federal inability to offer a national umbrella capable of safe-guarding wildlife. National wildlife policies are impossible in Canada. There can be no hope for an integrated, nationwide wildlife strategy or for a national platform of reform or change. The allocation of control of most wild species to cash-strapped provinces with strong rural constituencies tends to maintain status quo values.

Wildlife as a Renewable Resource

Yet, despite the above, some consistencies are present federally, provincially, and territorially – consistencies that mirror the belief system. All jurisdictions deny the capacity of wild creatures to engage in conscious subjective experiences that belong to them individually, or if they do, such experiences are deemed too inferior to matter morally. The designation of wildlife as a renewable resource is justified under this highly contestable rubric. Arguably, the concept of wildlife as a resource is longstanding and bound up in differing concepts of access and scope, as evidenced by the various historic regulations and laws respecting forests, hunting rights and franchises, and game laws.[48] However, the modern designation of wildlife as state property has narrowed its perception to one of pure utility. Furthermore, the integration of wildlife into land management and stewardship issues has tended to mute their existence as living creatures. The identification of wildlife as a state resource has neutered them in the same way as domesticated food animals have become identified with a consumer product. As a renewable resource, autonomous wild creatures become objects, collective entities, things.

The view of wildlife as a resource is part of Canada's long resourcist tradition, which dates to colonial times. This unfortunate association derived its validity primarily through a lucrative fur trade that for some time was the economic linchpin of a colonial economy. In the subsequent ongoing frontier tradition of resource extraction, the fur trade was pushed into the background. But the damage was done. Livingston sums up the impact of designating wildlife as a resource in a single sentence:

"Once wildlife is seen as a resource, one faces the impossible burden of demonstrating its utility in the human interest."[49] Historian George Colpitts contends that early-twentieth-century boosters and promoters equated wildlife with natural resource abundance and used photographs and taxidermy to advance the inexhaustible resource richness of western Canada.[50] Colpitts's point that wildlife were seen as a metaphor for other resource richness is well taken. Canada's place as a global economic force is dependent on its exploitation of natural resources like minerals, fossil fuels, agricultural products, and lumber. Being way down on Canada's resource hierarchy in terms of human benefit, wildlife are very minor players. Moreover, with their habitat requirements, wildlife often impinge on other resource extraction. Decisions as to winners and losers in these situations are not difficult to predict.

This context suggests another commonality. Although some advances have been made, wildlife policies, especially at the provincial and territorial levels, are still geared toward a few species. The appeal of wildlife as an exploitive resource in government policies refers to the few species who do qualify. These include commercial and recreational fish, furbearing species, and in a modern context, game animals like ungulates, wildfowl, and their predators. It is this group of species that is exploited in the human interest and this group that justifies the classification of wildlife as a renewable resource. This is where the historic conservation focus has lain. Despite very recent indications of change, the official mindset, which equates wildlife with game and furbearing animals, remains entrenched, even though they generate significantly lower revenues and jobs in the bigger resource picture.

In their totality and beyond these few species, wildlife really bring little to the resource table beyond aesthetics and intrinsic value, and neither will cut it as a criterion for priority as a human resource. The designation of wildlife as a resource is wrongheaded because the vast majority of wildlife do not fit the resource paradigm. The arthropods, amphibians, reptiles, many smaller mammals, and most birds and fish do not make money. Some are classed as vermin. Many are not even aesthetic, and their specific ecological role and value are largely unknown and often ignored. In fact, by classifying wildlife as a human resource, Canadian governments are unable to follow coherent policies. On the one hand, they budget for spending on a resource that in totality offers limited aesthetic and underappreciated ecological value. On the other hand, they also try to generate indirect and direct revenues by exploiting a few species that in the big resource picture are very minor players. Promising no short-term results, the former is underfunded, and the latter generates limited revenues and jobs when measured against other resource development. The inept enforcement of the Species at Risk Act is a classic example. Canadian governments, with their anthropocentric belief system, seem unable to divorce wildlife as a national living trust from its neutered status as a resource.

The fact that demonstrable value cannot be ascribed to the majority of wildlife has put Canadian governments in an untenable position. Their reaction has been to publicly affirm the impossible. Apparently, despite accommodating commercial human interests that hinder their ability to behave ethically and responsibly toward their wildlife, Canadian governments believe that they can combine their own low budgetary allocations with revenues from hunting, trapping, and tourism to ensure that all species are preserved, that substantial habitat is restored and maintained, and that biodiversity and ecological integrity are enhanced. The current Biodiversity Strategy, for example, promises far more than it can ever hope to deliver.

The definition of wildlife as a resource objectifies them. They are managed in the same way as any other resource, which means that in the government's eyes, a salamander is no different from a lump of coal and a deer no different from a sheaf of wheat. Even more than domesticated animals, many of whom benefit from human interactions, wildlife are stripped of individuality or selfhood and have entered the belief system as a neutered species-specific resource. But wildlife are not a human resource. If the word "human" must be used, as seems to be the case in a human-centred belief system, the word "trust" seems more appropriate. Trust connotes guardianship and obligation, not an ongoing right. Wildlife are not a renewable human resource. Only in a belief system that fails to recognize animal consciousness or individual lifestyles that parallel our own in their experiential nature can an aggregate of living beings be equated with truckloads of coal.

Wildlife as Species

The classification of wildlife into species for management purposes is understandable. The issue here concerns the irrelevance of the individual. Generally, policies in human organizations focus on the group dimension. However, individuals do matter, and their voices are considered in human management protocols. But when the focus is on a resource like coal or wheat, or any neutered group, the individual dimension is not present. Who cares whether a single piece of coal falls off a laden rail car? The belief system cannot assign individual worth to wildlife because value is set against their aggregate as a species. This is neither valid nor rational. Philosopher Paul Taylor, for example, in arguing for a biocentric ethic, suggests that "the principle of moral consideration prescribes that, with respect to each being an entity having its own good, every individual is deserving of consideration."[51]

The discourse about animals prejudices their individuality. Wildlife management discourse is about species. It is never about individual animals and their worth as living beings with their own life courses. According to ecological linguist Arran Stibbe, animals are mediated through discourses that encode a particular model of reality. Their messages are embodied in language through context-specific words and casual phraseology. For example, the human-nonhuman divide is routinely emphasized in discourse by the pronoun "it," the noun "thing," or common pejoratives like "being treated like an animal," "we are not animals," and "the beast within us."

Stibbe includes scholarly literature in discourses of otherness that stress animals as objects for human-centred discussion rather than like creatures with shared characteristics. He notes that "discourse conducted at the level of collective nouns has the side-effect of distracting attention away from direct relationships with individual animals: an individual can be seen, heard, and empathized with, but a 'species' cannot."[52] Almost invariably, well-researched, peer-reviewed articles (cited frequently in this narrative) treat wildlife as neutered species-specific things. From a purely scientific perspective, this is understandable, if not wholly necessary. There is always an animal dimension to discussions about animals. However, a recent trend in wildlife studies concerns the human dimension, which focuses on public knowledge levels, expectations, attitudes, and activities concerning wildlife and habitat, as well as on their implications for wildlife management and practice.[53] These articles in part explore the human affective element in the human-nonhuman relationship and, by implication, might be expected to portray the nonhuman dimension more inclusively and sensitively. Unfortunately, the vast majority do not do so.[54] A partial explanation is seen in environmental scholar Timothy Leduc's provocative article on interdisciplinary studies that focus on environmental issues. Leduc points out that the humanistic ethical dimension appears only peripherally in academic disciplines that pertain to the environment and surprisingly is not being carried through sufficiently at the interdisciplinary level. He discusses the merits of a qualitative dimension, or a new way of thinking about environmental and ecological issues in interdisciplinary studies, one that would involve a focus on intrinsic value, including that of wildlife.[55]

The practice of managing wildlife in terms of species has the effect of trivializing individual lives. Whether due to hunting, culling, or other human interests, the deaths of individual animals count for little in the wildlife management calculus. The belief system it represents envisions them as nonconsequential things, not as conscious living beings. Only the species counts and, even then, solely as an aggregate of things.

WILDLIFE MANAGEMENT AND POLICYMAKING

The belief system influences wildlife policymaking through the enduring anti-Darwinist belief that humans stand outside nature and need to manage it in accordance with principles that either aid or do not prejudice their interests. So, despite changes in emphasis through time, from game to wildlife generally and then to ecosystems and biodiversity, wildlife policymaking always includes the human dimension. Three streams of thought and activity are illustrative. The first relates to the selective focus on a few species. The second is the integration of hunting into the management paradigm. The third concerns the structure of management itself.

Management by Selected Species

Management by species is a selective process because most do not matter unless they intrude on human comfort zones. Management plans for skunks, porcupines, or garter snakes are nonexistent, not because they do not require oversight and protection but because they are not worth it. The only species that matter are the high-profile fur or game species, namely ungulates, waterfowl, and iconic predators like bears and cougars, or the problem species like wolves and coyotes. As wildlife biologist Vince Crichton has so aptly noted, "Wildlife managers typically concentrate on the high profile species."[56] Regardless of rhetoric to the contrary and positive action in other areas, the prime focus of Canadian wildlife management has always been on the game and problem species. Those belonging to the rest of the wild domain exist at the behest of private landowners and depend on the judicious practices of lessees of Crown land.

In the first sixty years of the twentieth century, wildlife officials managed nature by encouraging the preservation of game animals – ungulates and wildfowl – while persecuting their predators. This perception of nature could be seen as early as 1886 when William F. Whitcher, former Dominion fisheries commissioner, in his assessment of national parks, recommended that "the lupine, vulpine and feline vermin that prey on furred and feathered game" be exterminated.[57] In 1914 William Hornaday, a noted wildlife authority and the director of the Bronx Zoo, advised that wolves "be killed as quickly as possible" and that cougars "be hunted down and destroyed regardless of cost." The same applied to minks, skunks, raccoons, opossums, and weasels. He described sharp-shinned hawks and Cooper's hawks as "companion[s] in crime" and "equally deserving of an early and violent death." As for the later endangered peregrine falcon, Hornaday said, "First shoot the male and the female, then collect the nest, the young or the eggs … They all look best in collections."[58] In these years, wardens in the fledgling national parks system supplemented their income by trapping predators and selling their pelts.[59]

Sixteen years later, in 1930, the Alberta Fish and Game Association passed two motions. The first asked the provincial government to place snowy owls (on the short list in 2016 for designation as Canada's national bird), great horned owls (now the provincial bird of Alberta), and goshawks on the Vermin List; the second commended the government for its "splendid efforts" in encouraging the destruction of crows and magpies.[60] As late as 1953, E.S. Huestis, Alberta's fish and game commissioner, saw the rabies outbreak in northern Alberta as an opportunity to intensify "the war" against wolves, coyotes, foxes, and cougars in order to leave more "big game" for hunters.[61] By the mid-twentieth century, the wholesale slaughter of eagles, hawks, owls, foxes, wolves, coyotes, cougars, bears, gophers, crows, and magpies, the unregulated introduction of game fish and wildfowl, and the conscious cultivation of desirous "game" animals were hallmarks of wildlife management.

Amid growing scientific knowledge about ecosystem relationships, attitudes toward predators changed, and by the 1960s most of the big terrestrial predators had been legitimatized as quasi-game – or more accurately, trophy – animals. However, despite growing research indicating the crucial and pivotal role of predators in structuring natural ecosystems, the prejudice against them remains. In fact, it has been argued that modern predator management is as much a socio-political issue as a biological one.[62] Lethal predator control is seen as essential to livestock owners and trophy hunters. Moreover, the overexploitation of predators, which led to their extirpation in some areas of the country, has resulted in overabundance in ungulate populations and to policies based on erroneous assumptions that hunters can substitute for apex predators. In the absence of the wolf, the role of moose hunting in Newfoundland and Labrador has not resulted in perceived balanced ecological states.

Despite modern assertions about paradigm shifts in wildlife management from individual species to a holistic ecosystem approach, an examination of policies at the provincial level reveals an ongoing major focus on the need to maintain a renewable balance between game animals and their predators through regulated hunting. Environmental historian Stephen Bocking is right when he observes that the emphasis on commodity production is more important in modern management practices than is habitat preservation.[63]

"Problem" animals continue their prominence in wildlife management policy and practices. In that there is no such thing as a problem animal in truly natural environments, the word itself is a social construct and refers to levels of human tolerance and in some cases to past human miscalculations. Bounty programs targeting wolves and coyotes are current and ongoing in several provinces. Management plans for wolves, coyotes, bears, beavers, and deer include options for culling and extermination to protect human interests. They include lethal solutions for big predators who broach urban areas and human habitation. In Alberta, private landowners are allowed to shoot "problem animals" like red foxes, skunks, raccoons, rabbits, hares, and even badgers and bobcats indiscriminately. No licence is needed, and no management is necessary. It does not seem to matter that skunks and raccoons play important roles in the ecosystem, both by helping to maintain healthy insect and small rodent populations and by distributing seeds, or that porcupines act as ecosystem engineers by disturbing the soil when foraging and by changing plant communities through their diets.

Since only selected species qualify for management concern, other mammals and native birds, arthropods, amphibians, and reptiles are generally ignored unless classified under the Species at Risk Act. The efforts expended on behalf of ecological integrity or biodiversity tend to obscure a longstanding reality. Aside from species at risk (and debatable even within that context), wildlife management in Canada is heavily concerned with balancing populations of desired species and persecuting "problem" animals, while devoting limited attention to the rest of the biotic community, which is prejudiced by contaminants, habitat loss, and destruction through other anthropogenic disturbances.

Wildlife Management, Hunting, and the Belief System

The practice of hunting wild animals, regardless of its many exculpatory rationalizations, demonstrates the "thingness" of animals and is the best normative example of the dominant belief system as it applies to wildlife. Its respectability and even esteem, particularly in wildlife-rich western Canada, took shape amid a climate of behaviourist norms in the early conservation movement when it was insinuated into fledgling management policies. The singular success of its alignment with official priorities is a fitting example of political scientist and environmentalist Robert Paehlke's observation that "the very private interests which were to be controlled by public servants ... came themselves to dominate the resource management agencies."[64] From the very beginning of early wildlife management, the hunting lobbies successfully pressed their cause on wildlife managers and legislators. Although referring to only a few game species, the Alberta Fish and Game Association's mission statement in 1907 envisaged the association as a promoter of and educator on the merits of conserving fish and wildlife through hunting.[65]

Hunting's place in history is multi-layered and textured. The many books and studies on the subject discuss its relation to humans, human nature, human values, and human design but rarely contest the fundamental beliefs that justify it. Matt Cartmill's *View to a Death in the Morning* (1996), which stands high among the best books ever written on hunting, examines historical human development through hunting and its various roles, rationalizations, functions, and rituals to demonstrate its enduring place in explaining human relationships with the natural world. Discussing the discredited "hunting hypothesis," which essentially argues that hunting transformed hominids into humans, as well as hunting's close link with war and the nature-human divide, Cartmill situates hunting within changing societal and social contexts. Although he does not advocate an alternative belief system, Cartmill does suggest that it might lie within the willingness of humans to equate animal existence with the best of what they see in themselves.[66]

The lore of hunting has timeless roots in Canada. It also has powerful modern cultural and social associations. For example, Canadian historian Tina Loo has shown how hunting was integrated into a twentieth-century concept of nature.[67] With their nostalgic yearning for wilderness experiences and strong lobbies with sympathetic governments, sport hunters created a narrowly focused cultural artifact, or the "sportsman's paradise." This wilderness environment promised a market-driven encounter with nature and, according to Loo, was the outcome of the emerging science of game management, accepted and supported by state bureaucracy.[68] Rife with rationalizations about primal instincts, group identity, putting food on the table, mystical sojourns, acting out one's own mortality by killing a surrogate, or bonding with nature, hunting attracts loyal adherents, or about 8 per cent of Canada's population, who managed to kill 2.5 million waterfowl in 2014 and, a year earlier, 120,000 white-tailed deer in Ontario and Alberta alone.[69]

There was no doubt that the conservationist vision, with its objective view of nature, was compatible with hunting, or more accurately, a certain form of hunting. In fact, wildlife's place in the conservation ethos was the direct result of the massive reduction in wildlife numbers during the nineteenth century in the United States and Canada. The causes were overhunting, due primarily to unregulated plunder through lax game laws, especially in areas with railway access. For example, the Canadian North-West Territories Ordinance (1895) allowed hunters a seasonal allocation of six deer, six big horn sheep, six mountain goats, and twenty grouse a day.[70] The established hunting fraternity took the high moral ground and laid the blame for wildlife depletions on the game meat hunters and on wasteful overhunting by Aboriginals. By adopting the gentlemanly term "sportsmen," formal hunting associations advocated sustainable hunting governed by the code of ethical, restrained, fair chase endorsed by US president Theodore Roosevelt, a celebrity conservationist and ardent hunter who proclaimed, "In a civilized and cultivated country, wild animals only continue to exist at all when preserved by sportsmen."[71] Even the British-born zoologist, Canadian Dominion entomologist (1909–1920), and friend of wildlife C. Gordon Hewitt included a hunting code in his ground-breaking book *The Conservation of the Wildlife of Canada* (1921).[72] However, historian Don Wetherell argues that the code was honoured far more in the breach than in the observance, as evidenced by his accounts of the wanton barbarity and callousness of hunters.[73] Through the first half of the twentieth century, the hunting lobby integrated itself into the conservation movement by influencing game laws, hunting licences, and the establishment of sanctuaries and wetlands where game could breed and thrive. The resulting revenues from licences and economic spinoffs in local and regional economies created two-way benefit flows that permanently linked hunting with government policies. As the Saskatchewan game commissioner noted in 1933, "Revenue is the one and only thing."[74]

Furthermore, under the influence of celebrity hunters like Theodore Roosevelt and Jack Miner, as well as ecologists and land ethicists like Aldo Leopold, the notion of hunters as true conservationists and nature's guardians became a popularly accepted truth and an entrenched component of wildlife management.

The North American Model of Wildlife Conservation (2001) is a good example of this continuing acceptance of hunters as conservationists and hunting as a wider agent of ecological good, even though this model's primary focus is on hunting game animals according to Leopoldian principles. The model comprises "a set of [seven] principles" that, according to its influential multi-stakeholder founders, "has led to the form, function, and successes of wildlife conservation and management in the United States and Canada."[75] Accepted as the basis for many US wildlife policies, the model reflects a Canadian presence through numerous representatives on its Technical Review Committee and through the pioneering work of noted University of Calgary zoologist Valerius Geist, who spearheaded its establishment. The model contends that adherence to its principles in wildlife management policies will result in the preservation of species, habitat enhancement, and biodiversity health. In calling for broad societal funding, public education, ongoing dialogue, and citizen engagement, and in promoting a new normative ethical guide, the model casts hunting as a positive agent of societal ecological awareness. By so doing, it purports to integrate modern hunting more securely and positively into contemporary norms.[76]

A similar, modern, high-profile advocate of hunting as a necessary, sustainable practice is prominent Canadian conservationist Eugene Lapointe, former president of the International Wildlife Management Consortium's World Conservation Trust, president of the World Conservation Trust Foundation, and secretary-general of the Convention on International Trade in Endangered Species of Wild Fauna and Flora (1975).[77] In promoting the ivory trade, whaling, sealing, and pretty well any other lethal wildlife measure if it benefits humans, Lapointe adheres to the early conservationist dictum that the fate of wildlife is linked to public acceptance of their use as a sustainable human resource. Naturally, Lapointe is a hunter, one who believes that hunting is as good for animals as it is for the people who kill them. His following statement is a classic example of modern speciesism as it applies to wildlife: "These people trying to stop hunting don't understand elephants. A hunter's bullet spares the elephant from suffering of natural mortality. It's for their own good, to be hunted and used. The problem is misinformation. The reality isn't what we see on television. The reality is that's an animal that has to be contained. That's an animal that has to be controlled. That's an animal that tramples people. That's an animal that threatens people. You have to give it economic value. You have to use them."[78] In quoting the above, author Matthew Scully, in his penetrating indictment of contemporary attitudes and practices toward animals, writes of Lapointe, "God spare the creatures from this grim little tyrant and his kind. Grant them this sanctuary, and many more across the world from cruelty and avarice and the pride of man that knoweth no bounds."[79] Lapointe's argument that the illegal, exploitive use of wildlife poses the real threat to their survival and that sustainable management via lethal control is their sole recourse hearkens back to early conservationism and the sport hunters who saw Indigenous people and market hunters as the "bad guys" and themselves as saviours.

The hunting mentality is imbued in the majority of wildlife officers in the field.[80] The close link between hunters and wildlife management is explored by American sociologist Helene Lawson, whose research involves conversations with wildlife managers, game wardens, and hunters in several US states.[81] Given Canada's similar hunting cultures and wildlife management practices, Lawson's findings are applicable to Canada as well. Her conclusions are not surprising. Wildlife managers personify the dominant belief system about the human-nonhuman relationship. Lawson contends that it is endemic in the wildlife management profession itself to "dismiss those who would, through a growing realization of the 'humanness' of wild animals, include wild non-human animals into the community."[82] They hold steadfast to the classic hunter-as-conservationist mentality and argue that to preserve the natural order, humans must assume a predatory role.[83] Without exception, all of the wildlife managers interviewed by Lawson, male or female, were hunters themselves, having been socialized into hunting at an early age.[84] In other words, wildlife management philosophy and personnel are inseparable from the hunting mentality.

And with good reason. Hunting boosts rural economies in Canada by more than $2 billion annually and helps to defray the costs of wildlife management. A 2014 report on the multiplier effect concluded that the outfitted hunting sector in Alberta contributed $2.60 to the provincial gross domestic product for every dollar it spent. It also added 1.7 jobs to the provincial workforce for every job held in the sector itself.[85] In 2012 the Canadian Tourism Commission, seeking economic spinoffs for the tourist industry, urged the need to bring more American big game hunters and anglers to Canada, noting that "Canada has only tapped in[to] a small fraction of the avid game hunters and enthusiasts for sport fishing from the US."[86] The following comment by the Ontario government reflects the Canadian-wide provincial sentiment about the worth of hunting: "The Ontario government appreciates hunters' commitment to conservation. Hunters and anglers contribute to the management of wildlife [through] their licence purchases[,] with all licence revenues deposited to the Fish and Wildlife Special Purpose Account. This account funds two-thirds of the ministry's wildlife and fish management activities."[87]

The wholesale support that hunting receives from all Canadian governments, the continuing presence of a strong hunting lobby, and an indifferent public, most of whose members do not hunt but who acknowledge hunting as a normal and environmentally sound practice, all contribute to the widespread acceptance of hunters as conservationists.[88]

But the contention that hunters are conservationists warrants serious qualification. Critics of the North American Model of Wildlife Conservation contend that its simplistic notion of hunters as conservationists is outdated and that the focus on ungulate abundance creates an ecological imbalance.[89] Population assessments and predator-prey balances are complex and very difficult to establish. A six-year controlled experiment involving white-tailed deer on Anticosti Island in the St Lawrence River found that hunting was not an effective method of population control and that local control of abundant deer populations through sport hunting was problematic.[90] Similar studies on black-tailed deer on Vancouver Island showed that using hunters to control the predator-prey balance was not effective.[91] The dynamics of prey switching by predators and dispersal by prey are not well understood. According to environmental professor Adrian Treves, a lack of attention to complexities in the social systems and behavioural patterns of carnivores can lead to inaccuracies in establishing hunting quotas.[92] Other variables like compensatory and additive mortality factors are important considerations in the predator-prey relationships and are sometimes used misleadingly in management plans.

According to recent research, sport hunting is anything but sound conservation practice. Noting that little is known about the evolutionary effects of sport hunting, biologist Marco Festa-Bianchet observes that selective hunting may lead to a loss of genetic variability, which in turn has probable negative effects on the target species' ability to survive environmental changes over the long term.[93] Studies in "contemporary evolution" have demonstrated that evolutionary trends can occur within decades. Biologists warn that selected harvesting of the fittest animals can induce contemporary evolution, resulting in a rapid loss of genetic variation.[94] According to a 2009 study, exploited species transform on average three times faster than those in areas where hunting is absent, becoming smaller and breeding earlier. Biologist John Thompson sees the overlap in the timescales of ecological and evolutionary processes as having implications for "the short-term relationships between diversity, food web connectedness, and stability."[95] A recent study concluded that hunters cannot substitute for carnivores as providers of ecological services and are in fact agents of unsustainability, or super-predators who kill the adult prey essential for population stability at rates as high as fourteen times greater than other predators.[96] This rapid trait change has negative implications for normal ecosystem functions and for wildlife managers.[97]

American historian Karl Steel argues that, over time, humans reinforced their uniqueness and separation from animals through acts of violence and subjugation.[98] This violence toward animals took three forms: subjective violence involving individual acts, objective violence whereby the status quo either sanctioned or ignored it, and symbolic violence, or the violence inherent in the discourse of language itself.[99] Steel's observations apply to hunting today as much as they do to hunting in mediaeval times. Wildlife are subject to the individual violence of weapons, to the violence that collectivizes them as a resource, and to the symbolic violence that trivializes their lives and deaths through euphemisms like "culling," "game management," "population control," and "hunters as conservationists."

Structural Management Issues

Wildlife are penalized by other broad beliefs, strategies, and practices in wildlife management, or more precisely, by the specific interpretations of what they mean. Examples discussed here are ecological integrity, adaptive management, and the role of science. All are crucial elements in wildlife management, and all are less effective in practice than in theory. Differing notions about ecological integrity, the specifics of adaptive management, and the selective use of "best scientific practice" have all resulted in negative impacts on wildlife. The subjective element that surrounds ecological management, the collateral damage implicit in adaptive management principles, and misleading references to sound scientific practice combine to penalize individual wildlife. Although it could be argued that specific prejudicial actions toward wildlife are the exception rather than the rule, there can be little doubt that all three reinforce the "renewable resource management" syndrome.

ECOLOGICAL INTEGRITY

Managing for ecological integrity – the essence of ecosystem management – is a highly complex process subject to many variables and discourses. It is also very difficult to achieve because it needs to operate within the residual imbalances caused by anthropogenic disturbances. Indeed, contemporary thinking about managing for ecological integrity, or the ecosystem approach, stresses the need for holistic practices that also incorporate human social and economic priorities.[100] At the management-planning level, the goal of ecological integrity is subject to several approaches and emphases. At the operational level, however, it emerges as far more simplistic and, in many cases, as prejudicial toward certain species of wildlife.

In Canada managing for ecological integrity is based on normative principles and discourse, which assume that humans stand outside nature and that ecological issues can be addressed without compromising current human norms and practices.[101] Within this parameter, ecological integrity is based on the degree to which an ecosystem can deviate from a perceived norm without reaching irreversibility. This approach is typical of North American wildlife management and is reflected primarily in a desire to maintain equilibriums, or with respect to wildlife, balanced populations of species based on subjective determinations.

This management approach assumes a fixed-in-time perception of ecological integrity, or as Parks Canada states, "A condition that is *determined* to be characteristic of its natural region."[102] It involves the establishment of baseline conditions within a prescribed area in order to measure changes.[103] Although wildlife managers recognize that ecological states are never static in the evolutionary continuum, they micromanage relatively small areas to achieve a perceived ecological balance while accommodating contemporary social, economic, and political pres- sures.[104] The point is that wildlife managers pursue remediation policies when conditions detract from a subjective assessment within specific areas and timeframes. The Canadian Biodiversity Strategy, for example, equates rehabilitated landscapes and wetlands with ecological integrity rather than acknowledging that this assessment is, at best, an educated guess. The resort to regular culling of deer is an example in point.

Essentially, the long-range implications of a baseline, or fixed-in-time perceptions of ecological integrity based on subjective determinations, translate into tenuous attempts to control nature. Decisions that arise from varying interpretations of the definition of ecosystems, the complexity of the nature of eco-regions and their boundaries, and biases toward specific characteristics result in particularistic management applications.[105] Of course, it could be argued that managing from baseline perceptions is the only practical course open to wildlife managers since urgent time- frames and external human factors prohibit more evolutionary pro- cesses. However, in adjusting their policies to address perceived threats to ecological integrity, wildlife managers frequently make members of the "offending" species pay the ultimate price. Lethal moose-control programs in Newfoundland and Labrador are designed to mitigate the negative effects of overbrowsing on the ecological integrity of forest landscapes. Yet it could be argued that in opening up more canopies of light, the moose are contributing to the evolution of a landscape that is increasingly dominated by grasses and shrubs, plant communities attractive to new species variety, which would in time regulate moose numbers. But this is not going to transpire. The trouble is that given the belief system about animals and even allowing for some understanding of their ecological roles, policies based on normative perceptions about ecological integrity and the way to maintain it will and do penalize offending species of wildlife in the easiest, cheapest, and worst way.

Other human factors have become integrated into a perception of ecological integrity. Management decisions are influenced by economic

and social considerations that draw on the overarching respectability of
the term "ecological integrity" to disguise actions prejudicial to wildlife.
It is common practice for wildlife managers to increase the number of
ungulate hunting licences in grassland areas under stress in order to
restore their ecological integrity rather than removing the grazing cattle
that precipitated said stress in the first place. The way that double-crested
cormorants are being managed on Middle Island in Point Pelee National
Park (to be discussed) is a prime example of the interplay between human
factors and interpretations of ecological integrity. So is the wild horse
issue in Alberta, for that matter.

Currently, well under 1,000 wild horses – compared with over 8,000
range cattle – roam the foothills of southern Alberta, and although consensus suggests that horses are native to North America, the foundations
of the existing herds date to acquisition of Spanish breeds acquired by First
Nations groups in the early 1700s. Public interest in the horses dates to
the 1990s when the Alberta government, following reports of inhumane
capture methods, instituted a Horse Capture Regulation (1994) under the
Stray Animals Act (1980). Then, in 2011 and 2012, ostensibly in response to
reports about the increasing number of wild horses by disaffected grazing
and logging interests, Alberta Environment and Sustainable Resource
Development (ESRD) authorized the capture of 216 horses under the Horse
Capture Regulation. Following strong negative public reaction led by the
Wild Horses of Alberta Society, the government was forced to defend
itself by blaming the horses for creating significant ecological imbalances:
"Feral horses might look at home on the landscape – but because they're
not native species, they put pressure on the ecosystem."[106] Yet a report
commissioned by the ESRD in 2013 on stakeholder perspectives revealed
disagreement on the environmental impacts of the horses and a consensus
that the decline of grasslands was attributable to multiple factors.[107] The
report, however, indicated that the vast majority of the stakeholders felt
that population management was necessary, including some who felt
that since wildlife were managed through attrition and hunting, "horses
should be subject to the same."[108]

Reinforced by the report and an abiding assumption that local human
interests hold high precedence in resolving contentious wildlife issues,
the government proceeded predictably, announcing in 2016, "Since the

horse population is expanding, a population management program is necessary to ensure there are minimal adverse effects on other landscape users (i.e. wildlife, forestry, livestock and recreationalists). A balance has to be met between all landscape users and the land in a way that does not degrade the long-term viability of the landscape and vegetation. To proactively manage the horse population, an adaptive round-up program has been utilized to maintain an ecologically sustainable population on the landscape."[109]

Despite its rhetoric about the horses' singular role as contributors to ecological degradation, the Alberta government has not been forthcoming with conclusive scientific evidence to prove its case. Although the consultation report made broad reference to various research studies between 1975 and 2012 that suggested the feral horses posed a management issue affecting rangeland, reforestation, public safety, wildlife distribution, and habitat, it neither mentioned nor cited any specific source. Similarly, a document search of the websites of the ESRD and Alberta Environment and Parks revealed no available scientific study on the negative impact of wild horses on the environment.

In contrast, a comprehensive ninety-page review in 2015 by conservationist biologist Wayne McCrory based on extensive research found no scientific evidence that the wild horses were causing ecological damage.[110] McCrory even secured an admission from the ESRD and Alberta Environment and Parks that "they cannot point to any sites where free-roaming horses had damaged the range."[111] The review castigated the government for policies that lacked scientific rigour and credibility, for its strong bias against free-roaming horses in favour of range cattle, for inaccurate and inflated population estimates, and for a lack of transparency in withholding relevant information from the public, the media, and the independent scientific community.[112]

Another report, this time by wildlife ecologist and wild horse expert Craig Downer, which involved significant onsite research over an eighteen-month period and included thirty-eight ecological evaluations of diverse habitats and numerous interviews, concluded that the wild horses were impacting the landscape negligibly compared to anthropogenic disturbances and moreover were making positive ecological contributions. In stressing that the horses could not be considered an invasive species, the author believed that they "should be allowed to fill their ecological niche and treated with the respect due a returned North American native species of ancient and very long-standing precedence."[113] His overall conclusion was clear: "It is my specific recommendation that the wild horses who have adapted over the generations here be allowed to fill their ecological niche and play their natural role. If so allowed they will greatly aid in the healing process of soils and site stability, of waters and hydrological function, and in restoring the biotic integrity and ecosystem well-functioning at all levels."[114]

The subjective element in assessing for ecological integrity comes through loud and clear. The horse culls are linked to ecological degradation when in reality they are more about appeasing human stakeholders. It was also blatant given the extensive science-based analysis in the two reports and the lack of transparency from the provincial government about its own scientific findings or evidence to the contrary. Interestingly, only one scientist, a rangeland expert from the University of Alberta, sits on the fifteen-member provincial Feral Horse Advisory Committee, on whose advice the various culls are implemented. In the context of the wild horse issue, the misplaced use of ecological principles to disguise a human-interest agenda is a good example of Stephen Bocking's contention that the term "ecological integrity" can and is used "to justify nearly any action."[115]

ADAPTIVE MANAGEMENT

The adoption of what is known as adaptive, as opposed to tightly structured, management is now commonplace in resource management. Its principles were articulated as early as the mid-1980s by University of British Columbia professor Carl Walters in *Adaptive Management of Renewable Resources* (1986).[116] Originally conceived as a process for the design of creative resource management and policy alternatives by integrating the scientific method into management approaches, adaptive management has been broadened to embrace the notion of continual improvement. It accepts the uncertainty of knowledge about complex systems as well as the uncertainty of the outcomes of experiments involving them.[117] Properly implemented, adaptive management is a six-stage process that identifies uncertainties in resource dynamics and then designs diagnostic management experiments to reduce these uncertainties.[118] More than other management systems, adaptive management involves stakeholders – those impacted by a specific project – as participants in all aspects of decision making.[119] With its emphasis on local control and its flexibility in the form of ongoing testing of alternative hypotheses – which is usually trying to prove something to be false – adaptive management is widely accepted as the most effective knowledge-gathering tool informing modern wildlife policymaking. However, it is far from perfect, as has been noted: "The malleable nature of adaptive management is a double-edged sword. On the one hand, it allows for the concept to be utilized in a wide variety of situations. On the other hand, the fact that it is subject to such a wide array of interpretations is an effective barrier to its implementation."[120] A lack of definitiveness and clarity has resulted in confusion respecting exactly what the approach entails, the management context in which its use and application are appropriate and feasible, and the extent to which it has been applied successfully.[121] It has also resulted in uncertainty itself – about risk and cost, about credibility loss if things go wrong, about stakeholder commitment, and about ecological impacts.[122] Expenses, risk amenability, optimum timeframes for projects, stakeholder biases, and socio-political considerations are additional mitigating factors.

Due to its flexibility and nimbleness, adaptive management is firmly entrenched in Canadian wildlife policy and management. Applied properly and consistently, adaptive management can direct managers toward higher levels of efficiency and environmental enhancement. For example, adaptive management principles are being applied successfully in forestry management in British Columbia. Its application to wildlife, however, is highly selective. An adaptive management program, for example, that tries to find the most effective way to construct channels in order to increase the survival of salmon fry has merit; in contrast, trials that involve killing a certain species of wildlife to test its impact on another species do not. In fact, especially with regard to vulnerable species, many see adaptive management as far too risky.[123]

The most crucial element in adaptive management for wildlife and especially vulnerable species is its acceptance of uncertainty as an experimental determinant. The following comment at the Peter Yodzis Colloquium in

Fundamental Ecology at the University of Guelph in 2012 stresses the risks associated with a management system that relies on uncertainty: "The notions of treating policies as hypotheses and conducting management by experiment remain far from generally understood or widely accepted for reducing uncertainty that threatens to impede sustainability of renewable resources, biodiversity in general and, particularly, species at risk."[124] Regardless of other variables, adaptive management is a formal process for learning by doing that allows managers to legitimatize pretty well anything they want to do. The current wolf cull in British Columbia and the spring bear hunt in Ontario (both to be discussed) are outstanding examples.

Adaptive management also flies in the face of the precautionary principle inherent in wildlife management. The precautionary principle calls for withholding the initiation of proactive measures in the absence of scientific certainty about the outcomes. In terms of wildlife, the precautionary principle is a crucial guideline that seeks to minimize mistakes (and prevent deaths). The precautionary principle is enshrined in Canadian environmental policymaking. The Committee on the Status of Endangered Wildlife in Canada is guided by the precautionary principle in its assessments and designations of which wildlife species should be protected. The precautionary principle is stressed in the preamble to the United Nations Convention on Biological Diversity (1992),[125] of which Canada is a signatory. It is specifically mentioned in Ontario's Endangered Species Act (2007) and is coded in the federal Species at Risk Act (2002), as noted by the courts in the 2009 decision involving the endangered Nooksack dace in British Columbia.[126] Furthermore, the use of multi-hypothesis testing inherent in adaptive management can work against the precautionary principle. According to a study on wolves in the Algonquin Park area, an alternate testing hypothesis based on a short timeframe drew misleading conclusions about the impact of a limited ban on hunting.[127]

Unfortunately, the practical application of adaptive management principles is often deficient, and although not admitted as such, it has emerged as a modern label that edifies standard practices and justifies "trial by error" experiments. In the Yukon Wolf Conservation and Management Plan (2012), for example, adaptive management means no more that adjusting bag limits and seasons and changing bylaws.[128] Ontario's adaptive management plan for wildlife offers few details about the six-step process and simply lists harvest planning and allocation as well as hunter activity and harvest monitoring under its adaptive management guidelines.[129]

Parks Canada's adaptive management plan for dealing with hyper-abundant species stipulates lethal measures only as a last resort and predicates all actions on ongoing science-based programs of research, monitoring, and evaluation to incorporate new knowledge into management.[130] Yet the following statement in 2011 by the Canadian Environmental Assessment Agency, endorsing Parks Canada's plan to lethally cull moose in Gros Morne National Park in Newfoundland, inferred that the plan was doing the exact opposite: "Following the principle of adaptive management, the plan also allows for park staff or contractors to harvest moose if the volunteer harvest is unsuccessful at removing sufficient numbers. Parks Canada will continue to explore other management approaches throughout the course of the program as conditions such as animal wariness and cost-per-unit effort change or other forms of mitigating moose impacts become available."[131] In other words, only if the moose culls were not effective would parks management "consider including re-planting trees and other kinds of restoration," which it should have done in the first place if it had been following parks policy instead of using adaptive management to legitimatize the easiest and cheapest solution.[132]

An example of the uncertainty principle inherent in adaptive management concerns the impact of noise on mountain goats caused by low-flying recreational helicopters. According to a report based on research in southeast British Columbia, the acceptable measure of risk to mountain goats impacted by helicopters carrying recreationists should be set against long-term population trends in nonaffected areas.[133] In other words, regardless of helicopter-noise disturbance, which can affect mountain goats by inducing elevated heart rates, rapid flight, a decrease in forage activity, and even short-term range abandonment, an adaptive management approach would allow the flyovers and measure the level of acceptable risk to the mountain goats by conducting long-term research on population differentials in affected and nonaffected areas.[134] One wonders how long it will take to decide on an "acceptable" number of traumatized goats.

More serious is the practice of applying adaptive management principles in order to kill animals on a "see what happens" basis.[135] Or to quote Tom Ethier, an assistant deputy minister of the BC Ministry of Forests,

Lands and Natural Resource Operations, on the 2015 wolf cull, "We're really trying to figure out: does this work?"[136] Another lethal and unethical adaptive management strategy for mountain caribou in British Columbia involved an experimental moose-killing program in the Hart Ranges of the Rocky Mountains to gauge its effects on wolf populations and, by implication, caribou survival.[137]

Interpretations of ecological integrity and adaptive management are very subjective and are fitting examples of Benjamin Franklin's statement that a reasonable creature can find a reason for anything he wants to do.[138] When one manages caribou numbers by killing moose to gauge the effect on wolf populations or disguises economic-based motives in ecological terms to mount campaigns against wild horses, the outcomes are clear: individual wild lives are the casualties of selective human design.

THE RELIANCE ON SCIENCE

Scientific knowledge forms the backcloth of decision making in industry, institutions, and public policymaking. The belief that good science will always show the way or that scientific analysis draws upon the force of disciplined and trained minds to overcome speculation and guesswork remains largely intact, if somewhat eroded. Wildlife policymaking and management are no exceptions. Given that the role of science is to inform, not to dictate, wildlife policymaking, its actual misuse is difficult to identify. Generally, this misuse occurs on three levels.

The first is not the fault of science itself but the overreliance on a discipline that is anything but exact, correct, or rigorous. Or to quote two biologists, "If 10 biologists were asked to define a single term commonly used in wildlife science, they likely would invoke 10 different definitions."[139] When wildlife practice is compromised by a lack of scientific rigour, the results can be negative. Management of the wild horses in Alberta is a good example. More significantly, scientific knowledge is used by managers and politicians as a comfortable fallback catchword to justify or defend controversial wildlife decisions. The manner in which the federal government justified the uncertainty in its strategy for boreal woodland caribou (to be discussed) comes to mind.

Another major issue is the lack of transparency involving the availability, use, and validity of scientific knowledge and opinion in wildlife management. Wildlife managers often refer to scientific validity but do not produce evidence. In its current defence of grizzly bear trophy hunting, the BC government is scarcely forthcoming with its scientific rationales. According to Laura Beans of EcoWatch, the science behind government science-based decisions respecting grizzly bear management in British Columbia is neither transparent nor subject to independent third-party peer review.[140] A related problem concerns the way that expert opinion is integrated with scientific research to reach management solutions with no specific indication of how one was balanced against the other in reaching decisions. Again, BC grizzly bear management practices are illuminative. According to a 2015 report on grizzly bear harvesting in the province, expert opinion often overrode scientific methods in estimating bear densities.[141]

A final point concerns scientific bias in wildlife management. Bocking contends that when science operates on an authoritarian basis, it tends to mirror the belief system by supporting a conservative view of the world and thus rejects alternative visions like the relationship between humans and other species. He also argues that science reflects political and economic interests and thus tends to be aligned with stakeholder positions.[142] In short, the accepted role of scientists as neutral and objective is undermined by the social and political contexts in which they operate. His conclusions were reflected in a study on the delisting of grizzly bears in the Greater Yellowstone Ecosystem that found scientists employed by federal and state agencies were two to three times more likely to recommend delisting than those in academic institutions. The authors concluded that assessments of risk were not scientific-neutral and that "supposed scientific judgments may well be heavily influenced by socially segregated groups and their associated beliefs."[143] That the government-employed experts were more sanguine than the academics over bear survival under less-protected conditions is revealing.

Although it is true that wildlife policies are structured within professional guidelines and in the main are genuinely directed toward the benefit of wildlife, they are also driven by their fundamental assumptions about animals. Wildlife policymaking in Canada operates from a fractured jurisdictional base. It considers wildlife to be a neutered species-specific resource, rejects consciousness in animals, and accepts the myth of hunters as conservationists. It interprets ecological integrity from a subjective baseline perspective, applies loose and misleading adaptive management practices in violating the precautionary principle, and uses the term "best scientific practice" to selective advantage. All reflect the dominant belief system.

CHANGING ATTITUDES

During the preparation of this manuscript, I had many discussions with those who thought that I was wrong in contending that the belief system about animals was unchanging. In a way, they have a point. People today take a great deal of pleasure from learning about wildlife, whether it be at zoos, in documentaries, in structured close encounters, or simply when enjoying chance sightings. Public interest and involvement in animal issues and advocacy are on the rise. Accounts of people going to great lengths and even risking their lives to assist individual animals in danger or distress are commonplace. The mounting general sensitivity to issues of species loss and environmental degradation has reached levels unimaginable in the first half of the twentieth century. Proactive efforts by groups such as the Nature Conservancy of Canada are evidence of a strong restorative impulse and a desire to protect nature and its inhabitants. So even if these changing attitudes and practices are not overly reflected in wildlife management and policymaking, they are working to modify the belief system about animals, and especially in this narrative, they warrant some discussion.

Undeniably, the transition away from game to a wider concept of wildlife as manifested in the federal Wildlife Act (1973) indicated a changing management climate. For example, serious research was conducted on a variety of wildlife and habitat. The tolerance of predators was one early outcome. Wildlife sanctuaries and reserves were expanded, and with the North American Waterfowl Management Plan (1986), some 243,000 hectares of wetlands were secured under joint regional ventures. In 1981 Canada entered the Ramsar Convention on Wetlands (1975)[144] and currently has thirty-seven sites designated as "wetlands of international importance," or Ramsar sites, with a surface area of 13,086,767 hectares.[145]

The impact on wildlife of toxins in the Great Lakes was addressed. The opening of interpretive centres encouraged wide public interest in the lives of wild animals. Interest in endangered species began with the formation of the Committee on the Status of Endangered Wildlife in Canada in 1977 and led to the launching of the program Recovery of Nationally Endangered Wildlife in 1988. The ensuing decades saw more refinements. Management for ecological integrity and biodiversity enhancement meant that the whole biotic community was now in play.

Currently, the federal government participates in a wide variety of activities, projects, partnerships, and initiatives designed primarily to improve biodiversity and wildlife through sustainable practices. Since 1989 the Great Lakes Sustainability Fund has leveraged nearly $400 million from the public and private sectors for habitat restoration projects. It has also contributed approximately $110 million to more than 900 partnered projects in order to improve water quality in several areas. Results are impressive and include over 3,640 hectares of forests and wetlands, 584 kilometres of riparian habitat, 8 kilometres of shoreline, and 200 hectares of tallgrass prairie, as well as the mitigation of twenty-seven fish barriers. Between 2000 and 2015 the Habitat Stewardship Program for Species at Risk invested over $151.5 million to support more than 2,400 local conservation projects and to improve habitat for more than 420 species at risk, while leveraging an additional $397 million. The program has also established over 460 partnerships with Indigenous organizations, landowners, resource users, nature trusts, provinces, the natural resource sector, community-based wildlife societies, educational institutions, and conservation organizations. In partnership with the Nature Conservancy of Canada, the federal government is working to ensure the protection of over 200,000 hectares of sensitive land. The Aboriginal Fund for Species at Risk has invested over $29.4 million in 790 projects that involve more than 200 communities and benefit more than 280 listed species through increased Indigenous awareness of species at risk and through the development of strategies, guidelines, and practices. Until recently, the Department of Agriculture was responsible for the provincially delivered environmental farm-planning programs to decrease the impact of agricultural practices on biodiversity and the environment. By 2008 approximately 34 per cent of annual crop producers and 40 per cent of livestock producers had developed environmental farm plans. In 2014 this translated into over 70,000 farms and ranches.[146]

All official surveys indicate that Canadians are aware of and value their wildlife. A good example is the 2012 Canadian Nature Survey conducted by the federal, provincial, and territorial governments. More than 2 million Canadians reported donating money to support recovery of a species at risk, and over 227,000 undertook regular volunteer duties in a wildlife-support facility. Just under 7 million paid $874 million in membership fees or in donations to nature conservation organizations. Over 1 million spent money on maintaining, restoring, or purchasing land for wildlife or to conserve, enhance, or restore a natural setting, and almost 320,000 Canadians reported that they had personally donated their own land or signed an agreement with a land trust or other organization for conservation through an easement or other protective measure within the past five years. Perhaps the most telling statistic concerned problem wildlife on private property, which showed that for every person who chose the lethal option to eliminate the threat, more than ten either took no action or followed humane removal strategies.[147]

The numerous organizations that focus specifically on wildlife or that are indirectly supportive are astoundingly impressive in their range, focus, and proactivity.[148] Estimated at well over 1,800, these activist organizations are so diverse that any attempt to categorize them is, as one writer has observed, "an exercise in pounding square pegs into round holes."[149] Mostly nonprofit and with meagre staffs that are supported by dedicated volunteers, these organizations work tirelessly in the field and in political, social, and legal arenas on behalf of wildlife and their habitats. For example, NatureServe Canada, a nonprofit charity, and its network of Canadian Conservation Data Centres work together and with other government and nongovernment organizations to develop, manage, and distribute authoritative knowledge regarding Canada's plants, animals, and ecosystems. Currently, its database contains information on over 38,000 species and 2,200 ecosystems.[150] Rehabilitation groups nurse injured wildlife back to health. Others raise funds for land conservation and habitat protection and restoration. Legal groups lobby for protective legislation and challenge laws that put wildlife at risk. Some groups focus on specific species and their habitats. Several of these are almost academic in the depth of their knowledge and investigations and are invariably represented in hearings regarding proposed activities that impact their species. These advocacy groups often work in collaboration with each other and other stakeholders, including governments, on a long-range basis to secure mutually beneficial agendas. With their regular newsletters, website information, and direct communication, these wildlife support groups provide impressive communication networks that extend beyond provincial and national borders.

Loosely, these activist groups fall into three main areas. Groups devoted solely to wildlife usually have a tight focus. World Wildlife Fund Canada and Wildlife Preservation Canada concentrate on vulnerable species. The latter also focuses on captive breeding programs. The Atlantic Salmon Federation works cooperatively to conserve, protect, and restore wild Atlantic salmon runs and the ecosystems that sustain them. The Association for the Protection of Fur-Bearing Animals tackles cruelty to furbearers through conservation, advocacy, research, and education. Organizations like the Toronto Wildlife Centre, the Alberta Institute for Wildlife Conservation, and the Northern Lights Wildlife Society in British Columbia rehabilitate injured or orphaned wildlife for release back into the wild.

Advocacy groups work toward raising public awareness of wildlife issues by challenging unacceptable practices and securing greater measures of protection. Animal Alliance of Canada and the Animal Defence League are powerful forces advocating more protection for animals and a harmonious relationship between humans, nonhumans, and the environment. Ecojustice, formerly the Sierra Legal Defence Fund, is a nonprofit law organization that, in addition to advocating for more protective laws, provides legal services (often free) to environmental groups seeking to contest government policies or corporate actions in the courts. Currently, it is working to restore lost protections and to strengthen the overall reach of five environmental laws currently under federal review. Focusing on animals both in the wild and in captivity, Zoocheck Canada "endeavors to promote animal protection in specific situations and strive[s] to bring about a new respect for all living things and the world in which they live."[151] Its powerful advocacy on behalf of the Alberta wild horses is an excellent example of Zoocheck's proactive diligence.

In terms of broad and lasting benefit, the groups engaged in land and habitat conservation are undertaking vital work. Some government leadership is being provided here. For example, the federal and some provincial governments offer tax benefits for land donations under initiatives such as the Ecological Gifts Program, which encourages Canadians to donate ecologically significant land for conservation. As of October 2016, over 1,260 ecological gifts, mainly in the form of conservation easements valued at more than $807 million, had been donated, protecting over 180,000 hectares of wildlife habitat.[152] Land is also conserved by privately operated land trust organizations. The largest, the Nature Conservancy of Canada, has protected 1 million hectares through purchase or donation, as well as securing 2,000 hectares to add to protected land in BC's Great Bear Rainforest.[153] Significant wildfowl habitat protection is undertaken by organizations like Ducks Unlimited, which has acquired over 2.4 million hectares and completed 9,000 habitat projects.[154] Since its inception in 1963, the Canadian Parks and Wilderness Society has been involved in measures to protect over 500,000 square kilometres. The Wilderness Committee focuses on biodiversity enhancement through research and education.

The above discussion merely touches on the depth and range of public attention to the plight of wildlife and the willingness to engage in proactive measures. However, whether these collective efforts translate into a change in the belief system about animals is debatable. Although the figures may look impressive, the number of Canadians actually involved in wildlife and related issues as revealed in the 2012 Canadian Nature Survey is quite low overall, at well under 20 per cent. Similarly, public donations to environmental causes are minuscule compared to overall charitable giving in Canada. In 2010 the 1,155 registered environmental organizations nationally had total revenues of $959 million. Private donations amounted to $289 million of this amount, which, when set against a total of $15 billion given to charitable causes, translates into only 2 per cent.[155]

The vast majority of these organizations operate from an animal welfare position. Although they seek to improve the lot of species and individual animals, most do so on compassionate, environmental, or ecological grounds, or on the indirect duties rationale. The World Wildlife Federation, for example, endorses hunting as long as it does not affect endangered species. Ducks Unlimited spends millions on waterfowl habitat primarily for the purposes of maintaining recreational hunting. These welfare groups do not stress ethical treatment based on human parallels nor the closeness of the human-nonhuman relationship. They accept the instrumental use of animals as long as it is humane and necessary. Many hesitate to become too proactive in their efforts for fear of losing their charitable tax status, a weapon freely used by the federal government to silence those who take their cause too far. In short, most welfare wildlife support groups do not challenge the belief system. They simply want to soften it.

As indicated, governments and politicians are strongly resistant to animal advocacy groups and issues that go beyond the indirect duties position and that call for reforms prejudicial to human interests. The following statement from Lesley Fox of the Association for the Protection of Fur-Bearing Animals sends its own clear message: "The Association for the Protection of Fur-Bearing Animals was touring Canada and Europe, showing people the horrific reality of traps ... And then the government decided they'd had enough. The Canada Revenue Agency contacted The Fur-Bearers, along with four other organizations who were speaking out against the fur trade. Their message was simple: stop or we'll revoke your status. For the other four organizations, the financial implications were too much – they quieted down. But the Fur-Bearers stood strong and took the blow on the chin."[156] Recently, Animal Alliance of Canada reported on the existence and work of an informal bipartisan group of members of Parliament known as the "Outdoor Caucus." According to director Liz White, this group has been working to block humane, evidence-based legislation since 2006, achieving success against the Modernizing Animal Protections Act (Bill C-246) in 2016 and now setting its sights on blocking the Ending of Captivity of Whales and Dolphins Act (Bill S-203).[157]

Clearly, the need exists to lift the restrictions on animal advocacy groups. A study by the International Fund for Animal Welfare in 2008 applied nine criteria respecting animal cruelty legislation in fourteen countries, including Poland, Ukraine, Portugal, Malaysia, Croatia, and the Philippines.[158] Canada had the poorest cruelty legislation, being non-compliant in 6 of the 9 categories compared to an overall average of 1.8. The report slammed Canada for being the only country that had no explicit definition of an animal, for excluding wildlife from protection, and for making it virtually impossible to prosecute cases of neglect.[159]

In noting that over 99 per cent of acts of animal cruelty go unpunished in Canada, the report urged legislative changes to bring Canada in line with modern international standards.[160]

In contrast to the Association for the Protection of Fur-Bearing Animals and Animal Alliance of Canada, which are both animal rights organizations, an increasing number of animal welfare groups have become so fervour-driven, goal-oriented, and vociferous that they are conflated with the animal rights organizations that are asking for a different belief system and that in the main have failed to gain traction. Almost all animal advocacy groups are described in the media as animal rights activists when in fact most operate from an animal welfare position. It is a common, revealing ploy for governments and critics to align any powerful voice on behalf of domestic and wild animals with the pejorative term "animal rights." The public was led to believe that the International Fund for Animal Welfare was an animal rights group during its heated campaign against the seal hunt in the 1970s and 1980s. In fact, some who are calling for a change in the belief system maintain that the animal welfare position is actually detrimental to animals. For instance, prominent animal rights philosopher Gary Francione laments the co-option of animal rights by animal welfare: "As long as the animal movement perpetuates the confusion that permits even well-meaning animal advocates to believe that animal rights and animal welfare are substantially similar concepts and that 'animal rights' is merely a 'rhetorical' term to be used only as a political slogan, the animal protection movement will continue to march in one direction – backwards."[161] Canadian sociologist and animal studies professor John Sorenson is only slightly more hopeful: "To ensure that animal rights is no longer unthinkable but sensible, normative, and inevitable, we must overcome not only the deeply rooted ideology of human exceptionalism and the corporate-funded propaganda that encourages animal exploitation, but also the various forms of conservative, obscurantist, and welfarist thought that have been dominant in the field of animal studies."[162]

However, animal welfare might not be as separate from animal rights as the above quotations suggest. The number of people who continue to accept the instrumental, humane use of animals as a cultural norm but who would never consciously harm any living creature is growing. So is the number of those who recognize a wild being's inalienable claim to life. In this context, I am reminded of a comment by Bernard Rollin, a philosopher of consciousness and animal rights advocate: "It is reasonable to predict that if societal concern for animal welfare continues to grow, and to demand practical ethical changes in animal use based in that concern, attention to the legitimacy of the study of animal mind will also continue to grow."[163] Has he got a point? At the broader societal level, public attitudes toward support of wildlife and toward wildlife issues are changing and more nuanced. Popular opinion is more favourable toward wild animals today than at any time in the past. Indeed, it might be valid to assume that since private views often do not translate into public or even private behaviour, one cannot assess the depth of the changes in people's beliefs about animals in Canada.

Regardless, these positive sentiments have little impact on wildlife policymaking mainly because wildlife rarely figure prominently in the life courses of Canadians, most of whom presume that wildlife are being managed humanely and properly and in ways that protect public safety and the public interest. But approving of wild animals and wanting to see them thrive in the wild, while trusting wildlife management to use the tools of science and common sense to strike a balance between human interests and wildlife health, is not the same as demanding that wild animals be treated as individuals, that lethal solutions be abandoned, and that ethical standards apply to nonhumans. So although the belief system is being modified, it is not being transformed.

JOHN LIVINGSTON

Are there any prominent Canadian proponents of an alternate belief system when it comes to wildlife? Groups like People for the Ethical Treatment of Animals, Animal Alliance of Canada, the Association for the Protection of Fur-Bearing Animals, and the Animal Liberation Front operate from the animal rights position, but their focus is primarily on animals in the food and fashion industries, factory farms, and testing laboratories and on wanton cruelty and negligence generally. For a particular and eloquent alternate voice for wildlife, one that stands in sharp contrast to the almost universally accepted Leopoldian view, there is no better modern example than Canadian naturalist John Livingston (1923–2006), who rejected the belief system as a state of mind implacably indifferent to wildlife and so anthropocentric that the term "wildlife preservation" was a misnomer.[164]

Livingston's view of wildlife conservation as "the preservation of wildlife forms and groups of forms in perpetuity for their own sakes, irrespective of any connotations of present or future human use," is the direct antithesis of modern wildlife management. In his seminal work *The Fallacy of Wildlife Conservation* (1981), Livingston showed that wildlife conservation practices had little or nothing to do with the interests of wildlife. His main criticism stressed how the rational humanistic tradition, with its rationalizations and certainty about human superiority, values, and practices, had compromised wildlife conservation.[165] "But it is one thing to pretend and another to make the pretence *rational*," he wrote. "We have a neat way of doing it. Since wildlife cannot or will not see us in a dominant light (we are not of their species, therefore we are socially irrelevant), all we have to do is see wildlife in a human light. Then everything falls into place ... Because our standards are specific to us, no other species can possibly meet them. Man is thus the rational measure of all things."[166] On these grounds, the application of ethics to wildlife had no practical utility.

Livingston felt that humankind had abandoned the natural world and therefore lacked the level of compliance found in nature. For him, there can be no rational argument for wildlife preservation. It must be approached from elsewhere, from a willingness to open ourselves to more individual and qualitative experiences. In short, a new belief system. Livingston felt that it was necessary to see nature as all inclusive rather than as an external entity to be managed according to human-centred rational principles. His central point that "wildlife preservation is a state of being" rested on the belief that human relations with wildlife needed to involve a willingness to reach out and recognize other beings as unique, as well as on the conviction that management needed to be more qualitative and more attuned to the inner lives of its wild charges instead of pursuing quantitative, impersonal agendas.[167] He was also under no illusion about the prospects of any significant change, one that he admitted would "turn western metaphysics inside out."[168] After recognizing that humans should embrace their place in the beauty of existence, Livingston acknowledged that the "difficulties are formidable. Such an act – a conscious and willing act of self-recovery – would require the re-cognition of options that have long been masked from us by our accumulated tradition ... It would be the dissolution of the ancient western divorce from nature ... Implacably and relentlessly, our culture keeps us blinded to the qualitative sensory options that are ever at our hands and infinite in number."[169] As environmental activist David Orton has so wisely noted, "For Livingston, supposed cultural objectivity was actually riddled with cultural subjectivity."[170]

In summary, the Canadian governments stand squarely in the dominant belief system about animals in their policymaking and management practices. To them, wild animals lack conscious self-awareness and, unless listed as "threatened" or "endangered," have no individual value and are ethically entitled solely to a humane death. They are countered by a couple of thousand organizations that seek the reform of existing practices, that want to see more habitat preserved, and that wish to speak for those who cannot speak for themselves. Yet it appears that their numbers are too few, their financial resources too limited, and their individual ambitions too disparate to constitute or even influence a paradigm shift in the way people generally perceive their relations with animals. But they are there, speaking with their actions as well as their voices, and they embody one of Robert Paehlke's foremost environmental values, namely "a sense of humility regarding the human species in relation to other species and to the global ecosystem."[171] This stance is good because currently a lot of speciesism permeates wildlife policymaking. The welfare-oriented Canadian advocates are doing their best to keep it in check.

On a final note, it would be ridiculous, unfair, and plain wrong to suggest that wildlife managers, operating within the belief system, do not approach their tasks professionally and diligently. Any cursory examinations of their reports and practices will reveal serious, conscientious work on behalf of wildlife and their habitats. My point is that those entrusted with the responsibility of setting policy and practice are constrained by a belief system that refuses to acknowledge animals as selves. Through their human-centred worldview, these legislators, bureaucrats, administrators, and field practitioners are unable to see their wild charges both as kin and as integral parts of the same evolutionary unfolding that brought life and diversity to the unique planet we all call home.

Managing
Apex Predators

We want people to open their eyes and see the other animals
as they really are – our kindred and our potential friends with
whom we share a brief period of consciousness on this planet.
RICHARD RYDER

To philosopher Paul Taylor, "human actions affecting the natural environment and its nonhuman inhabitants are right (or wrong) by either of two
criteria: they have consequences which are favorable (or unfavorable)
to human well-being, or they are consistent (or inconsistent) with the
system of norms that protect and implement human rights."[1] He is so right.
Specific wildlife policies in Canada prioritize human interests. The intent
in the following discussion, which focuses on several species, is to show
how they are managed, the assumptions and depths of knowledge that
guide wildlife managers, how hunting quotas are set against uncertain
populations statistics, how political, economic, and cultural considerations count far more than the animals, how opponents are vilified, and
how anthropocentric views consistently override the interests and lives
of animals.

The application of traditional set-in-time attitudes toward wild animals
in Canada is best evidenced by the various management frameworks that
deal with a narrow range of species. Defined loosely as game animals,
problem animals, or commercial marine animals, these species are managed as renewable resources, with individuals being morally irrelevant
and species survival being the only norm. Translated into practice, this
means removing an annual percentage under a quota system set against
assessed overall populations. In short, Canadian governments primarily

deal with their high-profile wild animals by asking themselves only one question: how many individuals can be culled – removed, hunted, or euthanized – without putting overall numbers in jeopardy?

The current moratorium on hunting under the Management Plan for Mountain Goats in Alberta (2003) is a good example of the above. The plan admits that goat numbers are down, that accurate population assessments are problematic, that the impacts of anthropogenic disturbances in the form of logging and road construction are unknown, and that the goats are very sensitive to hunting pressure, have low recruitment rates, and are not recovering from overhunting as anticipated.[2] It further acknowledges that the death of a single female can have catastrophic implications for herd survival and that even experienced hunters often kill females by mistake. Yet the plan's intention is quite clear: "Alberta mountain goat populations have been very sensitive to hunting pressure in the past, but the demand for recreational hunting of mountain goats remains high. A protocol needs to be developed to evaluate when mountain goat seasons can be opened and how the seasons will be managed."[3] In other words, regardless of the goats' sensitivity to extirpation, wildlife managers anticipate the day when "a variety of [goat] hunting opportunities will be available for the recreational benefit and enjoyment of Albertans."[4] According to this view, past mistakes were made in assessing mountain goat numbers in Alberta, mistakes that, once corrected, will safely allow an annual mountain goat harvest. That accurate population assessments for wild species are extremely difficult and problematic is an understated reality in wildlife management, especially for wide-ranging, highly mobile, and elusive species.

Trophy hunting represents wildlife abuse and a threat to genetic diversity. Although prized victims include wildfowl species and members of the ungulate family, the most sought-after are the apex predators. Management plans in western Canada focus primarily on their popularity and value as creatures of the hunt. They tend to downplay the mounting evidence that apex predators are vital regulators of ecosystem health and balance and that their own population estimates are far less certain than advertised. In theory, wildlife managers may recognize that their fundamental role is to protect wilderness for its own sake in part by preserving ecosystems regulated by apex predators. In practice, however, the emphasis in management plans seems to be on the commercial, recreational, and revenue-raising advantages associated with killing an optimum number of apex predators annually. The grizzly bear in British Columbia and the cougar in Alberta are managed primarily within hunting parameters. The same applies to the polar bear in the Arctic, albeit with added dubious cultural considerations. The wolf is managed less as a trophy animal than as a despised but formidable foe. Although it might be an exaggeration to suggest that wildlife policies for apex predators are really about catering to a human craving for conquest and trophies, it is a thought worth considering.

GRIZZLY BEARS IN BRITISH COLUMBIA

The grizzly bear, a subspecies of brown bear, is an iconic animal whose awesome strength typifies the wildness and power of nature.[5] Stephen Herrero, an authority on grizzlies, describes them as "indicators of sustainable development." In addition to regulating prey numbers, grizzly bears maintain plant and forest health by dispersing seeds of many plant species, by aerating the soil as they dig for food, and by moving spawning salmon carcasses into the forest, where trees and other plants absorb their high levels of nitrogen.[6] Previously ranging across almost all of North America, the grizzly's habitat is now confined to the western United States and Canada. British Columbia is second to Alaska in overall North American numbers, and although its population is down over 40 per cent since the arrival of Europeans, the province is still home to over half of Canada's 25,000 grizzly bears. Due to their low reproduction rate, grizzly bears are slow to respond to impacts that produce a change in status. According to a report by the BC Ministry of Environment, Lands and Parks in 1995, a negative impact of hunting in one year is not felt for another six.[7] In short, grizzly bears constitute a crucial and vulnerable umbrella species whose status warrants close and careful scrutiny. In 2012 the Committee on the Status of Endangered Wildlife in Canada (COSEWIC) listed them as a "special concern."[8] As with predators generally, bear populations are very difficult to assess accurately, and if Alberta Environment is any example, official estimates will err on the high side.

In 2000, according to Alberta Environment, there were 850 grizzly bears in the province. In sharp contrast, noted scientist and bear expert Brian Horejsi gave an estimate of less than half that number.[9]

The province's first grizzly bear strategy was released in 1995 in response to a COSEWIC warning five years earlier that over 60 per cent of grizzly bears in Canada were either vulnerable or threatened and that all were at risk.[10] *A Future for the Grizzly: British Columbia Grizzly Bear Conservation Strategy* (1995) affirmed that "no other creature better represents the wilderness in British Columbia than the grizzly bear" and that "nothing is a better measure of our success in maintaining biodiversity than the survival of this species."[11] Yet for all these lofty statements, it was a broad document that promised merely to establish management areas and to work with stakeholders in the private sector. The strategy also noted, "Government recognizes hunting as an important part of our heritage that is enjoyed by thousands of British Columbians, has spiritual and cultural significance to First Nations and others, provides food for many people and generates more than $100 million in revenue."[12] Interestingly, a background report published as a companion document to the strategy warned about the ill effects of recent overhunting and the very difficult process of assessing overall bear numbers in terms of available habitat.[13]

Criticism ensued. Following allegations about inaccurate population assessments, overhunting, and population declines, the BC government, under the New Democratic Party, announced a three-year moratorium on grizzly bear hunting in February 2001. The moratorium was lifted five months later by the newly elected Liberal government, which cited sustainable bear numbers and the dollars brought into the economy by hunters. Two years later, a review by University of Alberta biologist Phillip McLoughlin found that hunting quotas were too high and concluded that in many areas grizzly bear populations had a 50 per cent chance of declining at rates exceeding 20 per cent over thirty years.[14] Under criteria set by the International Union for Conservation of Nature, this statistic met the standard for a threatened species.[15] McLoughlin also felt that current harvest rates were unsustainable and that the province could not maintain a 2.8 to 3.8 per cent annual harvest without more accurate population estimates.[16] This position was reinforced in an independent report commissioned by the BC minister of water, land and air protection, which found that no practical method existed for estimating bear numbers.[17] Noting the increasing grizzly bear mortality rates due to human influence, the report recommended urgent and aggressive remedial action.[18] Another report in 2004 by a group of scientists, including Horejsi, concluded that under current management practices, grizzly bears in British Columbia were facing extinction.[19] The authors were highly critical of the government's haphazard approach, arguing that the Grizzly Bear Management Areas were poorly designed and too small to maintain viable populations.[20] In their conclusion, the authors questioned the merits of hunting grizzly bears, stressing that "to date there has been no comprehensive analysis that includes current trends in habitat loss and which accounts for demographic and genetic stochasticity [probabilities] … To prevent this decline, the cessation of grizzly bear sport hunting must be considered."[21]

Even though in 2010 the province placed the grizzly on its Blue List (the equivalent of COSEWIC's "special concern" designation), it was for naught. Grizzly bear hunting continued in 135 hunting zones distributed throughout the 57 Grizzly Bear Population Units. Close to 70 per cent of the province's area was open to hunting, half of which allowed the maximum 6 per cent mortality rate.[22] According to one official source in 2010, a mortality rate of 9 per cent was sustainable in some areas.[23] Policies were relaxed to allow hunting in population units numbering fewer than 100 bears when the boundaries to adjacent units were "soft."[24] In 2012 this translated into hunting in a unit that contained only eighty-eight bears on the assumption that in-migration would be a compensating factor.[25] Between 2008 and 2012, the grizzly bear population in British Columbia dropped by almost 7 per cent.[26] As with wildlife generally, the accuracy of population estimates is problematic. A Canada-US study on assessments of black bear populations found that state-wide or province-wide black bear population estimates were not sufficiently precise or rigorous to provide accurate information on population trends.[27] In an extensive scholarly study carried out on wolves in Idaho, the authors affirmed that with large carnivores "few efficient and reliable methods exist for estimating populations and fewer still have been formally tested."[28]

The government's commitment to grizzly bear hunting was reflected in its trenchant attitude toward opposing voices. In 2005 the Raincoast Conservation Foundation raised $1.3 million to buy the commercial trophy hunting rights across 24,700 square kilometres of the Great Bear Rainforest, followed by an additional 3,500 square kilometres in 2012. The government responded by reallocating the lost harvest totals.[29] When ten frustrated First Nations groups tried to impose their own ban on grizzly bear hunting on the central and north coasts in 2012, they were told by provincial authorities that hunting was profitable to the province, and since enough traditional Native lands were already closed to hunting, they could not expect to have everything their own way.[30]

Nor was provincial officialdom impressed with the comprehensive study carried out by Stanford University through the Center for Responsible Travel, which reached the "overwhelming conclusion" that bear viewing in the Great Bear Rainforest "generates far more value to the economy, both in terms of total visitor expenditures and GDP and provides greater employment opportunities and returns to government than does bear hunting."[31] The study showed that, in 2012, bear-viewing companies in the Great Bear Rainforest generated in excess of twelve times more revenue in visitor spending than did bear hunting: viewing expenditures were $15.1 million, whereas guided nonresident and resident hunters generated $1.2 million. The bear viewers also went home happier if a thirty-year comparative study in Colorado was any indication. The study found that between 1982 and 2013 nonconsumptive recreationists consistently reported significantly higher levels of satisfaction from their interactions with nature than did hunters.[32] The Stanford report was also critical of the government, noting that its management and monitoring systems were unable to determine the number of bears lost to hunting within the Great Bear Rainforest.[33] Government officials were disappointed with the report and, in a bizarre rationalization, claimed that since bear watching and bear hunting were compatible activities, the report had created an "artificial divide."[34] Actually, the opposite is true. The Commercial Bear Viewing Association of BC is currently lobbying for protected viewing zones and an outright ban on hunting grizzly bears.[35] In 2015 one bear-viewing business operator chose to forfeit more than $60,000 in revenue by cancelling plans to guide tourists in an area frequented by hunters. He explained, "We can't, with a clear conscience, take guests into a valley where bears are being hunted … They are spending a lot of money locally, and they are doing that with an aim of seeing bears."[36]

The most serious challenge to the government's position on grizzly bear hunting came in an academic article published in November 2013. Authored by several scholars from three major universities in British Columbia and based on extensive research, the article argued that grizzly bear managers paid insufficient attention to the uncertainty factor in setting their sustainable mortality rates, resulting in significant over-mortalities, especially among females.[37] The authors concluded that proper consideration of the uncertainty factor warranted an 81 per cent reduction in hunting quotas and more no-hunting zones.[38] In short, shooting over 300 grizzly bears a year was way too many. Furthermore, as reported by Laura Beans of EcoWatch, the science behind government management studies was neither transparent nor subject to independent third-party peer review.[39] In fact, over the years, the BC government had been frequently criticized for its secrecy with respect to data on the grizzly bear populations and for the shaky science on which they are based.[40] In 2004, for example, grizzly bear researcher Barry Gilbert and colleagues questioned the serious lack of government documentation and noted the "lack of public and independent, scientific peer consultation on government management plans."[41]

The province reacted to the 2013 "uncertainty" article by expanding the 2014 grizzly hunting season through increased quotas and licences and by reopening the hunt in two population units that had previously been closed because of overkills.[42] In announcing the expanded hunt in a press release in December 2013, Steve Thomson, BC minister of forests, lands and natural resource operations, justified his decision by referring in part to the findings of a published report on grizzly bear densities in western North America: "The study released today reaffirms that grizzly populations in B.C. are being sustainably managed and with the best available science."[43] This is misleading. The report made no such state-ment. Actually, the authors concluded, "Current methods of predicting density in areas of management interest are subjective and untested." They predicted fewer bears in British Columbia and felt that their study demonstrated "the uncertainty in extrapolating animal densities, even for species for which there is considerable inventory data and a good understanding of the population biology." The authors further concluded that it was impossible to remove subjectivity from decisions respecting bear densities and suggested that twelve management units in British Columbia had annual kill rates higher than that allowed by policy.[44] In responding to queries in the BC Legislative Assembly with respect to the two aforementioned articles, Thomson was dismissive: "We continue to make decisions that are based on best available science, population estimates that are combined with a conservative grizzly bear mortality rate, to make sure that we continue to maintain the sustainable population of the province."[45] In November 2015 the Ministry of Forests, Lands and Natural Resource Operations, without prior debate and based on no specific rationale other than a desire to see more bears killed, tripled grizzly bear hunting quotas in the Peace River area of the province.[46]

In March 2016 the Ministry of Forests, Lands and Natural Resource Operations received a very interesting report on grizzly bear harvest management authored by three academics.[47] The fifty-five-page report found that "the grizzly bear harvest management procedures has attained a high level of rigor with a solid scientific underpinning modified, as necessary, by professional judgment. We believe that adequate safeguards have been established to ensure, with a high degree of confidence, the sustainability of this harvest."[48] In a subsequent press release, Minister Thomson informed the public that "the panel confirmed that B.C.'s population estimates are second to none."[49] Yet any close reading of the report revealed that it was anything but a clear endorsement of its grizzly bear harvesting policies. The authors found a lack of transparency in the preparation of harvest estimates.[50] They contested the way population estimates were taken and made particular reference to the uncertainty inherent in the mark-recapture model and to the reliance on expert opinion over scientific modelling.[51] Revealingly, the authors found that managers simply lacked the financial resources necessary to fund "proper population monitoring and assessment."[52]

The twenty-plus years of grizzly bear policymaking in British Columbia reveal a hidebound commitment to hunting even though population estimates are far from certain, numbers are declining in some areas, the vast majority of citizens in both urban and rural areas oppose the hunt, and bear watching is more popular and profitable than bear hunting. For example, a poll conducted in January 2017 found that 74 per cent of BC residents in rural ridings with a strong hunting tradition opposed trophy hunting of grizzly bears.[53] A simple answer suggests that British Columbia's reigning Liberal politicians cleave to the belief system more staunchly than their constituents. It was Premier Gordon Campbell's Liberal government that lifted the moratorium on grizzly bear hunting in 2001. Influential Liberal caucus member Bill Bennett made it known publicly in 2012 that he would continue to support the right of hunters to kill grizzly bears, and in 2015 Premier Christy Clark received the President's Award from the Guide Outfitters Association of BC as a gesture of thanks for recently amended regulations that supported trophy hunting.[54] Predictably, the politicians do not want to anger the strong hunting lobby and the outfitters who make money from the trophy hunt. Nor do they want to make a dent in the $350 million annual windfall from hunting.[55] When it comes to killing its iconic apex predator on the rationalized grounds that it is an environmentally good human thing to do to a good animal, the BC government seems out of touch with the times. Chris Genovali, executive director of the Raincoast Conservation Foundation, sums it up accurately: "Although attempts are made to dress the province's motivations in the trappings of proverbial 'sound science,' they are clearly driven by an anachronistic ideology that is disconcertingly fixated on killing as a legitimate and necessary tool of wildlife management."[56] Apparently, for BC policymakers, the iconic grizzly is just too iconic to be allowed to exist unmolested by humans.

This is disquieting given that part of the public tolerance for government policies in support of hunting rests on a residual fear of grizzlies. To many people, they represent ferocity and danger, inducing a fear that borders on paranoia. Yet, if Canadian naturalist Charlie Russell and photographer and artist Maureen Enns are right, the grizzly bear is anything but a menace to humans. Their two books, which document their six-year summer experiences living with grizzly or brown bears on the Kamchatka Peninsula on the northeast coast of Russia, are vivid testimonies to the reality of positive human-bear interactions. Russell, whose experience with bears spans decades, was inspired to undertake his unprecedented experiment by a cathartic experience on the Khutzeymateen Inlet in the Great Bear Rainforest when he was joined on a moss-covered log by a female grizzly, who, in a gesture of trust and friendship, gently touched his hand.[57]

From their experience living among the Kamchatka grizzlies, Russell and Enns learned that when treated with respect and understanding, grizzly bears are trustworthy, affectionate, and playful companions "with whom it is feasible for humans to be more generous and sharing in terms of land."[58] Interestingly, they link grizzly bear unpredictability in Canada to current management policies that inspire mistrust of, rather than rapport with, the bears.[59] They have a point. For instance, between 2011 and 2015, conservation officers chose the killing option over relocation of "nuisance" grizzly bears by a ratio of three to one.[60] Russell and Enn's message, buttressed by a vast array of incredible photographic evidence, is one of restrained optimism: "Hopefully, we have revealed that there is another way to relate to these awesome animals. With luck, we've also shown that fear is the most crippling obstruction to exploration – not only fear of the grizzly, but also fear of trying something new. The question remains whether entrenched human behaviour and beliefs can change quickly enough to make a difference."[61] It is a challenge that BC policymakers should be considering rather than bowing to clamorous trophy hunters and vested interests.[62]

WOLVES IN BRITISH COLUMBIA

The wolf in British Colombia is a different creature of the hunt in that he is not primarily a trophy animal. Wolves fill the same roles as other apex predators but are perceived as marauders by ranchers and farmers. Tough, intelligent, and very difficult to hunt, wolves, although furbearers, are combated as enemies.

No animal has had a more complex relationship with humans than the wolf. Environmentalist Ian McAllister has noted that perspectives on wolves are so different that is "difficult to imagine that they are held by the same species on the same planet and the same continent."[63] He also contends that any creature whose reputation is encoded in so much myth, misconception, and lore must be endowed with "immense spirit, mystery and intelligence."[64] Indeed, many consider the wolf to be the most charismatic symbol of the wild, a highly intelligent being whose complex social patterns reflect compassion, empathy, and moral behaviour.

Biologist and wolf expert Paul Paquet sees the wolf as providing "a test of how likely we are to live sustainably in the natural world."[65] Philosopher Mark Rowlands, in his poignant account of his life with the wolf he raised, writes that "the wolf is art of the highest form and you cannot be in its presence without this lifting your spirits."[66]

Unfortunately, this group is in the minority. Historically, wolves have been demonized, feared, and anthropomorphized through pejoratives like "mean," "unrepentant," and "murderous."[67] The North America experience has been one of constant warfare against them, resulting in extirpation from most of their ranges.[68] A 2012 study showed that wolves influenced political and social discourse at a highly emotional level, mostly on the negative side.[69] Similarly, a ten-year study involving over 30,000 comments on wolves in American and Canadian media revealed a strong bias toward negativity, with the greatest antipathy found in those areas containing wolf populations.[70] Currently, several municipalities in northern Alberta maintain a futile bounty program on wolves.[71]

In Canada the presence of large wilderness areas has enabled wolves to survive in most provinces, although without much public love, especially in British Columbia, where the wolf population is thought to hover around 8,000. In 1979 the first provincial management plan described wolves as the most polarized of all species in terms of public perception and recommended shooting, trapping, poisoning, and more liberal hunting seasons and bag limits to reduce wolf problems.[72] Similar sentiments in the management plan of April 2014 and the official sanction given to a wolf-killing contest in 2013 show that nothing has changed.[73]

Wolf policies and programs in British Columbia have been remarkably consistent.[74] A bounty system on wolves operated for almost fifty years, from 1907 to 1955. In the 1950s bait laced with cyanide and strychnine were distributed at bait stations and dropped from planes in remote locations. Selective poisoning continued until 1999. In the late 1970s and 1980s, 1,000 wolves were poisoned and shot from helicopters in northeast British Columbia in an unsuccessful attempt to reduce prey mortalities.[75] Trapping was introduced in 1926, discontinued in 1966, and then reinstated ten years later when wolves were designated as furbearers.

In addition to residual fear, the opposition to wolves and their resulting persecution has two rationales. The first is political and likely the pivotal reason behind the recent management plan. It concerns the perceived threat posed by wolves to the billion-dollar livestock industry. Over a half-million cattle graze on 26 million acres of private and Crown land in wolf country, most of it in the Cariboo region and in the more northern area of the Nechako and Peace Rivers, which has seen the most dramatic increase in cattle numbers over the past forty years. It is difficult to attach an accurate financial figure to wolf depredations on livestock. The value of livestock losses from all predators in 1978 totalled a meagre $57,572.[76] From 2012 to 2013, cattle mortalities caused by all predators totalled 168, a figure that represented 0.07 per cent of all cattle grazing on Crown land in British Columbia.[77]

The livestock industry paints a very different picture. In 2012 ranchers estimated wolf depredations at $15 million, a figure that, at existing cattle prices, translated into a loss of 19,736 head, or the equivalent of the entire provincial herd of one-year-old steers.[78] Another inflated assessment was provided in 2011 in a report by the BC Agricultural Research and Development Corporation, partly funded by the BC Ministry of Agriculture. Quoting annual predation figures of 6,000 calves and cows, while laying the onus of blame on the wolf, the report set an annual revenue loss of $4 million to farmers and ranchers and $9 million to the provincial economy.[79] In emphasizing the economic threat posed by wolves and other predators, the report superimposed the traditional attitude of ranchers and farmers onto the general citizenry by rationalizing that "the public has the sense that the number of predators meets or exceeds the social carrying capacity and that further preservation is not in the best interests of the general population."[80] That the report made no mention of the ecological role of predators and that it dismissed the wolf entirely in terms of positive human interest are facts that speak for themselves. Regardless of its biases, the report, with its industry-based value system and government endorsement, represented a strong statement by an influential lobby.

The second rationale for opposition to wolves is that they are seen as threats to other wildlife species and are blamed for the decreasing numbers of boreal woodland and mountain caribou.[81] The major culprit, however, is not the wolf but humans, whose resource development activities open up corridors that increase predator-prey interactions. A 2008 study on these caribou by Environment Canada concluded, "Modern commercial forestry creates new early seral forest stands which benefit primary prey species," such as moose and deer, but which also allow easy access by wolves, "resulting in increased predation rates on secondary prey like caribou."[82] Eight years earlier, the BC Ministry of the Environment had admitted that the main issues facing boreal woodland and mountain caribou were the loss of lichen-producing winter ranges, habitat fragmentation, and anthropogenic disturbance and hunting. As for predators like wolves, it was noted that habitat should be managed to keep them away from caribou. No mention was made of culling programs.[83] For Paquet, "Humans are the ultimate cause of endangered mountain and boreal caribou through cumulative habitat degradation imposed by resource industries and ongoing recreational access and activities."[84] In acknowledging that killing wolves to recover caribou might work in the short run, the conservation group Wolf Awareness underscores the real problem (which is not the wolf): "To date, what has been protected for BC Mountain Caribou is too small and isolated to ensure self-sustaining herds."[85]

In 2009 a report on mountain caribou prepared for the BC Ministry of the Environment recommended intensive action against wolves, suggesting that if caribou herds were to recover, wolf numbers should not exceed 1.5 per 1,000 square kilometres, a number far below the average estimated wolf densities in northern British Columbia.[86] In was also noted that conventional methods of hunting and trapping were inadequate and that measures like shooting the wolves from helicopters were the most cost-effective.[87] In releasing the report, Chris Ritchie, the species at risk recovery coordination manager, described it as a significant accomplishment and one that would "guide government in moving forward with Mountain Caribou Recovery."[88] The "moving forward" translated into regular culling programs where wolves were shot unethically and cruelly from helicopters.[89] In 2015 a five-year, multi-million-dollar culling program was undertaken, encouraged by the logging industry, which feared that unless wolf numbers were reduced, it would be forced to set aside more forest under the federal caribou recovery strategy.[90] Noting a need to step up the number of wolves killed in the second year of the program and ignoring a 200,000-signature petition by Pacific Wild to stop the slaughter, Tom Ethier, an assistant deputy minister of the BC Ministry of Forests, Lands and Natural Resource Operations, underscored the official attitude in a statement that emphasized both the worst aspects of adaptive management and insensitivity in wildlife policymaking: "We're really trying to figure out: does this work?"[91] This self-damning comment lends credence to Paquet's observation that "manipulative conservation management should be well grounded in ecology and environmental ethics. Wolf culls have neither."[92]

British Columbia's forty-eight-page Management Plan for the Grey Wolf (2014) was a tentative, self-contradictory document that reflected more ignorance than knowledge of wolves.[93] It offered little guidance beyond population reduction and, according to one critic, was nothing more than a "wolf killing plan."[94]

The plan was based on uncertain knowledge of wolf populations, a fact that was openly admitted and then inadequately qualified.[95] The plan referred to direct census as being "infeasible" due to the secretive nature and high mobility of wolves,[96] but it then noted the merits of indirect census, which assessed wolf populations according to two criteria. One involved loose extrapolations based on estimated numbers per 1,000 square kilometres,[97] and the other measured wolf numbers against the presence of ungulate prey. The validity of using ungulate numbers to correlate wolf populations is questionable. Research based on thirty-two sites in North America found that wolf populations are self-regulated rather than limited by prey biomass. "Our analysis," wrote the authors of one article, "shows that intraspecific strife, territoriality, or some other regulatory mechanism is relevant and likely plays an important role in wolf population dynamics."[98]

On these two criteria, the management plan concluded that the number of wolves in the province could be anywhere between 5,300 and 11,600. This meant, apparently, that the real number was half-way between the two. Ergo, there are 8,500 wolves in British Columbia. To make matters worse, officials were forced to acknowledge that in the absence of a mandatory reporting system, the number of wolves being killed each year by resident hunters and trappers was unknown.[99]

The most damning admission and one that virtually destroyed its credibility appeared toward the end of the plan. The section entitled

"Knowledge Gaps" conceded that the wolf was very much an unknown quantity: "The role of wolves in the dynamics of B.C.'s multi-predator, multi-prey systems remains the most significant knowledge gap. These predator-prey systems are characterized by complex dynamics between and among predator and prey species, with resultant time lags, stochastic events, and changing local conditions, which makes generalizations difficult."[100] The plan's focus on adaptive management as a "learn as you go" solution, or put bluntly, a rationale for unsupported decision making, is not encouraging for wolves or for those who value them.[101]

Thus the plan recommended that opportunities for "economic, cultural, and recreational uses of wolves" be pursued, that the "impacts on livestock caused by wolves be minimized," and that specific predatory packs or individuals that were "likely preventing the recovery of wildlife populations" be managed.[102] Supported by generous hunting quotas, no limit on killing females or pups, no bag-limit zones, long and sometimes open year-round hunting seasons, no licence requirements for residents, and open options on other "solutions," the management plan represented a war on wolves.[103]

So, in the face of opposition, the British Columbia government implemented a wolf management plan that emphasized maximum mortalities in spite of very subjective population estimates and no science-based knowledge of the wolf's vital ecological role in regulating smaller carnivore numbers, ungulate distribution and robustness, and overall biodiversity health.[104] In June 2016 the government removed seasonal limits and increased bag limits in the Thompson region, parts of which already had year-round hunting and no bag limits.[105]

One should not be surprised. Two years earlier, the government had declined to overrule its own Gaming Policy and Enforcement Branch, which had refused to stop a wolf-killing contest in Fort St John. In an affirmation of speciesism, the contest encouraged hunters to go out and kill up to three wolves and submit them for adjudication. Cash prizes were awarded to winners, including a booby prize for the smallest wolf. Promoted in an exaggerated poster that depicted the wolf as viciousness incarnate, the contest drew wide public criticism and defensiveness from its organizers.[106] The Ministry of Forests, Lands and Natural Resource Operations distanced itself, and the Gaming Branch upheld the legality of the contest on the grounds that it was a test of skill.[107] The whole exercise was another example of residual contempt for wolves. As for the three-month contest, the sixty hunter-entrants managed to shoot a total of six wolves,[108] proving one inescapable fact that continues to frustrate those who want them dead: of all North America's apex predators, wolves are by far the hardest to kill.

Growing field-based research on wolves is evidencing the complexities and social dynamics of individual wolf families, including higher-order cognition, self-awareness, advanced parenting skills, empathy, and a sense of justice.[109] Yet the BC government is intent on killing as many as possible by shifting the blame for caribou depletions from humans to the wolves and by bending to the wishes of the livestock industry. In his thought-provoking book *Of Wolves and Men* (1978), author Barry Lopez delves into the complexities that surround attitudes toward wolves. He sees wolves as evocative animals who have exerted "a powerful influence on the human imagination."[110] But to Lopez, they do far more than touch the imagination. They are windows into humanity itself. The following eloquent comment about human antipathy toward wolves should be read and digested by those who prepare management plans. "The motive for wiping out wolves," Lopez writes, "proceeded from misunderstanding, from illusions of what constituted sport, from strident attachment to private property, from ignorance and irrational hatred. But the scope, the casual irresponsibility, and the cruelty of wolf killing is something else. I do not think it comes from some base atavistic urge, though that may be part of it. I think that we simply do not understand our place in the universe and have not the courage to admit it."[111] It is unfortunate that the dominant belief system embedded in government thought disallows everything Lopez has said.

COUGARS IN ALBERTA

The cougar is the largest member of the cat family in Canada. Cougars are magnificent animals whose acute sensory perception, speed, and athleticism make them efficient survivors in their home ranges. Cougars rarely prey on livestock, and research has shown that their presence does not impact ungulate populations. Perennially viewed with fear and mistrust, cougars have been largely extirpated in eastern and central Canada, and in many provinces they are protected from hunting. Not so in Alberta, where "the cougar resource" is managed as a game animal for the benefit of Albertans.[112] Although cougars are shy, solitary animals, increasing human habitation is precipitating human conflict situations. The province's management plan was prepared in 2012 with two overriding goals. The first was to accommodate growing hunting interest, and the second was to provide a framework for handling cougar interactions with humans.

The Management Plan for Cougars (2012), which presented the cougar as a prime game animal, was an expansive, seventy-two-page, research-based document, replete with figures, graphs, and an impressive bibliography.[113] The focus was on the cougar's adaptability and on Alberta as the animal's ideal environment. The plan stressed that cougars were wide-ranging, flexible in habitat and prey selection, and at home in an expanding range that had brought about a threefold density increase in two decades. The plan noted their high reproduction capacity and a good survival rate enhanced by immigration. The plan also commented on their resilience and capacity to withstand anthropogenic intrusions and the visible human presence.[114] For a pro-hunting government that saw killing its wildlife as a public benefit, the presence of an iconic, adaptable, and apparently fecund predator like the cougar was as good as it got.

Hunting was front and centre in the plan, being described as a "quality recreational experience."[115] The interests of hunters were pivotal in four out of the six management objectives, which stressed benefits to all Albertans, even though only a tiny minority of said Albertans shot cougars.[116] The plan expanded the areas open to hunting, reduced licence costs, gave private landowners the right to kill cougars on their property year-round, and set an overall harvest rate as high as 20 per cent.[117] The plan also hinted that the two-phase, four-month hunting season in fall and winter might be extended and supplemented by additional seasons. A bow-hunting component was also under consideration.[118] As for harvest quotas, the fall hunting season had none, nonhunting mortalities were not included in quotas, and the practice of balancing overquota harvest in one year with reduced quotas in the next was abandoned.[119]

In short, although it might not have been open season on cougars, the plan came close to sanctioning it. The following comment by a local outfitter speaks volumes about the plan's intent and mentality. After exulting over the recent killing of one of the largest cougars in the world, the Double Diamond Outfitters went on to say, "Alberta cougar hunting is truly beyond compare. Not only is Alberta blessed with the largest subspecies in North America, the largest specimens documented, have been from Alberta as well. Add to that, cougars in Alberta occupy habitat that is more accessible than that found in many other places. Therefore, regardless of your physical condition, your odds of success are likely higher in Alberta than anywhere else."[120]

The manner in which the plan addressed the issue of cougar-human conflict reflected overreaction and a willingness to use the lethal option. Here, the emphasis was on public safety because cougars were not staying where they should. One wonders about the plan's use of the term "conflict." Cougars are rarely aggressive toward humans, and like wild animals in general, they will flee rather than attack. Only seven people in Canada have lost their lives to cougars over the past century and only one in Alberta.[121] The emotional dimension, as opposed to real threat, is seen in the sixty-three official "cougar interactions" recorded by the province for the year 2013. Apparently, fifty-one of them involved sightings in developed areas, another eleven involved closer proximity to human habitation, and one resulted in the death of two dogs. To its credit, the plan appeared to take the enlightened route by emphasizing the importance of education in developing cougar-awareness behaviours and in elevating public tolerance levels. Yet by referring to public-opinion surveys that indicated "an almost irrational fear of this large cat," as well as to comments that evidenced people's terror, fear, and paranoia, the plan's authors were clearly less sanguine about the prospects of an enlightened citizenry than their words suggested.[122] So the emphasis was put on allaying public fear by persecuting "offending" cougars.

Although the plan mentioned aversive conditioning and relocation as desirable solutions to conflict situations, the lethal option was everpresent. Hazing techniques to frighten cougars, such as the use of rubber bullets, dogs, or loud noises, were not even mentioned, and aversive conditioning was itself dismissed as largely ineffectual. As for relocation, the plan was vague in discussing its effectiveness but left the impression that it was a commonly used option. However, according to the plan, offending cougars were being killed rather than relocated at a ratio of almost three to one.[123] The reason lay in an extremely broad interpretation of what constituted a threat to human safety. Since cougars only have to be perceived as posing a threat for the lethal option to be exercised, the mere presence of a cougar in the vicinity of concentrated human settlement often meant a death sentence. As the plan rationalized, "These removals are not considered a threat to overall population viability, and are necessary to balance public tolerance with cougar conservation."[124] So here we have an official plan that not only encouraged humans to slaughter hundreds of cougars in the wild for fun but also endorsed death for any cougar who might be perceived as a possible threat to human safety. In practice, highly subjective decisions that set the value of a cougar's life against public safety are pretty easy to make. As geographer Chris Darimont of the University of Victoria notes, "A bullet reduces the chances of more conflict between humans and a particular cougar to zero and is 'much cheaper' than tranquillizing and relocating."[125]

A few examples will suffice. In 2014, after park officers in the Cypress Hills shot three cougars for the "unusual behaviour" of killing dogs, one summed up the official rationale: "It's fairly standard practice for a land manager that has cougars, that when you start seeing unusual behaviour, that's when you step in and have to destroy the animal."[126] A fish and wildlife officer in Canmore, Alberta, shot a female cougar that had killed an off-leash dog. He then inflicted the same fate on another young cougar in the vicinity who "would not give ground." His rationalization about public safety was in line with policy: "We now have a habituated cougar that feels comfortable walking around houses, being close to people and targeting dogs ... We now have a cougar that is now just one step away from possibly making contact with a person."[127] In Calgary, in September 2014, fish and wildlife officers shot a cougar who was lying in long grass near the recently completed South Calgary Health Campus on the city's outskirts not far from the Bow River corridor. Although the cougar was displaying no aggression and, according to one source, was licking his paws in the morning sun, he was deemed too agitated to tranquilize and, on "public safety" grounds, was shot several times.[128] A video taken by a private citizen from a hospital window showed the cougar lying quietly in the grass just seconds before the first shot jerked his head backward. In January 2017 three cubs were shot out of a tree in Penticton, British Columbia, and their mother killed because they were hunting deer in an urban neighbourhood and showing disregard for humans. The conservation officer's rationale was simple: "Human safety has to take precedent."[129]

Alberta's Management Plan for Cougars left much to be desired. Given that the cougar is one of the most reclusive of wild creatures, one should be wary of the validity of a management plan that included cougar viewing as a recreational opportunity and a strategy for the future.[130] Several issues were either ignored, misleadingly presented, or superficially discussed. The plan contained nothing on intraspecies social interactions and dynamics. Nor did it deal seriously with the ecological importance of cougars. True, the word "ecological" appeared nine times in the plan, but five were in the bibliography, and the other four were followed by the noun "factors," "role," "importance," or "integrity," with no elaboration and nothing about ecological processes. The plan's confidence, even smugness, about the robust future of the cougar was misplaced. Cougar population is a good example. The plan gave optimistic provincial estimates of around 2,000 cougars, even though no comprehensive reliable measurement tool has ever been developed for this wide-ranging, highly mobile, and elusive cat.[131] The plan was silent about factors driving prey selection, prey switching, and killing rates, as well as about how dispersal and immigration impact population dynamics.[132] Or to quote the plan, "Due to the difficulty and expense of doing so, the department has not attempted to collect systematic data on cougar population trends, densities, or predatory behaviour."[133]

The plan reached widely into North American literature on cougars. It had to since only two in-depth studies exist on cougars in Alberta.[134] The first was conducted in the Sheep River area in southwest Alberta between 1981 and 1989 in two phases and was primarily financed by government.[135] The second, out of the University of Alberta, took place between 2005 and 2008 in Clearwater County on the east-central slopes of the Rocky Mountains.[136] Some interesting observations were made in these studies that were not included in the management plan. A 144-page draft of the commissioned Sheep River study, presented to the Alberta Fish and Wildlife Division in 1988, noted that the importance of cougars lay not in their being hunted but in their public status as enduring symbols of the wilderness.[137] In stressing the absence of relevant studies, the authors noted the lack of knowledge of the cougar's breeding dynamics in established population clusters.[138] A later article on the study, written by two of the original investigators, pointed out the subjective nature of harvest quotas: "It is unknown what annual harvest rate could be sustained and still allow for stability or growth in the population size."[139] The authors also referred to ignorance about the ecological conditions that influenced cougar population densities.[140] The second study, in Clearwater County, did not focus on hunting but emphasized predator-prey and interspecies dynamics. In a cautionary statement, not evident in the management plan, the authors noted that "cougars remain difficult to manage." Indicating serious knowledge gaps and an uncertain future for cougars, the authors further stated, "Our foresight regarding cougars in Canada is clouded by unanswered questions about cougar ecology, conservation, and management."[141]

The management plan's focus on hunting misleadingly endorses the compensatory mortality hypothesis. This hypothesis predicts that when hunters kill adult cougars (mostly males), the reduced competition for resources induces a compensatory density-dependent response that results in higher maternity and reproductive success, increased cub survival, and lower natural mortality. In other words, hunting is sound practice because natural compensating factors neutralize its impacts, or as the plan notes, "Compensatory mortality is central to sustainable harvest of wildlife populations because it provides increased opportunity to harvest a population without causing long-term decline."[142] However, researchers tested the compensatory mortality hypothesis on heavily and lightly hunted cougar populations in Washington State over the five-year period 2002–2007. They found that in the heavily hunted area, male populations remained unchanged, but female numbers and kitten survivals declined.[143] The reasons were linked to dispersal patterns. Male cougars, who have very large and overlapping home ranges, replace and balance the number of killed by hunting. In contrast, female cougars do not disperse as widely, and hunting reduces their numbers. Kitten mortalities also increase when young are orphaned or when they are killed by the immigrating males to induce estrus in their mothers for breeding purposes.[144] The authors conclude, "The compensatory mortality hypothesis may not be appropriate for modeling hunter harvest for cougars and other large carnivores that exhibit long-distance dispersal." Unfortunately for cougars, Alberta's Management Plan for Cougars is not on the same wavelength.[145]

The Management Plan for Cougars raises serious concerns about the cougar's threat to public safety but offers very few ideas regarding what to do about it, beyond salving public disquiet by removing offenders, preferably in the most permanent way.[146] The authors of the plan were either unaware of or chose to ignore research that posited a correlation between cougar hunting and cougar-human conflict. For example, three Washington State University scientists suggested that sustained cougar hunting coincided with increased cougar-human conflicts because less-experienced younger males moved in to replace the more human-wary adult males shot by hunters.[147]

The plan included no specific strategies to address cougar interaction with humans, even though research suggests that risk-awareness factors are complex and differentiated.[148] A survey of public attitudes toward cougars in Montana concluded that perceptions of risk from cougars exceeded reasonable estimates and were linked to cognitive and affective factors. The level of knowledge about cougars was a crucial cognitive determinant, and irrational fear of carnivores generally, along with the visual imagery associated with a cougar attack, however rare, impacted affective attitudes. The researchers stressed programs that addressed both the cognitive and affective domains to induce a higher level of risk awareness.[149] Similarly, a survey on risk perception of cougars among rural-urban fringe residents in the southern Alberta foothills revealed variations associated with location. Although the tolerance levels were positive overall, residents in areas frequented by cougars were the least afraid of them, whereas the converse was true for those living in new fringe urban areas. Respondents to the survey felt that they were not well informed about wildlife issues in their communities and that there was a lack of public participation in wildlife management, and over 70 per cent expressed a desire to be more involved.[150] The Management Plan for Cougars does not tap into these elements.

Moreover, research suggests that the behaviour and physiology of cougars, combined with human psychological factors, warrant a specific educational focus to secure positive attitudinal change.[151] Education should focus specifically on cognitive, practical, and knowledge-based responses. Local residents can help to implement programs, create habitat, conduct biological surveys, offer educational programs, lead tours, and raise funds. Examples do exist. A successful program in California educates the public about local wildlife by teaching residents how to respond to wildlife intrusions using methods based on animal behaviour. This program has successfully diminished the overall number of wildlife complaints and reduced most of the remaining complaints, from panic-based to knowledge-based ones.[152] Although viable options exist to facilitate a more knowledgeable and tolerant citizenry, they apparently fall outside the purview of Alberta's Management Plan for Cougars.

In short, the Management Plan for Cougars emphasizes very little beyond its aim to maximize the "recreational benefits and enjoyment to Albertans from the cougar resource through the provision of a variety of recreational opportunities, including viewing and hunting."[153] Given the implausibility of viewing cougars, the "recreational benefits and enjoyment" refer solely to hunting, which can include hunting with dogs. As described by the Double Diamond Outfitters, "During the hunt we will travel the back country using four wheel drive trucks and snowmobiles to locate a suitable track. From there the pursuit will be on foot with hounds."[154] What this means is that after a jaunt on a snowmobile, the hunter tags along until the outfitter's dogs finally tree the cougar. This done, the exhausted, defenceless animal is then blasted out of the tree to become someone's trophy. The plan clearly stipulated that this callous, unethical act constituted a recreational benefit that all Albertans could enjoy, a contention that is as disturbing as it is wrong.

Alberta's Management Plan for Cougars represents the objectification of wildlife typical of management generally. It repeatedly referred to "the cougar resource." It associated cougar existence with human recreational benefit and endorsed an ignominious death, which is ethically undeserved by any living creature. It sought death-dealing options for cougars who came into contact with a human without balancing cause or assigning blame. In short, the plan was a speciesist document representative of an outdated mindset and a belief system that refuses to recognize the dignity of nonhuman lives.

POLAR BEARS IN THE NORTH

Given Canada's northern orientation and historical association with the Arctic, the polar bear is the country's most iconic and symbolic animal. These awe-inspiring, beautiful creatures, with their great strength and incredible endurance, are synonymous with the harsh and timeless land they inhabit.[155] However, even more than the other big mammals that make up Canada's tapestry of apex predators, polar bears are vulnerable giants. As a "resource," they join the rest of Canadian wildlife as instruments for human use. In that they are subject to serious threats to survival, fractured management frameworks, unique cultural-political discourse, and relentless hunting, the plight of polar bears is a sad testimony to the value of animal life in Canadian policymaking.

According to current approximations, Canada is home to about 16,000 polar bears, which is about two-thirds of the global population, or in human terms, an average attendance at a National Hockey League game. Considered a terrestrial rather than marine species, polar bears are scattered throughout the North in thirteen subpopulations (some sources refer to nineteen) and across seven jurisdictions, which include four provinces, the two northern territories, and Nunavut, the latter being home to over 80 per cent of Canada's polar bears.[156] Polar bears subsist primarily on blubber from seals, which they catch on the sea ice between autumn freeze-up and spring thaw. When on land, polar bears eat very little and can fast for months while waiting for freeze-up, when they can return to the ice platforms that sustain them. Their reproduction rate is low, with females denning every three years and giving birth in late fall, usually to twins. Despite their impressive size, polar bears are very mobile predators and excellent swimmers. Insulated by 10 centimetres of blubber, they can withstand intense cold and actually begin to overheat at 10 degrees Celsius. Their preferred habitat is the annual sea ice covering the waters over the continental shelf and the Arctic's interisland archipelagos. Ranges vary. Individual polar bears have been seen swimming 200 kilometres from land-fast ice, and the range of female polar bears tracked with satellite transmitters is up to 600,000 square kilometres.[157]

Responsibility for polar bears in Canada is shared between federal, provincial, territorial, and Aboriginal governments.[158] In this multi-jurisdictional system, only Manitoba and Ontario list the bears as "threatened," thus banning hunting and other commercial activity in body parts. Elsewhere in Canada, except Nunavut, the bears are listed as a "special concern" (or its equivalent in the provinces and territories), a category that means little beyond the requirement to present a management plan specifying the measures to be taken to prevent declines. Since most of the Arctic is governed by constitutionally guaranteed land claims agreements, the Inuit and First Nations have major control over polar bear management in the North, and because Nunavut has over 80 per cent of Canada's polar bears and is convinced that any listing of polar bears is unnecessary, federal involvement in the protection of this iconic species at risk has become increasingly problematic and political. Put simply, the federal government sees itself as having little choice but to keep the bears' "special concern" status since raising them to "threatened" status would end sport hunting and commercial activity, putting the government on a collision course with the Inuit and First Nations, something it is not prepared to consider. All of this exacerbates the already serious plight of the polar bears.

The greatest threat to polar bears is climate change. In 2008 warming trends were sufficiently significant for the United States to classify polar bears in Alaska as "threatened" and to further predict imminent endangerment across all their ranges, some of which are shared with Canada.[159] Overall, the ice cover in the Arctic has receded from 75 per cent in the mid-1980s to 45 per cent in 2011.[160] In 2017 the Arctic's sea ice had contracted 100,000 square kilometres from 2016 levels.[161] Populations are threatened. According to Polar Bears International, continued warming trends could see a two-third reduction in global numbers within the next eighty-five years.[162] Between 2001 and 2010, Beaufort Sea populations dropped by 40 per cent from 1,500 to 900 bears.[163] A detailed scientific demographic analysis of polar bears in the Beaufort Sea found that the ice-free period increased by approximately 50 per cent between 2001 and 2005 and was exceeding 127 ice-free days, or the vital tipping point beyond which polar bear survival and reproduction are compromised.[164] The authors concluded that "global warming is likely to have profoundly negative effects on future growth rates of polar bear populations" and that, at current trends, "there is a high probability that the Beaufort Sea population of polar bears will disappear by the end of the century."[165] A capture-release study in the southern Beaufort Sea between 2001 and 2006 involving 627 polar bears offered the following dire prediction: "Because this region includes *c.* 7500 polar bears, one-third of the current world population, our findings in the southern Beaufort Sea were considered relevant to the extinction risk facing a large portion of the world's polar bears."[166] Steven Amstrup, chief scientist at Polar Bears International, summed up the situation well: "It is difficult to get away from the conclusion that as the sea ice goes, so goes the polar bear."[167]

Projected warming over much of the polar bear range and reductions in the extent of sea ice are adversely impacting habitat and prey availability.[168] Earlier ice breakups are affecting polar bear weight and conditioning, which negatively impacts reproduction rates and mortalities. In the western Hudson Bay region, where bear populations have declined over 20 per cent in the past twenty years, a recent study on polar bear migratory patterns by four Canadian scientists using satellite-linked telemetry data from 109 collared bears concluded that changes to the timing and rate of sea ice breakup and formation were depriving the bears of access to calorie-rich marine mammal prey, resulting in "additional reductions to body condition, reproductive success and population numbers."[169] For example, studies have shown decreased weight, length, and skull size of female polar bears in the western Hudson Bay.[170]

Although the serious threat to polar bears posed by climate change is recognized by the scientific community, little is being done to help them, partly because no one really knows what to do. The Draft Nunavut Polar Bear Management Plan (2014) was in a state of denial. Noting that "the impacts on polar bears [are] not clear at this time," the plan was quick to point out that polar bears were neither endangered nor threatened.[171] An updated version, the Nunavut Polar Bear Co-Management Plan (2015), gave a clear indication of the Inuit position and, by implication, the major role of the Inuit in the plan they were preparing co-operatively with the federal government: "Pressure from national and international environmental and non-governmental organizations, climate change advocates, and the general public at large to conserve and protect polar bears has created contention about whether polar bear populations will need to increase, despite the fact that Inuit believe that there are now so many bears that public safety has become a major concern."[172] Not mentioned was that the overpopulation of bears around settled areas is a consequence of global warming trends rather than evidence of increasing populations.

Newfoundland and Labrador's Management Plan for the Polar Bear (2006) rationalized that climate change would affect distribution more than numbers and that in the short run the province might be advantaged since more ice would drift free and increase the polar bear numbers in the south.[173] The Canadian government made the following less-than-reassuring statement on climate change when it affirmed in the 2011 draft of its management plan (one still uncompleted) that "there is a need for focused research to understand the ecological conditions that are important to polar bear, and that inform conservation and management actions."[174] The strategy also admitted to limited information on "sea ice, habitat, and other environmental characteristics with which to build adequate models at a polar bear–relevant scale in Canada."[175] According to a 2013 assessment report by the Canadian Arctic Northern Contaminants Program, "much further work" is needed to establish the impact of climate change on the transport of contaminants to the Arctic.[176]

Polar bears are also subject to human-caused contamination. Toxic chemicals from worldwide industrial activities are carried to the Arctic by air currents, rivers, and oceans. Researchers also worry about the effect of climate warming on the releases of contaminants presently sequestered in permafrost and glaciers.[177] Polar bears, being top predators, are exposed more acutely to especially high levels of toxic substances through biomagnification, with negative long-term effects on their health and longevity. Arctic seals have particularly high levels of organochlorines concentrated in their blubber, and since polar bears mainly feed on seals, these toxins become even more concentrated in their fat layers. This potentially leads to an increase in cub mortality rates. An intensive investigation in 1991–1992 involving over 700 samples of polar bear fat from twenty-four arctic regions found major residues of polychlorinated biphenyls (PCBS) and other contaminants, and a later study revealed increasing levels of brominated flame retardant and other brominated substances in east Greenland bears.[178] A more recent study revealed that high-latitude ecosystems have a heightened potential for atmospheric mercury, which acts as a nerve toxin affecting the brain, especially in the foetus and the young.[179]

To its credit, the federal government responded to the contaminants threat with the formation of the Canadian Arctic Northern Contaminants Program (CANCP) in 1992.[180] In addition to its human-health component, which is focused on providing information to northern communities on contaminants in traditional food sources as an aid to diet choices, the program monitors, samples, assesses, and recommends with respect to persistent organic pollutants (POPs) in the arctic biota. Despite the best efforts of the CANCP, the polar bear remains highly vulnerable to toxins. The CANCP assessment in 2013 documented the presence of new toxic compounds and raised concerns about the impact of climate change on the transportation of contaminants.[181] With respect to polar bears, the assessment noted that they continued to be the species most affected by POPs and that, through the process of biomagnification, they were subject to "some of the highest POPs concentrations of any arctic species or any species on the planet."[182] New POPs such as perfluorooctane sulfonate were found in the livers of polar bears at levels higher than any other arctic animal.[183] The assessment also felt that the addition of harp and harbour seals to polar bears diets as a result of climate change would result in even higher contaminant levels.[184]

Although this program is viewed positively in government circles, its reports are not reflected in the various polar bear management plans. No mention was made of the CANCP in the federal polar bear draft management plan, which admitted in its ten lines devoted to contaminants in the forty-two-page document, "The effects of pollutants on polar bear are only partially understood."[185] Similarly, the Northwest Territories and Nunavut polar bear plans make no mention of the CANCP. The Northwest Territories' *Species Status Report* (2012) took the same route when it observed that the "effects of various compounds in the tissues of polar bears or of the seals they feed on [remain] largely unknown."[186] The Draft Nunavut Polar Bear Management Plan (2014) might have been referring to the CANCP when it concluded that "a combined magnified response to these and other stressors is likely expected."[187] Yet the CANCP's 2013 report gave no such assurance. In fact, it emphasized the pressing need to address the issue of POPs differently by focusing on "the multiple ecological, biological, and physical (natural and anthropogenic) variables ... when analyzing contamination in species and when comparing data between studies."[188]

The advance of other human activities in northern Canada negatively impacts polar bear population and habitat. These activities include anthropogenic disturbance through mining and oil exploration and development, energy transmission infrastructure, hydroelectric power generation, defence operations, marine transportation, as well as on-site human presence. At least a dozen mining projects in Nunavut are located in areas frequented by polar bears. Similarly, increasing oil and gas exploration activity in the Mackenzie River Valley, the Beaufort Sea, and Nunavut have implications for habitat degradation through noise disturbance and toxic pollution. In 2015 the Federal Court of Appeal ruled against an application filed by Inuit groups to block a five-year seismic-testing project off the east coast of Baffin Island.[189] Documented studies are lacking on the impact of marine transportation, energy transmission infrastructure, and defence operations.

Yet, despite these threats, Canadian jurisdictions are optimistic about the future of polar bears, referring to reliable population estimates that predict increases in several of the thirteen population units. The trouble is that these population estimates, which are primarily based on the methods of mark-and-recapture and aerial-survey inventory are not as accurate or comprehensive as made out. Biases, errors, and inadequate information are inbuilt qualifiers.[190] For example, aerial surveys cannot provide estimates of age-structure and age-specific reproductive rates or survival rates.[191] Moreover, several population units are classified as "data deficient," which means that no one really knows how many bears there are. For example, the Polar Bear Specialist Group of the International Union for the Conservation of Nature (IUCN), using estimates carried out before 2010, set the combined population of Davis Strait and Foxe Basin at 4,743.[192] However, Environment Canada noted a year earlier that polar bear population trends in the same area were unknown.[193] Someone is wrong. Others have obsolete status reports that date to the 1990s.

According to Mike Gill, the chair of Environment Canada's Circumpolar Biodiversity Monitoring Program, "Despite the sustained attention given to polar bears and concerns raised regarding the impacts of climate change, we have only limited baseline information on most populations and a poor understanding of how polar bears have and will continue to respond to a rapidly changing climate. Effective conservation actions require not only an understanding of polar bear trends across the Arctic, but a clear understanding of the mechanisms driving those trends."[194] Using nineteen subpopulation units, the same report lists fourteen as either declining or data deficient.[195] Mortality rates among polar bear cubs are high. A study by the US Geological Survey estimated that in the years 2001 to 2005 only 43 per cent of cubs survived their first year, compared to 65 per cent in the early 1990s.[196] According to another study, cub survival in the first year in the western Hudson Bay region was only 44 per cent.[197] These figures are subject to more variables than current survival estimates allow. A recent study concluded that assessments of sustainable harvest yields of polar bears based on assumptions about litter sizes may be wrong. Scientists Donald DeMaster and Ian Stirling suggest that litter sizes are more dynamic than current assessments allow and that "small biases in either litter size or cub survival could result in serious errors in estimates of sustainable yields."[198]

The plight of the bears is exacerbated by the fact that the Inuit rely on traditional knowledge more than science to set the population estimates, which determine their total allowable harvest. This approach translates into liberal assessments. Environment Canada thinks so, certainly with respect to how many bears there are in Baffin Bay: "There is disagreement between science and Inuit Knowledge as to the trend of Baffin Bay subpopulation – the best available scientific information indicates there is cause for concern and Inuit Knowledge indicates that there is no cause for concern."[199] One has only to note the 2014 draft of the Nunavut Polar Bear Management Plan. Clearly reacting to their obligations under the Species at Risk Act (2002), the authors of the draft plan expressed their displeasure and, by implication, their mistrust of the federal government and its scientists: "Inuit support the Nunavut's polar bear management efforts but it is Inuit who are impacted by reduced quotas and polar bear damage."[200] In an updated 2015 version of the plan, Nunavut spokespersons were more explicit. In referring to existing scientific modelling and monitoring of polar bear populations, the plan stated, "This method has been effective and will continue to be used, but it has not allowed the full participation of the Inuit … Improving the collection and use of Inuit Qaujimajatuqangit (IQ) [Inuit traditional knowledge/technology] and higher levels of Inuit participation in all aspects of management are central to the goals of this plan."[201]

Even the listing of polar bears as a species of "special concern" under the Species at Risk Act is at odds with the Inuit perspective, and despite the listing, Inuit do not believe that there is a serious conservation concern, a position strongly reaffirmed in the 2015 draft of the plan.[202] After referring to the fact that polar bears were versatile and omnivorous in their diets, the 2014 Nunavut plan downplayed climate change by observing that "the reduction of large areas of multiyear ice that is known to be of low productivity is being replaced with more productive first year sea ice."[203] According to Nunavut's draft assessments of the thirteen population units, none was declining, even though six of the thirteen had no status based on traditional knowledge.[204] The Northwest Territories' *Species Status Report* (2012) focused on the viewpoints of both science and Indigenous people.[205] Here, the Indigenous viewpoint did not jibe with that of the scientists, who predicted overall declines in polar bear populations due to disappearing sea ice. Instead, the traditional knowledge perception held that the bears would adapt in the long run by locating farther north and inhabiting year-round sea ice.[206] Given the strength of the Inuit's policy over polar bear hunting, their confidence about abundance and survival is a cause for concern.

In a way, the trenchant stand of Inuit and First Nations against what they see as direct federal involvement in polar bear issues is understandable. As historian John Sandlos has shown, the Native experience with Ottawa bureaucrats and politicians over wildlife management in the North has not been positive.[207] The federal policies in the mid-twentieth century, which militated against Native rights and access to northern bison, caribou, and musk ox, represented a clash of cultures over wildlife use. This could help to explain why modern Inuit and First Nations are resistant to any unwanted federal input on polar bear issues and management and why the federal government is reluctant to act more forcibly.

Uncertainty exists about polar bear populations and future trends. Furthermore, scientific and Inuit opinion are at odds over the seriousness of the situation. Several other factors put the plight of the polar bear in greater jeopardy. Jurisdictional issues have resulted in the weakening of federal authority in favour of the Inuit, who are much more positive about the future of polar bears. Commercial exploitation is impacting their numbers. Environment Canada admits that "some subpopulations are over harvested and current management mostly seeks the maximum sustainable harvest," adding that about 28 per cent of Canada's polar bears have a high risk of declining by 30 per cent or more within thirty-six years.[208] Yet the federal government has not stepped into the breach by declaring the polar bear a "threatened" species. Instead it defies international conservationist and scientific opinion by emphasizing both the commercial interests of the Inuit and a stable future for polar bears.

In 2011 the US-based Center for Biological Diversity complained to NAFTA that Canada was not following its own rules under the Species at Risk Act, first by ignoring scientific evidence in refusing to change the status of the bears from "special concern" to "threatened" and second by failing to produce compulsory management plans.[209] In 2013 the *Vancouver Sun* reported that the Secretariat of the Commission for Environmental Cooperation, "after conducting a year of study and hearing a full response from Environment Canada," found that there were many unknowns in Canada's polar bear policies and that there were "valid assertions" that, under NAFTA, Canada was not effectively enforcing its environmental law.[210] Noting inadequate population assessment methods and a lack of attention to enforcing the provisions of the Species at Risk Act, the secretariat recommended a full investigation. However, in ruling against the investigation, NAFTA's Commission for Environmental Cooperation felt it unnecessary to second-guess Canadian policymaking.[211]

The Committee on the Status of Endangered Wildlife in Canada assessed the polar bear as a "special concern" in 2008, but the species was not listed under the Species at Risk Act until November 2011. Even three years later, when the requisite jurisdictional management plans were to be in place, not one was operational. Soon after listing the polar bear as a species of "special concern," the federal government noted, "While the various jurisdictions have been working towards a unified approach, there is currently not a consistent, integrated approach to either the timing or financing of monitoring studies across the various jurisdictions in Canada."[212] Something needs to be done. As recently as

April 2017, NatureServe Canada added the polar bear to its growing list of globally at-risk mammal species.[213]

As of 2017, the federal management plan for the polar bear is still not in place and in all likelihood will not be until at least 2019, more than a decade after the original "special concern" listing. Part of the reason has to do with the intense and complex negotiations with the various jurisdictions, whose own plans involve lengthy consultations with individual Inuit communities, hunters, trappers, and other affected groups. Nevertheless, the federal intention is quite clear regardless of the impending implications of climate change: according to a 2016 progress report, the federal plan when complete "will reflect the reality of polar bear management in Canada and result in appropriate and effective delivery of conservation measures while allowing for a sustainable harvest."[214] In short, business as usual.

POLAR BEARS AND INUIT CULTURE

The uncertain future facing the polar bear is also rooted in historical events and policies that resulted in a shift of power to Canadian northern Indigenous peoples, specifically to Inuit economic and cultural considerations. Today, it translates into the human-induced deaths of between 600 and 800 polar bears annually in Canada.

For centuries, polar bears and Inuit functioned in a typical hunter-gatherer symbolic relationship. However, being dangerous and very difficult to kill, polar bears were not a favoured prey. They have never factored into the diet of Inuit in any significant fashion and, according to archaeological studies, "accounted for less than one-tenth of one percent of the diet of pre-modern Inuit."[215] As food, polar bears were far less important than seals, and their major contributions to Inuit subsistence culture came later.[216] The arrival of Europeans and their rifles were the change agents, but although Inuit did indulge in sporadic trade in skins, the polar bear was not an important component in Inuit hunting culture until the third-quarter of the twentieth century.

International interest in polar bears was spurred by unregulated hunting primarily in Alaska by North American trophy hunters, who used planes, helicopters, snowmobiles, and high-powered rifles to kill thousands of polar bears in the 1950s and 1960s.[217] By the late 1960s, the alarming death tolls spurred an international response. The five-nation Agreement on the Conservation of Polar Bears (1973) was signed by the Governments of Canada, Denmark (now represented by Greenland), Norway, the Union of Soviet Socialist Republics (now Russia), and the United States.[218] The agreement represented a joint commitment to coordinate national measures aimed at protecting the species and to collaborate on polar bear research and conservation initiatives. Although the agreement marked a significant step in the interests of polar bears, it did allow hunting, albeit only by Indigenous peoples for subsistence needs.[219]

A little over a year later, in ratifying the agreement, the Canadian government gave notice of a specific interpretation of two clauses in article 3 that in its opinion permitted "a token sports hunt."[220] Neither of the two clauses made the slightest reference to a sport hunt or even hinted at it, the Canadian case resting on a very liberal interpretation of the term "traditional rights." No other party to the agreement held the same interpretation, leaving Canada to stand alone as the only country to allow sport hunting of polar bears. It was in part a political move in that it involved federal recognition of Indigenous peoples as an organized political force primarily through the Aboriginal land claims processes unfolding in the 1970s. In this context, the federal government saw sport or trophy hunting as a source of revenue much needed by a cultural group with limited economic options. Thus, when the historic James Bay and Northern Quebec Agreement (1975) was settled, it specifically recognized sport hunting by non-Natives.[221] Beginning in the 1980s, the Ministry of Economic Development and Tourism developed contacts with outside big game outfitters and established several programs to train and certify Inuit as guides and to help develop community-based outfitters by providing start-up funding.[222] So while the 1973 conservation agreement was designed to protect polar bears, the Canadian government saw it as an opportunity for a specific human-centred program.

Today, through their wildlife management boards, Inuit governments regulate the hunting of polar bears by establishing annual hunting quotas based on population estimates. After being divided among jurisdictions, the total allowable harvest is generally further allocated among local communities within jurisdictions. Each jurisdiction's management board retains the right to allocate its hunting tags independently, resulting in diverse practices overall. Although most hunting tags are taken by the Inuit hunters, a certain number, sometimes reaching as high as 50 per cent, are reserved for non-Inuit sport hunting. These hunters, many of them from outside countries, pay a fee for these tags and then, after contracting with local outfitters, must conduct their hunt using an accredited Inuit guide.

This commercial exploitation of polar bears is seen by some as consistent with the Inuit subsistence culture.[223] Anthropologist George Wenzel, perhaps the foremost authority on Inuit culture, takes this view. Locating his arguments in his personal experiences, primarily with Inuit on the east coast of Baffin Island, Wenzel contends that the modern Inuit are simply taking advantage of contemporary technologies and capitalist norms to maintain their traditional culture by engaging in a longstanding symbolic activity.[224] He supports his argument by referring to the hunter-gatherer paradigm, where the relationship between hunter and prey constitutes a bond between symbolic equals. In Wenzel's context, the polar bear is aware of the Inuit hunter's intent and becomes complicit if the proper respect is exhibited.[225] Thus the hunting of polar bears, an enacted ritual played out against a background of equality and respect, cannot be equated with outright commercialism. In short, Inuit engagement in polar bear hunting is an important cultural component steeped in tradition and a subsistence lifestyle.

This rationalization of "subsistence" is at best a stretch given Wenzel's personal reinterpretation of the word and given that the traditional symbolic hunter-gatherer relationship with prey is being violated on several levels.[226] Nevertheless, it helps to justify Inuit commercial activity on time-honoured cultural grounds with respect to polar bear pelts, body parts, and guided hunts. Encouraged by the 2010 decision of the Convention on International Trade in Endangered Species of Wild Fauna and Flora (1975) not to tighten its rules on the polar bear trade, European and Asian hunters and markets replaced the American.[227] An annual average of 3,200 items made from polar bears, including skins, claws, and teeth, are exported and re-exported from several countries.[228] Rising prices and a strong international demand mainly from China are sending prices sky-high. According to one report, the number of polar bear skins selling at auctions rose 375 per cent between 2007 and 2012.[229] The same report contended that over half of the polar bears killed annually in Canada end up overseas either in whole or in part. In 2013 the *National Post* reported a polar bear skin going for over $20,000.[230] A year later, a stuffed polar bear trophy fetched $108,000 in China.[231]

Sport hunting is an increasing area of interest to Inuit. Hunters from Canada, Europe, and China are willing to pay substantial sums for the right to hunt a polar bear. A non-Native wanting to kill a polar bear must be willing to pay at least $30,000 for a hunting tag, a trained Inuit guide, and a dog team. According to anthropologist Martha Dowsley, the number of transferred hunting tags exceeds 50 per cent in some communities.[232] Given the economic importance of the polar bear trade to Inuit, it is not surprising to see the demand for increased quotas or to discern an underlying reason for the Inuit's rationalization that polar bears are under no threat whatsoever.[233] For example, in advising against a proposal by Nunavut to increase its total allowable harvest (TAH) three-fold for the 2012–2013 season, the IUCN's Polar Bear Specialist Group noted, "Proposing an increase in the TAH, in a subpopulation where the scientific information suggests the subpopulation is declining and where there is no indication it could be supported, is not consistent with the 'precautionary principle,' widely accepted by conservation organizations around the world."[234]

Polar bear lives are being sacrificed in the interests of a subsistence culture in the twenty-first century. Despite serious threats from climate change, toxins, overhunting, a lack of consistent management, and an unclear knowledge of population numbers and other variables, the federal government refuses to safeguard the bears by listing them as "threatened" under the Species at Risk Act. Furthermore, the need to kill polar bears to support Inuit culture is overstated. According to a 2011 detailed study commissioned by Environment Canada on the socio-economic import-ance of polar bears, the annual value derived from polar bear watching was $7.2 million.[235] In contrast, sport hunting contributed $1.3 million a year in revenues. The sale of polar bear skins and meat, plus its consumption value to Inuit households, added a modest $600,000. In fact, the importance of polar bear meat as a food source is exaggerated, or as one authority admitted: "In food terms, polar bear, especially when compared to seal, are at best of minor importance."[236] Parasitic, and with increasing toxic contaminant residues, it is not surprising that most polar bear meat ends up as dog food.[237] The implications are clear for the Canadian federal government to commence the process of transitioning Inuit culture from a consumptive to a nonconsumptive use of polar bears. The idea that the polar bear is integral to Inuit culture is true. It always has been but largely in a symbolic and nonconsumptive capacity. The dependence on polar bears for meat and skins dates primarily to the European-contact period.

In 2010–2011, 816 polar bears were slaughtered globally. Canada killed 628 of them. Given that Canada houses two-thirds of the global population of polar bears, we are doing more than our share of removing them from the planet. Are we killing too many? The consensus, of course, answers in the negative. Although quota and gender violations are admitted, they are brushed off as isolated and easily remedied. Others simply refer to statistics affirming population abundance. The Inuit are convinced, at least officially, that there is nothing to worry about and that killing polar bears will continue as a time-honoured practice and cultural right. Scientific opinion sees a need to align hunting practices with ongoing habitat loss through climate change. A rare official comment that referred to a need to reduce killing polar bears overall came in the Northwest Territories' *Species Status Report* (2012), where, in recognizing the impossibility of countering climate change, the authors suggested that "direct mortality due to human activities may be more easily reduced and managed."[238] The evidence seems to support this conclusion.

Polar bears join grizzlies, wolves, and cougars as victims of the hunting mentality and its rationalizations about viable management practices. However, polar bears stand outside their fellow predators in terms of Canadian wildlife policy. Here, we have a former minor component of a hunter-gatherer subsistence-based economy now thrust onto a twenty-first-century stage and promoted by the Inuit as a deeply rooted hunting ritual and by the federal government as a primary revenue source and a mainstay of Inuit culture. Vulnerable and threatened as they are, the iconic polar bear is an economic asset to Inuit and a pawn in federal political policymaking.

Canada's big predators are demeaned by policies that rationalize their persecution. As their management plans attest, the existence of the grizzly, cougar, and polar bear is predicated entirely on their instrumental value, primarily as prey for hunters. Grizzly bears and cougars exist in these plans as creatures of the hunt. Their deaths are associated with recreation, status, and a romantic mystique. Of the four species, wolves represent the war against wildlife in its most unabridged form, the rationale for their slaughter being, ironically, that they apparently do the same sort of things to other animals that humans do, albeit with far less frequency and greater need. Not only do polar bear policies equate the iconic white predators with the hunt, but they also integrate them into cultural norms that arguably penalize them more than the grizzly or the cougar.

The population of these predators is relatively small, and in spite of the optimism inherent in their management plans, they face a precarious future. Population estimates of wide-ranging apex predators are unreliable, and in light of their shrinking and degraded habitats, wildlife managers would be wise to set conservative hunting quotas or even to disallow hunting altogether, concerning themselves instead with the place of predators in ecosystems and with exploring ways that they can be reintroduced to areas where they have been extirpated or can be of added value in regulating ecosystems.

Managing Other Wildlife

Human beings possess a species-specific nature
and morality which occupy only a tiny section in
the space of all social and moral conditions.

EDWARD O. WILSON

This chapter's discussion shows how the human element works to penalize other wildlife. The hapless deer is hunted for human enjoyment and culled to salve human anxieties. In the issues involving the spring bear and the mourning dove hunts in Ontario, the power of the hunting lobbies and the cooperation of government agencies were clearly obvious. Coyotes in Saskatchewan were needlessly slaughtered by the thousands to accommodate a specific human-interest group. The federal government's promotion of the seal hunt is linked to dubious cultural considerations, and the killing of thousands of moose annually in Newfoundland and Labrador is advertised as a cultural identifier. The needless culling of urban wildlife is a by-product of human intolerance. Additionally, the force of external factors or higher agents of government is a further example of how wildlife more readily become victims of human interests.

DEER

In terms of larger high-profile mammals, none faces hysteria about over-abundance more than the deer. Although appropriated in the past for sport by nobility and for food by peasants, deer today are available to anyone with a licence and a gun – and sometimes to those with neither.

Deer management plans in Canada are little more than hunting templates. Both the white-tailed and mule deer are hunted with frequency and enthusiasm. In Alberta this translated into the deaths of over 57,000 animals in 2013.[1] Recently, however, another death-demanding dimension is being added to the lowly deer's woes. Apparently, deer numbers have reached unprecedented levels and are undermining ecological integrity. According to an American article, "White-tailed deer likely impact every landscape east of the Mississippi River. The damage has been insidious – both slow moving and cumulative."[2] A biologist with the Royal Botanical Gardens in Ontario, referring to degraded eco-lands in the gardens, lamented, "In order to sustain a forest with an understory of wild flowers and shrubs, rich in diversity, the deer population would need to be reduced by two-thirds."[3] Discussing rising deer populations in BC's Gulf Islands, a University of British Columbia conservation biologist said, "If we don't address this issue pretty quickly, we are likely to end up with more rare and endangered species in the future, leading to all kinds of social costs."[4] These individuals are not alone. Several academic articles attest to the long-range negative impacts of deer on forest ecosystems and song bird populations.[5]

Natural mortality cycles are also significant. For example, research has shown that historical deer populations likely were much higher than have been estimated and that what is referred to as overabundance is cyclical in nature, as well as linked to human incursions and social perceptions. For example, the number of white-tailed deer in North America was only slightly higher in 2000 than it was in 1500. In 1700 the number had decreased by about 7 million from the 1500 figure.[6] Similarly, the 2014 population had 5 million fewer animals than did the 2000 population. Yet management solutions are overly reactive and focus on reducing deer numbers by increased hunting activity and through official culls. There seems to be little inclination to restore predator-prey balances, likely on the grounds that human economic interests and personal safety would be prejudiced. Public opinion generally seems divided on the issue.[7] Other nonlethal solutions, such as removing and relocating deer to areas of less abundance or implementing immunocontraception programs, are not widespread in Canada due to cost and time commitment.[8] Reducing numbers by lethal methods is simpler, easier, and cheaper.

In fact, deer are seen as so abundant that negative trends pass by unnoticed. This seems clear in the case of mule deer. Alberta's Management Plan for Mule Deer (1989) is no exception, as witnessed by the following comment about the provincial perception of the real worth of mule deer: "Their major value stems from the thousands of days of recreation they provide for both hunters and nonconsumptive users."[9] Despite the add-on, the comment referred primarily to hunting. In its section on uses for the mule deer, the plan devoted twelve pages to hunting and two paragraphs to aesthetic experiences.[10] Indeed, the plan's first management goal was to provide a variety of recreational hunting opportunities that would hopefully result in the annual deaths of over 17,000 mule deer by 1996.[11] Not surprisingly, the plan predicted significant population gains and was rosy in its forecasts for the future of the highly popular game animal. That the plan is now more than a quarter of a century old should tell us something about the extent to which the province is in tune with mule deer dynamics. The plethora of websites advertising bountiful experiences hunting mule deer affirms that the official "green light" to hunters is as bright as ever. Almost 90,000 applicants were registered to hunt mule deer in 2012, many more than for elk or moose.[12]

However, the situation facing the future of the trusting ungulate with the big ears is more problematic than officialdom is prepared to acknowledge. Although it is very difficult to obtain reliable population statistics, indications are that mule deer populations are declining in several US states and across the Canadian prairies.[13] Mule deer populations in Colorado dropped 36 per cent in the decade from 2005 to 2014. Their numbers in Saskatchewan were halved between 2001 and 2014.[14] In British Columbia their numbers have also declined in certain areas.[15] A committee of biologists confirmed in 2002 that mule deer numbers and distribution "have been declining throughout the West since the latter third of the 20th century."[16] Even in Alberta, where mule deer abundance is taken for granted, evidence suggests otherwise. Several wildlife management units in Alberta have reported significant decreases in mule deer numbers. Aerial surveys conducted by the Alberta Conservation Association in 2012 and 2013 showed mule deer declines in three of the four blocks surveyed. In two of the three surveys, which included both mule and white-tailed deer, the latter had the advantage of a population density five to eight times higher than that of the former.[17] A worrying trend was attested by statements like "Mule deer observations were exceptionally low in number, making stratification for this species difficult" and "Mule deer in WMU 506 were extremely low in numbers, with only 35 individuals observed during the intensive survey."[18] By 2013 hunters in Alberta were killing four white-tailed deer for every one mule deer. As a participant in a hunting forum commented in 2014, "Where are the mule deer?"

Apart from generous hunting quotas, which take heavy tolls, other factors are at work, including competition with elk for food, snow depth in winter, and lack of flexibility in diet.[19] Fire control practices have reduced the early successional habitat favoured by mule deer.[20] Conversion to farmland and forage crops militate against mule deer diet, which is far more selective than that of white-tailed deer. The encroachment of the more numerous white-tailed deer into mule deer territory poses another threat. For example, in areas where the two species interact, the mule deer is the favoured prey of cougars, leading to population imbalances and a decrease in mule deer numbers.[21] White-tailed deer have more resistance to various parasites and to diseases such as brain worm, and they carry many diseases to which mule deer are highly susceptible. Since they breed at a younger age, white-tailed deer also have a higher reproductive rate. Moreover, white-tailed buck will breed with mule deer doe at a significantly greater frequency than mule deer buck will breed with white-tailed doe, leading ungulate expert Valerius Geist to predict that hybridization between the two species could mean the ultimate loss of the mule deer.[22]

Despite these trends, the abundance mentality seems undisturbed in Alberta. The solution to decreases is to simply adjust the hunting quotas in specific areas and assume that numbers will rebound.[23] Apparently, rationalizations about perceived abundance and an affinity for letting the guns roar reduce any need for Alberta to review its ideas about the friendly, trusting "muley." Of course, it could be argued that cyclical natural mortality factors are at work, but even then it would seem wise to monitor short-term patterns and trends more closely.

ONTARIO SPRING BEAR HUNT

With the black bear in Ontario, we see another predictable reaction to the abundance factor. In the case of the spring bear hunt, the issue of public safety was linked to social perceptions about overabundance and to the readiness of other groups to capitalize on the hunting solution. Unsurprisingly, officialdom was only too willing to cooperate.

Black bears are seen as an abundant species in Canada. They are smaller and far less iconic than the grizzly bear, with whom they share many characteristics, including a sensitivity toward female survival, vulnerability to overhunting, and slow recovery rates from low population levels. In these contexts, the hunting of bears in the spring is both undesirable and unethical since it imposes undue risk to female bears and their cubs born during the hibernation period. Upon emergence from hibernation, hungry, foraging females usually hide their cubs before approaching a visible, often baited food source, and although spring hunting regulations apply specifically to male bears, difficulties in distinguishing gender result in unacceptably high mortality rates among mother bears, as well as almost certain death for their cubs, who, left alone, face starvation or predation. Furthermore, black bears are opportunistic and more prone than grizzlies to live in proximity to humans. Yet they are rarely aggressive, are afraid of dogs, and will usually run from a human voice or movement. The above notwithstanding, and despite the fact that only sixty-three North Americans have been killed by black bears in over a century, they continue to inspire fear and terror in people.[24] That these negative sentiments are socially constructed norms is reinforced by research showing that personal experience ameliorates fear of black bears, whereas alarmist media messages enhance it.[25]

The issue of a renewed spring bear hunt in Ontario is a classic example of the willingness of governments to exploit wildlife in the interests of public pressure groups. It is especially distressing to find this happening in Ontario, a province whose policies toward wildlife have been considered somewhat more enlightened than those of other Canadian jurisdictions. For example, in grading Canada's laws on species at risk, Ecojustice, a legal-support organization for environmental enhancement, put Ontario at the top, with a grade of C+. Not high, mind you, but first nonetheless.[26]

Black bears are found in most Canadian provinces. Population estimates in the late 1990s put the total above 300,000 and the annual hunting mortalities in excess of 26,000.[27] The Government of Ontario maintains that its 100,000 bears are valued citizens. According to its Framework for Enhanced Black Bear Management (2009), "Black bears are highly valued and unique members of Ontario's wildlife heritage, symbols of wilderness, an integral part of a functioning ecosystem, and an important component of Ontario's biodiversity."[28] As to be expected, the framework overall was not as effusive in stressing a balanced management approach that penalized the bears more than humans. However, in dealing with hunting seasons, it dwelled only on the traditional fall season. Neither the framework nor its accompanying document, Backgrounder on Black Bears (2009), made any reference to a spring bear hunt. The latter's more detailed discussion referred to the former spring bear hunt, how it had involved the deaths of more bears than the fall hunt, and how it had been abandoned in 1999 "to address concerns about the potential orphaning of cubs during the spring at a time when they are very dependent."[29] At the time, the Conservative Party's natural resources minister, John Snobelen, assured Ontarians that his government "would not tolerate cubs being orphaned by hunters mistakenly shooting mother bears ... Stopping the hunt is the only protection for the animals."[30] The province acted positively by establishing a $34.5 million Bear Wise Program to reduce potential human-bear conflicts through education, bear-awareness protocols, and trap-and-relocate strategies despite also instituting "right to hunt" legislation in 2002.[31] Over the years, the Bear Wise Program was highly successful. In 2012 Deputy Minister of Natural Resources David O'Toole reported that "awareness of Bear Wise is high and many municipalities have good, robust bear wise strategies in place," writing that "the public is better educated about what to do when they encounter a bear."[32]

Given the above, the issue of the renewed spring bear hunt in Ontario shows how official support was easily secured for unnecessary and unethical actions prejudicial to individual animals and, in this case, to bear cubs as well. An early sign was the erosion of the progressive Bear Wise Program in 2012 through a $50 million budget cut over three years. Officials intimated that the program was irrelevant since it had done its job in affirming personal responsibility in dealing with bears.[33] A year later, following rumblings about "nuisance" bears in northern Ontario, the issue of renewing the spring hunt came to the fall session of the Ontario Legislature through a private member's bill from Thunder Bay's Bill Mauro. On 14 November 2013, without due consultation or reference to responsibilities under Ontario's Environmental Assessment Act (1990), the Liberal Party's natural resources minister, David Orazietti, the long-serving member of the Legislature for Sault Ste Marie, announced that a spring bear hunt would go ahead in selected wildlife management districts around Timmins, Sudbury, Thunder Bay, North Bay, and Sault Ste Marie between 1 May and 15 June in 2014 and 2015.[34]

The hunt was rationalized as a public safety issue. In Minister Orazietti's opinion, many northern Ontario towns were under virtual siege by black bears who were endangering citizens. Citing vulnerable school children at recess guarded by teachers armed with bear whistles, Orazietti aligned his perception of public alarm with government responsibility.[35] He obviously felt that the very real risk of shooting a female bear and orphaning and dooming her cubs was well worth it if one could kill a male bear who just might be on his way to a school playground where he just might inflict Ontario's ninth black bear fatality in 130 years, the previous eight of which had occurred in remote areas.[36] (In contrast, in 2013, the City of Toronto reported 79 homicides, and Ontario had 476 road fatalities.) It was a tidy, believable rationalization, for when it came right down to it, the renewed spring bear hunt had more to do with appeasing the many avid hunters and stakeholder organizations in northern Ontario, and securing their electoral support, than with ridding communities of a marauding presence.[37] Put simply, killing bears in the spring translated into additional opportunities for hunters, more moose for them in the fall, and $44 million in hunting-related revenue for northern Ontario communities.[38]

In spite of a petition signed by around 100,000 citizens opposing the hunt, Orazietti was encouraged by the support of forty-two northern Ontario town councils and by the fact that the province's premier, Kathleen Wynne, was onside given her sentiments about "public safety and human-bear conflicts."[39] On 5 February 2014, Orazietti requested a regulation under the Environmental Bill of Rights (1993) to reinstitute a spring bear hunt through a two-year pilot project. The regulation proposal noted appeals of concern from northern Ontario communities about public safety and conflicts with bears, specifically stating that the reason for the pilot project was "to help address this conflict with problem bears."[40] By the end of April, 2,300 hunting licences had been issued.[41]

However, a few days before the hunt was to begin, two animal advocacy groups, Animal Alliance of Canada and Zoocheck Canada, challenged Orazietti's constitutional authority to issue the regulation by serving him and the Attorney General of Ontario with a notice of application for judicial review and a notice of constitutional question. Together, the notices challenged the constitutionality of the regulation on the grounds that it failed to satisfy conditions in the Environmental Assessment Act and the Environmental Bill of Rights, the former for not conducting the mandatory environmental assessment and the latter for failing to give due consideration to specific responsibilities under the bill's Statement of Environmental Values.[42] The plaintiffs also claimed that the regulation was *ultra vires* because it conflicted with the animal cruelty provisions in the federal Criminal Code.

In dismissing all three claims against the constitutionality of the regulation and in refusing the request for judicial review, the three justices of the Ontario Divisional Court did not follow traditional practice and delivered the decision orally so as to allow the hunt to go ahead.[43] First, the justices agreed with the government's argument that it had legally bypassed the need to conduct an environmental assessment by invoking an exemption granted in 1985. Second, the court felt that the government had complied with requirements under the Environmental Bill of Rights, including the requisite submission of Statements of Environmental Values. Third, the judges interpreted hunting as normally accepted behaviour that therefore fell outside federal Criminal Code provisions respecting animal cruelty.[44] So the spring bear hunt proceeded in 2014. Almost 200 bears were killed, but no statistics were given on probable cub deaths.[45] Extrapolations from figures for 1990 to 1998 suggest that about twenty cubs might have died.[46]

The reasons for the decision provide a clear example of the legal biases against animals. The dismissal of the Criminal Code challenge was predictable given the burden of proof of cruelty based on wilful intent and conscious negligence, as well as the acceptance of hunting as a normally accepted practice, even though a sympathetic interpretation might have associated cruelty with deliberation in that the respondents were well aware of the high likelihood of undue suffering. The other two reasons were more conjectural. The rationale for the exemption of 1985, which allowed the government to bypass the need for an environmental assessment, had nothing to do with public safety, which was the reason given for the pilot project. Rather, it had listed population control, protection of game and nongame species, and habitat improvement.[47] The judges, without giving reasons, were apparently satisfied that public safety issues were valid under the above criteria and instead focused on the fact that due process had been followed in the posting of the requisite regulation.[48] In noting that the minister of environment had chosen not to intervene and order an environmental assessment, the judges failed to take into account that the exemption of 1985 specifically directed the minister to order an environmental assessment if the proposed activity "generate[d] an unusual amount of public or Government concern" or had "unusual or significant potential environmental impacts not adequately treated in the pertinent planning exercise."[49] Both circumstances applied to the spring bear hunt.

The court also rejected the applicant's claim that the regulation did not follow stipulations in the Environment Bill of Rights, ruling that proper ministerial discretion had been exercised under the bill and that the rules had been followed regarding the submitted Statements of Environmental Values.[50] The rules had been followed but very perfunctorily. None of the four selected statements pertained to the issue, let alone on public safety grounds.[51] One has only to note the minister's biased reasoning when he read public safety into the following environmental value: "The planning for and management of natural resources should strive for continuous improvement and effectiveness through adaptive management of natural resources."[52] Possibly, his justification was implied in a very broad interpretation of the flexible adaptive management principle, the application of which had nothing to do with testing an uncertain hypothesis.

The decision respecting Ontario's spring bear hunt sent four messages to those who seek to protect wildlife under the legal system. First, a successful constitutional challenge on behalf of wildlife under animal cruelty provisions in the Criminal Code is highly unlikely. In the code, animals are classed as property, and the burden of proof based on intent is very difficult, being well-nigh impossible in the case of wild animals. Second, with animals generally, and certainly with wildlife, provincial courts tend to interpret regulations broadly in terms of their consistency with the enabling statute rather than based on their possible outcomes, worth, or ethical considerations. Third, statutory provisions allowing exemptions and ministerial discretion afford government executives significant latitude and protection from the courts. Fourth, Canada's legal system as it pertains to wildlife is built around the dominant belief system about animals and in large part is interpreted within anthropocentric parameters.

The two-year pilot project was extended in 2015 for another five years through a notice of regulation demonstrating that the hunt's reinstitution in 2014 had little to do with public safety issues.[53] The extension now included nonresident hunters and was applied to all wildlife management areas in Ontario that had a fall bear hunt. For the hunt to be expanded on the basis of the original pilot project, black bears had to be evincing menacing tendencies toward school children in the eighty-eight areas added to the spring bear hunt eligibility list. Not so, apparently. The reason for the extension in time and scope was to allow a test for uncertainty, as per adaptive management, by compiling "additional data with which to assess the impacts of the spring black bear hunting season and help inform long-term black bear management activities."[54] No mention was made of data collected in the two-year pilot. Nor were there any statistics related to cub mortalities. Moreover, baiting was to be regulated not due to any concern about added bear vulnerability but due to the dangers to humans through food habituation. The notice of regulation also revealed how the crude application of adaptive management principles – in this case, learning by doing – can and is used to justify actions that penalize wildlife, including baby bears.

The real reason for the extension was, like the pilot project, a political sop to the hunting industry but more blatant. As the notice of regulation stated, "The establishment of an early black bear season would provide increased economic benefits to tourist outfitters that provide services to non-resident and resident hunters and to local communities."[55] Mike Commito, a researcher with the Northern Policy Institute, acknowledges that the spring bear hunt adds millions to the provincial economy but also believes that it holds environmental risks to the black bear population.[56]

The dominant belief system can rationalize cub mortalities away with no problem: baby bears are things; hunters are humans.

MOOSE IN NEWFOUNDLAND AND LABRADOR

The issue of overabundant moose in Newfoundland and Labrador is a classic example of the "blame the victim" syndrome, where a species of wildlife is penalized for faulty human decisions. As an introduced species, moose flourished in the boreal forests on the island, and by the second half of the twentieth century, they had reached what many thought were unsustainable numbers. By the new millennium, the provincial government was faced with a three-sided dilemma as to what to do about the moose. The first concerned the research that pointed to their negative impact on ecosystems. The second concerned the social alarm over the frequency of vehicle collisions caused by moose. And the third concerned the hunting interests, which saw moose abundance in terms of opportunity.

The moose is the largest species of the deer family and inhabits boreal and mixed deciduous forests of the Northern Hemisphere in temperate to subarctic climates. Moose are large, solitary animals who browse on terrestrial and subaquatic vegetation, and although generally slow-moving and nonthreatening, they can be a formidable presence if startled.[57] Moose arrived in Newfoundland in 1878 when a single pair was released in the Gander Bay area. Twenty-six years later, two pair from New Brunswick were set free near Howley, not far from present-day Gros Morne National Park. In the presence of highly favourable habitat, moose rapidly colonized the province. By the 1990s 150,000 moose occupied all eco-regions on the island. The extent of moose abundance is unarguable. With less than 2 per cent of the continent's moose range, Newfoundland accommodates over 10 per cent of North America's moose population.[58]

Although ideal habitat doubtless influenced the rapid growth of the moose population, the human presence was paramount. First, it was no accident that moose had been introduced to the province. According to historian Allan Byrne, their introduction was an attempt to attract investment capital to the province in the form of wealthy sport hunters and their equally prosperous social and business contacts.[59] And for most of the century, the more moose, the better. The "sportsman's paradise" described by Tina Loo was very much evident in Newfoundland.[60] Regulated hunting began in the 1930s, and by the mid-1950s, hunters were killing over 5,000 moose per year in the province's boreal forests. Second, the sports mentality extended to other species. The wolf, the only predator on the island capable of balancing moose numbers, was hunted to extinction. Third, the presence of the logging industry facilitated new growth succession and created an ideal food source for moose that supplemented old-growth vegetation.[61]

In Leopoldian terms, the proper response to a human-induced problem with wildlife numbers involves a punitive human management solution. Invariably, this approach calls for harsh action against representatives of the "offending" species. The hunters fitted nicely into this paradigm since, for many Newfoundlanders, moose existed solely for the hunt. The scientists who worried about the impact of moose on the ecosystems and the motorists who collided with them on provincial roads also wanted to see fewer moose in the forests. Although humans were directly responsible for the "moose situation," nonlethal solutions were not popular. The victim was to pay the price. For example, little thought has been given to reintroducing the wolf to Newfoundland, probably for the same reason as researchers found in New Brunswick. A survey carried out on attitudes toward wolf reintroduction in that province found strong opposition from hunters and relative disinterest elsewhere.[62]

Scientists, worried about the impact of moose density on the forest ecosystem, put forward several arguments. Concerns were expressed that moose consumption of hardwoods had affected forest regeneration to the point where regrowth rarely exceeded a metre in logged forests with high moose densities.[63] Trampling by moose inhibited growth of smaller low-growing plants and contributed to soil erosion. It was argued that changes to forests caused by moose also affected other wildlife. Forest songbirds dependent on hardwood and balsam fir trees were put at risk, as were tree lichens with specific habitat requirements.[64] This perception of the moose in negative ecological terms was enough to galvanize Parks Canada into action. In Terra Nova and Gros Morne National Parks, the federal government instituted management plans for "hyper-abundant moose," which amounts to giving licences to kill a certain number of moose annually in specific areas in order to allow forest regrowth, or to quote Bill Brake, the field superintendent at Terra Nova National Park, "Parks Canada is taking proactive steps to address these hyper-abundant, non-native moose populations to preserve the native diversity of the forest ecosystem."[65] Since the program began in 2011, Gros Morne National Park has increased its hunting areas from 20 per cent of the park to 90 per cent, which in 2013–2014 translated into the deaths of about 1,000 moose.[66]

Generally, although the scientific consensus seems to favour population reductions through hunting, it is not in favour of all-out war on the moose. According to one study, more work needs to be done on density, which is more pivotal than overall numbers. The authors of one study argued that sustainability of the provincial moose population should not be linked either to upping the hunting quotas or to issuing more licences in easy-to-access areas. Rather, licences and quotas should be distributed along density lines.[67] Wildlife biologist Vince Crichton sees the issue differently. He contends that moose are an important species who play a major role in conservation of biodiversity. Although he acknowledges some negative impacts of moose on forests, Crichton focuses on foraging ecology and on the long-range positive effects of selective browsing in terms of both nutrient cycling and the altering of carbon-nitrogen balances to influence plant compositions and regrowth acceleration. He also sees the moose as an umbrella species and cites a Manitoba experiment demonstrating that managing for moose habitat accommodates the habitat needs of 62 per cent of other boreal wildlife species.[68] A Swedish study of moose density, which analyzed the whole plant community, including unbrowsed plants, found that the extra light afforded by browsing resulted in an increase in the reproduction and growth of grass species. In other words, an ecological transformation was precipitated rather than environmental degradation. The study concluded, "Indirect effects such as changed competition among plants or habitat modification may be just as important as direct effects when understanding plant community responses to herbivory."[69]

Yet, for all the scientific cautionary concerns, the hunting fraternity, led by an outfitting industry valued at $35 million a year, is interested in maintaining moose numbers at high levels.[70] According to Byrne, moose hunting in Newfoundland is a firmly embedded, annual, local tradition. "The social and cultural elements of the hunt," Byrne writes, "are immortalized in local song, literature and folklore from all parts of the island, and the practice of hunting and eating moose has become a cultural identifier."[71] Between 2002 and 2012, an average of 20,000 moose fell to hunters' guns every year. In 2012–2013 hunting licences were issued for over 30,000 moose, a very high number considering expected harvest levels of 70 per cent or more.[72]

Moose-caused collisions on provincial highways are inducing calls for reduction of numbers. Quoting an average of 650 accidents a year involving moose, one source estimates an annual cost of $20 million to the economy. Wildlife biologist Anthony Clevenger is critical of the government's limited response, which involves driver education, enhanced signage, and clearing of roadside brush.[73] The more than $1 billion to erect protective fencing is considered prohibitively expensive.[74] Clevenger believes that the Newfoundland and Labrador government seems to lack the will to address the issue adequately, even though successful moose mitigation strategies are pursued elsewhere.[75] In 2011 a class action suit was launched by 135 plaintiffs claiming negligence on the part of the government in failing to control the moose problem. In September 2014 a Supreme Court judge dismissed the suit for lack of "evidence to prove that moose population management or moose-vehicle collision risk mitigation were irrational or done in bad faith."[76] The defeat, although a blow to the plaintiffs, was seen by their lawyer as just heightening the seriousness of the issue in the public mind.[77]

Finally, the long-awaited and brief Moose Management Plan (2015) was released. Not surprisingly, as evidenced by the following comment, its primary focus was on hunting: "Effective moose management on the Island is dependent on the active participation of the hunting community to continue the moose hunting tradition ... Hunters remove approximately 25,000 moose annually and their continued participation is critical to successful long-term moose management."[78] There was no discussion of moose ecology in the larger biotic community or anything that revealed the moose as a living being. Aside from the familiar ameliorative measures to address vehicle collisions, there was nothing in the plan that suggested anything else beyond systematic slaughter as a cherished cultural norm. Accompanied by a visual of an exulting family in photographic pose with a dead moose, and a warning about the urban values of people who oppose hunting, the plan emphasized the need to preserve and guard what it saw as "an integral part of the province's social fabric."[79] Although Newfoundland and Labrador's Moose Management Plan followed the same tired lines of others across the country, it was unique in that it not only embedded the slaughter of a single animal firmly in the provincial cultural fabric but also warned against those who thought otherwise.

Arguably, even more than the big predators, moose are victims – of being labelled stupid, of human miscalculation, and of human unwillingness to shoulder the blame. Moose in Newfoundland must take the entire blame for damaging the boreal forest ecosystem. They are implicated for damaging vehicles and for the deaths of their drivers. They are victims of a hunting culture that allows over 30,000 humans an annual opportunity to kill them, and their deaths are associated with cultural enhancement. They are even seen as agents of global warming through their methane emissions. They are not even secure in the sanctuary of two national parks. They are safe, however, from the exterminated wolf. But restoring the predator-prey balance in this manner has little currency in the province, especially among hunters. Neither have ameliorations like fencing or immunocontraception.

THE COYOTE CULL AND BOUNTY IN SASKATCHEWAN

If the wolf is hated and feared, the lowly coyote is hated and despised. In rural Saskatchewan, this wily, intelligent predator is at the top of the "most unpopular list" of the majority of farmers and ranchers. Labelled as an official "nuisance" and seen as a major predatory threat to calves, lambs, poultry, and pretty well everything else small enough to make a meal, coyotes constituted a menace sufficient enough for the Saskatchewan government to declare outright war on them in 2009. It was a nasty, unwarranted war reminiscent of the official campaigns against predators waged in the first half of the twentieth century. As in those years, Saskatchewan's war was emotional, ecologically unsound, and ultimately futile. By resorting to the antiquated and barbaric bounty system, Saskatchewan's lethal control program in 2009–2010 provided a graphic example of how little things have changed for wildlife, especially those with the mental and physical capacities to threaten human equanimity.

The coyote is a medium-sized canine with the general appearance of a German shepherd dog but about half the size and slimmer, weighing 10 to 14 kilograms. Once limited to prairie habitat, coyotes took advantage of agricultural expansion and the extirpation of the wolf to extend their range throughout North America and today are no strangers to rural and urban areas. In fact, coyotes are an incredibly adaptable species and one of the very few able to keep pace with the spread of human settlement. Although primarily a carnivore, coyotes can subsist on fruit, berries, insects, carrion, and anything that is available. In addition to being very wary of humans, coyotes enjoy low mortality rates, possess acute vision, hearing, and smell, are able to run up to 70 kilometres per hour, swim well, and hunt efficiently alone, in pairs, or in packs.[80] They are also highly intelligent and, with a brain-size 12 per cent larger than that of their dog counterparts, are capable of keen levels of learned behaviour.[81] Coyotes are described by wildlife managers as perhaps the most challenging of all North American carnivores and extremely difficult to manage effectively.[82] This helps to explain why they are anathema to ranchers, farmers with livestock, and people who give their cats and dogs free rein.

The rural province of Saskatchewan has traditionally been, and still is, no place for coyotes. It is open season on them year-round. No licence is required. Their situation worsened in November 2009 when, in response to concerns about coyote livestock depredations raised by several organizations, including the influential Saskatchewan Association of Rural Municipalities, the government placed a bounty on coyotes. The Coyote Control Program (2009) was touted in terms of public safety. Referring to a recent coyote-inflicted fatality in Nova Scotia, Minister of Agriculture Bob Bjornerud was determined that a repeat event was not going to occur on his watch: "If we had waited until something like that would have happened ... I think then I would have been criticized on the other side for not taking some kind of action."[83] As it was, the minister's political instincts were working overtime. The two "coyotes" that killed the young woman in Nova Scotia had more than 80 per cent dog DNA in their genes.[84]

Under the Coyote Control Program, the province paid a bounty of $20 to every individual who submitted four coyote paws to a rural municipality. Although it was expected that the coyotes would be shot or trapped, poison was also an option under certain circumstances. By the time the program had run its five-month course, the province had paid out $1.5 million for the deaths of 71,000 coyotes. It was a staggering number, one that did not concern the Saskatchewan government, which justified the deaths in sustainability terms even though no one in the Ministry of Agriculture seemed to know how many coyotes there actually were in the province.[85] In announcing the end of the program, Minister Bjornerud hoped that it "helped to reduce both the predation issues facing livestock producers and the potential danger posed to farm and ranch families."[86]

In retrospect, it is difficult to determine any valid reason for the program beyond a knee-jerk reaction to emotionally charged political pressure by agricultural stakeholders in a rural province. The program was ecologically indiscriminate. Critics insisted that coyotes were a "keystone species" whose loss could trigger adaptations in other resident species, resulting in dramatic habitat alteration.[87] Biologists and conservationists described the program as disruptive of "nature's balance by removing a predator that helps keep gopher, fox or deer populations in check."[88] According to Lorne Scott, president of Nature Saskatchewan, "Biologically it's simply not a good way to manage wildlife. We still maintain that the bounty is non-selective. It removes animals that are actually the farmer's friend. Most coyotes are beneficial to landowners."[89] Noting that the elimination of over 71,000 coyotes ensured the survival of more than 130 million rodents, biologist Paul Paquet, a member of Project Coyote's Scientific Advisory Board, referred to other vital ecological contributions by coyotes: "If we also consider the sheer number of insects coyotes eat, the sick animals they remove from the gene pool, and carrion they clean up, it's not a stretch to say we're clearly working against ourselves when we kill coyotes in mass numbers."[90]

Worse was the fact that the program was a useless exercise, whose failure was compounded further by apparent official ignorance as to its futility. Coyotes exhibit strong compensatory responses to lethal control. According to Shelley Alexander, a prominent coyote researcher at the University of Calgary, "Research has shown when you persecute coyotes with a cull, you're simply removing individuals and breaking down the social structure and what can happen, is you end up having higher levels of reproduction to try and fill the habitat."[91] Citing internationally recognized coyote authority Dianne Wittner, one article explains, "Contrary to popular belief, most coyotes are pack animals with a very strict social structure. Only the alpha male and female breed, producing four or five pups a year. Only the alpha female ovulates. However, if one of the alphas dies, all of the females in the pack ovulate, which can result in 12 or more pups."[92] Wittner states, "Right off the bat, if you take out an alpha, you'll have three times as many pups."[93] Eighteen months after the program ended, a southeast Saskatchewan trapper observed an increase in litter size and in the number of young coyotes.[94] Anyone with practical experience, let alone a research background in the field, knew that lethal control against coyotes would not work. Except for the government of Saskatchewan. Or did it?

In early 2010 just before the bounty program ended, the Province of Saskatchewan made a surprising announcement. On 11 March federal minister of agriculture Gerry Ritz and Saskatchewan minister of agriculture Bob Bjornerud gave out the news of overall enhancements to the province's Wildlife Damage Compensation Program. Under a $5 million partnership with the federal government, the province promised to fully compensate producers for livestock killed or injured by predators.[95] In other words, a prime reason for the bounty was now no more. It is difficult to believe that this startling development had not been in the works for some time. "We are continually working to improve our programs to benefit producers," said Bjornerud, who was "pleased to partner with the federal government to provide this compensation."[96]

So here we have a provincial government choosing to kill 71,000 coyotes just months before it adopted a program that largely negated the perceived need. Although evidence is not available, it is possible, even likely given the nature of provincial-federal dialogue, that the issue was at the discussion level or on the negotiating table at the time the Coyote Control Program was adopted. One wonders, too, why a futile lethal control program was implemented in the face of existing expert opinion. It is difficult to believe that scientists in the government's employ were unaware of coyote biology and its implications for culling programs.

The $1.5 million spent on the program, or the $500,000 later allocated to control rodents in the aftermath of the cull, could have been utilized in assisting livestock owners to adopt nonlethal methods of control.[97] According to Alberta's Ministry of Agriculture and Rural Development, "pro-active measures to prevent or reduce coyote predation" include "close supervision of stock, proper carrion disposal," and the "use of guardian animals, predator-proof barrier[s] of electric fences, [and] scare devices."[98] Apparently, it doesn't work that way for "nuisance" beings like the coyote in Saskatchewan, as witnessed by the ongoing, persistent agitation for a renewal of the program by disaffected groups.[99] In the exercise of political power, wildlife have no chance against voters with a gripe.

ONTARIO'S RENEWED MOURNING DOVE HUNT

Sometimes, lethal responses to species abundance require no rationalizations whatsoever. They do not call on public safety issues. Neither are they tied up in cultural considerations. They have nothing to do with arguments about the limits of biological carrying capacity or with social perceptions about overabundance. Sometimes, they represent nothing more than pure speciesism in action. The mourning dove hunt in Ontario, renewed in 2013 after a fifty-eight-year hiatus, is one such example. The decision to go ahead and turn the hunters loose on a bird, seen by many as a song bird, is bad enough. That the hunt's renewal hinged on the go-ahead given by the Canadian Wildlife Service in the absence of perceived need or appropriate public consultation is a damning indictment of the federal government's attitude toward its wildlife.

Mourning doves are medium-sized, seed-eating, migratory birds who mate for life and who range throughout the United States and into southern Ontario and parts of British Columbia and Alberta. They derive their name from their plaintive owl-like call. Mourning doves spend a lot of time on the ground, where they forage for seeds, and with their quiet beauty, gentle nature, haunting call, and wide seed preferences, they are very welcome visitors at birdfeeders. They are also the most hunted bird in North America. In forty of the US states where hunting is allowed, more than 17 million meet their deaths every year.

Some groups rationalize mourning dove hunting as a social experience. An article in the *Human Dimensions of Wildlife* on mourning dove hunters in Alabama concludes that the hunt is more about the socializations embodied in family traditions and that the mentoring and initiating of children into hunting are far more important than bag limits.[100] On this rationalization, killing mourning doves in Alabama is a worthwhile family rite of passage. Others claim that mourning doves are no more than "cheap skeet," or in plainer terms, target practice for hunters.[101] Despite these rationalizations and the appalling death toll, a sizable number of Americans, including those in the populous state of New York, oppose the hunting of mourning doves. Other state legislatures have faced legal challenges to the hunt. One survey of public opinion on hunting, conducted by the research firm Responsive Management, showed that mourning dove hunting induced the most negative responses. According to the survey, almost 80 per cent of Americans were in favour of deer hunting. When it came to mourning doves, the percentage was halved.[102]

Whereas British Columbia has had a mourning dove hunting season since 1960, the seasonal hunt occurred only once in Ontario before 2013. In 1955, 300 birds were taken amid public opposition and low hunter interest. However, it was just a matter of time before the hunting lobbies, noting dove abundance and the enduring popularity of mourning dove hunting in the United States, felt that it was about time Ontario played catch-up. Spearheaded by the 80,000-strong Ontario Federation of Anglers and Hunters, and by the research-oriented private organization Long Point Waterfowl, the hunting cohorts began making a case for the restoration of the hunt in the province. Being a migratory bird, the mourning dove is under the control of the federal government, or more specifically, the Canadian Wildlife Service (cws). It was toward this steward of wildlife that the hunting lobbies turned their significant influence and energy.

Although the cws began receiving entreaties to allow the legal hunting of mourning doves early in the new millennium, the major impetus occurred in 2007 in the form of a research-based technical report from the pro-hunting organization Long Point Waterfowl, which concluded that a mourning dove hunt was justified on sustainable grounds and, furthermore, was supported by public opinion.[103] Unsurprisingly, the cws gave the report serious attention due to the reputation of Long Point Waterfowl for its work on research, conservation, and education in the Great Lakes area. Moreover, the nonprofit organization is affiliated with the University of Western Ontario in an active two-way relationship. Scott Petrie, Long Point Waterfowl's executive director, teaches an undergraduate course at the university on wildlife ecology and management, and Long Point Waterfowl staff supervise undergraduate and graduate students with field studies and major research projects at its 40-acre facility southwest of Simcoe on Lake Erie.

The Long Point Waterfowl report was pivotal to the CWS in its decision to evaluate the feasibility of opening a mourning dove hunting season. In this context, two points are relevant. First, in terms of research, Long Point Waterfowl has nothing to do with mourning doves. The doves are outside its purview and mandate, which, as its name suggests, concerns waterfowl and aquatic ecology.[104] Second, Long Point Waterfowl is a very active promoter of hunting. Scott Petrie, for example, is affiliated with the Ontario Federation of Anglers and Hunters, which, in presenting Petrie with one of its most prestigious awards, lauded him for introducing "a new generation of young people to the experience of waterfowl hunting."[105] Barry Kent MacKay, an outspoken naturalist, artist, and animal advocate, describes Petrie as "a staunch proponent of killing doves."[106]

The CWS released its assessment in 2011. Not surprisingly, it concluded that "a Mourning Dove hunt in Ontario is biologically justifiable and feasible at the present time."[107] It was an interesting document for several reasons. It was long on population analysis and graphs, US mourning dove hunting frameworks, and endorsements from pro-hunting organizations. It was short on information from the general public and gave no information on official public consultation for the simple reason that none had taken place. As to the morality of initiating a hunt on a gentle bird, the assessment had only the following to say: "Some segments of society regard this species as a beautiful song bird or a symbol of peace that should not be hunted."[108] Then, quoting the Long Point Waterfowl report, the assessment affirmed, "A recent public opinion poll showed that a majority of Ontario residents would not be opposed to reinstating a Mourning Dove hunt if the population could sustain harvest."[109] The latter was not a matter of issue given that, in terms of current sustainability criteria, there was no difficulty in justifying the hunt based on population abundance. The moral grounds might have given the cws more trouble since there was no compelling basis for the hunt. But its assessment did give the impression that public opinion was in favour, and this is where it gets interesting.

Essentially, in relying on the Long Point Waterfowl report, the cws had equated public approval with a single telephone survey from the private sector. In a separate government document, the cws admitted that it was basing its recommendation on "a relatively small public opinion survey conducted by a non-governmental organization."[110] Unacceptable as this was, it did not end there. What Long Point Waterfowl's authors did not make clear was that the telephone survey used in their report had been designed a year earlier by a University of Western Ontario undergraduate student as part of her honour's thesis.[111] In fact, sections of the report on the telephone survey were taken almost verbatim from the student's thesis. Yes, the student's co-authorship of the report was acknowledged, albeit after two of her supervisors and another honours student. However, her paper was not in the bibliography. Nor was it mentioned that the survey was her work. The intent here is not to undermine the student's work or integrity but to suggest that, in a decision of this magnitude, the authors misled the cws on an authenticity issue. As for the survey itself, it comprised 400 respondents chosen at random. The number was adequate for extrapolation but barely. Although the survey had some small merit, it was far too inconclusive to justify the emphasis that the cws put on it. Ten questions were asked, four on attitudes toward wildlife, five on hunting generally, and only one on the mourning dove hunt specifically.[112] Further, as the author herself had noted, the survey was biased toward hunters. The percentage of hunters in the survey, at 23 per cent, was over four times the national hunting average of 5 per cent.[113]

With the ready approval and cooperation of the Province of Ontario, and amid opposition from groups that were never consulted, the mourning dove hunt was reinstituted in September 2013. The press reported the hunt indifferently, as the following comment in the *Toronto Star* attests: "The Canadian Wildlife Service believes there are enough mourning doves for all Ontarians – from those who watch them coo at the backyard feeder, to those who like to shoot, clean, and pair them with a wild rice pilaf."[114] Opponents condemned the hunt as cruel, unnecessary, and

unworthy, or as one writer noted, "Mourning doves? Come on, really? …
Mourning doves as a game bird?"[115] Anne Bell, the director of conservation
and education at Ontario Nature, summed up official neglect when she
told the *Globe and Mail*, "The federal government has been listening to
the hunters who have been lobbying for it, and they haven't adequately
consulted the rest of us."[116] MacKay challenges the culturally embedded
disallowance of moral worth in animals when he writes, "No dove will
ever create great art, pen profound thoughts, develop a scientific theory
or contribute to a just cause … I get all that; honest. But why should they
therefore suffer or be killed for, what, sport? Why should their lives be
ended? Why should they suffer?"[117] Like MacKay, the Animal Alliance of
Canada appealed to a different belief system in urging people to protest
the hunt to Canada's prime minister and Ontario's premier: "Doves have
a Right to Live as a species, each of them as an individual enjoys the same
right, as do we all. Because each of them – as a consequence of the Right
to Live – also has a will to live, as do we all. We have in common with all
life this will to live. It binds us."[118] The trouble is, when one looks through
that lens or that belief system with respect to Canadian wildlife policies,
the view is unwaveringly bleak and hostile.

In summary, what transpired was a cws decision to open a mourning
dove hunting season that was based on no ecological grounds and was
societally justified by a limited and inadequate public opinion survey
prepared and administered by a university undergraduate student. It
was irresponsible and high-handed. Public consultation was lacking in
that oppositional, informed stakeholders and the general public were
denied adequate input. Noting correctly that it was "a purely political
decision aimed a throwing a 'bone' to the sport hunting lobby," the Animal
Liberation Front lamented the lack of consultation on a decision "made
very quietly, so as to restrict public input."[119] It is bad enough that the
mourning dove hunt was reinstated on these grounds. It is more appalling
to realize how quickly and positively the cws, a body charged with the
protection and welfare of migratory birds, reacted to the clamours of a
hunting lobby. Indeed, the several attachments to the cws assessment
were all from pro-hunting groups. In light of the needless demise of
nearly 20,000 mourning doves and the fact that nonhunting and other
wildlife advocate groups were not afforded adequate opportunity to speak

for them, naturalist and author Alexander Burnett's statement about the cws's exceptional service to Canadians and Canada's wildlife is, in this case at least, unfortunately in error.[120]

THE ATLANTIC SEAL HUNT

The Atlantic seal hunt is the most prominent example of current federal policies linked to outright commercialization, on the one hand, and to cultural accommodations, on the other. Unlike animal experimentation, which takes the high moral ground and is hidden, or factory farming, which caters to high consumer demand and is hidden, the annual seal hunt off the coast of Newfoundland and Labrador and in the Gulf of Saint Lawrence can claim no moral high ground nor high consumer demand.[121] Nor can it be hidden. In setting its significant death toll against a backdrop of public visibility and anthropocentric commentary by government, vested interests, and private citizens, the seal hunt has become the most graphic demonstration of the rigidity of the human-nonhuman relationship.

Although seals, primarily harp, have been hunted for subsistence by Inuit for centuries and commercially for oil by Europeans since the seventeenth century, the modern seal hunt began in the 1950s in response to a strong European market for pelts to serve the fashion industry. Hundreds of thousands of seals were taken annually between 1950 and the late 1970s,[122] before the market collapsed in 1983 due to rising public protest over visible testimony of the hunt's bloody nature and due to a ban placed by the European Union on the import of the most popular pelts, those from newborn pups, or whitecoats.[123] Although the federal government believed that the ban lacked "a scientific, legal or other credible basis,"[124] public outrage resulted in a successful boycott of Canadian fish products in the United Kingdom.[125]

Following a royal commission in 1986 that endorsed the seal hunt subject to refinements,[126] it was invigorated and renewed by substantial federal financial support in the 1990s and the early 2000s, as well as nurtured by local, European, and limited Asian markets for the pelts of "older" seals, 98 per cent of whom were under three months in age.[127]

Then in 2009 the European Union, noting that "seals are sentient beings that can experience pain, distress, fear and other forms of suffering," extended its ban to all seal products.[128] Again, the market collapsed, and this time the downturn was more serious and long-lasting. The federal government appealed the ban to the World Trade Organization on free trade principles, only to be denied twice, first in 2013 and again in 2014 on appeal.[129] With poor demand, low prices, and international mistrust, the Canadian seal hunt, for the time being, is a shadow of its former self. On 17 April 2015, amid stockpiling of sealskins in the absence of buyers, and noting "challenging times" and "restrictive market opportunities," the Canadian Sealers Association announced that it was scaling down its future operations.[130] Doubtless its troubles were somewhat assuaged four days later when the federal minister of finance announced a five-year budget of $5.7 million, commencing in 2015–2016, "to help secure new market access for Canadian seal products."[131]

The above brief summary vastly understates the controversy surrounding the hunt and the abundance of books, articles, studies, and reports that have focused on the issue from both sides. Put simply, the federal government, which has constitutional and legal authority over the seal hunt, sees it as a viable way to support the economic and cultural needs of marginal Atlantic and Inuit communities. They also point to very high harp seal numbers and their alleged unsustainable impacts on fish stocks. Opponents, led by various animal-support groups, including the International Fund for Animal Welfare and Humane Society International/ Canada, argue the opposite. They see the hunt as inhumane and of little economic merit. They also contest the claim that seals eat too many cod, as well as the fish that cod like to eat. Both sides have indulged in strategies to win over public opinion, which understandably varies with location but which, on the whole, opposes the hunt both internationally and in Canada.

On the surface, the issue polarizes on practical grounds and over two questions: whether the seal hunt is humane and whether it is economically viable and ecologically necessary. Although the practical answer to both questions is negative, their implications are more revealing. Those who see the hunt as inhumane are attacked as urban, sentimental anthropomorphists, out of touch with the real world. Those who argue that the hunt is nonviable economically are portrayed as undermining human cultural traditions and, in putting seals before people, are admonished for advocating a new world order of animal equality with humans. These two critical viewpoints have effectively transformed an animal welfare concern into an animal rights issue.

The argument that the seal hunt is humane is a stretch given its visible presence, the efforts made by the federal government to keep critical observers away, and most significant, the word "humane" itself. Being located on open pack ice, the commercial seal hunt is a visible undertaking. It occurs after the whelping, or birthing, season when thousands of very young harp seals crowd the ice for a very short period, prior to following their mothers into the ocean. The hunt is conducted from boats by licensed sealers with rifles and by landmen, also licensed, who use clubs called hakapiks to bludgeon very young seals, who are, if nothing else, fair game aplenty.[132] The open nature of the hunt has allowed limited onsite observations denied in slaughterhouses, factory farms, and animal experimentation practices, and despite what the critics suggest about staged and/or altered images, sufficient visual material exists on the seal hunt to show that it is anything but humane. According to Rebecca Aldworth, the executive director of Humane Society International/Canada, videos depict wounded seals crawling on the ice in their own blood, many of whom have been shot several times while conscious: "It's very much the kind of killing that we film every year," she added.[133] Other reports attest to baby seals being skinned while still alive.[134]

Regardless of the good intent of some sealers, physical factors like uneven ice, poor visibility, and rough seas constrain humane practices. The shortness of season and the desire to fill quotas as quickly as possible induce haste and inefficiency. According to a review by an independent group of veterinarians, "The competitive nature of the hunt and large number of licenses and vessels may result in undue haste. This reduces the potential for the humane killing of each seal."[135] Even an article supporting the humaneness of the seal hunt notes that neither the club nor the rifle "offers a complete guarantee of instant death."[136] The authors also admit that many illegal rifles are used on the ice and that seals shot in the water may suffer if not retrieved quickly and efficiently.[137] Interestingly, the authors defend the humaneness of the hunt in a self-defeating rationalization by comparing it favourably to slaughterhouse practices.[138]

In an excellent article that appeared in *Marine Policy* in 2013, veterinary scientist Andrew Butterworth and animal welfare expert Mary Richardson rely on extensive veterinary studies, post mortems, anatomical and physiological data, and authorized videos of the hunt to demonstrate that "cruelty takes place on a large scale during the Canadian commercial seal hunt." Noting the visible distress exhibited by baby seals before they are clubbed, incompetent clubbing practices, and excessively high wounding rates with rifles, the authors are unequivocal in their conclusion that the seal hunt is in violation of international humane standards: "The evidence, which continues to be available year on year, through observer data, video material, and veterinary study is clear ... There are unacceptable (and unlawful) things being done to animals for profit in this hunt."[139] These are strong statements, and I wonder how many Canadians, if forced to witness what is done to baby seals every year on the ice, would disagree. Not many, I imagine.

Moreover, it is revealing that the federal government is very sensitive about observers to the hunt. Since it occurs on public, unoccupied space, observers cannot legally be denied access. However, a legal decision in 2005, pursuant to a constitutional challenge by Paul Watson of the Sea Shepherd Conservation Society, ruled that although his Charter rights had been violated by denying him right of access to the hunt, the infringement was justified on the grounds that the sealers had a right to earn a livelihood without disruption.[140] Today, observers are tightly screened through background checks and strict on-site conditions and are issued licences "only if the Minister determines that the issuance of the licence will not cause disruption to a seal fishery."[141] In July 2015 the Maritime Mammal Regulations (1993) were amended to double the distance observers must maintain from the hunt to 1 nautical mile, making it impossible for observers without high-tech equipment or a helicopter to film the hunt.[142] Conservative member of Parliament Greg Kerr, in introducing the bill, noted that it was a gesture of government support for the hunt and then rationalized that it was also a way of allowing those with clubs and rifles to do their jobs "without fear of disruption."[143] One article was on the mark when it likened this constraint on public viewing to the US "ag-gag" laws that hide cruelty practices in slaughterhouses and factory farms by making it illegal for inside workers to expose them.[144]

Finally, there is the question of what constitutes humane practices. The federal government ignores stress, distress, and fear, while equating humaneness in the seal hunt solely with speed and painlessness, an end that cannot be anywhere near fool-proof given the number of animals involved and the physical circumstances of the hunt itself.[145] This means, of course, that humane standards have a statistical component that tolerates a degree of noncompliance or collateral damage. "Humane" is a relative term both by definition and on the pack ice. Furthermore, given the number of sealers on the ice, the terrain, and the spatial differentials, it is impossible to enforce humane standards. Canada's seal management plan, for example, is silent on the degree of oversight needed to ensure accountability and optimum humaneness, as well as on how it can be achieved. Its frequent use of the word "humane" assumes, but comes nowhere near guaranteeing, humane compliance. So, although the federal government may indeed want the hunt to be humane, its supportive proclamations reflect a wish, not a reality.

In economic terms, the seal hunt is not viable. Evidence suggests that the seal hunt's economic importance is minimal. International demand for seal products is weak and shows no sign of recovering. The current price of seal pelts is barely enough to cover the costs of the sealers' fuel and insurance.[146] The market is closed in many countries, and others are hesitant to become involved due to the hunt's marginal reputation. For example, China is stalling on a three-year Canadian initiative to buy seal meat because of concern over the hunt's international acceptability.[147] Exports are down significantly. In 2008 over $6.5 million in seal products went to overseas markets. In 2010 the figure was $813,000.[148] According to the federal government, the landed value of seals in 2012 was 98 per cent below that in 2006.[149]

The value of sealing to local economies is overstated. In comparison to income from the seal hunt, Newfoundlanders in 2005 made 10 times more from shrimp, 50 times more from tourism, and 500 times more from oil and gas.[150] An extensive study carried out as early as 2001 concluded that "commercial sealing represents less than 0.06 per cent of Newfoundland & Labrador's Gross National Product (GNP) and employs less than 1,000 people for no more than a one-month average per year ... making it hard for sealers to justify their economic participation."[151] The above dismal percentage has likely dropped to less than 0.01 per cent.[152] In terms of the fishing industry itself, the seal hunt is a very minor player. According to a detailed report by the International Fund for Animal Welfare (IFAW) in 2009, the landed value of seal pelts in Newfoundland and Labrador accounted for 1.2 per cent of the total landed value of Newfoundland fisheries, an industry itself reeling under the impact of vastly depleted cod stocks. The study also reported that about 75 per cent of sealing communities in Newfoundland derived less than 5 per cent of their income from sealing.[153] University of Guelph economist John Livernois estimated that net average earning per sealer in 2008 was $281.[154] An IPSOS Reid poll conducted in 2011 showed that only 14 per cent of Newfoundlanders thought that the fishing industry, let alone the seal hunt, was a pressing provincial issue. More significantly, over half favoured ending the seal hunt through a buy-out of sealing licences, with compensation for lost income, providing that funds were made available for economic alternatives.[155]

However, there is the cultural dimension. To the federal government and the Newfoundland and Labrador government, the economic component of the seal hunt cannot be separated for the cultural. According to this view, the seal hunt is economically important to a portion of a human population whose culture is attuned to sealing as a traditional practice. John Crosbie, a former Cabinet minister with both governments, sees the seal hunt as an experience that "has been etched into our collective memory."[156] According to one journalist, "Anyone outside the province who is against the hunt is dismissed as a money-grabbing, mainland lunatic. If you suggest from inside the province the hunt might be on the way out, you're branded as an 'anti-rural Newfoundland traitor.'"[157]

The federal government has supported the seal hunt financially for decades. In lean times, it seems equally determined to prop it up by defending it as a cultural activity that must be preserved. Or to quote its own management plan, the seal hunt is important "to Inuit and Atlantic Canadians for community cohesion, nutrition, and well-being."[158]

The presence of Inuit sealing practices is a further exacerbating factor in that opposition to the seal hunt is often portrayed as an attack on Indigenous cultures, when in fact the Inuit seal hunt and its commercial counterpart farther south are two completely different activities. Inuit seal-hunting products were always exempt in the European Union's bans.

Its 2009 regulation banning sealing products stated, "The fundamental economic and social interests of Inuit communities engaged in the hunting of seals as a means to ensure their subsistence should not be adversely affected. The hunt is an integral part of the culture and identity of the members of the Inuit society ... Therefore, the placing on the market of seal products which result from hunts traditionally conducted by Inuit and other indigenous communities and which contribute to their subsistence should be allowed."[159] The IFAW, the foremost opponent of the seal hunt, made its position clear: "The IFAW's campaign against the commercial seal hunt has never targeted subsistence hunting, by Inuit or anyone else."[160] The failure of the federal government to publicly delineate the modest Inuit sealing practices from the mass cruelty, needlessness, and waste of the commercial seal hunt has led to misconceptions about the real focus of opposition to the seal hunt.

The federal government seems willing to defend the common argument that seals are detrimental creatures in that they are preventing the replenishment of cod stock decimated by overfishing. In 2011 a report by Fisheries and Oceans Canada concluded, "The weight of indirect evidence suggested that grey seal predation could account for much of the high natural mortality of southern Gulf cod."[161] In 2016 Fisheries and Oceans Canada maintained that grey seals were likely responsible for 50 per cent of large cod mortalities in the southern Gulf of Saint Lawrence.[162] Conveniently forgotten was that humans caught an annual average of 300,000 tonnes of cod between 1902 and 1958, as well as landing a staggering figure of 800,000 tonnes in 1968.[163] As Dean Bavington has shown, the ruination of the cod fisheries had little to do with seals.[164]

The federal government's stance is contradicted by other evidence. In 2001 its own eminent panel found a lack of evidence that seals were severely impacting fish stocks.[165] The most telling argument refers to the intricacy of marine ecological environments and the unreliability of assuming a simple seal-cod relationship.[166] Since ocean ecosystems exhibit complex interactions among many species, simplistic problem-solving involving two species could well have serious unintended consequences.[167] One has only to note the above-mentioned report by Fisheries and Oceans Canada, which duly noted in its concluding remarks, "Seal predation may be a less important source of mortality than suggested here ... There is a high natural mortality for cod ... that is unexplained and additional hypotheses were not examined to determine the importance of other mortality sources."[168] In other words, we do not know, so why contemplate killing 200,000 grey seals in the Sable Island sanctuary for no scientifically established reason?[169]

No animal issue in Canada forces the belief system to defend itself more forcibly and emotionally than the seal hunt. Quebec senator Céline Hervieux-Payette, who hosted the first seal meal in the parliamentary restaurant in 2010, justified the hunt by putting humans back into the ecological food chain as predators acting on their natural instincts.[170] The following comment in the Newfoundland and Labrador Legislature in 1998 by Minister of Fisheries and Aquaculture John Efford forced the Speaker to call for order: "As, far as the IFAW is concerned, Mr. Speaker, they do not exist. They are not a topic of my conversation or thoughts whatsoever. I do not care what they think. But, Mr. Speaker, I would like to see the 6 million seals, or whatever number is out there, killed and sold, or destroyed or burned. I do not care what happens to them ... and the more they kill the better I will love it."[171] That Efford was railing against a vociferous critic raises a salient issue about concerted attacks on human-based enterprises involving animals. Because a group like the IFAW (and others) questioned a specific need for animal exploitation, it was interpreted as a challenge to the belief system itself. The fallback defence was to associate all critics with the mistrusted and derided animal rights movement. The federal minister of fisheries and oceans, Gail Shea, lashed out at those who had been "brainwashed by decades of propaganda from fringe animal rights groups and radical environment-alists."[172] Anthropologist George Wenzel, in *Animal Rights, Human Rights: Ecology, Economy, and Ideology in the Canadian Arctic* (1991), contended erroneously that the animal rights lobby was responsible for the European Union's ban in 1983, claiming that it had brought the Inuit to their knees by denying them a traditional right to hunt seals.[173] The main opposition came from animal welfare groups, and the European Union had excluded the Inuit from in its ban.

Others defend status quo beliefs by falling back on anthropocentric sentiments. Here, opponents of the seal hunt are portrayed by critics as animal rights urban dwellers who are "out of it" in their ignorance of the real world and in their unwillingness to see that young seals are no more than potential coats and boots, bottles of omega oil, or a hearty meal. They view those who perceive seals as living beings capable of eliciting emotions of empathetic kinship as sloppy sentimentalists imbued with the infantile Bambi syndrome. Extracts from the following media articles are typical. In contending that animal rights had co-opted animal welfare and animal conservation, and in reference to the Bambi syndrome, one writer lamented, "The animal rights movement is an urban-based phenomenon whose ultimate goal is the ending of man's use of animals ... Seals are merely a means toward achieving a larger goal. It's seals today. But what about tomorrow? Will it be sheep, lambs, cows?"[174] This article further accused "animal rights fanatics" of using the Bambi syndrome to advance their goal of ending humans' use of animals, noting that sealing was the perfect vehicle because of graphic bloody visuals and the misleading sight of "cute and cuddly" animals.[175] Even political scientist Donald Barry, in his well-researched study of the early seal hunt controversy in the 1970s and 1980s, seems to think that the IFAW drew more people to its cause by portraying the seal hunt as visually repugnant than by proving it was inhumane. In referring to Brian Davies, the founder of the IFAW, Barry writes that Davies "quickly recognised the powerful emotional appeal of cuddly newborn harp seals ... His main weapons in the battle for public opinion were images of grim-faced sealers bludgeoning adorable 'baby' seals."[176]

The point is that the seal hunt is not about animal rights at all. Opposition to the seal hunt comes primarily from the animal welfare viewpoint, not from current animal rights philosophy as articulated by Peter Singer, Tom Regan, Gary Francione, and others discussed in this book's introduction. Although some groups, like People for the Ethical Treatment of Animals and Animal Alliance of Canada, oppose the hunt from an animal rights position, the bulk of the opposition comes from animal welfare groups. Organizations like the IFAW, Humane Society International, Greenpeace, and others simply believe that the needless, mass clubbing and shooting of young sentient mammals is in violation of ethical human standards and therefore should be discontinued.[177] They are not arguing from the animal rights position, which stresses the inherent rights of animals and the discontinuance of all instrumental use. By seeing all opposition to the seal hunt in terms of animal rights, the federal government and other seal hunt supporters have transformed a debate that is essentially about humane ethical practice into a confrontation between normative cultural values and a perceived "nut fringe" philosophy.

Since wildlife in Canada are primarily under provincial jurisdiction, the controversy surrounding the seal hunt is significant in that it affords insights into the federal government's attitude toward its wildlife. Unsurprisingly, its attitude matches, and arguably exceeds, its provincial counterparts in terms of active speciesism. In defending the worst global example of mass slaughter of wild, defenceless, very young mammals, the Canadian federal government epitomizes status quo speciesism. Its justification of the seal hunt as humane demonstrates a combination of ignorance, hypocrisy, and fanciful rationalization. It derisively dismisses legitimate animal welfare concerns by misconstruing their rationales. Finally, the federal government's trenchant willingness to sacrifice hundreds of thousands of sentient beings in order to gratify the marginal economic interests of a specific human group is a pertinent example of wildlife's instrumental place in our national life.

URBAN WILDLIFE

Nowhere is the belief system about wildlife and the ambiguities associated with their management seen in more graphic contrast than in the interactions between humans and the wild creatures in urban environments. Today, urban wildlife biology is an emerging discipline, and at the educational and awareness levels, the Urban Wildlife Working Groups of the Wildlife Society are striving to bridge gaps in public perceptions about wild animals in the city. Depending on species and their adaptive capacities, the degree of presence and permanence of wildlife in urban environments is related to the availability of food sources occasioned by migratory patterns as well as by natural habitat loss and fragmentation.

In a broad sense, urban ecosystems and their components aid biodiversity by providing food for migrant avian and other species, by creating corridors for animals moving through cities, and by furnishing ecosystem services such as pollination, improvement of soil and air quality, and even carbon sequestration. They also allow people to connect more meaningfully with nature, and it can be argued that urban green spaces will increase in importance as natural areas continue to be degraded. At the same time, urbanization contributes to habitat loss and fragmentation through road densities, recreational activity, and alterations to hydrologic regimes. Buildings, roads, domestic cats, and power lines are death traps for birds. According to one study, they account for more than 250 million bird fatalities a year in Canada.[178] Moreover, biotic communities in cities tend to be more homogenized and to include more non-native species. The competition for food in restricted urban areas reduces the evenness of diversity, resulting in the imbalance of winners and losers.[179] Urban wildlife are exposed to a new array of stresses compared to their rural counterparts. Some are forced to change dietary habits and hunting and foraging patterns. Species react differently to the intensity of pollution and contamination. Adaptation to new and novel stresses may induce evolutionary shifts within a few generations.[180]

Although urban wildlife comprise many taxa, they may be usefully categorized into the following groups in terms of how humans perceive them. The most welcome are the migratory and perennial song birds, like robins, warblers, chickadees, and bluebirds, along with the amphibians who take advantage of urban wetlands. The most common group, which is much less popular, includes sparrows, magpies, Canada geese, bats, gulls, squirrels, raccoons, possums, rabbits/hares, skunks, and mice, all of whom live permanently among humans, taking advantage of natural and, more often, human food sources, like gardens, garbage, pet food, or other human offerings. A third group, which promotes curiosity, fear, anxiety, and wariness, includes coyotes, ungulates, cougars, foxes, and hawks. They do not live in urban areas but are usually accidental, transitory, or short-term food-seeking visitors. A final miscellaneous group comprises permanent residents, like insects and spiders, who are either accepted, ignored, or eliminated as pests, depending on type.

Management of urban wildlife is, in the main, under the control of the specific urban jurisdiction but is constrained by provincial or federal policies. For example, migratory birds are under federal control. Wildlife generally are under provincial control, but in Alberta, for example, municipalities are allowed to manage species regarded as "pests."

The province also limits the size of municipal reserves, which further constrains habitat.[181] Generally, wildlife in cities are accepted as a minor by-product of urban life. However, when urban wildlife threaten comfort zones by allegedly endangering human health, by damaging property, or by becoming too bold, too numerous, or too dangerous, lethal options inevitably emerge as solutions.

A study on opinions about problem urban wildlife showed that public safety was the greatest factor in determining whether a "problem" animal should live or die.[182] Yet public safety is a subjective issue and is often invoked as a means of rationalization. For example, do crows threaten life and limb when they swoop on people who are too close to their nests? Are deer in gardens inherently dangerous? Do raccoons in attics directly threaten household health? Or are concerns over the former more about human tolerance levels and a right not to be exposed to worrisome animals. We only have to note the Toronto columnist who – confronted by the "evils" of urban Canada geese, whose feces littered parks and playgrounds, and by the "evils" of deer, who collided with vehicles – concluded that "there's only one predator that can control urbanized geese and deer populations. We need to get on with that job, and soon."[183] Rabbits, deer, squirrels, raccoons, coyotes, beavers, geese, magpies, and crows all face hostility and the ultimate solution in urban areas if public intolerance levels are high enough. Fortunately, this is avoided in many cities by residents who are not impacted, who possess higher tolerance levels, and who are morally disquieted by the notion of exterminating the creatures who live among them, albeit not always harmoniously. But their sentiments often do not prevail, as witnessed by the culling of beavers in Prince Edward Island, rabbits in Canmore, Alberta, and deer in Oak Bay, British Columbia.

Yet it is encouraging to see that the websites of major Canadian cities reveal a strong level of interest in their urban wildlife and an intent to manage them sensibly through policies that promote public tolerance and, where necessary, humane aversion techniques. Nonetheless, if the City of Calgary is any indication, there are limits to human kindness toward urban wildlife. In discussing beavers, the city noted their positive environmental role but warned about the dangers associated with increasing numbers and the impossibility of relocating them. The city's solution is death by trapping.[184] Contemporary research is generally in agreement that urban dwellers place more intrinsic value on wildlife than do their rural counterparts.[185] However, when it comes to urban wildlife, the divide between the two is narrower, primarily because of the universal human-interest factor.

CONCLUSION

The foregoing discussion has argued that although wildlife management policies reflect a stated awareness of the importance of species survival, they reserve a lot of leeway for ending the lives of an unacceptably high number of animals. Their vaunted scientific bases for dealing out death are not so scientific in terms of accurate population estimates. Ecologically, their interventions are subject to assumptions more than understanding. Lacking in ecological contexts and dependent on revenues from the consumptive use of game animals, wildlife management policies are far more receptive to the interests of hunters and of other influential stakeholders who lobby for the removal of offending species than they are to those who challenge the belief system's assumptions. Despite invoking wise use, carrying capacity, stewardship, sustainability, and scientific practice, management plans for the notable species can be little more than templates for hunting. Their discourse of species objectification disallows management policies that recognize shared characteristics with humans or that acknowledge research on the presence of conscious mental states in nonhumans.

The wildlife discussed in the preceding two chapters represent those exploited in the human interest. The plight of urban wildlife is more about human tolerance thresholds. Yet many would argue that the discussion proves nothing beyond the fact that governments are attempting to keep their numbers stable through culturally accepted conservation strategies. But this is the whole moral point. Why kill other sentient beings when life within our own species is valued so much? Where is any sense of kinship with the creatures under policy management? Where is the celebration of life, or even an awareness of the complexities inherent in wild domains? And, above all, why is an affinity for inflicting death on the defenceless superficially rationalized as stewardship? Regrettably, such thoughts belong to a belief system not evident in Canadian government management policies, which defer to Aldo Leopold, not John Livingston, and which, despite their rhetoric to the contrary, see wildlife primarily as aggregates of things for human exploitation.

PART TWO:
CONSERVATION OF SPECIES
AND THEIR HABITATS

4

The Species at Risk Act

One year from now [in 2008], Parliament is required to
review the effectiveness of SARA [Species at Risk Act (2002)].
Bureaucrats are now beginning work on the file. They will
be hard-pressed to spin this law as a success story.

AARON FREEMAN

In his thought-provoking book *Apocalyptic Planet: Field Guide to the
Future of the Earth* (2012), Craig Childs sees the loss of biodiversity as a
major global threat. "Numbers of lost and declining species are rapidly
rising with no end in sight," he writes. "Some researchers offer outside
estimates that as many as half of all remaining species may disappear
within the next century. Since declines on this scale have happened only
a handful of times in the fossil record, this point in earth's history seems
pivotal."[1] Compounded by the lack of understanding about the ways that
human beings are tied to the remainder of life, the task ahead is daunting
and will demand efforts that involve a new belief system, not just about
animals, although that will be part of it, but also about how humans should
live in an interdependent world.[2] Evolutionary sociobiologist Edward O.
Wilson is on the mark when he says that we need a better understanding
of human nature and "a more powerful and intellectually convincing
environmental ethic based upon it."[3]

Canada's efforts to deal with the challenges of enhancing biodiversity
reflect the limits of the belief system. Proper commitment to addressing
this crucial issue demands enormous capital investment and a willingness
to make significant sacrifices in the interests of wildlife, their habitats,
and the natural environment. None of these directions is palatable. The
chosen course is ameliorative. Put simply, whether it be conservation of

species or proper allowance for wildlife habitats, human priorities must be considered in any way forward. Insufficient funding, the lack of political will, and social costs have thus far thwarted the task of redressing wildlife declines and the ongoing diminishment of habitats.

According to official statements, the Canadian federal and provincial governments began moving away from their limited vision of wildlife management around 1970. The Wildlife Act (1973) empowered the federal government to conduct research on any species or its habitat, to acquire or lease private land for the same purposes, and to enter into agreements with the provinces in the interests of education or other aspects of wildlife preservation.[4] In practice, however, not a great deal changed. Despite some focus on species at risk through the Committee on the Status of Endangered Wildlife in Canada (COSEWIC), formed in 1977, and the Recovery of Nationally Endangered Wildlife program, launched in 1988, as well as on habitat preservation, parks expansion, contaminant control, and public education, the emphasis on nuisance-animal control and on revenue-raising game and furbearing animals continued to dominate wildlife management, certainly at the provincial level, where most policies are framed.[5] In fact, some provinces resented the federal Wildlife Act because of fears about its impact on provincial control of hunting and fishing.[6] Twelve years later, fears were expressed that the real reason behind the federal government's 22 per cent reduction in Canadian Wildlife Service staff was due to a belief that wildlife and education were provincial responsibilities, not federal.[7]

However, to give the federal government its due, a major policy change did occur in the 1990s when Canada made an international commitment to do its share in preserving global biodiversity. When it released the Canadian Biodiversity Strategy (1995), the federal government included a statement that envisioned a society where humans were responsible agents and where wildlife were valued as integral components of the natural world. Officially, Canada's goal was to become a "society that lives and develops as a part of nature, values the diversity of life, takes no more than can be replenished and leaves to future generations a nurturing and dynamic world, rich in its biodiversity."[8] With this slice of rhetoric, over the top even by political standards, Canada formally announced the dawn of a new era in policymaking where wild creatures apparently were to be valued not as living instruments for human use but as fellow contributing members of the wider biotic community. Yet, twenty years later, the "society that lives and develops as a part of nature" seems more distant than ever. As far as wildlife are concerned, the forces that have always borne badly on them just do not seem to be backing off.

THE CANADIAN BIODIVERSITY STRATEGY

Part of the problem in dealing with biodiversity is its immense scope. Biodiversity refers to the totality of all plants, animals, fungi, and micro-organisms present in any given area and includes all their individual variations and interactions. The quality and quantity of food, water, air, and other life-support materials are linked to ecological integrity and the biodiversity that sustains it. Currently, these materials are being impacted negatively on a global scale by habitat loss, overexploitation, climate change, and pollution.

Although the importance of biodiversity is recognized, knowledge gaps exist. Scientists estimate that the total number of species on earth may be as high as 14 million. However, only 1.75 million have been identified, and far fewer have been assessed for their ecological role. This is worrying, not just because overall biotic interactions are not well understood but also because extinctions are occurring at a rate 100 times greater than that of the fossil record and, furthermore, are expected to rise.[9] The US National Sciences Board predicted in 2000 that one-quarter of the world's species could be lost within twenty years.[10] In other words, insufficient knowledge exists about most species in the biotic community, some of whom are becoming extinct before anything is known about their interdependent roles.

International recognition of the importance of biodiversity to ecological integrity and global health dates to the late 1980s, particularly to 1987, when the World Commission on Environment and Development (Brundtland Commission) released its report *Our Common Future*, a landmark document that argued for a sustainable approach to balancing human needs with resources.[11] This essentially economic approach to managing the environment was, to quote John Livingston, simply a way "to plunder nature and get away with it."[12] Yet it resonated well with Canada's resource mentality and with general global sentiment, which was seeking a more environmentally friendly forward path. Following preparation of the United Nations Convention on Biological Diversity (1992),[13] Canada showed its commitment by being the first industrialized country to ratify the convention. At present, 194 countries are parties to the convention.

As part of its obligations under the convention, Canada prepared the Canadian Biodiversity Strategy (1995).[14] Wildlife were further recognized when the Accord for the Protection of Species at Risk (1996) was accepted by all Canadian jurisdictions.[15] Under the accord, participants agreed "to play a leadership role by developing complementary legislation, regulations, policies and programs to identify and protect endangered and threatened species and their critical habitats."[16]

The Canadian Biodiversity Strategy was an impressive eighty-six-page document that stressed the importance of biodiversity and outlined Canada's plans for implementation through a broad vision statement and several guidelines, goals, and strategic directions. The central place of wildlife was defined in goals that promised to maintain wild fauna in their habitats and ecosystems, to complete networks of protected areas, to restore and rehabilitate individual species and degraded ecosystems, to develop and implement plans, policies, and programs for agricultural, forested, and aquatic areas in support of biodiversity, and to reduce the adverse impacts of human population growth and settlement on ecosystems and species.[17]

However, a closer look at the Biodiversity Strategy shows that although its focus was ostensibly on biodiversity, and by implication on the need to restore and maintain it by enhancing natural processes, the inevitable human imperatives were lurking in the background. As with the related resource sustainability approach, which assumes that humans "can have their cake and eat it, too," the emphasis on biodiversity was really not much more than a wordy intent to encourage human restraint. After referring to the need for change, the strategy referred to "management approaches that integrate biodiversity conservation and sustainable use of biological resources with economic, social and cultural objectives."[18] This is extremely problematic given contemporary political ideology and practice, which continue to equate growth and prosperity with economic indices and the human interests they represent. Prominent Canadian geneticist David Suzuki put it another way when he said, "It is absurd for any species to aspire to take over 82–88 per cent of the land base of the planet and hope for sustainability."[19] In reference to the Convention on Biological Diversity (and by association, the Biodiversity Strategy), the Maritime Aboriginal Peoples Council noted, "For most western societies, predominantly modeled on *laissez faire* economics, and structured on the tenets of resource exploration and exploitation for economic development, particularly true in a resource rich and diverse country such as Canada," the Biodiversity Strategy "is a new and difficult concept to accept."[20]

The Biodiversity Strategy was short on specifics and long on the sidebars that showed how biodiversity health would aid humans. In many of the strategy's goals and directions, the economic, social, and cultural factors were paired with the more crucial ecological and biodiversity components. Pest management strategies had to consider both the economic and the ecological goals, which translated into lots of herbicide and pesticide use. Ecological and biodiversity planning had to integrate appropriate economic and social objectives, which obviously implied trade-offs. For instance, inclusionary clauses that permitted recreational activities and resource development in protected areas served to guarantee the human presence in places where it was neither wanted nor needed. There were also omissions, one of the most glaring of which was the failure to include or even mention genetically modified crops, biodiversity's main enemy on agricultural lands and in surrounding ecosystems.[21] After mentioning that forests were ecologically significant on a global scale, the Biodiversity Strategy stressed, "About 300 communities depend largely on forestry and more than 800,000 people work in the forest products industry or for organizations associated with it. In 1993, forest product exports contributed $22.4 billion to our net balance of trade."[22] Finally, the use of escape phrases such as "where practical" and "if necessary" offered clear indications that the implementation of the strategy was to be more human-centred and less enthusiastic than its rhetoric implied.[23] The Canadian Biodiversity Strategy was a naive document that mocked ecologist Larry Harris's contention that a high-level approach was needed to support ecological integrity, one that recognized and understood the intricate linkages in naturally functioning ecosystems, or as he wrote in 1984, "The strategy selected should not only ensure the conservation of spotted owls, but all the intricate linkages that are associated with natural populations of spotted owls in naturally functioning ecosystems. Many of these are as yet unknown."[24]

This chapter and the two that follow examine how wildlife have fared under the Canadian Biodiversity Strategy. They deal with the two inter-related factors impacting the health of wildlife in Canada: the conservation of species generally and the preservation of their habitat.

Canada is home to over 70,000 known species. The risk of endanger-ment has been determined for 10,332, including 43 per cent of all rep-tiles and 20 per cent of amphibians. The 12 per cent of fish at risk does not include the 60 per cent ranked as undetermined.[25] Many globally threatened species are endemic to Canada, including over one-third of mammals, almost half of freshwater fish, butterflies, and skippers, and around 20 per cent of birds.[26]

That it took almost a decade for Canada to comply with the Biodiversity Strategy and produce legislation to protect species under threat was an early indication that despite the strategy's enthusiasm, prompt attention to species' conservation was not a major priority. Jurisdictional wrangling between the federal and provincial governments, power battles between politicians and scientists over control of "species at risk" designations, and fears over the impact on private landowners prevented legislation from going forward.[27] Two federal endangered species bills died on the Order Paper when federal elections were called in 1997 and 2000. The same fate befell the Species at Risk Act when Parliament was prorogued in September 2002. The act was finally passed in December of that year.[28] Although in force by June 2003, more amendments were added before it became fully operational in June 2004. It had not been an easy birth. The act was opposed by government bureaucrats, by rural members of Parliament who worried about property rights, by livestock organizations, and by environmentally conscious backbenchers who thought it was ineffective. It passed only because of strong lobbies by environmental organizations with some backbencher support.[29] Nor did it pass with pub-lic fanfare. An article in the *Hill Times* commented on media disinterest and an uninformed public: "The long-overdue Species at Risk Act (SARA) was brought into force by the federal government. And no one noticed."[30]

THE SPECIES AT RISK ACT

In its broadest sense, the Species at Risk Act (SARA) functions as a federal tool for conserving and protecting Canada's biological diversity, or as Ken Harris of the Canadian Wildlife Service puts it, "SARA is the biodiversity emergency ward: it deals with species that are literally about to be eliminated from Canada's biodiversity."[31] Its stated purposes are to prevent wildlife species from extirpation or extinction, to identify and provide for the recovery of those species listed as "endangered" or "threatened" as a result of human activity, and to ensure that species of "special concern" are not further compromised. SARA relies on the Committee on the Status of Endangered Wildlife in Canada to assess and recommend the listing of species at risk.[32] It also maintains an ongoing public registry of all species listed as "extirpated," "endangered," "threatened," or of "special concern." Responsibility for the implementation of SARA is shared by Fisheries and Oceans Canada, Parks Canada, the Canadian Wildlife Service, and Environment Canada (now Environment and Climate Change Canada), with the latter holding the final authority to make recommendations to Cabinet on the listing of species. Following "endangered" or "threatened" listings, recovery measures, primarily through mandatory recovery strategies and action plans, are prepared cooperatively by the relevant jurisdictions and private stakeholders, with the federal component in the leading role. If a recovery plan already exists and meets the requirements of SARA, it may be adopted as the official recovery strategy. Although most recovery strategies focus on individual species, a multi-species, ecology-based approach may be undertaken at the discretion of the appropriate federal minister.

SARA's effectiveness is compromised on several levels. With an area of 9.985 million square kilometres, Canada is a vast federal state that contains almost 20 per cent of the planet's wilderness, 24 per cent of its wetlands, 20 per cent of its freshwater, 10 per cent of its forests, and an arctic ecosystem that covers a quarter of its landmass.[33] The task of structuring a workable, protective legal regime across fourteen jurisdictions presented formidable challenges. Unfortunately, the federal government chose a politically safe legislative path in passing a bill that limits its capacity to deal effectively with this difficult challenge. First, it chose to politicize the "species at risk" listing process by assigning final authority to Cabinet, not to the Committee on the Status of Endangered Wildlife in Canada, its arm's-length and respected scientific body. Second, the financial resources allocated to species protection were inadequate. Third, and most important, the federal government took the safe constitutional route by opting to protect species within a narrow jurisdictional framework that forces SARA to operate within the cumbersome confines of cooperative federalism. Underfunded, thwarted by a time-consuming and political process, and weakened further by an inability to mandate compliance, SARA flounders while at-risk wildlife suffer.

Essentially, SARA relies on voluntary compliance and a commitment to stewardship in order to protect the nation's at-risk species and their habitat.[34] Put another way, this approach means less centralized control of wild creatures of national interest. Direct federal control, which focuses on about 5 per cent of provincial land and on less than half of Canada's overall land area, is limited to species on federal land, to most aquatic species, and to birds listed under the Convention for the Protection of Migratory Birds (1916).[35] Control over all other species devolves on the respective provincial and territorial governments, whose own powers are constrained on privately owned land. To achieve its ends, SARA works cooperatively with these jurisdictions. Under the Accord for the Protection of Species at Risk (1996), wildlife ministers of provincial and territorial governments agreed to support SARA through complementary legislation and/or regulatory measures.[36] In 1998 they also joined the federal government in forming the Canadian Endangered Species Conservation Council, which acts as a coordinating agency for identifying and recovering species at risk on nonfederal land. The Canadian Wildlife Directors Committee supports interjurisdictional cooperation on species at risk through the development and coordination of policies, strategies, programs, and activities that address wildlife issues of national concern. The National General Status Working Group is responsible for completing the general status assessments of species in their jurisdictions.[37] Additionally, the Habitat Stewardship Program for Species at Risk provides incentives in support of voluntary stewardship initiatives by any government, organization, or individual. Special agreements also exist between four provincial governments and the federal government on the management of species at risk and on administrative issues.[38]

The decentralized nature of SARA is a major weakness in the implementation of recovery measures. An Environment Canada evaluation of SARA in 2012 acknowledged a lack of evaluative information on provincial policies and effective communication with the provinces. It also noted the confusion caused by overlapping jurisdictional consultations on species recovery plans, the need for bilateral agreements with the provinces, and the problematic financial capacity of some provinces to meet their obligations under SARA.[39] That this in-house audit was unable to endorse its own efforts was a sad testimony to SARA's first decade and a sobering foretelling of a bleak future.[40]

Once a species is listed as "endangered" or "threatened," and thus entitled to legal protection, recovery plans or strategies must be prepared within one year for "endangered" species and two years for "threatened" species. Recovery strategies identify the species' critical habitat and specify the goals, objectives, and activities necessary to arrest or reverse the decline of a species. Mandatory action plans flow from these recovery strategies and are focused primarily on the restoration, preservation, and maintenance of critical habitat. At the discretion of the federal government, recovery strategies may involve more than one species. Usually, recovery strategies are prepared cooperatively with those jurisdictions where the at-risk species is found. Once recovery strategies are complete, however, unless they concern federal land and waters or involve migratory birds, their implementation falls to provincial and territorial jurisdictions, which are guided by the recovery strategy itself and by the federal agency involved. These recovery measures are implemented at the provincial and territorial levels in various ways, including legislation, regulation, separate recovery strategies, management plans, agreements, and permits. The attention, detail, and commitment to these responsibilities under SARA differ widely across Canadian jurisdictions.

A good example of the problems facing at-risk species under SARA's mixed jurisdictional framework can be found in Ontario, where the provincial government seems bent on undermining its own Endangered Species Act (2007), a piece of legislation that was lauded as a "gold standard act" when it was first passed. In 2013 the Liberal government introduced amendments to the act that allowed exemptions sanctioning harm to endangered species and destruction of their habitat by forest, oil and gas, or mining operations following official approval of a management plan. The government defended its position, arguing that "the legislation balances the central concern of protecting at-risk species with social, economic, health and cultural considerations,"[41] sentiments echoed by Premier Kathleen Wynne: "We have to recognize there are businesses and the agricultural community that is dependent on being able to develop certain land and to manufacture goods."[42] Subsequent legal challenges by the conservation groups Ontario Nature and Wildlands League were denied by both the Divisional Court and the Appellate Court in Ontario, which agreed that the protection of endangered species had to be balanced against social and economic interests.[43] Not only are these unfortunate developments typical of official ambiguity over conserving vulnerable species, but they are also at odds with section 49(e) of the federal Species at Risk Act, which integrates socio-economic factors into official action plans only. Of course, the federal government can intervene if it deems that proper steps have not been followed. Such intervention, however, is rare and, in this case, extremely improbable given the courts' rulings that the appropriate minister had exercised sufficient oversight through the compulsory management plans.

Several issues demonstrate the price SARA pays for its reliance on cooperation and stewardship. The provinces and territories lack consistency and commitment to the intent of SARA. Not all provinces and territories have dedicated species at risk legislation. In Alberta, for example, no specific law exists to protect the habitat and homes of vulnerable species.[44] British Columbia, the other province without species at risk legislation, had identified over 1,300 species at risk by 2007, of which only 4 were legally listed and therefore entitled to the very weak protections afforded by British Columbia's Wildlife Act (1996).[45] Recovery strategies are not binding in Ontario, and they are at the discretion of the appropriate minister in Saskatchewan, where requirements are lacking to identify or protect critical habitat.[46] As of 2013, Manitoba did not require recovery planning, and implementation and provincial recovery strategies are almost nonexistent.[47] In Quebec recovery plans are discretionary, and in Newfoundland and Labrador they do not stipulate the protection of critical habitat. New Brunswick protects species at risk but offers little in the way of recovery mechanisms. Legislation in Nunavut has no listed species and therefore no recovery plans. The Yukon's laws do not provide for recovering species at risk, and as of 2013 no recovery strategies had been prepared.[48]

Although recovery strategies are mandated for all "endangered" and "threatened" species, their implementation at the provincial and territorial levels is inconsistent and in many ways problematic. Species listed under SARA often receive no corresponding designations in the relevant provincial or territorial jurisdictions.[49] Ontario, for example, lacks recovery strategies for over 200 listed species – some of which are linked with the unavailability of the corresponding federal recovery strategy, which the province intends to adopt.[50] Of the 298 SARA-listed species in 2011, 36 per cent were not listed under any provincial or territorial endangered species or wildlife statute or equivalent.[51] In 2015 wildlife-rich British Columbia, Alberta, and Saskatchewan together listed a total of 72 species in contrast to SARA's 191. The three territories in total list only 5 species of the 46 listed by SARA.[52] Most provinces have not implemented adequate recovery plans. For 76 per cent of species with federal recovery strategies in 2010, nothing had been done at the relevant provincial or territorial levels.[53] Two years later, only 26 per cent of SARA-listed species had provincial or territorial recovery strategies. Saskatchewan had only two underway.[54]

The identification and subsequent protection of critical habitat, the most important element in recovering an at-risk species, are compromised by jurisdictional constraints. A recent study by University of Victoria scientists found that inadequacies in the identification and protection of critical habitat meant that the status of 86 per cent of SARA-listed species has either deteriorated or stayed the same through time.[55] Critical habitat is identified in the recovery strategy, and within 180 days it becomes the legal responsibility of SARA through a protection order issued by the appropriate federal minister. Although a species' recovery cannot begin until critical habitat is identified and legally designated, recovery strategies are often prepared minus the identification of critical habitat, which leads to inordinate delays, stalemates, and legal challenges. Particularly in provinces that do not prepare their own recovery plans, thorough identification of critical habitat is often lacking. Furthermore, provinces are reluctant to identify critical habitat in the absence of federal assurance respecting compensation for private land taken out of production or use.[56] That SARA is silent on timeframes for provincial recovery measures makes matters worse. In 2010, according to forestry professor and environmental authority George Hoberg, only 31 per cent of the 322 species listed under SARA had recovery strategies, and of those, only 6 per cent had critical habitat identified.[57] Biology professor Scott Findlay said much the same thing when he told a federal parliamentary committee in 2010 that only six species had critical habitat identified.[58]

The mandatory action plans are not subject to timelines and are virtually nonexistent at the provincial level. The red-headed woodpecker was assessed as "threatened" by the Committee on the Status of Endangered Wildlife in Canada (COSEWIC) in 2007.[59] Following an official response statement, which reported that "there is no evidence to suggest that the population trend will be reversed," no recovery measures were undertaken until 2016, when the species was included in two multi-species action plans in the Great Lakes area.[60] In other words, it took almost a decade for a dangerously threatened bird to receive cursory mention in nonspecific action plans. According to the current Species at Risk Public Registry, complete federal action plans for at-risk species number fewer than twenty.[61] Although action plans must incorporate a socio-economic cost and benefit statement, those few that have been completed by the federal government follow a prescribed generalized template that offers no specifics. Critics also contend that the multi-species approach is driven by time and fiscal pressures and pays less attention to individual species.[62]

The time period for the initiation of appropriate action to recover a species at risk is too long. It can take years for the federal Cabinet to accept, reject, or require more study following a COSEWIC recommendation. Ministerial discretion and catch phrases like "biological and technical knowledge gaps" and "the need for best possible information" are synonyms for procrastination following a COSEWIC listing. For example, in 2012 COSEWIC had listed 630 species at risk compared to SARA's 513. It took three years for the federal government to list the polar bear as a "special concern" following a COSEWIC recommendation in 2008. Some species of lake sturgeon listed by COSEWIC as "endangered" or "threatened" in 2007 languished for more than six years before they were listed under SARA.[63] Even after a SARA listing, the requisite recovery timelines have not been met. The wolverine (eastern population) was listed as "endangered" in eastern Canada in 2005. It took until 2014 for a proposed recovery plan to be completed, and the action plan is not expected until the end of 2019.[64] After being listed as endangered in 2003, the burrowing owl had to wait until 2012 for its recovery strategy. Hopes were expressed for an action plan within two years, an objective that was only partially met by 2016.[65] Similarly, the endangered leatherback sea turtle had a recovery strategy in place in 2006. Six years later, the action plan was still being developed.[66] In 2014 Environment Canada admitted that 163 out of 192 federal recovery strategies were overdue, some by more than six years.[67] Fisheries and Oceans Canada has recovery plans for twelve at-risk marine species in Quebec but action plans for none.[68]

Even when threatened with extirpation, some species face the same delays. Endangered Atlantic salmon in the Bay of Fundy had to wait over eight years before a SARA recovery strategy was completed in 2010, and a further four years were given for the action plan, a delay that, according to one source, "is out of tune with the imminent extirpation of these populations from main rivers in its range of distribution."[69] This source's prediction in 2011 of a "foggy future" for said action plan was accurate. As of the end of 2015, it was still not in place.[70] Biologist Rick Smith, executive director of the national conservation group Environmental Defence Canada, puts it well: "If it seems to you that the adjective most often associated with SARA is 'delayed,' you'd be right. What's the bottom line? It will be years before most species now legally 'protected' by the federal government receive any help whatsoever in their recovery from near extinction."[71]

In 2012 Ecojustice, a Vancouver-based group that provides legal support and advice to environmental groups involved in litigation with governments and industry, evaluated the performance of Canada's various governments in fulfilling their responsibility to protect Canada's at-risk species and their habitats.[72] Its conclusion was unequivocal: "The analysis in this report paints a clear, though unsettling, picture. Across the board, Canada's federal, provincial and territorial governments are doing an abysmal job protecting our at-risk species and the habitat they need to survive and recover."[73] Twelve of fourteen jurisdictions received a grade of C– or lower, including four with an F. The other two grades were C and C+. Ecojustice contended that the primary reason for these poor performances was rooted in discretionary provincial and territorial wildlife laws and in a lack of leadership by the federal government in exercising its overriding authority.

Politics is also present at the listing level. In noting SARA's failure to protect critical habitat effectively, Joshua McNeely and Roger Hunka of the Maritime Aboriginal Peoples Council touch on the central problem with SARA, or any other issue concerning wildlife preservation, for that matter: "SARA recognizes that the machinery of government cannot or has not accepted the value of considering the conservation and sustainable use of biodiversity to be equal [to] or greater than exploration and exploitation for profit."[74] With regard to the down-listing of the humpback whale, COSEWIC member Andrew Trites commented that politics was involved and noted that "the Canadian government seems to be slow to list species we'd consider threatened or endangered, but they seem much faster when we go the opposite direction."[75] In cases where Cabinet has asked COSEWIC for more study on a species, its possibility of being listed is lower.[76] In 2007 published research that analyzed listing decisions under SARA concluded that marine and harvested species with commercial and subsistence value or with a northern orientation were less likely to be listed.[77] Using sturgeon as an example, the authors of this study argued that the green sturgeon was listed because it had no economic value, whereas certain populations of the white sturgeon were not listed because of their value as a sport fish.[78] In referring to the Nunavut Wildlife Management Board and its reluctance to accept the additional stewardship responsibilities required by SARA, the authors noted that the refusal to list the eastern Hudson Bay beluga whale posed an extinction risk and that consultation issues with Nunavut were delaying the listing of the wolverine, grizzly bear, and polar bear elsewhere in Canada.[79] Building on this research, Findlay and colleagues agree, emphasizing that of the twenty-one subsistence-harvested species submitted to Cabinet, only three have been subsequently listed, and then solely as a "special concern," the lowest risk category, where hunting and harvesting are allowed. The remaining eighteen species are either not listed or have been referred back to COSEWIC for extended review.[80] Eight aquatic species recommended by COSEWIC were not listed by Cabinet in 2006 in order to protect the fishing industry."[81] In 2012 it was admitted that commercially harvested species listed under SARA could not expect the same level of protection as noncommercial species.[82]

The status of the porbeagle shark is an excellent example of SARA yielding to marginal commercial interests. A cold-water but warm-blooded shark with a wide range of feeding preferences, porbeagles fill an important ecological role as high-trophic predators in structuring marine communities in the northwest Atlantic. They are also renowned for their high-quality meat. With overall numbers more than halved since 1961 due to overfishing, female populations having dropped as much as 77 per cent, and with only 1 percent of their range in a marine protected area, the species was listed by COSEWIC as "endangered" in 2004. SARA did not follow suit, refusing to list the species at all and preferring instead to rely on its own fishing controls.[83] The reason was simple. In COSEWIC's words, "It was not listed under the *Species at Risk Act* (SARA) because of economic losses associated with eliminating the directed fishery. Reduced catch levels were thought to be low enough to avoid jeopardizing the long-term recovery of the species."[84] In this particular case, the interests of a small number of fishers and the federal government's penchant for bypassing its own Species at Risk Act outweighed the necessity of using SARA to do as much as possible in order to protect an endangered species.[85]

The Atlantic bluefin tuna is a very large, migratory fish who feeds in Canadian waters in the Bay of Fundy and the Gulf of Saint Lawrence, as well as between Georges Bank off the coast of Nova Scotia to the Grand Banks of Newfoundland. In 2011 COSEWIC classified the western Atlantic population of bluefin tuna as "endangered," referring to a 69 per cent decline in the number of spawning adults over the past forty years, primarily due to heavy commercial fishery exploitation. In recommending the "endangered" designation, COSEWC observed, "While the cause of the decline, overfishing, is understood, it has not ceased and it is not clearly reversible." COSEWIC further noted that the chances of recovery were further compromised by the fact that the vast majority of the fish being taken (85 per cent in 2007) were immature.[86]

The federal government, however, acting on the advice of the minister of environment and the minister of fisheries and oceans, decided not to follow COSEWIC's recommendation to list bluefin tuna as "endangered." In fact, it decided not to list these fish at all, opting instead to manage them under provisions in the Fisheries Act (1985). The reasons were clear since it was expected that the bluefin's listing "as endangered under SARA and the subsequent closure of the directed and by-catch fisheries, including commercial harvesting, charter boat and Aboriginal commercial-communal fisheries, would result in significant socio-economic impacts on industry and communities in the region, including Aboriginal communities."[87] In responding to criticisms that listing the bluefin tuna would allow effective recovery of the species, the government went into a high-rationalization mode and contended that it would not do the species any good overall since the International Commission for the Conservation of Atlantic Tunas – an intergovernmental organization whose broad mandate includes establishing target stocks or allocations for specific areas – would transfer Canada's allocation to other countries, some of which did not have Canada's stringent tagging and catch-monitoring processes.[88]

The lack of protection afforded to the wolverine is also linked to special interest groups. Ranging across northern and western forested areas, alpine tundra of the western mountains, and arctic tundra, these stocky, fierce, reclusive, wide-ranging, and legendary carnivores resemble a small bear but in taxonomic terms are the largest terrestrial members of the weasel family. With their dependence on extensive connected ecosystems that support ungulates and create scavenging opportunities, wolverines act as important indicators of ecosystem health. They have a low reproductive rate, are sensitive to human disturbance, take a long time to recover from severe population depletions, and require vast tracts of secure areas to maintain viable populations.[89] Unsurprisingly, given their long, glossy, coarse fur, which varies from brown to black, wolverines are highly sought-after fur animals.

Currently, these reclusive animals are under several threats that bear careful monitoring. Although trapping is regulated, overharvesting occurs in some areas and according to COSEWIC has the potential to increase, especially with the growing use of motorized vehicles.[90] In more southerly ranges, habitat loss results from conversion for human land uses, including agriculture, ranching, and urban and suburban developments. Elsewhere, logging, mining, and associated infrastructure, plus transportation corridors that allow noisy snowmobiles, helicopters, and a growing number of backcountry skiers, are all intruding on wolverine habitat. A recent study in Alberta's forested areas, the first of its kind, found that human-modified landscapes induced stressful wolverine behaviour and more cautious hunting patterns.[91] A reduction in caribou prey is impacting wolverines in some areas, and since adequate snow cover is essential for wolverines, climate change is already affecting habitat in the southern ranges.[92]

Wolverine populations (eastern and western) are difficult to assess, more so than for other large carnivores given their wide range (up to 1,580 square kilometres), low density (5 to 10 per 1,000 square kilometres), and reclusive nature. Also, because most population data are derived from harvest records, many of which are unreported, actual accurate numbers are impossible to gauge. However, consensus suggests that wolverine populations are declining in much of Canada, particularly in the southern reaches of their range. The eastern population, found in Quebec and in Newfoundland and Labrador, is listed as "endangered" and has possibly been extirpated. The western population, found in Ontario, western Canada, and all three territories, has been virtually extirpated on Vancouver Island. Wolverine numbers are down in British Columbia, Alberta, and Saskatchewan. Although considered stable in the Yukon and Northwest Territories, they seem to be facing a declining trend there as well.[93]

Recognizing the implications of the ongoing threats to wolverine habitat health, COSEWIC designated the wolverine as the equivalent of a "special concern" as early as 1982. In 2003, following the division of the wolverine into two populations, COSEWIC listed the eastern population as "endangered" and maintained the western population's listing of "special concern." Over a decade later, in 2016, the federal government released its recovery strategy for the eastern subpopulation. It was not a forceful, proactive document. It lacked the crucial identification of critical habitat. In fact, according to the strategy, surveys were necessary "to determine if the species still persists in Quebec and Labrador." In addition, studies on critical habitat of the eastern subpopulation were generally necessary. Yet, on that basis, action plans for this endangered regional population of wolverines were not expected until the end of 2021.[94]

As for the western subpopulation, SARA did not follow up on COSEWIC's recommendation in 2003, in part due to concerns expressed by the Nunavut Wildlife Management Board. As noted by COSEWIC in reference to its "special concern" listing in 2003, "the Western Population was not added to the SARA list in order to further consult with the Nunavut Wildlife Management Board (NWMB) and the Nunavut government. Issues for the NWMB centred on the lack of ATK [Aboriginal traditional knowledge], inadequate consultation, issues with [the] land claims agreement, and evidence of increasing population in Nunavut. The consultation process occurred in 2005; however, the Minister of Environment did not issue a recommendation."[95] In this case, it was more important for the federal government to acquiesce to the wishes of a single territory than to recognize negative trends in wolverine populations in Canada generally. Nothing changed when COSEWIC reassessed the western subpopulation in 2014. Although COSEWIC reaffirmed its "special concern" status, the federal government again declined to list the species under SARA. The merits of this decision are questionable. In its assessment, COSEWIC gave wolverine population estimates that varied by over 50 percent, ranging from 15,688 to 23,830, and it further noted that the estimates were predicated on stable trapping harvests, which are far from predictable, and on relatively uniform wolverine densities across the species' entire ranges, which must have been based on an assumption given the uncertainty caused by climate change and ongoing anthropogenic disturbance.[96]

The "special concern" listing has become a political tool used for economic and other purposes. Unlike the "endangered" and "threatened" categories, which legally bind governments to specific actions and restrictions, the "special concern" category demands a management plan and little more. For example, COSEWIC listed the black-tailed prairie dog as a "special concern" five times after 1978. Nothing was done, eventually prompting an up-listing to "threatened" status in 2011.[97] Under the "special concern" status, the opposite trend should have occurred. For example, the polar bear's listing as a "special concern" allows for hunting, whereas a listing as "threatened" or "endangered" would not. Although a "threatened" listing is more appropriate for the polar bear, it would put the federal government on a collision course with the Inuit, who see polar bear hunting as an economic lifeline. Similarly, by downgrading the humpback whale from "threatened" to a "special concern," the federal government is not forced to protect critical habitat, which makes it easier to clear environmental barriers in the way of the proposed Enbridge Northern Gateway Pipeline in British Columbia. The "special concern" category is meant to be a "red flag" necessitating the close monitoring of a declining species. Unfortunately, it has also become a useful way to honour the intent of SARA while allowing for the continued exploitation of a vulnerable species. For example, a government report in 2012 admitted that only 26 per cent of species listed as a "special concern" had their requisite management plans in place.[98]

Another major stumbling block to SARA's effectiveness is its limited ability to protect species on privately owned land. This is particularly difficult in the Maritimes, where most land is in private hands. Depending on ideology, political considerations, and inclination, provinces vary greatly in their willingness and capacity to involve themselves in issues concerning private landowners, especially in areas of dispute. The Sprague's pipit, for example, a threatened prairie grassland bird, enjoys protection under SARA in Grasslands National Park in Saskatchewan. On private land in Alberta, however, the bird's critical habitat has not been adequately identified.[99] This is a case where SARA's reliance on stewardship should be seen operating to best advantage, with all stakeholders, including landowners with at-risk species, voluntarily and consistently working together to implement the recovery strategies and action plans primarily through cooperation, conservation agreements, and special permits.[100]

Several factors, however, are at work that militate against effective protection of at-risk species on the above basis. First, the voluntary approach doubtless asks for more than it can expect.[101] Many private landowners are resistant to unapproved government intrusion on their land. Second, as political science professor Andrea Olive has shown, not all landowners have a stewardship ethic, and the majority of those who do have one possess minimal knowledge of at-risk species or how to monitor them. In reference to assisting the endangered Lake Erie water snake, she writes, "Quite simply, they [landowners] lack the knowledge as to how to use their own land in ways that could benefit these species."[102] A study on Saskatchewan ranchers found a low knowledge of species at risk and concluded, "Species at risk programs could achieve success by recognizing rancher stewardship for native prairie and rewarding ranchers with economic support or incentives for the ecosystem goods and services they provide."[103] This latter point is significant because although the voluntary approach implies shared responsibility and financial ownership, the matter of any monetary compensation remains a shadowy uncertainty. Provision for compensation is specified in SARA under section 64.1 but only for "extraordinary impact," which apparently does not include reimbursing landowners for loss of land set aside as critical habitat. One wonders why. In 2012 Environment Canada's Audit and Evaluation Branch, in referencing the Species at Risk Advisory Committee, noted that the absence of compensation was a barrier to successful negotiations with private landowners and industry.[104] Not surprisingly, landowners upset at being treated dismissively are losing some of their enthusiasm for their stewardship duties.[105]

SARA, THE BLACK-TAILED PRAIRIE DOG, AND THE BLACK-FOOTED FERRET

The interdependent plights of the imperilled black-footed ferret and the threatened black-tailed prairie dog show the limitations of SARA when applied to private and even Crown land. Although a tentative solution is unfolding, much more needs to be done in order to guarantee the survival of both species.

Black-tailed prairie dogs, a diurnal member of the squirrel family, live in large colonies in broad, flat river valleys or upland grasslands. They construct burrows, where they sleep at night, seek protection from weather, hibernate, breed, rear their offspring, and escape predators. In Canada they number between 6,000 and 9,000 and are found only in southern Saskatchewan adjacent to and within the lower Frenchman River Valley in the area of Grasslands National Park. In 2010 Canada's population of black-tailed prairie dogs consisted of eighteen colonies on approximately 12 square kilometres.[106]

Parks Canada states, "Prairie dogs play an important ecological role for many species. They influence biodiversity, nutrient cycling, environmental heterogeneity, hydrology and landscape-level processes." Their communities support a high "diversity and density of small mammals, terrestrial predators and avian species," while enhancing species richness and abundance by furnishing "important habitats for multiple trophic and taxonomic groups of arthropods." Their burrows provide important breeding sites for a number of species, and the terrain of their colonies is used as habitat by more than 100 vertebrate species, including the black-footed ferret and the burrowing owl.[107]

The black-footed ferret is a nocturnal, intermediate-sized member of the weasel family and a prairie species that has inhabited North America's semi-desert shrub lands and short-grass and mixed-grass ecosystems for the past 800,000 years.[108] Currently extirpated from Canada, the historical range of black-footed ferrets included southwestern Saskatchewan and southeastern Alberta. Currently, efforts are underway to reintroduce the black-footed ferret into the wild through a controlled breeding program in Grasslands National Park in southern Saskatchewan. Black-footed ferrets are one the world's most specialized carnivores in that prairie dogs comprise over 90 per cent of their diet. They also utilize and adapt prairie dog burrows, which can be more than 4 metres underground and extend over 20 metres in a horizontal and vertical network of burrow systems.[109] The dependence of black-footed ferrets on the prairie dog is so great that they rarely leave the confines of prairie dog colonies, and to quote one source, "As the prairie dog goes, so does the ferret."[110]

And herein lies the problem. The black-tailed prairie dog is itself a highly vulnerable species and is listed by COSEWIC as "threatened." Not so under SARA, where the current "special concern" listing does not preclude hunting or lethal control measures. The reason is simple. Farmers and ranchers consider the black-tailed prairie dog to be a pest. As the Management Plan for the Black-Tailed Prairie Dog (2009) noted, "Across their entire range they are considered to be pests that are not welcome on most lands due to competition with grazing livestock and the possible loss of income from this competition. Many land managers hunt and poison prairie dogs and are determined to continue to do so."[111] Thus, under the plan, black-tailed prairie dogs are managed within tightly controlled and restricted areas to appease human interests. They will be allowed to breed and thrive in Grasslands National Park but will be at risk if they establish colonies outside park boundaries, where, according to the plan, "Neighbouring landowners should contact the Government of Saskatchewan if they wish to apply for a permit to kill prairie dogs that have expanded onto their land."[112] In the case of what are primarily Crown lands in the form of community pastures, their numbers will be regulated at a specific threshold solely through lethal control.[113] This means that if black-footed ferrets are reintroduced successfully, they will be confined to the park and, in limited numbers, to two adjacent community pastures.

The isolation of these two imperilled species within specific management areas and the tight control of black-tailed prairie dog numbers greatly limit both species' chances of securing sufficient habitat to allow healthy widespread recovery. For example, the entire black-tailed prairie dog colonies in Grasslands National Park can support only thirty ferrets.[114] This is further compromised by the fact that both species are highly susceptible to periodic outbreaks of the contagious and deadly sylvatic (bubonic) plague, which has hindered successful reintroduction of the black-footed ferret in the United States.[115] Thus far, Canada has been spared an epizootic outbreak of the disease.[116] Nevertheless, the threat is very real, and given the tight concentration of prairie dog colonies in the current management areas, a major outbreak of a disease with 90 per cent mortality rates would be devastating.

The successful reintroduction of the black-footed ferret, an extirpated species in Canada, depends on the health of the black-tailed prairie dog, a species that itself is vulnerable to declines because of its small numbers, limited habitat, susceptibility to sylvatic plague, and geographic location at the northern edge of its range. Yet the vulnerability of black-tailed prairie dogs (and by association black-footed ferrets) is amplified by their negative reputation among private landowners, federal disinclination to afford them additional protection under SARA, and ranching activity in the two community pastures set aside for them. As for range and habitat expansion, COSEWIC is not hopeful, noting that "expansion would be limited by threats that would likely occur for animals beyond the regulation zone. These threats are associated with habitat loss or degradation from road construction, conversion of grassland to cropland or forage crops, commercial and industrial development primarily through oil and gas development, and human persecution."[117]

Finally, although SARA contains overriding provisions in section 80 for instances where protection of an at-risk species is deemed inadequate on provincial or private land, federal authorities thus far have been very reluctant to interfere. According to one study, a large number of SARA-listed species are not being adequately protected on nonfederal lands, and "SARA is failing to play the critical safety net role that was promised when the Act was introduced."[118]

FUNDING SARA

In light of the Canadian Biodiversity Strategy's grand design, the Species at Risk Act is grossly underfunded.[119] Accurate figures on overall expenditures on at-risk species are difficult to locate in budgets and financial statements, partly because they are merged with related wildlife management programs within the appropriate ministry and/or are incorporated into other spending programs in another ministry. Federal funds for SARA were reasonable in the first decade of its existence, averaging around $48 million annually between 2007 and 2010.[120] Since around 2011, when the government of Prime Minister Stephen Harper began reducing funding for environmental issues, the funds available for SARA have been drastically reduced. Some broad assessments show the current low priority given to wildlife generally and to species at risk. The federal government's expenditures were around $241 billion for 2015–2016.[121] Of that total, $25 million, or around one-hundredth of 1 per cent, went toward species at risk programs.[122] The Province of Ontario's expenditures for 2015–2016 were set at $126.7 billion, of which $5 million was allocated to species at risk.[123] Newfoundland and Labrador allocated $410,000 for endangered species and biodiversity out of its spending budget of $7 billion for 2015–2016.[124] Alberta's expenditures in 2014–2015 were around $42 billion, of which $32.5 million went to the Ministry of Fish and Wildlife.[125] British Columbia was projected to spend about $46 billion in 2015–2016, of which $28 million was to support environmental protection and sustainability.[126] These figures are pitifully low, and those of Alberta and British Columbia are not specifically dedicated to species at risk. As has been suggested, species at risk might benefit from other programs, but actual dollar amounts come nowhere near one-tenth of 1 per cent of government spending. If they did, Canada would be devoting $241 million, Ontario $126 million, British Columbia $46 million, Alberta $42 million, and Newfoundland and Labrador $7 million to biodiversity and the recovery of species at risk.

The plight of the endangered blue racer snake is a good example of the impact of financial constraints on a species' survival. The blue racer is one of eleven subspecies found in North America, and although histor-ically located in extreme southwestern Ontario, it is now only found on Pelee Island in Lake Erie. The species was designated as "endangered" by COSEWIC in 1991 and by SARA in 2004. The provincial recovery strategy was completed in 2015 and the federal addendum in 2017. Although no population assessments have been undertaken since 2002, the current numbers are estimated at 250 adults and likely declining. Suitable blue racer habitat on the island is fragmented and further degraded by urban and agricultural development activities, increased road traffic and tour-ism, intentional human persecution, disease, and possibly the predatory presence of the recently introduced wild turkey.[127] Although recovery efforts are ongoing, the habitat necessary for expansion and growth on a small, increasingly developed island is extremely limited.

The possibility of relocating the blue racer to additional suitable sites on the mainland has been explored and rejected. Expense is a major reason for not going forward. According to the Recovery Strategy for the Blue Racer (2017), "A substantial commitment of resources is required for the long-term monitoring of any introduced Blue Racer population to evaluate the success of repatriation efforts. Under current funding formulas for species at risk projects, such a commitment to [a] long-term (ca. 10 year) project is highly unlikely. Considering the amount of resources and expertise required for repatriation, and the limited resources currently available for recovery, resources would be better spent on recovery actions with a higher probability of success."[128] Clearly, playing it safe by conserving scarce resources to protect a critically endan-gered species in a limited habitat on Pelee Island was the preferred and understandable choice. If the money were available, additional suitable and protected land could be secured, and the long-term assessment of key habitat variables could be undertaken. Maybe the blue racer would have a better chance of recovery in a larger protected area. The current approach also runs counter to the intent of section 1.10 of the Canadian Biodiversity Strategy, which states: "When only a single population of a species exists and it is in a highly endangered state, it may be necessary to move all of its members to ex situ conservation facilities in order to build up its numbers and eventually re-establish in situ populations."[129]

Downsizing due to budget cuts has hurt species at risk recoveries. Hundreds of scientists with Environment Canada lost their jobs in 2011 under federal fiscal restraint measures.[130] In 2014 the Harper government announced further cuts to Environment Canada's budget, which would result in a 35 per cent reduction in funds for biodiversity programs by 2016–2017.[131] Parks Canada lost almost 1,700 positions in 2012.[132] Two years later, it saw its budget cut by $27 million.[133] Fisheries and Oceans Canada has endured thousands of job losses and hundreds of millions of dollars in budget cuts. Whole departments have been gutted or eliminated.[134] Overall, spending on species at risk was cut by $12.5 million in 2015.[135] Ironically, cuts in staff in some cases have meant that even the modest spending allocations to the three pertinent ministries have not been fully utilized.[136] The federal Habitat Stewardship Program for Species at Risk, which provides about $12.2 million annually for private projects in support of species at risk, requires recipients to match its contribution.[137]

Some insight into the uncertain financial malaise that plagues SARA can be seen in the federal government's Partial Action Plan for the Blue, Fin, Sei and Pacific Right Whales in Pacific Canadian Waters (2016). Since this action plan also included the British Columbia government, the usual nontransparent federal cost and benefit template could not be used. In terms of federal costs, the plan opted for the low-end spending scale of less than $1 million annually and sought to solicit as much in-kind financial and resource-based support as possible. Or as it states somewhat unconvincingly, "Such activities may result in in-kind support from partners and collaborators in terms of staff time and resources for discussion, meetings and research. It is anticipated that education and stewardship activities would be funded from existing government sources, with the possibility of in-kind and financial support from partners."[138] In other words, the plan lacked precision regarding the financing of long-term protection measures for four endangered or threatened whale species.

A hidden financial issue, with potentially significant implications for SARA and wildlife generally, concerns the current interest in applying monetary worth to nonmarketable resources. Although the allocation of a dollar value to these services is complex and subject to several variables, it is now generally accepted that an estimation of the value of nonmarketable commodities is an important component of environmental policymaking.[139] In terms of species at risk, the government has no trouble putting a monetary value on their consumptive use and, as has been argued, is often loath to list such species under SARA. For species with nonconsumptive value, the process by which a specific value is placed on a nonmarketable good is far more problematic. One common approach is contingent valuation, whereby hypothetical markets are constructed to ascertain the consumer's willingness to pay (WTP) for potential benefits or for the avoidance of their loss. WTP usually involves surveying representative members of the public to determine a dollar amount they would be willing to pay to sustain, protect, and maintain a specific nonmarketable commodity.[140] Policymakers are subsequently guided by these results.

Certainly, it can be argued that assigning monetary worth in this way can be a foil against the commercial development of critical habitat. However, it can also influence the listing process itself and lead to reduced spending on threatened species with low appeal.[141] For example, WTP is much higher for eagles and owls than for the sage-grouse, let alone lesser known and more esoteric endangered species like the white flower moth or the gray ratsnake. Nonmarket assessment through WTP, if administered carefully, can provide useful information on noncommercial and nonconsumptive public interest in threatened species. For example, a WTP study carried out for five species at risk in the Milk River watershed in southwest Saskatchewan found that respondents did not favour conservation strategies that either stressed or excluded the human presence. Instead, and perhaps surprisingly, they chose a moderate approach that primarily involved paying for conservation easements on private land.[142] Nonetheless, if deployed for political and/or economic purposes, WTP-based actions could hasten extinctions rather than avert them.

The use of WTP as a valid instrument is controversial. Critics argue that it demands a sophisticated survey design and strong respondent awareness and integrity, that it fails to consider the socio-economic status of respondents in terms of WTP, and that hypothetical responses are exactly that, hypothetical.[143] Economist Steven Edwards argues that it also fails to isolate the respondents' ethical motivations.[144] In any case, the idea of assigning monetary worth to any species in a hypothetical survey is at best an individual, reflective exercise and, for the survey administrators, only an imprecise gauge of public sentiment. However, the most relevant point about estimations of the nonmarket value of an at-risk species is not whether it is valid but that it exists in the first place. Canada's biodiversity strategy stresses the integrity of the biotic community and the living creatures who comprise it. WTP-thinking aims to quantify the unquantifiable by assigning a dollar amount to a vulnerable species or habitat, or to quote University of Calgary law professor Shaun Fluker, "We do not assess our own worth by calculating the costs and benefits of our existence, so why do we insist on doing so for other species – particularly those for which we have accepted an obligation to protect?"[145]

Yet despite these uncertainties, the federal government is using WTP as a guide to ascertaining a dollar value for vulnerable species and their habitats, or more specifically, the amount of money to be spent on their recovery. The preamble to SARA specifically recognizes socio-economic factors in the implementation of recovery measures, and section 49 mandates the evaluation of socio-economic costs and benefits in the subsequent action plans.[146] As early as 1985, Environment Canada attempted to place an economic value on recreational wildlife through WTP. Using the opinions of over 100,000 respondents in a national survey, Environment Canada showed that the value hunters placed on the animals they hunted was around 40 per cent more than what they spent on hunting them.[147] The authors concluded that wildlife constituted an important and profitable asset and that any decline in numbers would have serious economic repercussions. In a solid endorsement of WTP, the authors emphasized, "The findings provide senior government decision-makers with economic criteria that could be used in evaluating wildlife conservation programs ... and charting emerging policies affecting conservation."[148] Fisheries and Oceans Canada measured WTP with respect to the establishment of a protected marine wildlife area on the BC coast in 2011.[149] Benefit transfer – a reliance on information from existing studies involving similar species – based on the WTP for the US wild turkey was used to set a WTP of $23 per household to protect the greater sage-grouse.[150] A meta-analysis model arrived at a WTP preservation value of $508 per household to protect the polar bear.[151]

Questions remain about WTP. Given that accurate figures for actual spending on recovery of at-risk species are virtually impossible to verify, one wonders how often WTP is used as a gauge and, more important, how significant it is in determining actual dollar amounts. It seems that it depends on the species. According to the federal government, "It is not always necessary to quantify the benefits of protection in order to determine their likely magnitude in comparison to the costs imposed on Canadians."[152] Furthermore, information gained from WTP varies with the scope and range of the survey, and if the study on WTP for the recovery of the Alaska stellar sea lion is any example, Americans generally were far more prepared to shoulder the financial burden for recovery than those actually affected by it.[153] Taken further, this indicates that when WTP is applied broadly to include passive or nonuse value, the full costs of recovery will likely be much higher than the government is willing to spend.[154] If this is the case, WTP surveys at the local level among those most impacted by the issue will probably furnish a more feasible option and a cheaper guide. For instance, according to one account, citizens and the business community on Plum Island in Massachusetts were opposed to beach closures in order to protect threatened piping plover nesting sites.[155]

The belief system about wildlife (and animals generally) is starkly revealed in an emerging debate about the merits of applying the system of triage to recovering species at risk. According to this view, recovery efforts should be directed toward those species deemed to be more valuable in terms of evolutionary uniqueness (i.e., a lack of close relatives), rarity, ecological role, aesthetic appeal, or specific value to humanity.[156] A system that assigns priority to vulnerable wildlife based on their perceived value to humans or ecosystems is short-sighted because it defaults to fixed-in-time baseline perceptions about worth or ecological integrity. It is also human-centred and dismissive of life forms that have "no value." One would hope that any wildlife triage movement fails to gain traction.

Although the problems respecting the identification of at-risk species and preparation of federal recovery and action plans are due to SARA itself, the jurisdictional malaise that defies uniformity and conformity is not. Did it have to be this way? Was the federal government bound by its own constitutional limitations? A negative answer leads one to wonder whether the federal government was consciously amenable to enacting legislation that threw the financial burden for protecting the bulk of Canadian wild species onto the provinces.

First, the need for a narrow interpretation of the Canadian Constitution is conjectural. Former Supreme Court justice Gerard La Forest and distinguished University of Manitoba law professor Dale Gibson feel that the protection of endangered species is a national concern and therefore falls under federal jurisdiction.[157] According to the National Environmental Law Section of the Canadian Bar Association, the federal government possesses the constitutional authority to enact broad endangered species legislation. Citing three legal precedents, the association argues that shared jurisdiction over environmental matters is the rule rather than the exception and that protection of the environment constitutes a legitimate public objective in federal criminal law.[158] The association concludes, "General federal legislation concerning protection of all endangered species in Canada would be found constitutional as being part of the rule, and not constitute an exception. We believe the principal constitutional authority for such legislation is found under the federal government's 'peace, order, and good government' power, particularly the power to address matters of 'national concern,' and under the criminal law power."[159] The argument that SARA represents the federal government's avoidance of its responsibility to its wild domain is worth considering in light of its lofty ideals under the Canadian Biodiversity Strategy.[160]

Second, as already indicated, SARA includes a mechanism that allows for discretionary federal action in the case of provincial or territorial delinquency in protecting a species or its critical habitat.[161] Ecojustice, formerly the Sierra Legal Defence Fund, is of the opinion that even though the provision is consistent with federal environmental law, its implementation is unlikely.[162] Indeed, the federal government so far has been very reluctant to intervene on behalf of wildlife at risk. Examples include the woodland caribou in Alberta and the spotted owl in British Columbia, where environmental groups were unable to persuade the federal environment minister to exercise overriding powers.[163] So far, the federal government has intervened only twice, first in 2014 through an emergency protection order respecting the greater sage-grouse following a court decision that gave it little option and again in July 2016 through an emergency order that protected the tiny endangered western chorus frog from commercial development in its wetland habitat in the Montreal area after the provincial government had declined to intervene.[164]

Nothing better illustrates the federal government's delinquency in fulfilling its duties under SARA than the several successful legal challenges mounted by various nongovernmental organizations. An outstanding example was the 2012 application for judicial review brought by five organizations against Fisheries and Oceans Canada and Environment Canada for their failure to prepare recovery strategies for three threatened and one endangered species.[165] The judicial review, heard by federal justice Anne Mactavish, was illuminative on three levels. First, although the four recovery strategies were on average more than four years overdue, notice of litigation prompted their completion in the seventeen months before the actual review. It was a desperate face-saving political scramble that simply proved the plaintiffs' point. Second, in arguing their case, the two federal ministers contended that SARA's timelines for recovery strategies were discretionary rather than mandatory, a preposterous assertion given SARA's specific language on timelines in section 42.[166] In rejecting this claim, Justice Mactavish was not happy with what she saw as a clear violation of the intent of SARA:

> To state the obvious, the *Species at Risk Act* was enacted because some wildlife species in Canada *are at risk*. As the applicants note, many are in a race against the clock as increased pressure is put on their critical habitat, and their ultimate survival may be at stake. The timelines contained in the Act reflect the clearly articulated will of Parliament that recovery strategies be developed for species at risk in a timely fashion, recognizing that there is indeed urgency in these matters. Compliance with the statutory timelines is critical to the proper implementation of the Parliamentary scheme for the protection of species at risk.[167]

Third, the decision itself sent a pointed message in declaring the ministers' failure unlawful and noting that the threat of litigation had prompted the completion of the recovery strategies. Justice Mactavish found, "It is simply not acceptable for the responsible Ministers to continue to miss the mandatory deadlines that have been established by Parliament."[168] In recognizing a wider overall neglect of responsibility by both ministries, Mactavish underscored the critical issue in the implementation of SARA:

> It is, moreover, apparent that the delays encountered in these four cases are just the tip of the iceberg. There is clearly an enormous systemic problem within the relevant Ministries, given the respondents' acknowledgment that there remain some 167 species at risk for which recovery strategies have not yet been developed … Indeed, it is reasonable to assume that the acceleration of progress on these four cases in response to the commencement of this litigation could well have caused further delays in the preparation of recovery strategies for other species.[169]

Interestingly, following her decision, Justice Mactavish retained her jurisdiction over the case, which meant that she could reopen it if not convinced that the ministers were following proper direction. In 2013 the conservation groups Ontario Nature and Wildlands League challenged an Ontario regulation that exempted a wide range of industrial activity from the prohibitions of Ontario's Endangered Species Act (2007), threatening more than 150 vulnerable species.[170]

SARA AND THE GREATER SAGE-GROUSE

The plight of the critically endangered greater sage-grouse on the Canadian prairies provides a good example of the problems endemic to SARA. Despite the fact that COSEWIC in 1998, Saskatchewan in 1999, and Alberta in 2000 had all imposed pre-SARA "endangered" listings, the situation of this unique grasslands dweller under SARA continued to worsen.

Greater sage-grouse, the largest Canadian grouse, inhabit the mixed grassland eco-region in southeastern Alberta and southwestern Saskatchewan near the Montana border. They are regarded as an "indicator species" in that their status functions as a red flag to other species' health. Sage-grouse are dependent on silver sagebrush for food, nesting, and wintering habitat, and they concentrate at leks, or breeding grounds, located in relatively flat areas near creek valleys, where richly plumed males congregate and perform their incredibly balletic courtship dances to entice a mate.

The sage-grouse population in western Canada in the late 1980s was estimated at around 900.[171] Further decreases by the time the Species of Risk Act came into force should have spurred urgent and concerted recovery action. Not so. Reduced to 7 per cent of their range, the sage-grouse adult population in 2012 was estimated to be between 93 and 138, a reduction of over 89 per cent since the 1980s.[172]

The reason behind this appalling statistic relates to human encroachment on habitat and the unwillingness of SARA to address it. Although sage-grouse are threatened by droughts, fires, disease, and predation, the dominant impediments to their survival lie in crop disturbance, ranching, and oil and gas activities.[173] Sage-grouse are extremely sensitive to habitat disturbance and will vacate nesting sites when threatened by infrastructure and noise. They will not build nests less than 800 metres from a power line. Mortality rates increase 1.5 times for every energy well visible within 1 kilometre of the brood. Breeding is abandoned in response to the presence of active energy wells or roads within 6.4 kilometres of the nests. Sage-grouse will also avoid or abandon habitat essential for their survival during the winter if oil and gas development exists within 1.9 kilometres of their habitat.[174]

Alberta presented the first official post-SARA sage-grouse recovery plan in 2005. It was a weak document in that it relied on existing guidelines, was remiss in identifying critical habitat, and limited its recommendations to broad, long-range goals linked to population monitoring and the preservation of range health.[175] The Province of Saskatchewan did nothing, preferring to rely on a plan prepared in the early 1990s. As for the federal government, it displayed a lack of leadership by waffling. When it was released in January 2008, the federal recovery strategy was severely deficient. With full knowledge of the serious plight of the sage-grouse and the urgent need to begin habitat protection measures, the strategy admitted that critical habitat had not been identified nor would be inside another three and a half years.[176] In short, the federal government was saying that under its own legislation to protect its vulnerable species, it needed over eight years to figure out where imperilled greater sage-grouse lived in southern Alberta and Saskatchewan.

It took private, nonprofit environmental organizations to force the government's hand. In July 2009 four groups mounted a legal challenge to Environment Canada by securing a judicial review of why no critical habitat had been identified in the 2008 recovery plan. In his decision, Justice Russell W. Zinn disagreed with Environment Canada's argument that the delay was reasonable due to insufficient knowledge of breeding, nesting, brood-rearing, and winter habitat, finding that, based on scientific evidence, critical habitat could be identified for three out of the above four criteria. He allowed the review and ordered that the relevant section in the recovery plan be rewritten accordingly.[177] The long delay in achieving this directive meant that little was done on the ground to help the birds.[178]

Worried about the provincial reluctance, especially in Alberta, to act on the sage-grouse's behalf, private organizations again took action. In 2011 several environmental groups wrote to Minister of Environment Peter Kent, asking him to exercise his power under SARA and issue an emergency order protecting the birds. In 2012, after Kent hedged and failed to reply, the issue went to the courts, where it languished, partly because of Kent's refusal to disclose his planned actions on the grounds of Cabinet confidentiality.[179] In August 2013 the Federal Court of Appeal rejected Kent's arguments and ordered Environment Canada to clarify its position and intentions. Forced with the unpalatable options of denying the plight of the sage-grouse or admitting that her department had no strategy at all, the new environment minister, Leona Aglukkaq, had no choice but to back down and opt for an emergency protection order.[180]

Five months later, in February 2014, the emergency protection order, the first federal intervention under SARA, came into effect, forbidding the disturbance of ground cover, loud noises during certain times of the year, and the construction of new roads, tall fences, or high objects in a total area of 1,672 square kilometres in Alberta and Saskatchewan.[181] The order's rationale noted that some species at risk had cultural importance but omitted ecological implications. It gently chastised the two provinces for existing measures that were neither mandatory nor sufficiently targeted to protect the habitat of the sage-grouse. The environment minister's opinion that compliance with the order was "anticipated" to contribute to habitat protection, which "should in turn increase the probability of maintaining the species in Canada," offered more hope than confidence or commitment.[182]

It is easy to see why. The emergency protection order was primarily about limitations and lacked a clear protective intent. It contained too many exceptions to ensure sage-grouse comfort zones. The order applied only to Crown and provincial lands, and even then it excluded grazing activities on those lands. Some noise exemptions were applied to agricultural lands. Other loud machines could be operated for ten hours a month for ten months of the year. Height restrictions did not apply to any existing structures. Specifics were lacking on oil and gas activity in lek locations.[183] Mark Boyce, a University of Alberta biologist, was less than enthusiastic when he said, "All we can do is hope that this new order will have some promise and the remaining bits of habitat will provide a sufficient base for population recovery."[184] University of Calgary law professor Shaun Fluker went further, noting that the exemptions compromised the sage-grouse's chance of recovery.[185]

Almost as soon as it was announced, the emergency protection order came under attack. Although they were affected only marginally, ranchers were up in arms.[186] Noting the poor track record of government in managing species numbers, one rancher warned that "this order will restrict our ability to make a living ... but it's not really going to help the bird too much."[187] Even before the order came into effect, the City of Medicine Hat and LGX Oil and Gas jointly applied for and were granted a judicial review.[188] In the fall of 2014, the City of Medicine Hat launched a lawsuit against the federal government claiming $42 million in compensation for loss of revenue from its oil operations.[189]

The three current recovery strategies, despite their stated ambitions, are not forceful documents. As noted in the updated Alberta plan, overseen by a team of ten people, half of whom are from the ranching and energy industries, "The current Alberta population of sage-grouse is likely too small to increase on its own to a size necessary to support recovery of the species."[190] The plan also advises that economic activity will continue in sage-grouse country. In fact, the major goal of the plan is to secure sustainable numbers of grouse for recreational viewing and hunting.[191] For example, Alberta hunters killed over 1,100 sage-grouse between 1986 and 1989.[192]

In Saskatchewan reliance is placed on secure locations, like Grasslands National Park, and little hope is held out for fragmented habitat areas. Like Alberta, Saskatchewan has made its position clear: "Protecting all potential Sage-Grouse habitat is likely not practical and prioritizing habitat for protection is of significant importance, especially considering increasing development activity in southwest Saskatchewan."[193]

More than a decade after its endangered listing, the critical habitat of the sage-grouse was finally defined and delineated in the federal Amended Recovery Strategy for the Greater Sage-Grouse (2013).[194] However, this was not a hopeful document. Recognizing the need for urgency amid anthropogenic threats that were not going away, the strategy made relocation and captive breeding programs major priorities.[195] The strategy also noted the tight concentration of sage-grouse in small geographic areas, their continued high risk of extirpation, and the fact that final action plans could be four years away from completion.[196] It also concluded that it was "not possible to quantify with certainty the number of adult Sage-Grouse required for a self-sustaining Canadian population."[197] Yet it set a long-range population goal of 2,595 without advising how the number could be sustained if the human presence was not considerably constrained.[198] Finally, one might speculate on the federal government's spending priorities with respect to the sage-grouse given that it had already ascertained a low WTP compared to more exotic avian species.[199]

SARA has not protected the greater-sage grouse. The jurisdictional malaise endemic to SARA resulted in the unwillingness of either level of government to shoulder the burden of protecting the species. Despite the fact that the birds were endangered from the outset, recovery plans were delayed and then poorly implemented. Critical habitat was not identified, and coordination was lacking between federal and provincial authorities. Political considerations stood in the way of federal intervention, which occurred only because of a court decision initiated by private, nonprofit environmental groups. The recovery plans are marginally ameliorative in that their primary focus is not on the healthy survival of the sage-grouse but on how to protect the species while allowing, even encouraging, human economic activity in sage-grouse habitats. This is the situation with all species and the main predictor of failure for SARA. Species like the sage-grouse with high sensitivity to anthropogenic habitat disturbance are prime candidates for extirpation, proving biologists Jeremy Kerr and Josef Cihlar's point that SARA does little to protect overall habitat for endangered species.[200]

Current statistics tell us much about SARA's failure to halt or even slow down species decline. The most significant is that since SARA's inception, no endangered species has ever recovered sufficiently enough to warrant downgrading. That SARA, with all its intent and power, has failed to guarantee the survival of at least one endangered species after years of trying does not bode well for the future. Figures on mammals, birds, amphibians, reptiles, fish, and arthropods are not reassuring. The number of endangered fish, for example, has increased threefold over the past thirteen years and now stands at twenty-seven. COSEWIC's list of endangered species rose from 77 to 176, or by 128 per cent between 2003 and 2014. The number of species listed by COSEWIC as "endangered," "threatened," or a "special concern" increased from 237 to 430 during the same period. Moreover, COSEWIC's lists clearly indicate the level of inactivity at the political level, where the final listing decisions are made. In 2014 SARA's list of 126 "endangered" species contained 50 fewer designations than COSEWIC's, and if all three categories are considered, SARA's lists contained 150 fewer species. Generally, rhetoric trumps action in government, with the SARA experience proving the point.

SARA AND THE OREGON SPOTTED FROG

Another downside to SARA is its lack of success with less prominent species. Reptiles are in serious decline, as are amphibians. Endangered reptiles are up threefold since 2003, and amphibians classified as at-risk have increased by almost 70 per cent. Amphibians are important indicator species and provide a major mechanism of energy transfer between aquatic and terrestrial ecosystems, or as herpetologist Leslie Anthony describes the ecological exchanges in river valleys and wetlands, "Solar energy blooms algae in the water; tadpoles eat the algae, then transform into frogs that consume enormous numbers of insects; snakes eat the frogs, and then birds and a few carnivorous mammals eat the snakes. Why would you want to get in the way of that?"[201]

As concerns amphibians, the seemingly irremediable plight of the Oregon spotted frog shows the weakness of SARA and, more significantly, the formidable barriers that confront endangered localized species under relentless ongoing anthropogenic threats.

Amphibians are threatened globally. In Canada at-risk listings under SARA have increased by almost 70 per cent in the past fifteen years. Likely the most imperilled is the Oregon spotted frog, a warm-water marsh specialist who prefers floodplain wetlands, side channels, and sloughs near permanent water bodies. The Oregon spotted frog is an indicator of the health of shallow, warm wetland habitats, a top predator of aquatic invertebrates, and a food source for reptiles, mammals, and birds. It is found in four populations in British Columbia's Fraser River basin, one of which faces imminent extirpation, and a further three populations have already been extirpated. Accurate population estimates are difficult to achieve, but according to the BC government's Conservation Data Centre, populations declined by approximately 35 per cent between 2000 and 2010. Currently, the adult population at the three remaining sites is estimated at around 350 adults. The data centre offered a dire prediction: "None of the populations may remain viable over the long term."[202]

Recovery of the endangered Oregon spotted frog under SARA has followed a familiar belated pattern. Although COSEWIC assessed the species as "endangered" as early as 1999, the provincial recovery strategy was not in place until 2012. The federal government adopted the BC strategy, added its own addendum, and released both as the federal recovery strategy in 2015. This strategy admitted that the existing 67 hectares of critical habitat was insufficient to sustain the species and further that the government had not yet identified additional critical habitat sufficient to sustain growth. Omitting the fact that identification of critical habitat was a prerequisite in a recovery strategy, the government looked to the future: "A schedule of studies … has been developed to provide the information necessary to complete the identification of critical habitat that will be sufficient to meet the population and distribution objectives. The identification of critical habitat will be updated when the information becomes available, either in a revised recovery strategy or action plan(s)." The timeline for these studies was given as 2015 to 2022.[203] In other words, up to seven more years were needed to identify adequate critical habitat for a species already on the verge of extirpation.

Although SARA's administrators have been remiss in developing timely recovery strategies and action plans, it is also possible that even if they had done so, the plight of the Oregon spotted frog would have remained unchanged. The levels of anthropogenic and other disturbances of vulnerable species located in small, closely contained areas are simply too great to ensure their survival. This is especially true for amphibians, whose habitats are fragile and impermanent.

Already constrained by very limited critical habitat, the Oregon spotted frog faces numerous and varied threats. These include the continuing loss of suitable wetlands, habitat fragmentation, population isolation, and the absence of readily available habitat due to private land ownership. Other threats include the alteration of site hydrology, which affects egg-laying habitat and increases egg mortality. For example, females require locations with rare combinations of water depth and exposure to the sun in the late winter in order to lay eggs. These locations are usually on the edge of wetlands, which are subject to higher rates of alteration by flooding, drought, and in the long run, climate change. Contributors to habitat loss and degradation as well as to direct and indirect mortalities include pollution from agricultural and industrial activities and from human sewage and waste water; aquatic fungal diseases, such as chytridiomycosis; iridoviruses, which are linked in part to captive-reared populations; and predators or competitors like introduced green frogs and American bullfrogs. As noted by Environment Canada in 2015, habitat loss due to human influence was a limiting factor at all sites occupied by the Oregon spotted frog.[204]

The point is that despite interventions between 2000 and 2011, which included egg mass enumerations, habitat maintenance, and captive breeding programs, the combination of the above threats was probably beyond the redressive power or capacity of SARA. Although species recovery is more difficult for at-risk amphibians occupying limited, fragile habitats, it is also true that wildlife policymaking to assist vulnerable species can be, and often is, severely compromised by external factors. There exists an urgent need to strengthen SARA by way of significant overriding powers with respect to habitat protection measures. Species like the Oregon spotted frog do not stand much of a chance otherwise.

SARA AND ARTHROPODS

Arthropods – insects, spiders, myriapods, crustaceans, mites, and their relatives – are likely even more significant than reptiles and amphibians both in terms of range and scope. Yet the proportional attention they receive under SARA is less than any other species, probably because so little information exists on them. In fact, COSEWIC admits that the number designated is small due to inadequate knowledge.[205] Not surprisingly, arthropod declines have continued in Canada. In 2003–2004, SARA listed seven species of arthropods as either "endangered," "threatened" or a "special concern." In 2016 the number was thirty-four, of which twenty-three were "endangered."

No one really knows how many species of arthropods exist. Insect species alone number between 4 and 5 million, of which around 80 per cent remain unknown to science. It has been estimated that the insects, springtails, mites, and other land-dwelling arthropods outnumber humans by as much as 250 million to 1.[206] In Canada there are over 30,000 species and at least that many more waiting to be discovered. It has been estimated that between 6,000 and 8,000 arthropod species can occupy a single peatland bog in Canada's boreal forest.[207] The same figure is given for insects living in the Suffield National Wildlife Area in southeastern Alberta, of which 15 per cent represent new discoveries.[208]

Arthropods fill many crucial ecosystem functions. Insects are the pollinators upon whom the existence of plant-life depends. In addition to enabling the reproduction of 90 per cent of the world's flowering plants, pollinators are vital to creating and maintaining the habitats and ecosystems that many animals rely on for food and shelter. By feeding on dead plant and animal matter as well as dung, which are broken down through digestion, insects accelerate the process of decay that frees nutrients to nourish future plant growth. Arthropods also help to mix soil with organic matter and nutrients. For example, ants and termites move tremendous amounts of soil through burrowing and tunnelling. Plant-feeding insects convert plant biomass to animal biomass. In turn, they serve as the primary source of food for other insects, birds, fish, and mammals. Insects are the prime determinants of plant life, generally through feeding on and dispersing seeds.[209] With their high functional and unmatched biological diversity, arthropods are valuable indicators of ecological health and are "ideal candidates to monitor the subtle effects associated with habitat fragmentation."[210]

The Biological Survey of Canada released a brief in 1996 that suggested the wide diversity of arthropods makes them well suited for the sort of baseline information that allows for biodiversity monitoring and measurement. In other words, information derived from arthropod species assemblages could be used to characterize accurately the existing state of almost any aspect of an ecosystem. The brief advocated that "the acquisition of ecosystem baselines of arthropod biodiversity should be viewed as an integral component in the implementation of Canada's biodiversity strategy."[211] A paper published a decade later agreed with this assessment but noted that information gaps continued to hinder progress and that "much effort is yet required to identify robust arthropod ecological indicators for biomonitoring."[212] Three years later, the Alberta Lepidopterists' Guild stated that arthropods were so diverse and poorly known in Canada that the vast majority of species had not been assessed for protection under SARA.[213]

SARA listed five arthropods, all butterflies, in 2003–2004. Three were "endangered" and two "threatened." It took four years for the first recovery strategy to be completed in 2008 (island blue), another four for the second (maritime ringlet), and a further four years for the third (Behr's hairstreak). A fourth (Taylor's checkerspot) was incorporated into a multi-species recovery strategy in 2016. At this time, no recovery strategy exists for the fifth, the "threatened" dun skipper. As of 2015–2016, twenty-three arthropods were listed as "endangered" and five as "threatened": eleven butterflies, eleven moths, four beetles, one dragonfly, and one bee. Final recovery strategies were not in place for almost half. The minimum wait for a recovery strategy following a SARA designation was four years. The endangered Aweme borer moth's recovery strategy is still delayed, nine years after it was listed. Many of these delays are the result of a lack of information on numbers and habitat, as well as difficulties associated with the necessary coordination of the federal government with the provinces and other relevant jurisdictions. The Biological Survey of Canada has begun a serious attempt to develop baseline information on the rich and highly diverse taxa of grassland arthropods.[214] One hopes that its projected multi-volume series (two completed) will provide information that enables SARA to fulfil its responsibilities toward at-risk arthropods more effectively.

In 2012 the federal government completed an evaluation to provide program management and senior decision makers at Environment Canada, Fisheries and Oceans Canada, and Parks Canada with evidence-based information on the relevance and performance of efforts to support the implementation of the Species at Risk Act. The evaluation stressed a climate of uncertainty and inactivity within the three "competent" ministries, noting the backlog related to delivering recovery strategies, action plans, and management plans, as well as the lack of activity in implementing priority actions, monitoring, and evaluation. More significantly, the evaluation concluded, "It is not clear at this point how the departments are planning on moving forward to address all three objectives of the Act."[215] This is unfortunate since SARA does possess the mechanisms to be a champion for vulnerable wildlife. For now, "SARA struggles alone, crawling inch-by-inch, against an overwhelming tide of 'Business as Usual.'"[216]

On a final note, the Species at Risk Act is flawed in its present form because of its reactive approach to management. This approach is especially problematic since most species at risk in Canada live in southern regions, where fragmented and settled landscapes significantly reduce prospects for remediation and habitat restoration. A more proactive approach might be to concentrate on the focal species in any isolated landscape whose needs define the conditions that must be present if that particular biotic community is to meet the requirements of the species that live there.[217] This approach might be effective if attention was paid to sensitive habitat for amphibian and reptile species before they reached at-risk status. As environmentalists Karen Beazley and Nathan Cardinal have shown, this difficult and complex process of quantification, although valid, is far from easy to undertake.[218] It is also expensive, time-consuming, and presumptive of isolated habitat as ongoing and self-contained.

As a piece of legislation, the Species at Risk Act demonstrates an intent to protect at-risk wildlife. In practice, this intent is severely constrained by human priorities. The sage-grouse and woodland caribou would face a much more certain future otherwise. As evidence of how blatant these human priorities are, all one has to do is consult the Species at Risk Act itself and a 2012 amendment to section 77. Hitherto, under this section, developers who wanted to go ahead with activities that impacted critical habitat could not do so before consultation with and approval from the appropriate federal authority under the act. The amendment exempted the National Energy Board from this requirement.[219] This means that the National Energy Board can intrude on habitat crucial to vulnerable wildlife and that, even under the Species at Risk Act, the interests of animals at risk are deemed less important than habitat impingement in the human interest.

In 2016 the Green Budget Coalition, a consortium of fifteen environmental groups that included Nature Canada, the Canadian Parks and Wilderness Society, Greenpeace, and the World Wildlife Federation, put forward a recommendation to the Government of Canada that it more than double its spending on species at risk over the ensuing four years. Noting the failure of policymakers to properly implement SARA, the coalition stated, "In the absence of full implementation, SARA cannot effectively meet its objective of protecting species at risk in Canada. The failure to implement a full suite of SARA policy tools and flexibility mechanisms creates tremendous uncertainty for project proponents and leaves Canada with an impaired species protection regime."[220] Stressing Canada's international obligations to biodiversity health and legal responsibilities, the coalition warned, "The ongoing failure to properly protect species at risk represents a breach of Canada's commitments under the U.N. Convention on Biological Diversity, and also leaves Canada open to a challenge before the Commission for Environmental Cooperation. After years of political neglect federal leadership is needed, especially with respect to species for which the federal government has constitutional responsibilities such as migratory birds and marine species, to deliver on the full potential of SARA."[221] Unfortunately, despite this sound advice, the first budget of Prime Minister Justin Trudeau's government, tabled in 2016, made no mention of species at risk or programs specifically designed to support them. A year later, NatureServe Canada reported 116 vertebrates in Canada of global concern. Significantly, one-third had no listing under SARA, of which fourteen were native to Canada.[222]

Threats to Terrestrial and Marine Habitats

Wildlife conservation is the preservation of wildlife forms and
groups of forms in perpetuity, for their own sakes, irrespective
of any connotation of present or future human use.

JOHN LIVINGSTON

In 2013 the Canadian Wildlife Service released its third edition of *How Much Habitat Is Enough?* Its goal was to provide science-based information and guidelines related to habitat and biodiversity in wetlands, riparian areas, forests, and grasslands.[1] It was a comprehensive, solid text that spoke of good intentions. However, if it was not meant to be a wake-up call, then it should have been. Canada has already lost 99 per cent of its original tall grass prairie, 97 per cent of Ontario's Carolinian forest, 95 per cent of British Columbia's Garry oak meadows, and on average well over 70 per cent of the nation's wetlands.[2] In the same year as the aforementioned volume was released, the commissioner of the environment and sustainable development commented that all of Canada's habitats – forests, lakes and rivers, grasslands, ice, and marine – were either severely impaired or deteriorating and that a wide gap existed between the government's commitments and the results achieved.[3]

Loss or damage to habitat is easily the greatest threat facing Canadian wildlife, accounting for 94 per cent of the endangerment of terrestrial species.[4] In all Canadian provinces and territories, there are examples like that seen in Ontario, where loss of habitat has pushed the loggerhead shrike, a songbird, to the brink of extinction.[5] Agriculture, logging, industry, urbanization, and other human interference are responsible for well over

80 per cent of wildlife habitat loss and up to 98 per cent in some areas. These activities do not represent conscious attempts to subjugate wildlife, but they do assume that the lives of wild creatures and the ecosystems they inhabit are incidental to human ambitions. So although it might be unfortunate that intensive agriculture and grazing impact wetlands and reduce the vegetation necessary for nest survival of waterfowl and other birds, it cannot be helped. The welfare of the northern pintail, who likes to nest in standing stubble, is secondary to cattle grazing and beef production.[6] In many cases, the damage is done before awareness sinks in, and any remedial measures that are taken are compromises that only modify the human influence. No one really wants sage-grouse to go, but if they cannot coexist with restrained human interference in their habitat, then so be it.

Habitat deterioration is occurring on several levels. Agricultural expansion is one major cause. A study on habitat trends between 1986 and 2006 demonstrated how wildlife habitat richness was linked to the availability of unimproved land.[7] Development pressures are mounting in Canada's boreal forest, one of the largest intact forests on the planet, which is home to 5 billion land birds and the breeding ground for 40 per cent of North America's waterfowl population. According to Nature Canada, two-thirds of national wildlife areas and migratory bird sanctuaries are increasingly threatened by harmful public interference, including poaching, boating, use of all-terrain vehicles, hunting, and nest disturbance and loss.[8] Pesticides, herbicides, and fertilizers are contaminating wetlands and lakes, causing fish mortalities, killing off plant species, and resulting in reproductive failure and developmental impairment in various wildlife. Urbanization contributes to habitat loss and fragmentation through road densities and recreational activity and by altering hydrologic regimes. Buildings, roads, domestic cats, and power lines are death traps for birds. According to one study, these combined threats account for more than 250 million bird fatalities a year in Canada.[9] A recent article refers to pending global "biological annihilation" and notes that "dwindling population sizes and range shrinkages amount to a massive anthropogenic erosion of biodiversity and of the ecosystem services essential to civilization."[10] The emphasis on population shrinkages even among species of low concern is significant, as is the emphasis on habitat loss.

AGRICULTURE, WILDLIFE, AND BIODIVERSITY

Studies on Canada's ecosystems show that the percentage of suitable habitat and levels of biodiversity decrease in proportion to agricultural intensity. The large size of agricultural operations fragments the natural landscape and affects the abundance and diversity of herbivores and their natural enemies. Many species are affected by the conversion of grasslands to agriculture. Habitat is lost. Pesticides, herbicides, and fertilizers pollute remaining habitat, and intensive grazing diminishes vegetative cover. The dismal effects are clear. Habitat capacity in the prairie eco-zone, Canada's agricultural heartland, is well below 50 per cent, the lowest in the country. In 2003 only about a quarter of the original grasslands remained, and only 3.5 per cent of that was protected.[11] Fully 73 per cent of the boreal transition zone in Saskatchewan has been converted to agriculture since European settlement. The annual deforestation rate of 0.89 per cent over the past twenty-eight years is approximately three times the world average.[12]

Agricultural landscapes cover 7 per cent of Canada's land area and provide important habitat for over 550 species of terrestrial vertebrates, including about half of Canada's at-risk species. In the main, croplands are not conducive to ecological integrity in that they are genetically uniform and represent a simplified form of terrestrial biodiversity in competition with natural vegetation and other key ecosystem components.[13] Since 1970 bird populations in the prairie agricultural belt have dropped 40 per cent, including those of the popular meadowlark and bobolink, and aerial insectivores like swallows and chimney swifts are down 64 per cent.[14] The number of ferruginous hawks on the Prairies has decreased by half in the past fifteen years.[15] Not only do croplands reduce habitat suitability for wildlife, but the problem is compounded by herbicide and pesticide applications to increase yields by destroying weeds and insects. In this context, the prevalence of genetically modified crops on Canadian croplands constitutes a major threat to biodiversity.

Agricultural practices can push some species toward extinction. The current plight of the burrowing owl is a case in point. These small owls inhabit grasslands areas, where they serve a primary ecological role by preying on insects, gophers, and other rodents. They have been extirpated in British Columbia and Manitoba, and according to the Species at Risk

Public Registry, they could well disappear from the western plains within a few decades.[16] In Alberta their number is down from 243 pairs in 1991 to between 35 and 50. The main cause of these decreases is the conversion of grassland to cropland and the fragmentation and degradation of remaining unimproved land. Cattle trample through the owls' burrows, and farm machinery destroys them. The loss of burrowing owl habitat to agriculture is compounded by the use of chemical pesticides to control insects, which reduces food sources and forces the owls to range farther from their nests in search of food. The owls are further threatened by ingesting poisoned prey. Alberta's current recovery plan, in discussing prey management, seems at a loss to find ways of increasing prey population for the owls.[17]

Other species find adaptation very difficult. In its management plan for the McCown's longspur, a grey, sparrow-sized, insect-eating songbird whose numbers in Alberta and Saskatchewan have been decreasing steadily since the late 1960s, Environment Canada notes that the birds are trying to adapt to cropland habitat by feeding at small stubble fields. The plan is not optimistic, concluding that a shift in habitat use from rangeland to cropland will mean that a greater proportion of the birds are forced to breed in ecological sink habitats, where population declines are inevitable.[18] The management plan offers no strategies for the restoration of grassland habitat or even for its consolidation within crop landscapes. Instead, according to the plan, the McCown's longspur will apparently benefit from time spent on population monitoring, on researching knowledge gaps, and on conversations with private landowners respecting stewardship options.[19]

Wetlands are threatened by agriculture. They support a rich variety of species, including waterfowl, freshwater amphibians, fish, invertebrates, and aquatic flora. In Canada more than 200 bird species and over 50 species of mammals depend on wetlands for food and habitat. Between 50 and 88 per cent of several species of waterfowl breed on the small wetlands that dot the Canadian prairies. However, conversion to cropland has taken a heavy toll. Fully 75 per cent of prairie wetlands have given way to crops. In southern Saskatchewan and southwest Manitoba, about 350,000 hectares of wetlands have disappeared over the past fifty years, and in Alberta annual wetland loss rivals that occurring in the Amazon rainforest.[20] Over three-quarters of the original wetlands have been lost in the western part of the Lake Ontario watershed and about half in most of the remainder.[21] The Ontario greenbelt retains only 12 per cent of its original wetlands. In 2003 the Species at Risk Act (2002) listed twelve amphibian species, five of which were "endangered," five "threatened," and two of "special concern." In 2015 this figure had risen to twenty amphibian species, five being "endangered," eight "threatened," and seven of "special concern." Much of this increase was attributed to wetland loss.

Despite conservation efforts over the past several decades, wetland loss and degradation continue. Existing wetlands in proximity to croplands are severely compromised by chemical pollutants through transport from deposition, spray-drift, and surface run-off.[22] According to one study on prairie wetlands, the situation is worsening in spite of remediation by the North American Waterfowl Management Plan (1986). Results from this study clearly demonstrate high rates of wetland impact across the entire Canadian prairies. Not surprisingly, wetlands are negatively impacted more severely in agricultural lands, and recovery efforts are more success-ful in grassed and wooded areas.[23] Climate change is a further exacerbating factor. According to Environment Canada, small changes in temperature or water supply significantly affect wetland biota in the form of bacter-ial growth, undesirable plant species, and wildlife loss due to changes in seasonal water cycles. Although the ecological value of wetlands is now recognized, some researchers suggest that the financial protections afforded by government price-support and insurance programs induce farmers to clear wetlands that they might otherwise leave intact.[24]

Although monocultures are rewarded by economies of scale, their lack of crop rotation and diversification removes key self-regulating mechanisms and increases their dependence on high chemical inputs.[25] Regardless of type, pesticides have lethal implications for life forms. Although studies have claimed that pesticides, if applied carefully at the optimum field rate, do not impair microbial activity, they can and do alter microbial community structure. Fungal and bacterial biomass populations can become imbalanced. Ecological niches left by suppressed microorganisms may be taken over by others less suited.[26] Defenders of pesticide use note that, in modern-day practice, pesticides are integrated with biological control agents, which means that target pests are killed but not their natural enemies. However, although they may not die, these natural enemies and the entire ecological system in which they reside are compromised by negative longer-range impacts. The pesticide can result in reductions in lifespan, development rates, fertility, and fecundity, as well as changes in sex ratios and mobility and changes in prey consumption, searching, and egg-laying habits.[27] Moreover, as entomologist Raymond Cloyd has noted, "Many pesticide manufacturers and suppliers make unsubstantiated claims that pesticides are safe to natural enemies without any references to testing methodology, which fails to take into consideration that ... indirect effects may vary depending on concentration, natural enemy species, pesticide exposure time, developmental life stage(s) evaluated, and the influence of residues and repellency."[28] In other words, any pesticide use compromises life forms and ecological processes. Furthermore, the impacts of their ongoing use are not well understood since they presume a lot of predictive confidence based on knowledge, study, and awareness about commercial products.

The potential of pesticides to undermine ecological integrity increased dramatically in the mid-1990s when the new science of biotechnology produced commercially viable genetically modified crops. Designed to be herbicide-tolerant (HT) and to resist the insecticide *Bacillus thuringiensis* (Bt), these genetically modified (GM) crops gave growers a simple, flexible, and forgiving management system that allowed them to apply high levels of chemical agents to kill a broad range of weeds and pests without damaging their crops. Also commonly known as genetically engineered crops, they are now widely used in several countries for the cultivation primarily of corn, cotton, canola, soybean, and sugar beets.[29] GM crops are praised by supporters for simplifying farming practices and for increasing yields and profits. In 2014 a record 448 million acres of GM crops were planted globally, up 15 million acres from the previous year. However, despite ongoing research and refinements in technology and application, the large-scale use of GM crops remains problematic. A report by the United States Department of Agriculture in 2014 concluded that with respect to weed and insect resistance, the jury is still out with regard to the long-term impacts of GM crops.[30]

Concern exists over the implications for nontargeted plants and insects and over the potential of affected organisms to develop resistance. The accumulation of Bt toxins, which remain active in the soil after ploughing, means fewer soil bacteria and negative impacts for invertebrate health and nutrient cycling.[31] Furthermore, GM crops alter the ecological roles and population dynamics of species in cultivated areas and surrounding environments, resulting in species declines and irruptions, as well as changes in biotic structure and function.[32] Evidence also suggests that the biomass for species of weeds among HT crops decreases over time to the detriment of beneficial arthropods and birds. Researchers studying HT beet and canola found lower density levels of invertebrates who control pests and recycle soil nutrients.[33] Most GM crop fields are virtual deserts. As one author wrote about walking through a GM cornfield in Iowa, "In this cornfield, I had come to a different kind of planetary evolution. I listened and heard nothing, no bird, no click of insect."[34]

GM crops are believed to have negative effects on several species. The decline in an active pollinator like the monarch butterfly is linked to herbicide treatment of GM crops, which kills the milkweed, a major favoured food source of the butterfly. Ingestion of aphids on GM potatoes undermines the fecundity and longevity of certain ladybirds, a species recognized for their value in the control of plant mildew, mites, and other harmful insects.[35] One researcher has associated GM crops with "plant diseases and spontaneous abortions and infertility in pigs, horses, cattle and other livestock."[36] The plight of biodiversity-friendly wild bees is a source of major concern. Since they thrive much better on uncultivated land, their current decline in numbers is linked to agricultural production.[37] A recent study at the University of Guelph found that even low levels of pesticides impact the behaviour of bumblebees foraging on wildflowers, thus changing their preferences and hindering their ability to acquire the necessary skills to extract nectar and pollen.[38] They fare worse on GM cropland. Tests have linked bee loss to fewer flowers on GM beets. A study of wild bee abundance and pollination deficits that compared organic, conventional, and GM canola in northern Alberta found the lowest bee abundance and the highest pollination deficits with the GM crop.[39] One researcher has suggested that bees are compromised by pollen from GM crops, arguing that it induces disease in their digestive tracts.[40] Recently, the United States Fish and Wildlife Service announced that it was discontinuing the use of bee-killing pesticides (and feed-grain GM crops) in its wildlife refuges.[41]

Ironically, Canada began planting GM crops in 1995, the same year that the federal government released the Canadian Biodiversity Strategy. Six years later, Environment Canada was advised by one of its scientists that serious oversight was needed of potential ecosystem impacts of GM organisms: "We need to know the long-term cumulative impacts on biodiversity resulting from the dispersal of GMOs in the environment ... An Environment Canada program on potential ecosystem impacts of GMOs must be based on understanding their impacts, if any, on ecosystems and biodiversity."[42] Given the rapid growth of the GM crop industry and the encouragement given to the biotech companies, one presumes that this advice received scant attention. The Canadian Biotechnology Action Network, a coalition of stakeholder organizations concerned about food and environmentally related issues, is unhappy about deficiencies in the approval process and the implications of increased herbicide use. One of its 2015 reports linked GM crops directly to ongoing erosion of genetic diversity and to biodiversity loss, while criticizing the Canadian regulatory system for its failure to evaluate the risks of GM crops within the context of wider, complex ecosystems and agricultural use.[43] The report also warned about unforeseen longer-term, ecosystem-level impacts.

The record speaks for itself. Today, Canada is ranked fourth in the world in terms of GM acreage. In 2014 over a third of Canada's cropland acreage, or 29 million acres, was seeded with GM canola, corn, soy beans, and sugar beets, marking a sevenfold increase since 1997, a 400 per cent gain since 2008, and 7 per cent more than in 2013. Canada is the world's largest producer of canola, of which over 97 per cent is genetically modified, being worth almost $20 billion a year to the national economy.[44] GM corn accounts for 80 per cent of Ontario's production. It is obvious that the federal government does not see any inconsistency between its biodiversity strategy and the growing reliance on GM crops. Scientists Maria Alice Garcia and Miguel Altiera sum it up well: "As long as the use of these crops follows closely the high-input, pesticide paradigm, such biotechnological products will reinforce the 'pesticide treadmill' usually associated with genetic uniformity and reduction of biodiversity in agro-ecosystems."[45]

In his insightful article on the sustainability of GM crops, Brian Johnson, a senior advisor on biotechnology to British nature conservation agencies, put forward the idea of testing the potential impacts of GM crops by measuring fluctuations in native bird populations: "This link is vital if we are to preserve the function of biodiversity to deliver early warning of dangers in crops or the chemicals used to manage them."[46] One wonders what the application of a similar test using grassland birds in Canada would tell us about biodiversity health on GM croplands. However, the modern biotechnology proponents clearly do not feel the need for any such test. They contend that the GM crop revolution is producing its own magic, feeding the world with better and cheaper food, and leaving the land better-off and richer in biodiversity. For example, an article by research consultant Janet E. Carpenter, published in GM Crops in 2011 and supported by CropLife International, a federation of agricultural biotechnology companies, represented a strong research-based attempt to put GM crops in a favourable light. Carpenter's article was essentially a selective literature review that, in her own words, found "currently commercialized GM crops have reduced the impacts of agriculture on biodiversity, through enhanced adoption of conservation tillage practices, reduction of insecticide use and use of more environmentally benign herbicides and increasing yields to alleviate pressure to convert additional land into agricultural use."[47]

No specifically Canadian articles were included in the extensive bibliography, and Canadian examples were absent in her reference charts, as well as very lightly discussed in the narrative, all of which is surprising given Canada's strong GM agricultural presence. With respect to above-ground species, the article was inconclusive, admitting to the absence of birds in GM fields while offering qualitatively limited and at-variance information on others.[48] But this is not the point. That Carpenter was able to find many authors to make her case indicates not that she is right but that an abundance of widely divergent science-based information exists on an issue with enormous implications for biodiversity and for environmental, human, and nonhuman health. If for no other reason, the precautionary principle should call on stakeholders to err on the side of caution.

Strong recommendations for a cautionary approach appeared in a remarkable online book published in 2012 under the authority of the Swiss National Science Foundation. Titled *Valuating Environmental*

Impacts of Genetically Modified Crops – Ecological and Ethical Criteria for Regulatory Decision-Making, the 190-page study contends that the GM debate stems not primarily from a shortage of data but from the absence of criteria for assessing the effects of GM crops on biodiversity. In proposing a partly moral-based criteria and stressing unknowns with respect to risk factors and the long-run net benefit to agriculture, the authors argued that "current scientific risk knowledge does not yet suffice to justify the commercial release of GM crops."[49]

Obviously, Agriculture Canada does not agree with the more ethical, cautious, and realistic Swiss appraisal of GM crops. Neither do Canadians generally – although a current debate does exist on genetic engineering. This debate, however, is all about potential health risks from eating food derived from GM crops, not about the advisability of planting them in the first place or their impact on wildlife or biodiversity.

In 2011 Statistics Canada reported that herbicide use in Canada totalled 50.3 million kilograms, an increase of 130 per cent over 1994, and was impacting almost 70 per cent of farms across Canada.[50] In the first half of 2014, the value of chemicals in Canada was up by over 8 per cent to $4.2 billion, with much of the increase attributed to higher demand for pesticide, fertilizer, and other chemicals used in agriculture.[51] One of the most detrimental is glyphosate, a plant enzyme inhibitor discovered and developed by Monsanto and used in its Roundup herbicide. Its Roundup Ready product allows farmers to use glyphosate freely without damaging their GM crops. Research has linked glyphosate to birth defects and other serious abnormalities in laboratory animals. In addition, glyphosate is toxic to many beneficial soil dwellers, including earthworms, and is harmful to a wide range of microbes that "convert insoluble soil oxides to plant-available" nutrients.[52] Glyphosate can be retained and transported in soils, with long-lasting cumulative effects on soil ecology and fertility, especially in countries like Canada with long biologically inactive winters. The continued application of glyphosate-containing herbicides significantly reduces the number and diversity of plant species around field edges. Studies examining the effect of glyphosate spray-drift found negative effects on the growth and species composition of wild plant communities.[53] Glyphosate contamination of surface water is especially detrimental to amphibians, who absorb the chemical through their skins and eat contaminated food sources. One North American trial on tadpoles in artificial ponds found mortality rates as high as 96 to 100 per cent when glyphosate was applied at the manufacturer's recommended rate.[54] It is also the most popular herbicide in Canada, with about 35 million kilograms sold in 2010.[55] Today, Roundup is on sale in Canadian hardware chain stores.

The application of glyphosate has led to the emergence of glyphosate-tolerant weeds. In response, the biotechnology companies are now using glyphosate in combination with 2,4-D and dicamba to develop new, more tolerant crops. The end result will be an increased use of herbicides since there are at least four weeds in Canada already resistant to 2,4-D or dicamba. Canadian scientists Hugh Beckie and Linda Hall predict short-terms benefits to farmers and a perpetuation of the "chemical treadmill."[56]

A more recent chemical used in agriculture presents a significant threat to wildlife and ecosystems. Neonicotinoids (neonics) are nerve-poison members of a relatively new class of insecticides and are applied to crop seeds before planting. After planting, these insecticides spread into every plant cell and into plant nectar and pollen. The entire plant becomes toxic. They are especially toxic to invertebrates and have been linked to rapid declines in bird populations. A Dutch study has shown the negative impacts of neonics on the food chain: insects feed on neonic seeds, and since birds eat the insects, bird losses increase as the supply of insects for food declines.[57] Another author, in linking proportionate bird loss to crops planted with neonics seeds, suggests that "the environmental damage inflicted by these insecticides may be much broader than previously thought."[58] Others agree, citing the "massive declines in insect-feeding groups such as swallows, swifts, bats and frogs."[59] A 2013 study shows that neonic pollution is occurring in surface water and potentially undermining aquatic invertebrate life, food chains, and ecosystem functions.[60]

In spite of these disturbing trends, Health Canada has registered neonics for virtually every crop grown in the country. Over 300,000 kilograms were sold in 2010, and the widespread use of neonics led one commentator to remark, "It is difficult for Canadian farmers to buy seeds for major crops such as corn and soybeans (and soon, wheat) that aren't treated with these nerve poisons."[61] At present, all Ontario's canola, corn for grain, and about 60 per cent of soybeans are grown with neonics.[62]

In referring to neonics and other seed-treated insecticides, one senior scientist observed, "It is a consequence of the susceptibility of our overly-simplified, biologically-pauperized agricultural system, which relies on piecemeal pest control approaches like Bt and chemical insecticides rather than ecologically based systems that greatly reduce the opportunities for pests to get a foothold."[63]

The unfolding issue of neonics use in Ontario provides a graphic example of the tensions that surround this insecticide. A total of 37 million bees were killed in 2012, and the Canadian Honey Council reported a 35 per cent loss in the provincial bee population between 2011 and 2014, which scientists attributed to crops sown with neonic-coated seeds.[64] In response to these alarming figures, the province introduced regulations in July 2015 that required farmers to restrict the use of neonic-treated corn and soybean seeds to 50 per cent of their 2016 crops and to submit a pest assessment report before using any neonic-treated seeds in 2017.[65] It was a first in North America and followed the lead of the European Union, which had already banned neonic crops. A subsequent appeal to delay the implementation of the regulation by the Grain Farmers of Ontario (GFO) was denied by the Ontario Supreme Court on 23 October 2015.[66] Ten days later, the GFO lodged an unsuccessful appeal in the Ontario Divisional Court. GFO chair Mark Brock, inadvertently perhaps, underscored some of the central issues standing in the way of a concerted consensual approach to the implementation of the biodiversity strategy: "We see more issues coming down the road where government can react to public opinion and develop a regulation that may not have a lot of basis in science, but has a significant impact on (agriculture) the number two economic driver in the province."[67] Human interests are always at stake in biodiversity issues.

Health Canada has the final say on how the neonics issue will unfold. In a report released in January 2016 on how neonics affect pollinators, it found that neonic-coated seeds posed no potential risk to honey bees. The report also included native bees in the above assessment but was cautionary with respect to possible negative impacts on bumblebees and downright uncertain as to the effects on the 1,000 other varieties of native bees in Canada.[68] Despite this vindication of agricultural neonics use, Health Canada seems to be considering limiting or banning them.

In any case, even if it does act, several years will pass before neonics disappear from farms. Their residual impact on Canadian ecosystems will likely remain. Currently, Ecojustice is trying to protect the bees through a legal challenge, arguing that two neonicotinoid pesticide registrations, for clothianidin and thiamethoxam, are unlawful under the Pest Control Products Act (1985).[69]

Agriculture poses the greatest threat to a wide range of wildlife and biodiversity in Canada. Cropland is hostile to wildlife habitat, and depending on type and scope, grazing areas undermine habitat integrity. Furthermore, the widespread use of chemical toxins results in air, soil, and water pollution, with harmful effects for wildlife and their food sources. When applied as fertilizers and used in the control measures of commercial farms and ranches, acreages, hobby farms, road allowances, and rural recreational areas, chemical agents drift in the air, run off into streams, lakes, and wetlands, and inhabit the soil. All of this occurs with the approval and endorsement of government policymakers ostensibly committed to the Canadian Biodiversity Strategy. It should also be noted that although the highest wildlife death tolls occur on GM-treated farmland and in surrounding areas, the use of chemical toxins also rests easily with those rural and urban dwellers who want greener lawns, perfect golf fairways, fewer dandelions, and mosquito-free patios and decks. In a survey on pesticides conducted by CTV Calgary in June 2015, over half the respondents were opposed to any restrictions on their use in the city.[70]

FORESTS

Human encroachment into forest areas represents a serious threat to terrestrial wildlife globally and certainly in Canada. Anthropogenic disturbances in the form of logging and forestry activities, roads, seismic cuts, power lines, pipelines, buildings, and other infrastructure pose significant threats to wildlife, not all of which are understood. The elusive wolverine (previously discussed) is a case in point.

Canada is home to one of the world's greatest forest reserves, particularly to habitat-rich old-growth stands. With their understories, canopies, riparian areas, marshes, and wetlands, forests are global ecological engines. Well over half of Canada's land area is forested. Around half of this area is considered commercially productive, and a quarter is currently managed for timber use. A global leader in the production and export of forest products, Canada holds fast to an ongoing logging tradition that dates to the eighteenth century. Since Canada's forests are also home to an abundance of wildlife and biodiversity, and since both count for little in the economic calculus, environmental groups are fighting an uphill battle against powerful logging interests and the governments that back them. The issue over logging in British Columbia's Great Bear Rainforest, one of the last coastal temperate rain forests in the world, is an outstanding case in point.

The Castle Wilderness area in Alberta is another controversial site. In September 2015 when the New Democratic Party government announced a provincial park and a wildland area totalling over 1,000 square kilometres of habitat-rich forests and wildlife corridors in the Castle area in southwest Alberta, it was hailed as a major victory for biodiversity and for the nongovernmental organizations that worked for years to secure preservation of an outstanding, ecologically significant wilderness area.[71] Their joy was muted a month later amid fears that the subsequent management plan might allow off-road vehicles, livestock, grazing, and hunting.[72] Unfortunately, they were not entirely wrong.

In March 2017 the provincial government released its revised draft for managing the Castle area through the protection of 105,179 hectares of land in the form of a provincial park (25,501 hectares) and a wildland park (79,678 hectares). The plan was a carefully worded documented that reflected the contemporary sensitivity to values management in protected areas. Yet, despite applauding itself upfront for its intention to manage the two areas as world-class protected spaces with high standards of ecological values and conservation, the authors wasted little time before indicating that the ubiquitous human interest was paramount. Beyond a doubtless serious commitment to due oversight, even to the point of considering the merits of the precautionary principle, the plan was also adamant about promoting a management regime that provided "long-term economic benefits to the people of Alberta."[73] Thus grazing, hunting, trapping, sport-fishing, and other recreational activities were to proceed as usual. Although off-road motorized vehicles were to be phased out, it would take five years to do so, and even then they were to be relocated to nearby public lands. The merits of snowmobiling in winter were to be the subject of further research and consultation with stakeholders.[74] Yes, sound ameliorations were present. Commercial logging was out, and, in the main, so were the destructive off-road vehicles. But the fact remains that wildlife still have to coexist and die among humans in a protected wilderness forested area.

The Boreal Forest

Canada's boreal forests, 65 million years in the making, comprise Canada's largest set of ecosystems.[75] At first glance, the abundance of biodiversity in these vast landscapes seems impervious to threat. They account for 25 per cent of the worlds' boreal forests and cover 3.5 million square kilometres, stretching 10,000 kilometres across the breadth of Canada. The treed landscapes of white spruce, black spruce, jack pine, tamarack, balsam fir, balsam poplar, white birch, and trembling aspen are complemented by 200 million acres of surface water, including five major rivers and 1.5 million lakes. With 25 per cent of the world's wetlands, encompassing more than 1 million square kilometres, and with 9,000 square kilometres of peat lands, the mixed vegetation of the boreal forests and their interconnected groundwater and subsurface water systems provide an incredibly rich and diverse wildlife habitat. The world's largest populations of woodland caribou, bears, wolves, and many other species roam these green expanses. The wide variety of habitat allows 200 species of birds to breed there, including 35 species of waterfowl. In all, it is estimated that the birds breeding in the boreal region number over 5 billion.

Birds comprise more than 75 per cent of all terrestrial vertebrate species, and are the richest vertebrate taxon in boreal forests. Thirty-five families, comprising 186 species of land birds, regularly inhabit Canada's boreal regions. Over 80 per cent of the global population of fourteen species of land birds breed there, most being migratory warblers, sparrows, and thrushes.[76] As many as 500 birds can be supported by 1.6 square kilometres of forests, lakes, river valleys, and wetlands. With their varied plumage and appearance, with their songs and sounds, and indeed in their whole wondrous diversity, they represent an aesthetic beyond any human comparison. Whether they are permanent residents or short-range or long-range migrants, in acting out their lifecycles, boreal birds help the habitat that supports them. They provide the best measure of forest ecosystem health by integrating many structural and functional aspects of the forest ecosystem. They disseminate seeds and are agents for nutrient and energy cycling. Birds also promote forest health and growth by reducing insect densities and by controlling small mammal populations.[77]

Globally, forest birds are declining rapidly. Over 8 per cent of global undisturbed forests were lost between 2000 and 2013, with the greatest declines occurring in Canada's boreal forests.[78] According to the Breeding Bird Survey (1966–2001), bird numbers in the Canadian boreal forest dropped dramatically over a thirty-five-year period. Forty species were identified as declining in number, including migratory birds and permanent residents.[79] Among the declines are the rusty blackbird and lesser yellowlegs (90 per cent), the blackpoll warbler and Canada warbler (80 per cent), and the evening grosbeak and boreal chickadee (70 per cent). A dozen boreal birds have been listed by the Committee on the Status of Endangered Wildlife in Canada (COSEWIC) and/or under the Species at Risk Act (SARA). The specific reasons for these declines are not well understood. Extensive research on forest management and bird habitats has shown considerable levels of interactive complexities, including ecological relationships between forest composition, structure, and origin, as well as the difficulty of managing all habitat types by emulating natural disturbances.[80] Some birds, like wood thrushes, respond positively to single-tree harvesting but avoid clear-cut areas. In newer managed areas, for example, rose-breasted grosbeaks have a low rate of reproduction success. Furthermore, although bird population density may be a reliable indicator of specific habitat quality, it does not account for variations in species' needs and cycles.[81]

There can be no doubt, however, that anthropogenic disturbance is the major cause of wildlife declines, especially among birds. Approximately 41 per cent of the primarily treed boreal has already witnessed anthropogenic disturbances, and around 23 per cent of the boreal overall has been degraded or damaged. More than 30 per cent of Canada's boreal forest has been slated for some form of industrial development.[82] Over 95 per cent of the Canadian boreal forest is publicly owned and is available for human use, primarily logging through geographically defined tenures or long-term licences.[83] In 2002 over 60 per cent of logging in Canada occurred in the boreal taiga, where close to 600,000 hectares of trees were harvested.[84] Hydropower and mining companies are exploiting the southern limits and slowly moving north. Oil and gas exploration are fragmenting habitats with expanding networks of roads, seismic lines, and other infrastructure. Some statistics are already telling their gloomy story. Whether one is a deer, bear, wolf, wolverine, small furbearer, northern leopard frog, eastern garter snake, or water dweller like the snapping turtle, the mixed ecological environments of the boreal forests are home. Billions of lives are being eked out in one of the world's last vast, undisturbed tracts of habitat. But for how long?

An Alberta study found a 15 per cent decrease in black-throated green warblers and a 50 per cent decrease in ovenbirds following clear-cutting. Conservation biologist Bridget Stutchbury reports that "songbirds that prefer edges and open areas may be threatened by logging." Taking the example of olive-sided flycatchers, who nest in open areas such as forest edges, bogs, and burned forest, she cites a study in the western United States that "found that Olive-sided Flycatchers living in selectively logged forests had 50% lower nesting success than in natural habitat."[85] Wetlands are contaminated by mining and oil and gas activities. Roads, seismic lines, and pipelines fracture habitat.[86]

Cavity nesters are severely impacted by forestry activities.[87] In forest areas in British Columbia, more than forty species, or about 30 per cent of forest vertebrates, use cavities for nesting and shelter.[88] Clear-cut logging of older forests displaces cavity nesters, forcing them to move elsewhere or attempt to breed in regenerating forest. Yellow-bellied sapsuckers, an indicator species, excavate cavities that other birds use. Depletions in this species have implications for others. Three-toed woodpeckers, more abundant in old forests relative to the larger forest community, are the most sensitive to loss of habitat from logging and are in serious decline as a result.[89] The retention of some trees and snags is essential for the welfare of cavity-nesting birds. A study in western Canada comparing bird communities in recently burned areas with those in logged areas found that a harvest "that left 12–34% of the trees standing and some patches untouched came closest to attaining the bird community one would find after a fire."[90] Another study comparing wildlife habitat in regenerating 3-metre-high forest stands with that in mature old-growth forest found less abundance in the regenerating stands and recommended that "some mature forest stands should be maintained within managed landscapes for a complete logging rotation period."[91] Although cavity nesters prefer old-growth forests and snags, they also vary in their preferences. Red-breasted nuthatches like old fire-origin forests, but the bay-breasted warbler is more at home in the oldest managed forests.

Logging is not the only threat. According to Mining Watch Canada, mining activities in the boreal forest means the daily removal of tens of thousands of cubic metres of thin boreal soils. Put another way, the boreal forest is home to around 80 per cent of Canadian mining operations, totalling approximately 7,000 abandoned mines, 72 operating mines, and 14 smelters. In 2007 about 98 projects were in "advanced exploration" or under development, and thousands more properties were being prospected under mineral claims. Additionally, according to the Mining Watch report, "The acid-laden mine effluent and acid-laced air discharges of the mining industry overlay the thin and naturally acidic soils of the boreal, adding undue stress to these forest ecosystems."[92]

Oil and gas activity is a further ongoing threat to birds and their habitats. More than 272,000 gas wells are located in the boreal forest, of which around 87 per cent are within 5 kilometres of a lake or river. The western boreal has seen the most intrusions. Intensive drilling is occurring in British Columbia, the Northwest Territories, Alberta, and Saskatchewan, and prospects are for increased activity in the future. The implications of wetland and watershed degradation through leakage of toxins and pollutants into nearby watersheds are major causes for concern.

The development of bituminous sands – commonly called tar sands or oil sands – in Alberta is a death trap for thousands of birds. The development of bituminous sands involves the clearing of 300,000 hectares of forest and the construction of 30,000 kilometres of roads, leaving 80 per cent of the remaining forested area within 250 metres of a road, pipeline, or well site. The impact on birds is devastating. "Each year between 22 million and 170 million birds breed in the 35 million acres of Boreal forest that could eventually be developed for tar sands."[93] The Peace-Athabasca Delta alone supports "as many as 130,000 breeding waterfowl."[94] The Mackenzie Delta provides important nesting habitat for several shorebird species, including the American golden plover, whimbrel, and Hudsonian godwit, all identi-fied as "species of high concern" in the Canadian Shorebird Conservation Plan (2000).[95] Yet, according to a 2008 report, the projected strip mining of 300,000 hectares of forests and wetlands in the development area will adversely affect breeding habitat for up to 3.6 million adult birds, which will translate overall into an outright loss of 36 million birds over a twenty-year period.[96] The report further notes that restoration of habitat, when it does occur, is at a snail's pace. In the Athabasca boreal region, only 104 hectares of mined area have been certified as reclaimed. Even then, this single reclaimed area consists of overburden, and its management has not addressed the challenge of reclaiming tailings ponds. According to the report, "Provincial regulation of waste management, water withdrawals, water pollution, air pollution, and habitat destruction and reclamation [is] insufficient and not well enforced."[97]

FOREST RESIDENTS IN DECLINE

Despite serious efforts to monitor bird populations in the boreal forest, significant knowledge gaps remain. According to a 2011 academic paper, the very vastness of the boreal forest has created misconceptions about its vulnerability to habitat loss or to bird declines.[98] This uncertainty is reinforced by the federal Bird Conservation Strategy (2013), which reports that on the Boreal Taiga Plains,

> Population objectives are difficult to assess for many ... species due to limited or unavailable population trend data (e.g., evaluation of temporal patterns of change over multiple sample periods) for many boreal forest species. Existing monitoring programs (landbirds, waterfowl) are biased due to inadequate route coverage. Many landbird species (irruptive species, nomadic species, primary cavity nesters/woodpeckers, grouse, diurnal raptors, nocturnal raptors, species at risk), almost all waterbird and shorebird species, and cavity-nesting waterfowl species are not adequately monitored using existing monitoring programs.[99]

Boreal bird populations are also variable. Some species of waterfowl are increasing, whereas shrub and forest edge birds are showing serious decreases. All are impacted negatively by anthropogenic disturbance. For example, warblers who eat caterpillar larvae have suffered from the pesticide war against spruce budworm. More significantly, for at least 30 per cent of boreal birds, there is a lack of reliable information on population numbers. Of those species for which statistical information is available, over 20 per cent are decreasing, over half of them seriously.[100]

The Rusty Blackbird

The rusty blackbird is an excellent example of a boreal migratory species in dramatic decline. Rusty blackbirds are medium-sized passerines with long, pointed wings, pale-yellow eyes, black feet, and black bills that are slightly curved. They are found in every province and territory in Canada but are most abundant in northern portions of the boreal forest, where over 90 per cent breed in the wetlands and other riparian areas of the Taiga Shield, Hudson Plains, and Northwestern Interior Forest. Over the past forty years, the rusty blackbird has experienced a 95 per cent decrease in numbers, the most marked decline of any North American land bird.[101] Although many possible causes for this decline are recognized, consensus is lacking on why this particular bird should be so dramatically impacted. Currently, the Species at Risk Act lists the species as a "special concern."

The most common reason given for rusty blackbird depopulation focuses on its wintering areas in the southeastern United States, where conversion of land to agriculture has led to extensive loss of wooded wetlands. However, in the breeding areas of the boreal forest, habitat loss and degradation are also recognized, with particular emphasis on anthropogenic disturbance in the form of logging, mercury contamination, acidification, and wetland loss primarily in the more southerly regions of the forest. In the vast northern reaches of the boreal forest, where accessibility and the human presence are lacking, climate change is having an unnoticed and unknown impact. Rising temperatures increase the incidence of fire, disease, and severe storms in nesting season. Melting permafrost affects the chemical, physical, and biological properties of lakes and other wetlands. In short, global warming is causing major changes to the extent of boreal wetlands, the chemistry of the waters, and the structure of invertebrate communities. It is likely that climate change may be disrupting the food chain such that the emergence of invertebrates is out of phase with breeding rusty blackbirds.[102]

The mandatory Management Plan for the Rusty Blackbird (2015) was released nine years after COSEWIC's recommendation and six years after it was officially listed under the Species at Risk Act. Although it gave direction respecting monitoring activities, it also stressed severe knowledge gaps. Its stated aim was to maintain populations at 2014 levels. No actual yardstick was given, which was not encouraging since, according to COSEWIC's 2006 report, rusty blackbird numbers in Canada could be anywhere from 110,000 to 1.4 million.[103] In spite of the precipitous decline in numbers, the plan assessed winter habitat degradation as the only major threat to the birds' survival. As for the role of climate change in altering hydrologic regimes, the plan identified it as a medium threat while admitting a lack of knowledge about its impact on overall population levels.[104] In fact, given the plan's concluding observation that "wetland drying from climate change may reduce suitable breeding habitats," the rusty blackbird's future in the northern reaches of the boreal forest is far from assured.[105]

The Boreal Chickadee

The focus of the Species at Risk Act is on threatened species and the need to combat their declines. Thus, little or no attention is paid to species generally until alarm bells ring. Yet many species considered "secure" are declining. The previously discussed mule deer is a case in point. The boreal chickadee is another. One of the few North American birds who are permanent residents of the boreal forest, the boreal chickadee faces an uncertain future.

Although chickadees are permanent residents of the boreal forest, they are also familiar to Canadians farther south. Perky, tough, and known for their distinctive cheery song, chickadees are just about everybody's favourite avian visitor, lining up almost dutifully for their turn at a suet block or feeder filled with sunflower seeds. Like their fellows, the black-capped, mountain, and Carolina chickadees, boreal chickadees generally forage in the forest canopy by gleaning for insects on conifer branches or by probing into bark to extract larvae. They supplement their diet with seeds and berries. Chickadees have excellent memories and in the winter will subsist on food stored on the underside of branches months earlier.

Boreal chickadees have shown alarming reductions in eastern Canada and are highly vulnerable to changing forest landscapes. They are very sensitive to habitat disturbance and have shown steep declines in areas punctuated by anthropogenic linear features like seismic lines and pipelines. They thrive in old-growth forests and do not do well in managed stands until the trees are at least thirty years old. In Alberta, where boreal chickadee numbers are thought to be relatively stable, recent studies have shown an almost 8 per cent decline in mean habitat suitability.[106] A research-based study in 2006 concluded that boreal chickadee declines were attributable to the loss of winter habitat occasioned by forestry activities.[107] Forest health is another contributing factor. One researcher suggests that irruptions such as those caused by budworm infestations and their aftermaths take their toll on boreal chickadee numbers.[108] Others contend that the combination of reduced breeding populations and habitat availability is aligning boreal chickadees with the more numerous black-capped chickadee and triggering hybridization.[109] Overall, however, knowledge of their winter requirements is limited.[110]

International avian groups are not optimistic about the future of the boreal chickadee. According to the Boreal Avian Modelling Project, an international group of avian and forest researchers, accurate knowledge is lacking on boreal chickadee populations and the reasons for their decline.[111] Partners in Flight, a consortium of public and private groups that includes Environment Canada, has identified the boreal chickadee as an exceptional "Stewardship Species" in need of careful monitoring and attention.[112] Similarly, Birdlife International, a global partnership of international nature organizations, notes that boreal chickadee numbers are down by more than 70 per cent over the past forty years.[113] A 2008 article concluded that declines are due to the loss of high-quality wintering habitat caused by current forestry practices.[114]

In Canada, where over 80 per cent of the global boreal chickadee population live and where more than 90 per cent breed in the boreal forests, official apathy mingles with mild concern, resulting in inactive activity.

Environment Canada considers boreal chickadees to be abundant and widespread, noting that their affinity with forests in poor soils may give them some relief from forestry operations. Nonetheless, it acknowledges severe population depletions in eastern Canada, admits to ignorance about why a lesser trend is occurring nationwide, and ponders the need to preserve wintering habitat. With this conflicting information stated up front, Environment Canada is of the opinion that the boreal chickadee is a candidate for assessment by COSEWIC.[115] This is all very good, but when COSEWIC released its 2015 list of bird candidates for future assessment, the boreal chickadee did not even rank a mention on the lowest of three levels of priority.[116] Given this, and the ponderous workings of the Species at Risk Act, the little boreal chickadee is going to wait a long time before being noticed. Hopefully, not too long.

The Woodland Caribou

Caribou are another inhabitant of boreal regions and have become synonymous with Canada's northern environments. Also known as reindeer in North America, they are the only member of the deer family whose males and females both grow antlers. Uniquely adapted to the harsh northern climate, caribou are insulated from the cold by semi-hollow hair that traps warm air next to their skin. Their large crescent-shaped hooves spread when they walk to function like snowshoes or paddles, depending on terrain. An indicator species, these historically symbolic animals are found in three subspecies, the barren-ground, Peary, and woodland. All have listings under COSEWIC and SARA.[117] The former two occupy more northerly ranges, whereas the woodland caribou are located farther south and are found in every Canadian province, except New Brunswick and Prince Edward Island.

The precarious state of Canada's woodland caribou is a prime example of the impact of anthropogenic disruptions to habitat. They are a medium-sized member of the deer family and rich brown in colour with white necks. Unlike the great herds of barren-ground caribou to the north, woodland caribou are usually found in groups of only ten to twenty-five animals. They comprise four populations, all of which are listed under COSEWIC and SARA.[118]

That the woodland caribou is a threatened species destined for probable extirpation is bad enough. That this seems to be accepted in official circles is worse. Minister of Environment Peter Kent, for example, chose to ignore a court recommendation in 2012 directing him to revisit his decision not to issue an emergency order to protect Alberta's critically endangered caribou herds from extirpation. He believed that woodland caribou numbers were not threatened overall in Canada, or as he stated, "While there are threats to the recovery of certain populations, there is still sufficient time to take management actions that would achieve recovery objectives."[119] As for Alberta, the parlous state of Alberta woodland caribou was apparently not of particular relevance to the man responsible for the protection of the nation's fauna.

Woodland caribou are classified into several populations in Canada, the largest of which is the boreal. The following discussion focuses primarily on boreal caribou but is applicable to woodland caribou generally. Around 34,000 boreal caribou are listed as "threatened" under the Species at Risk Act and, although not listed as such, are actually endangered in Alberta. They are not listed in either the Northwest Territories or the Yukon. Boreal caribou require continuous tracts of undisturbed, mature coniferous forests, peat lands, and hilly areas that allow them to disperse widely and maintain low population densities in order to reduce predation risk. Like all woodland caribou, boreal caribou are extremely sensitive to habitat loss, primarily because of their specialized winter diet, which consists almost entirely of lichen in old-growth forest stands. Since no other large mammal can survive on this food source, they live in habitat that separates them from other deer and from their predators. Across Canada, boreal caribou live in fifty-one ranges. At the present time, only fourteen are classified as self-sustaining. The rest are in decline, most of them seriously.

These declines are the result of human disturbance. Any partial degradation of habitat constitutes a major threat since at least 300 boreal caribou are needed to maintain numbers in an undisturbed range of at least 15,000 square kilometres. They avoid logged areas, and any exposure to human activities induces them to abandon traditional wintering areas, even if the habitat itself is not disturbed by forest harvest or roads.[120] In addition to the loss of old-growth forests through logging, boreal caribou are also impacted by the harvesting of regenerated forests before they are mature enough to sustain lichen. Logging is not the only threat. Seismic lines, roads, pipelines, hydroelectric installations, and oil and gas activity disturb caribou during calving and overwintering. They also cause habitat fragmentation by creating linear corridors that allow increased predation. For example, wolves, who have lived in balance with caribou for thousands of years, now use these human-made open spaces to prey more liberally on them.[121] Statistics tell their own sad story. Habitat loss due to human interference is as high as 95 per cent in one range in Alberta, and the average loss of habitat in both Alberta and British Columbia across all caribou ranges is well over 70 per cent.[122]

Despite the extensive research carried out on woodland caribou and the expressed need to combat their decline, their chances of survival are slim in many areas. A 2013 report on the status of woodland caribou, prepared by the Canadian Parks and Wilderness Society and the David Suzuki Foundation, had little positive to say about Canadian jurisdictions.[123] Not all had recovery plans in place. Those plans that did exist were lacking or deficient. The Yukon, for example, seems more intent on development than on protecting caribou habitat. Newfoundland and Labrador has an outdated plan, is deficient in identifying critical habitat, and relies overly on predator control. Other plans are delayed. For example, although the Quebec government has received solid recommendations from its recovery team, it has failed to implement them.[124] In British Columbia, where 75 per cent of caribou habitat is given over to oil and gas development, extirpation in some areas seems accepted. Its 2011 implementation plan was expected to "benefit Boreal Caribou and support future recovery efforts while providing resource development opportunities."[125] Translated into practice, this meant that no habitat restoration was to be undertaken in one-third of the province's boreal caribou ranges.[126] In Alberta the government ignored the recommendations of its 2005 recovery plan, which called for a moratorium on oil and gas and timber leases in areas where caribou extirpation was imminent.[127] Instead, it went ahead and auctioned off or allowed intensification on over 3 million hectares, adding a further 490,518 hectares in boreal ranges between 2012 and 2014, and in the middle of 2014 it offered up another 1,235 acres, half of it in caribou habitat already in a crisis state.[128] An updated status report in 2010 noted bleakly that land-use guidelines for industrial activities militated against long-term caribou health and habitat conservation and that "guidelines for caribou habitat protection are currently not being applied in all caribou ranges within the province."[129] In the face of caribou declines of over 80 per cent in some areas, it was not surprising to see a government study in 2010 predicting extinction for local caribou within forty years.[130]

Insight into official attitudes toward saving the woodland caribou is provided by the federal recovery strategy, overdue by seven years and released in 2012.[131] The plan attempted to accommodate caribou habitat within the framework of ongoing logging, mining, and oil and gas development, and it embodied the usual disappointing mindsets. For example, no specific information was offered on how industrial development was to be managed, let alone curtailed. At the same time, the necessity of culling programs aimed at wolves came through loud and clear.[132] Significantly, the strategy advocated adaptive management, which accepts uncertainty as a basis for experimentation and presupposes high stakeholder cooperation and involvement, as well as rigorous ongoing oversight. The "probabilistic approach," as the strategy calls it, proceeds despite data deficiencies and information gaps, being based instead on hypotheses about probable outcomes that in turn inform new hypotheses.[133] For example, although it was expected that adaptive management experiments could ascertain habitat disturbance thresholds, it was also admitted that "there exists an intermediate range of disturbance levels over which outcomes for caribou local populations are highly uncertain."[134] This "learn as you ago" process is a risky exercise given the caribou's vulnerable status. In criticizing the strategy for setting "an insultingly low bar" and for defying "scientific evidence on what caribou need to survive," an Ecojustice spokesperson noted, "This is not a recovery plan. This is barely a survival plan."[135]

Ambiguities and confusing statements were present in the strategy. Extensive attention was paid to the need to develop range plans that would "outline how range-specific land and/or resource activities will be managed over space and time to ensure that critical habitat is protected from destruction."[136] In other words, these range plans were the main instruments for measuring and reconciling human disturbance with caribou populations. However, the strategy also admitted that "most boreal caribou ranges in Canada have not been fully described owing to a lack

of standardized animal location data and poor understanding of movement within and between ranges" and that "monitoring and assessment
programs to provide data on local population size, local population trend,
recruitment and adult mortality are required to improve understanding
of factors affecting boreal caribou survival and recovery."[137] Alberta's
initial status report on the woodland caribou, published in 2001, likewise
concluded that the number in Alberta remained "largely unknown."[138] It
seems reasonable to assume that measurement of habitat loss must be
set against the number affected by it, or to quote Environment Canada,
"Understanding the relationship(s) between caribou population condition
and the condition of the range is central to determining the amount of
habitat required to support a self-sustaining population."[139] These range
plans, therefore, are deficient as a primary management tool because
insufficient knowledge exists about caribou populations and movement
to allow accurate assessments of habitat loss.

As with recovery plans in general, the federal version for woodland
caribou was a feeble attempt to aid caribou through visible but largely
token amelioration under the guise of adaptive management. Essentially,
the strategy allocated 35 per cent of the boreal regions to industrial
development and placed the remaining 65 per cent under range plan
management.[140] Restoration of habitat in the thirty-one ranges where
human disturbance was greater than 35 per cent was mentioned as a goal
but essentially nullified by the observation that it could take a century
to achieve.[141] The strategy also specified that undisturbed habitat began
500 metres from any human disturbance.[142] The validity of this measure
seems questionable since an Environment Canada scientific review in
2008 cited studies that found that collared caribou moved from 8 to 60
kilometres away after the commencement of logging activities.[143] Worse
yet, the strategy admitted that the 65 per cent represented the lowest
threshold for caribou population maintenance in undisturbed habitat
and that, even then, there remained a 40 per cent probability that caribou
populations there would not be self-sustaining.[144] In other words, caribou
populations had only a 40 per cent chance of sustaining themselves in
undisturbed areas that were likely less than adequate in the first place.
Given that the average percentage of anthropogenic disturbance across all
caribou ranges was already over 30 per cent and that only twelve ranges

had stable populations, chances of healthy population recovery amid increasing human intrusion seemed slim.[145]

The method by which it was determined that caribou could survive and flourish in about two-thirds of their former habitats is a further source of concern. The threshold figures, which were projected over a twenty-year period, were qualitatively derived by assuming a statistical mean for the annual survival rate of females and combining it with habitat disturbance variables.[146] Details on degree of habitat disturbance were obtained from satellite imagery across all boreal caribou ranges, not all of which were sufficiently accurate.[147] This information was largely negated by the fact that caribou population estimates in less than half the ranges were classified as reliable.[148] The strategy further admitted, "In some cases, local population size estimates and trend data are based primarily on professional judgment and limited data, and not on rigorously collected field data."[149] For instance, no information at all was available for Saskatchewan's Boreal Shield range, the largest in area of all fifty-one ranges. Moreover, in line with adaptive management theory, management thresholds in individual ranges were set based on probabilities of risk and on likely outcomes, or as the authors of the updated scientific assessment put it, "The consideration of a management threshold is informed by science but determined by managers in accordance with decisions regarding the acceptable level of risk."[150] In theory, this means that when industrial activity intrudes into previously undisturbed boreal caribou habitat, decisions respecting the scope and size of the 35 per cent allowable habitat disturbance have to be made based on what amounts to a subjective assessment of probable risk to caribou numbers in the remaining 65 per cent, or in other words, on accurate knowledge of disturbance thresholds. Yet, as already indicated, these thresholds remain unknown. This is not good science. It lacks precision and is not accountable management. In practice, it will prejudice the boreal caribou far more than it will the human interests that represent money and jobs.

Provincial and other jurisdictions have three to five years to develop their own range, or action, plans to align with the federal strategy. On paper, Alberta is doing exactly that, noting its intention in July 2013 of working "cooperatively with Canada to develop one or more action plans setting out details on how the recovery strategy will be implemented for all Alberta's caribou populations by December 31, 2015."[151] It also admitted that, in order to do this, it needed to figure out a way to measure caribou population numbers and levels of habitat disturbance even though its own recovery plan dated to 2005.[152] By the middle of 2014, it apparently had done neither, for the province sold off about 1,200 hectares to oil and gas interests in a caribou range already ravaged by over 80 per cent habitat loss.[153] In an extensive review of current government strategies released in December 2015, the Canadian Parks and Wilderness Society concluded that not a great deal was being done to secure adequate habitat for the woodland caribou.[154] Given the heavy reliance of cash-strapped provincial and territorial governments on resource revenues, policies that give bureaucrats and politicians free rein in setting the survival of a species against "accepted levels of risk" are a blueprint for extirpation or worse.

A glimmer of hope for the woodland caribou, or at least for around 3,000 of them, is seen in the Manitoba recovery strategy released in 2015.[155] In seeking to set aside large tracts of forested areas and promising to preserve them in all management units at a level well in excess of the federal guidelines, the Manitoba strategy on paper is easily the best in Canada as far as the caribou are concerned. However, low populations in over half of the nine management units indicate that a lot of work lies ahead and that careful attention needs to be paid to identifying and protecting critical habitat.[156] The fact that approval has been given for a copper mine site in a prime area of caribou habitat and the intent to include restored logged land as part of "set-aside" caribou habitat tend to dampen hopes for a plan that on the surface seems sympathetic to the plight of the caribou.[157]

In the above context, the Canadian Boreal Forest Agreement (2010) deserves mention as an example of the compromise approach to addressing at-risk species. Signed by the twenty-one-member Forest Products Association of Canada and by seven leading environmental organizations, the agreement covers around 73 million hectares, or a little under one-quarter of Canada's total boreal forested area. It is also a truce of sorts, with the environmental groups agreeing to withhold negative action and publicity and the forestry companies opting to suspend logging operations on 29 million hectares of specifically designated boreal caribou forest habitat. Included in the six-goal agreement, in addition to sustainable forest management, are commitments to accelerate species at risk recovery efforts, with a particular emphasis on the boreal caribou.[158] Essentially, the latter means developing frameworks and working with government jurisdictions with respect to action plans in specific logging tenures in order to secure protected caribou habitat. It is a grand design and, in the words of the agreement, represents a "wish to demonstrate leadership in developing and implementing a globally significant model for conservation and resource management in Canada's boreal forests in a manner that sets the stage for joint action in relation to both boreal forest conservation and forest sector competitiveness."[159]

Described as ground-breaking, a new paradigm for resource management, and the most ambitious agreement of its kind in the world, the Canadian Boreal Forest Agreement faces enormous organizational and multi-jurisdictional challenges that have already resulted in the withdrawal of two conservation groups, a bitter dispute with one logging company, and very slow progress.[160] According to one conservation group in 2013, "Members have not been able to agree on a single joint recommendation for protection," and "all target dates have been missed and shifted."[161] As of 2014, although there were several planning areas, only one plan was in place, affecting 3 million hectares of the Abitibi River Forest north of Timmins, Ontario. Negotiations are ongoing for a second plan involving 9 million hectares in northwest Manitoba.[162]

With respect to the agreement's implications for wildlife and especially the boreal caribou, three points are worth noting. First, the agreement is not popular in settled areas with lumber mills. According to a Timmins news article, the plan will cost the logging industry over $100 million a year in lost revenue and will impose significant economic stress on local communities.[163] Second, for all its good intentions, the agreement reflects the overstated optimism inherent in the Canadian Biodiversity Strategy in its presumption that human commercial interests will coexist with wildlife voluntarily, benignly, and to equal mutual benefit amid a treasure trove of potential resource wealth.[164] Third, if the latter plan is any indication, one wonders how much habitat will be protected under the Canadian Boreal Forest Agreement. The Abitibi plan encompasses 3 million hectares, of which 2.2 million hectares will be open to logging, leaving less that 27 per cent permanently protected for caribou and other wildlife. Indeed, if everything goes as hoped, which is highly problematic, and all 29 million hectares of boreal caribou habitat designated by the agreement come under legal protected status, it will still leave more than 80 per cent of one of the world's most intact wilderness areas unprotected.

For the unfortunate woodland caribou, rusty blackbird, boreal chickadee, their fellow forest creatures, and the pristine habitat they occupy, the protections they can expect are few and tenuous. Scientific research on boreal birds is lacking compared to that in Europe. Furthermore, some researchers are unconvinced that human intrusion in boreal forests is causing drastic bird declines. Others see the main damage to birds coming from deterioration in migratory habitat farther south.[165] However, the various avian nongovernmental organizations do not agree, urging that action be taken in the boreal forests to protect vulnerable species before it is too late.[166] COSEWIC, too, attributes bird declines to habitat loss caused by logging.[167] As for the woodland caribou, no one knows how many there are or what constitutes critical habitat loss. The official approach to preserving their habitat is too vague and based on probabilities of outcome. Unless the Canadian Boreal Forest Agreement can demonstrate otherwise, which is highly problematic, the demise of the woodland caribou in Alberta, like the sage-grouse, will simply go down as an unfortunate by-product of progress. It is all such a familiar refrain: hesitancy to remediate vulnerable wildlife based on the absence of consensus, conscience, and money. Thus, the relentless intrusion into the boreal forest will continue, for in the official calculus, humans have first claim to the boreal forest, not the cheery boreal chickadee, the iconic woodland caribou, or the other billions of living beings who call it home.

A powerful argument for preserving wildlife and habitat by leaving the boreal forest intact was put forward by the Wilderness Committee, a Canadian nongovernmental organization dedicated to protecting wilderness areas and overall biodiversity. Noting that the limited research-based scientific knowledge of boreal ecosystems was inadequate to justify massive extractive-resource activity, the Wilderness Committee referred to studies that equated the carbon stored in the boreal forests with over 900 years of Canada's total greenhouse gas emissions. Equally significant was its claim that the nonmarket value of boreal ecosystems was 13.8 times greater than the combined value of all resource extraction. This figure included a $5.4 billion value placed on boreal birds for their contributions to pest control.[168]

Clearly, wildlife are prejudiced by anthropogenic pressures on their habitat. Since these pressures are in the main slow and often seemingly innocuous, it takes time for negative outcomes to be noticed and even longer for them to be addressed. Although the belief system may acknowledge damage done, and even the need to attempt repairs, it cannot accept solutions that unduly penalize human interests (usually translated as jobs). Fixing damage done, at best, means some sort of compromise, some level of human restraint, and a rationalized conviction that all will be well as a result. In these compromise arrangements, wildlife are mute victims of a belief system that devalues them and their lifestyles.

It is important to note that most threats to wildlife posed by agriculture and industrial activity in the boreal forests are outside the purview of wildlife policymaking. Although it could be argued that those responsible for wildlife management could be more interventionist and stronger advocates, the fact that they are not or cannot simply proves the point that wildlife are a minor resource in federal and provincial priorities. Unfortunately, and inevitably, wildlife depletions and habitat loss are indirect by-products of higher-order human needs and interests.

MARINE HABITAT

Marine habitat demonstrates fundamental flaws in managing wildlife. Marine critical habitat is very difficult to identify in terms of both geographical location and the biological components necessary to sustain the life of the species in question. Moreover, its location within federal waters often conflicts with shipping and other commercial activity. Unlike most terrestrial critical habitat, it falls directly under federal jurisdiction. Although Fisheries and Oceans Canada is responsible for the implementation of legal requirements respecting endangered and threatened species under the Species at Risk Act, it is also in charge of developing and implementing policies and programs in support of national economic priorities. The conflict of interests inherent in this dual role has proven prejudicial to marine wildlife, particularly to whales.

In 1996 Canada passed its Oceans Act. Coming hard on the heels of the Canadian Biodiversity Strategy's release in 1995, the Oceans Act announced the federal government's intention to take an active coordinating role in oceans policy and management, and like the biodiversity strategy, it aspired to place Canada at the forefront of global environmental leadership. The task of steering this new course was entrusted to the Department of Fisheries and Oceans. Renamed Fisheries and Oceans Canada in 2008, it has sole authority to conserve Canada's aquatic resources and manage their harvesting. This mandate to conserve and protect marine ecosystems and habitats while managing the resources within them has created tensions at Fisheries and Oceans Canada.

Bordering on three major oceans, Canada has a coastline of over 243,000 kilometres, the longest in the world. Its extensive marine area of 5.87 million square kilometres, of which 2.7 million square kilometres are nutrient-packed shallow waters of the continental shelf, is complemented by almost 1 million square kilometres of inland waters. Historically, fishing figured prominently in Atlantic Canada and is still an important industry, albeit one in decline due to overexploitation. A study published in 2006 found that overexploitation was the greatest threat facing Canadian marine species and that this trend outpaced those in other countries.[169]

Marine habitat is not easy to identify accurately and more difficult to manage successfully. According to an expert panel on biodiversity, adequate data on the physical and biological characteristics of Canada's marine habitats are lacking.[170] The most damaging elements to marine habitat are related to fishing and contaminants. Towed fishing gear that directly impacts the seabed, such as trawls and dredges, is responsible for most fishing-related alteration or destruction of habitat. Entanglements, collisions, chronic oiling, and noise pollution are on the increase, and contaminants from dumping, spillage, chemical run-offs, and nutrient overloads all contribute to habitat loss. A case in point is the Scott Islands just off the northwest tip of Vancouver Island, where habitat integrity is threatened by intensive commercial shipping. The islands are home to the largest Steller sea lion rookery in Canada and provide nesting habitat for over 2 million breeding sea birds, including more than half the global population of Cassin's auklets. Although the islands themselves are protected, the waters around them are not, and according to the Canadian

Parks and Wilderness Society, a proposed marine national wildlife area does not adequately ensure marine habitat protection for the islands' wildlife populations.[171]

FISHERIES AND OCEANS CANADA:
A DISMAL TRACK RECORD

The Department of Fisheries and Oceans (DFO) came under early fire from the Office of the Auditor General. In 2005 the commissioner of the environment and sustainable development found that implementing the Oceans Act and subsequent oceans strategy had not been a priority. In focusing on the DFO, the commissioner found a lack of organization, leadership, and guidance, characterized by inaction, randomness, and nontransparency. Performance indicators were not in place and coordination with Environment Canada and Parks Canada was inadequate. More significantly, the commissioner concluded that "Fisheries and Oceans Canada's development and implementation of integrated management and marine protected areas have lacked focus and fallen far short of meeting commitments and targets."[172] Although the DFO promised to do better, it failed. Two years later, a research-based academic article equated the DFO's unwillingness to list commercially valuable at-risk fish with "a reluctance to accept the additional stewardship responsibilities required by SARA."[173]

The DFO's less than stellar reputation as a steward of species at risk came under later fire from the scientific community. In February 2012 an expert panel that included nine university professors released a detailed assessment of Canada's marine diversity. Published under the auspices of the Royal Society of Canada, the 316-page report was not kind to the DFO, lambasting it for "the absolute discretion afforded to the Minister" and for a lack of stewardship in not completing the promised national network of marine protected areas.[174] The report condemned prevailing mentalities that perceived fish and other exploited marine organisms as commodities rather than as integral biological components of ecosystems, and in a telling comment, it accused the DFO of identifying "its 'clients,' 'partners,' and 'stakeholders' as members of the fishing industry rather than the Canadian public."[175] The report hammered the Species at Risk Act for failing to provide an effective legislative mechanism for the protection, conservation, and recovery of marine species at risk and felt that the Fisheries Act (1985) was unequal to the task of protecting marine diversity and required extensive revision or replacement.[176]

The Nooksack Dace

A specific example of this lack of stewardship concerns the Nooksack dace, an endangered small minnow found in shallow water on riffles and sandbars in four lower mainland streams in British Columbia. The Nooksack dace is an indicator species whose health signals the abundance of salmon and other species. They require oxygen-rich water and are thus very susceptible to threats posed by agricultural runoff, sediment deposits, disruptions or changes in stream flow and levels, and toxins. The number of Nooksack dace is unknown, but it seems that they are virtually extirpated in two of the four streams. One research study estimated about 7,000 altogether, well below recovery target numbers, and steadily declining.[177]

The Nooksack dace was listed as "endangered" under the Species at Risk Act in 2003, and a draft of the mandatory recovery plan was completed by a well-qualified scientific team and submitted to the DFO in 2005. Consistent with SARA's requirements, the draft included detailed descriptions and maps of critical habitat. Yet a year later, without consulting any of the recovery-draft team, the DFO posted the draft on the public registry but without the descriptions and maps of critical habitat or the details on activities likely to result in the species' extinction.[178] Despite attempts by the plan's authors to have the crucial elements reinstated, the DFO chose to violate SARA requirements by releasing its 2007 recovery strategy minus the crucial maps and descriptions of critical habitat. The strategy admitted unapologetically that critical habitat for Nooksack dace had not been mapped or specifically defined.[179] Its reason became clear in another telling statement. In a veiled reference to the Nooksack dace's limited nonmarket value, the strategy affirmed that "a quantity of proposed critical habitat sufficient to ensure the survival and recovery of the species will be designated through the action planning process, which will include socioeconomic analysis and consultation with affected interests."[180] Clearly, the DFO either agreed with or was reluctant to confront the private landowners whose interests would be compromised by costly measures affecting drainage facilities, waterline activities, and channelling operations for the benefit of a tiny fish who very few knew or cared about.

In August 2007, a month after the recovery strategy was released, several environmental groups began legal proceedings against the DFO on the grounds that SARA provisions respecting critical habitat identification had not been followed in the recovery strategy. Among the affidavits filed by Ecojustice were three by former members of the team that had prepared the draft plan in 2005.[181] The DFO unsuccessfully tried to derail the challenge by blocking the evidence contained in the incriminating affidavits and by trying to bypass SARA via a protection statement based on provisions in the Fisheries Act.[182] In a final unsuccessful attempt to avoid litigation, the DFO revised the strategy to include critical habitat identification.[183]

The judicial review was heard on 9 September 2009. The DFO's arguments about time constraints, lack of peer-reviewed studies, and specifics about critical habitat criteria were to no avail. Instead, the Nooksack dace became the first endangered species in Canada to benefit from a comprehensive legal interpretation of key elements of the Species at Risk Act. Justice Douglas R. Campbell agreed with the applicants that the account of critical habitat in the 2007 recovery strategy was inadequate in not including geospatial location and a description of identifiable features necessary to sustain the species' life processes.[184] He alluded to socio-economic costs and stressed that under the SARA they could not figure in the DFO's decisions at the recovery strategy stage.[185] His overall judgment was scathing: "This is a story about the creation and application of policy by the Minister in clear contravention of the law, and a reluctance to be held accountable for failure to follow the law." It was, he added later in his judgment, "fundamentally inconsistent with the precautionary principle as codified in SARA."[186]

Seven years after this decision, and over a decade removed from the initial recovery strategy, a proposed action plan for the endangered Nooksack dace was completed in late 2016 when the species were paired with the Salish sucker.[187] The plan stressed stewardship measures and was heavily reliant on voluntary cooperation from private landowners and other stakeholders, with voluntary activity and stewardship being mentioned sixty-two times in the twenty-two-page plan. Yet, according to the plan, both fish needed to wait another three years before measures would be taken to address hypoxia (oxygen deficiency), habitat fragmentation, sediment deposition, and toxicity through incentive programs and persuasive dialogue with landowners. Matters of financial compensation were not discussed, nor was the plan confident that recovery actions to maintain Nooksack dace populations would even be beneficial.[188]

Official attitudes toward the Nooksack dace – and toward the greater sage-grouse and the woodland caribou, for that matter – invite speculation that extirpation might be acceptable given socio-economic and other human considerations if the species in question is not at risk elsewhere. If so, the optional removal of a species from a habitat in which it is a contributing member represents a serious undermining of the overriding intent of the biodiversity strategy.

The Northeast Pacific's Northern and Southern Resident Killer Whales

The issue of critical habitat and protection also emerged in the recovery strategies for killer whales off the BC coast. Here, repeated attempts by the DFO to use ministerial discretionary provisions under the Fisheries Act in order to avoid following stricter SARA requirements for protecting critical habitat provide a further example of delinquent stewardship. It fell to the courts yet again to clarify the legal picture for the DFO in a case concerning the northeast Pacific's threatened northern and endangered southern resident populations of killer whales. Mindful of the importance of shipping activity in waters inhabited by the whales, the DFO sought to bypass SARA's strict provisions respecting legal obligations to protect critical habitat in favour of ministerial discretion in existing legislation, primarily the Fisheries Act. Arguably, the victory achieved with the 2002 enactment of SARA was more symbolic than real.

Killer whales are cosmopolitan mammals who generally concentrate in colder regions and in areas of high prey availability. In British Columbia, where they are classified loosely as transient or resident, they have been recorded in virtually all salt water areas, including many long inlets, narrow channels, and deep bays. Resident killer whales feed on fish, and their distribution is closely tied to peak abundance of various species of salmon, primarily Chinook. The two populations of resident killer whales, northern and southern, are small and have low potential rates of increase. The southern resident population has been growing only sporadically and is smaller now than in the 1960s. Slow increases were recorded following the cessation of live capture in 1973. Only 89 individuals were counted in 1998, 83 in 1999, 82 in 2000, and 78 in 2001. This population has declined by 20 per cent over the past six years and now faces extirpation.

Reminiscent of the Nooksack dace, critical habitat identification for the two populations was made by a team of scientists in 2004. This information was removed from the team's recovery plan by the DFO and then, upon pressure from the scientists, reinstated and subsequently edited and modified before being released in March 2008. This recovery plan admitted to an incomplete understanding of critical habitat and identified it specifically by geophysical surveys, or location, only.[189] On 10 September 2008, instead of fulfilling its obligation under SARA to release a direct protection order stating how the whales' critical habitat would be legally protected, the DFO chose to issue a protection statement outlining how critical habitat was already protected under existing legislation.[190] Faced with pending legal action, the DFO later reversed itself and, without going through necessary consultative channels, issued the required protection order on 23 February 2009, which gave only broad locational descriptions of sixty-two critical habitat areas.[191]

Eight environment groups applied for a judicial review, challenging both the protection statement and the protection order, the former for its reliance on nonbinding policy, existing legislation, and ministerial discretion and the latter for not including biological elements of critical habitat.[192] In December 2010 federal justice James Russell ruled that the DFO had erred in law in determining the whales' critical habitat was already protected by existing laws and that it was unlawful for the minister to have cited discretionary provisions of the Fisheries Act in the protection statement.[193] With respect to the protection order, Justice Russell found that it was unlawful for the DFO and Environment Canada, the latter included through Parks Canada, "to exclude the ecosystem features of Resident Killer Whales' critical habitat, including availability of prey and acoustic and environmental factors."[194]

Subsequent to these decisions, the DFO prepared another recovery strategy in 2011. It was identical to that of 2008, except for the reference to the February 2009 protection order and a footnoted explanation informing readers that the attributes of critical habitat noted in the 2008 version – geophysical disturbance, acoustic degradation, biological and chemical contaminants, and diminished prey availability – "are in fact a part of critical habitat."[195] However, the above "attributes" referred to in 2008 appeared not as attributes at all but as "activities likely to result in destruction of critical habitat" and its function.[196] This resort to semantics simply reinforces the fact that the DFO, satisfied with managing critical habitat by location only, did not take the time and energy to ensure that said critical habitat contained the biological integrity necessary to the whales' survival.

The above conclusion was reinforced in the DFO's response to Justice Russell's decision on ministerial discretion. In 2011 it launched an appeal, contending that the minister should be allowed to exercise his discretion based on the greater effectiveness afforded by the close alignment of his duties under both SARA and the Fisheries Act.[197] In dismissing the appeal on 9 February 2012, the Federal Court of Appeal ruled that the DFO is bound by SARA for the legal protection of critical habitat both in terms of location and in terms of the measures to guard its biological integrity. Speaking for the court, Justice Robert Mainville ruled, "This Court should not approve the substitution of the non-discretionary and compulsory critical habitat protection scheme of section 58 of the SARA by the discretionary fisheries management scheme established under the *Fisheries Act* and its regulations."[198] In other words, under SARA, killer whale critical habitat must be protected legally through protection orders that both identify location and ensure food source availability, acoustic integrity, and attention to biological contaminants and other disturbances.

Two years later, in March 2014, over a decade after the first recovery strategy was released, the first draft of an action plan was issued for the endangered southern resident killer whale and the threatened northern resident killer whale. It was less than impressive. In fact, it was a defensive plan whose impacts on a dangerously threatened species were admitted to be "unknown" and only "likely positive," although it was emphasized that recovery measures "may result in positive benefits to Canadians."[199] The plan's commitment to action mainly devolved on management undertakings geared toward a future safer habitat overall. Specific tangible measures to ensure immediate protection were lacking or tentative. The most pertinent called upon managers to "investigate strategic fishery closures as a possible tool to reduce Resident Killer Whale prey competition" and to "consider area-specific boating regimes (speed restrictions, restricted whale watching hours) to reduce acoustic impact as well as collisions."[200] Neither gave confidence of concerted action that would put the interests of the whales upfront.

A comprehensive analysis of the plan, submitted directly to the DFO by four environmental groups with the assistance of Ecojustice, found that it lacked "clear, concrete measures to address, mitigate and prevent identified threats" and that it was "often silent on key threats identified in the very Recovery Strategy that it is intended to implement."[201] The analysis referred to a lack of details on the specific actions to be taken regarding control of contaminants, prey-availability management, threats from shipping, and acoustic pollution. Noting that the DFO had not consulted with relevant nongovernmental groups, the authors underscored SARA's disconnect from potential supportive agencies in requesting that the DFO "prepare the Action Plan in cooperation with our organizations," which "have significant expertise with Resident Killer Whale conservation and recovery, and have access to legal expertise."[202] One doubts that their overtures were heeded.

The legal issues regarding the killer whales asserted the supremacy of SARA over existing legislation in matters involving the critical habitats of listed endangered and threatened species, and they implied that the DFO was more interested in protecting interests other than those of the whales. Yet little changed. True, the DFO must take action to protect the biological components of the whales' critical habitat. However, these measures are unfolding through the same mechanisms as would have been employed under the original protection statement, and since many derive their authority from the Fisheries Act, with its wide ministerial discretions, one wonders how much the intent of SARA is being honoured. SARA's weak compliance provisions and a general reluctance to enforce them do not improve matters.

CHANGES TO THE FISHERIES ACT

These adverse legal decisions doubtless were among the factors that led the DFO to strengthen its human-centred position by amending the Fisheries Act. Passed in 1985, the act empowered the DFO to directly protect fish and habitat in what constituted a blanket statement affecting all marine species and habitats. However, it also granted excessive ministerial discretion and did not provide sufficient details on habitat protection. According to Ecojustice, the Fisheries Act, being loosely enforced, had demanded little compliance. Yet, rather than heed the wake-up call and strengthen an act that at least recognized the integrity of all marine species, the DFO decided to do the exact opposite, and it did so without public consultation and against the expressed opinions of over 600 scientists and four former DFO ministers.[203] In the spring of 2012, amendments with crucial negative implications for marine diversity were inserted into the Fisheries Act via the controversial Bill C-38, a 425-page legislative behemoth that mocked the principles of democratic debate and process.[204]

Amid other provisions, the amendment changed section 35(1) from "No person shall carry on any work, undertaking or activity that results in the harmful alteration or disruption, or the destruction, of fish habitat" to "No person shall carry on any work, undertaking or activity that results in serious harm to fish that are part of a commercial, recreational or Aboriginal fishery, or to fish that support such a fishery."[205] In other words, most noncommercial fish and marine life and habitat in other areas were subject to no protection at all. In an off-the-cuff statement, DFO minister Keith Ashfield wrote that this only meant drawing a distinction between "vital waterways that support Canada's fisheries, and water bodies such as ditches and agricultural channels."[206] This unprofessional levity was countered by University of Calgary biologist John Post, who warned about the amendment's potential to eviscerate the ability to protect habitat for most of the country's fish species.[207] The provision was followed by subsequent stipulations that allowed the minister extreme latitude to decide what activities and measures constituted serious harm to fish or habitat.[208]

The amendments to the Fisheries Act constituted a blatant statement about the DFO's commitment to human interests over stewardship. In a letter written by Ashfield on 13 June 2012 and published in an article by journalist Mike De Souza, the minister succinctly outlined what the DFO was all about, and it had nothing to do with protecting marine inhabitants or their environments. In a brazen violation of the Canadian Biodiversity Strategy, Ashfield wrote, "The proposed amendments will support Fisheries and Oceans Canada's focus on protection efforts for fish that support fisheries that are of importance to Canadians and the threats to those fisheries ... Regulatory efforts will be directed to those impacts on fish that are part of or support commercial, recreational and Aboriginal fisheries."[209] In 2013 journalist Gloria Galloway referred to documents acquired under freedom of access laws showing that although the DFO had consulted with environmental groups and industry before preparing the amendments, it had heeded the latter to the extent of obtaining the actual wording of the amendment from industry associations.[210] As noted by Andrew Gage of West Coast Environmental Law, one of the environmental groups that were consulted by the DFO before the law was rewritten, "When laws are written to pander to particular industries, Canadians get weak environmental laws, and weak protection for our fish."[211] John Bennett, the executive director of Sierra Club Canada, commented that "the federal government ignored serious advice from environmental organizations and accepted undocumented knee-jerk advice from self-interest industry groups who could not substantiate their complaints."[212]

Scientific criticism was widespread. Fish conservationist Eric Taylor of the University of British Columbia remarked, "The one thing that fish need to persist is a safeguarding of the place they live, and that is no longer an explicit part of the fisheries act."[213] John Smol, an award-winning lake biologist at Queen's University, regarded the proposed changes as unbelievable: "It's a disconnect with science. Minnows are a part of the food chain. So what is an ecologically significant fish?"[214] Another damning indictment of the changes to the Fisheries Act came from Anthony Hutchings and John Post, two biologists who documented the negative implications of the DFO's brazen actions. They were appalled at provisions that essentially legalized the harmful alteration and disruption of fish habitat, putting more than seventy wildlife species of freshwater fish, or 80 per cent, at risk of extinction.[215] They also argued that in selectively favouring some species over others, the DFO violated its own stated objective to adopt an ecosystem approach to sustainable management and was therefore in contravention of the Canadian Biodiversity Strategy. Hutchings and Post also believed that, under the new rules, a downsized DFO had abrogated responsibility by allowing commercial interests to supply their own scientific validations when submitting applications for habitat disturbance projects. Their conclusion states a painful reality: "Politically motivated abrogation of the country's national and international responsibilities to protect fish and fish habitat suggests to us that Canada might no longer be up to the task."[216]

THE PACIFIC HUMPBACK WHALE

The case of the humpback whale off the coast of British Columbia provides an insightful glimpse into the operations of not only the DFO but also SARA and COSEWIC, the powerful, behind-the-scenes scientific body on whose assessments and recommendations the future of Canada's vulnerable species rests. The debates that unfolded between 2011 and 2014 showed unreliability in the assessment process for an at-risk species. With the looming potential of the Enbridge Northern Gateway Pipeline in the background, SARA rejected its own recovery strategy in favour of a dubious COSEWIC assessment.

Humpback whales are living treasures and testaments to the complexities of being. They are highly intelligent, playful, vocal, and acrobatic marine dwellers, reaching lengths of 14 metres and weighing over 40 tonnes. In Canada humpbacks are found on both the east and west coasts. The range of the North Pacific population extends along the full length of the west coast of British Columbia to northwestern Alaska, where they feed on krill and a variety of small schooling fish like herring and sand lance.[217]

The humpbacks were first assessed by COSEWIC in 2003 and designated as "threatened," with a special note being made of their high level of fidelity to feeding grounds, which made it highly improbable for repopulation to occur following extirpation.[218] Particulars on habitat were broad, and they concentrated on delineating breeding and feeding areas. No recovery strategy was put in place, and therefore critical habitat was not defined in detail. Over the next eight years, the only official attention given to the whales' status under SARA concerned a 2011 statement of an upward population estimate for 2004–2006.[219] Then, also in 2011, another COSEWIC assessment recommended downgrading the whales' status to "special concern" based primarily on numbers indicating healthy population growth, even though critical habitat for the whales had never been determined.[220] It was a strange assessment. It admitted that the whales were anything but secure and that the proposed Enbridge Northern Gateway Project posed "a potential threat." The assessment also acknowledged that habitat would continue to be degraded but would be properly identified in the subsequent recovery strategy.[221] In this respect, the wisdom of recommending a downlisting on the assumption that adequate critical habitat was available in spite of ongoing threats flies in the face of the precautionary principle embedded in COSEWIC's mandate.

Under COSEWIC's assessment guidelines, the estimated increase in population arguably might have given sufficient reason to recommend the redesignation. However, the habitat requirements were highly questionable. Under its quantitative criteria, COSEWIC measured the humpback whale's habitat location parameters in terms of threats both serious and otherwise.[222] Since critical habitat had never been identified for the whales in any of the four dominant whale concentration areas, COSEWIC had no habitat yardstick to justify downgrading.[223] Given the absence of any regulatory habitat protection under "special concern" status, one could argue that the precautionary principle should apply. And threats did exist. In a comprehensive three-part brief to the Joint Review Panel for the Enbridge Northern Gateway Project, charged with assessing the pipeline application, the North Coast Cetacean Society documented the crucial importance of Gil Island and how maternal site fidelity in this rich habitat could be destroyed by shipping threats.[224]

The long-awaited recovery strategy, based on the then "threatened" status, was released in September 2013, hastened by knowledge of a pending lawsuit.[225] The strategy reinforced the problems facing the humpback whale. No population estimates were available for BC waters. It echoed comments made in the 2003 COSEWIC assessment on maternal site fidelity. Commenting on the limited interchange between regional feeding areas, the strategy concluded, "This suggests that humpbacks may be very slow to re-colonize areas from which they have been removed and that anthropogenic actions and impacts to foraging habitat could have large effects on the population in B.C., even if activities occur in highly localized areas."[226] The identification of critical habitat focused only on location and acknowledged, "More information is needed on diet composition, prey availability and other habitat features of Humpback Whales in B.C. waters." The strategy further stated, "Clarification of habitat requirements, seasonal use, migratory corridors, and biophysical characteristics of habitat will aid in further identification of critical habitat, and contribute information to determine important biophysical features of critical habitat."[227] The strategy also affirmed that prey abundance and levels of acoustic disturbance in the four critical habitat areas had not been determined and that increased anthropogenic presence in the form of increased ship traffic, potential toxic spills, and overfishing posed additional risks to the whales and their habitat.[228] The strategy expressed moderate concern over prey reduction, toxic spills, and acoustic disturbance and high concern over vessel traffic. With respect to habitat and COSEWIC's adherence to the precautionary principle, this document gave no justification for downgrading the "threatened" status of the Pacific humpback whales.

Yet, in spite of the recovery strategy's cautious tone, SARA confirmed COSEWIC's 2011 recommendation in April 2014 by downgrading the status of the whales to "special concern."[229] The implications of removing the "threatened" status were enormous. As stated in the Species at Risk Act, "If a wildlife species has been classified as an endangered species or a threatened species by a provincial or territorial minister, no person shall destroy any part of the habitat of that species that the provincial or territorial minister has identified as essential to the survival or recovery of the species and that is on federal lands in the province or territory."[230] All the negative impacts outlined and discussed in the recovery strategy were now in play more forcibly and threateningly than ever given the dangers posed by an increasing anthropogenic presence among a vulnerable species. Who was to blame?

For the first time, a COSEWIC assessment and recommendation came under public fire from critics who felt that it had made the wrong decision in 2011.[231] In a letter to the SARA Directorate in May 2014, the Raincoast Conservation Foundation was critical of COSEWIC's scientific reliability and information sources, referring to inadequacies in population assessments, the acceptance of the single population unit, the decline in prey availability, the failure to consider oil projects, and the crucial factor of site fidelity and critical habitat.[232] It had a point. COSEWIC's assessment had acknowledged that "quality of habitat may be declining due to increases in physical and acoustic disturbance, and possible changes in prey distribution and/or abundance."[233] The assessment also affirmed the crucial role of site fidelity but then argued that although habitat quality was being degraded by physical and acoustic disturbance, it was not vital to whale survival since it was the quantity of habitat that mattered, or in other words, the whales just moved elsewhere.[234]

The integrity of the down-grading process itself was questioned. It was suggested that the decision was just too timely, coming only two months before the federal government's Joint Review Panel approved the construction of the controversial Enbridge Northern Gateway Pipeline in June. With the humpback whale listed as a "special concern," the oil-laden tankers passing through Douglas Strait from Kitimat to the Pacific Ocean would not be constrained by the legal habitat protection requirements demanded by the "threatened" designation. According to one critic, the federal government was hiding behind COSEWIC to make a political decision. Another felt that it was odd to reduce protection when the threats to the whales could only increase.[235] According to Ecojustice, "There is uncontroverted expert evidence that the project will create a greater than 50 percent probability that these whales will go extinct in this century."[236] In October 2015 several environmental groups mounted a Federal Court of Appeal challenge, arguing that the federal government had erred in granting approval to the pipeline on the grounds that the Joint Review Panel was in violation of its mandate to review all environmental effects of the project in failing to consult the humpback whale recovery strategy.[237]

The criticisms were countered by arguments that pointed to mitigation plans and to the fact that the whales would simply feed elsewhere.[238] Also stressed was that COSEWIC had recommended the down-listing three years earlier. Others took refuge in COSEWIC's integrity and the fact that specific guidelines were followed.[239] However, the timing does seem more than a little coincidental, particularly given the DFO's less than stellar record in preserving aquatic species, as well as considering the legal decision handed down months earlier that had found the DFO in default with respect to the humpback whale recovery strategy. Indeed, the DFO described the down-listing as "good news."[240] Yet by any cautious standards, COSEWIC had made a poor decision. The humpback whales' "threatened" status should have been retained, regardless of estimated population increases. Existing uncertainties about habitat variables, prey availability, and the added dangers posed by increased shipping traffic through feeding areas should have been enough to stay COSEWIC's hand.

But the criticism of COSEWIC went deeper. Two environmental groups raised the question of bias in the COSEWIC assessment of 2011, arguing that its author had connections to the oil and gas industry and lacked experience, contentions hotly denied by scientists with connections to COSEWIC and the author.[241] Yet the issue of bias, unfounded or otherwise, had nothing to do with the author.[242] The assessment was clearly inadequate overall, especially with respect to detailed critical habitat factors. The precautionary principle should have prompted COSEWIC to follow accepted practice and seek more detail. Moreover, the possibility that this widely respected body could be occasionally remiss in its deliberations concerning at-risk species is disquieting. In this case, it determined that humpback whales were in a recovery mode based primarily on population indices. Given the present and potential threats they are facing, the lack of conclusiveness about prey availability, and the implications of disturbance in fragmented habitats characterized by maternal site fidelity, COSEWIC's conclusions about the humpback whales' security were problematic.[243] The whales may be recovering, but they have not recovered. COSEWIC appears to believe that the "special concern" status, coupled with a speedily prepared management plan that does nothing more than monitor population trends, will grant the whales sufficient protection. If so, it has opted for a dismal approach.

The DFO has a record for giving human interests clear priority over the marine species in its charge. A report on ecosystem status released by the federal, provincial, and territorial governments in 2010 reached a bleak conclusion about marine species. Almost 20 per cent of Canada's freshwater fish were either endangered or threatened, and the decline in fisheries overall was significant.[244] Both outcomes were due primarily to anthropogenic disturbances. Between 2003 and 2013 COSEWIC's listings for endangered fish increased alarmingly from sixteen to fifty-seven. Even SARA's listings more than doubled to twenty-seven. Still, the fact that this figure is less than half of COSEWIC's should tell us something about the way that the DFO attends to its conservation duties. These high numbers are going to continue, especially given global warming and its implications for ocean acidification. That the DFO intends to stay the course and wave the human-interest banner over Canadian oceans, lakes, and rivers comes through loud and clear in its vision statement: "To advance sustainable aquatic ecosystems and support safe and secure Canadian waters while fostering economic prosperity across maritime sectors and fisheries."[245] Under this human-centred mantra, commercially exploited fish face an uncertain future, and lesser souls like the little Nooksack dace do not stand a chance.

Protected Areas

There's nothing to fear and much to gain by being open
to deep and reciprocal interactions with other animals.
MARC BEKOFF

Like all countries, Canada is committed to the establishment and oversight
of protected areas, both independently and as a mandated component
of the United Nations Convention on Biological Diversity (1992).[1] In its
Protected Areas Strategy (2011), Environment Canada seems clear enough
in stating the obvious: "Protection of wildlife and its habitat is the primary
purpose of a protected area. All activities on protected areas, on the land or
at sea, have to be considered within this priority." Furthermore, in giving
itself a pat on the back, Environment Canada seems equally transparent
about its intentions: "Environment Canada's protected areas are unique
because they are specifically designated and managed to protect wildlife and their habitat. This may include interventions such as habitat
restoration, especially for species at risk."[2] If they could communicate
with humans and were unaware of the belief system, cougars, bears,
moose, ducks, deer, and pretty well every other wild creature would nod
approvingly at the above. Sadly, they would be wrong.

An essential element of the Canadian Biodiversity Strategy (1995),[3]
protected areas in Canada are designated and managed by the federal,
provincial, and territorial governments, while differing widely in name
and scope. Both terrestrial and marine, they include parks, wilderness,
natural wildlife areas, ecological reserves, conservancies, sanctuaries, and
marine and other reserves. They exist ostensibly to preserve ecosystems,

wildlife, and the biodiversity they represent. Although seemingly mindful of this need, the framers of Canada's policies of protection are remiss.

The fate of many wild creatures in the vast majority of protected areas reflects the minor place of wildlife in the dominant belief system. The concept of protected areas for biodiversity and wildlife seems simple enough: they are places that offer protection from human intrusion so that ecological systems can play out their rhythms and wild animals can be free from fear of humans. Not surprisingly, Canadian governments have a very different and limited working definition of "protection." Rather than excluding humans from protected areas, Canadian policy, at best, mandates a limited form of restraint. It is very rare to find wildlife protected from hostile human intent in Canada's protected areas. It seems that the belief system just will not allow it.

Although protected areas may be designed to conserve species and biodiversity, they are not meant to shield wild animals or all ecosystems from harm. Therefore, like almost every other government initiative respecting stewardship over the land and its living components, the human-interest element is paramount in protected areas policy.

The designation of marine protected areas is a fitting example of the human-centred priorities that dominate decisions about biodiversity and species conservation. The National Framework for Canada's Network of Marine Protected Areas (2011),[4] which followed a 2005 predecessor,[5] took two years to prepare and presented itself in cutting-edge terms as providing "strategic direction for establishment of a national network of marine protected areas that conforms to international best practices and helps to achieve broader conservation and sustainable development objectives identified through Integrated Oceans Management and other marine spatial planning processes."[6] Its focus on networks of bioregions was designed "to fulfill ecological aims more effectively and comprehensively than individual sites could alone."[7] In other words, Canada's marine protected areas were to be embodied in networks differentiated by location and, more significantly, by ecological significance.

The human-interest element is seen in the meaning of the term "Integrated Oceans Management." Very much like adaptive management, it accepts an element of uncertainty by referring to "mounting evidence" that networks of marine protected areas can "achieve ecological benefits, which can translate into economic, social and cultural benefits."[8] However, this simply means a reliance on a lot of human judgments to decide how much anthropogenic disturbance will be allowed to interfere with a natural marine biotic community.

The 2011 framework therefore followed predictable lines. After admitting that "human use considerations come into play in the context of Integrated Oceans Management," the framework announced, "In planning a new [marine protected area], it will be configured and sited to accommodate socio-economic considerations to the extent possible without jeopardizing achievement of the conservation goal(s)."[9] While acknowledging that there may be areas where the ecological importance will outweigh socio-economic considerations, the framework added that "there may be areas of such high socio-economic significance that they are deemed inappropriate for setting aside as marine protected areas by decision-makers."[10] Two disturbing points arise from these rationalizations. First, the framework is discretionary, being based on essentially subjective determinations, ostensibly linked to scientific opinion. Second, and more worrying, ecological integrity and preservation are not stand-alone factors in delineating a marine protected area. The following statement in the Canada–British Columbia Marine Protected Area Network Strategy (2014) shows where its priorities lie: "Marine protected areas are public investments. The importance of such investments [is] determined and maintained by the benefits they provide and how they are valued by the public. [Marine protected areas] that offer a variety of recreational activities and learning experiences facilitate a personal connection between protected places and the people who visit them."[11]

Thus the term "protected areas" is misleading both in its definition and in its relationship to overall ecosystems. Protected areas in Canada protect wildlife far less than the term implies. Arguably, species are not safe in all protected areas. Unarguably, individual animals are victims of either human disturbance or lethal intent in the vast majority of protected areas. Furthermore, all protected areas are not representative of the entire range of flora and fauna typical of the region, and being surrounded by unprotected areas, they are indirectly impacted by anthropogenic disturbance.

The notion of protected natural areas is not new, dating back two millennia to sites in India. Although some early protected areas were sacred sites, the most common precedents were the hunting reserves of the Renaissance period. Later incentives for protected areas were inspired by the beauty of nature and the preservation of native flora, fauna, or significant natural features. Today, although protected areas may be established for natural, heritage, or other cultural reasons, the primary motive behind their existence is the need to preserve biodiversity. Protected areas globally and certainly in Canada vary greatly in size and function, but very few do not encourage an exploitive human presence.

Although Canada's interest in protected areas dates to the early twentieth century, a modern focus emerged in 1982 when the Canadian Council on Ecological Areas was established to encourage and facilitate the establishment and use of a comprehensive network of protected areas representative of Canada's terrestrial and aquatic diversity. In 1992 the United Nations Convention on Biological Diversity called for each participating country to establish "a system of protected areas or areas where special measures need to be taken to conserve biological diversity."[12] In 1995 Canada responded by promising to "make every effort to complete" its networks of terrestrial protected areas and to speed up the acquisition of marine protected areas.[13] A decade later, the Federal Marine Protected Areas Strategy (2005) was released, calling for immediate action to safeguard marine areas.[14] In 2011 Environment Canada produced its Protected Areas Strategy, in which it advertised itself as possessing the "flexibility needed to evolve and adapt the network in an ever changing ecological context."[15] Although the strategy stressed an intent to protect species, habitat, and diversity, it did not mention any need to exclude the human presence. In fact, the closest it came was a reference to an updated policy respecting "the permitting of activities."[16] In 2016, in announcing its new biodiversity goals and targets, Environment Canada told Canadians that by 2020 at least 17 per cent of terrestrial and 10 per cent of marine areas would be under some form of official protection.[17]

From a limited perspective, Canada has gone part of the way. Between 1990 and 2016 the amount of land and freshwater under some form of protection increased from 547,905 to 1,024,930 square kilometres, of which around half was under federal jurisdiction. The total protected land doubled from 5.5 to 10.3 per cent of Canada's area. These protected designations also fell within the management categories outlined by the

International Union for the Conservation of Nature. In the same period, marine protected areas also increased by 60 per cent.[18]

However, these positive statistics are misleading. Canadian protected areas do not measure up to global expectations. They are represented disproportionally in Canadian ecosystems. The term "protected areas" is interpreted so broadly and diffusely that respect for wildlife and their habitats is compromised. Intrusive activity, fringe interference, uncertainty of status, discretionary powers, and inadequate funding all militate against the well-being of wild creatures in protected areas. Ecologist Larry Harris underscores issues in the selection of protected areas: "Existing reserves have been selected according to a number of criteria, including the desire to protect nature, scenery, and watersheds, and to promote cultural values and recreational opportunities. The actual requirements of individual species, populations, and communities have seldom been known, nor has the available information always been employed in site selection and planning for nature reserves."[19]

In fact, even as it proclaims otherwise, Canadian officialdom might be less than confident in the future of protected areas. As the leading agency directing the disposition and management of Canada's federally protected areas, Environment Canada seemed somewhat tentative in its 2011 Protected Areas Strategy. The foreword referred to the widening disconnect between rising expectations and Environment Canada's capacity to meet them.[20] In fact, the strategy hinted at underlying tensions in offering this guarded appeal to the public: "Faced with competing economic interests, governments will be supportive of protected areas if the public understands their importance to society."[21] The strategy also warned of demands primarily from the resource sector that were stretching national ecosystems to the limit and threatening to intrude further into protected areas.[22] When one considers the federal government's 2020 Biodiversity Goals and Targets (2016),[23] these comments are scarcely reassuring, which may explain why the goals were stated so broadly and why there were no specifics as to how targets would be achieved or measured over time.

An evaluation by World Wildlife Fund Canada of the degree to which different types of landscapes are represented within protected areas showed that almost all areas were seriously deficient in protecting the full range of habitats and species.[24] In terms of protected terrestrial areas, Canada is below the global average by almost 3.5 per cent and more than 6 per cent lower than the United States.[25] Statistics Canada reports that Canada ranks 111th out of 201 countries reporting terrestrial areas under protection.[26] With 1.3 per cent of its marine areas under protection, Canada ranks last among countries with extensive coastlines and is dwarfed by the United States and Australia, which have set aside 30.4 and 33.2 per cent respectively of their ocean estates for marine protected areas.[27] Moreover, Canadian statistics on protected areas include those under interim protection even though they may or may not achieve legal protected status. A report published by Global Forest Watch Canada indicated that around 30 per cent of Canada's protected lands were under the uncertainty of interim protection in 2010.[28]

Protected areas do not adequately protect endangered species or bio-diversity according to a study by two University of Ottawa biologists who found less wildlife richness and fewer endangered species in northern eco-zones like the Taiga Shield and Boreal Cordillera compared to the habitat-richer but seriously degraded Mixedwood Plains.[29] Thus, even recognizing that it is challenging to secure protected areas in more popu-lous and prosperous regions and acknowledging the federal government's positive initiatives in encouraging conservation easements on private land, one must conclude that the nation's protected areas network is highly skewed toward regions with limited capacity to provide diverse wildlife habitat. For instance, in the wildlife-rich Niagara Escarpment, of which less than 3 per cent is under protection, acquisition of protected areas is severely compromised by lack of funding.[30] More than half of Canada's eco-zones have less than 10 per cent protection, and two out of every three of Canada's primary drainage basins have less than 5 per cent of their areas secured for protection.[31] Almost 40 per cent of the total area under protection in Canada is in Nunavut, the Northwest Territories, and the Yukon.[32] Less than 10 per cent of Canada's fertile eco-zones have protected designations, and around 70 per cent of the total land and freshwater in eco-zones nationwide are in arctic designations and mountain areas.[33] Of the 1 million hectares protected in national wildlife areas, 900,000 hectares are in Nunavut, and only one new area has been established in the ten provinces since 1995.[34] Canadian jurisdictions do not advertise these anomalies to their constituents when they stress the role of protected areas in enhancing wildlife and biodiversity.

The word "protected" is used in a variety of contexts and with various meanings. When one refers to wildlife and biodiversity, the definition seems simple enough. In a natural setting, they only require protection from humans. And here's the rub. Almost all Canadian protected areas allow some form of human encroachment. In short, the vast majority, if not all, of Canadian protected areas do not shield wildlife from unfriendly human intent. Human intrusion occurs in almost all protected areas, and in approximately 60 per cent of terrestrial protected areas, anthropogenic disturbance impacts over 25 per cent of their eco-zones.[35] Even strong proponents of protected natural areas accept some measure of human activity. The Canadian Parks and Wilderness Society, for example, has long advocated protection of the Castle area in southwest Alberta but is also in favour of what it terms "low-impact recreation."[36]

Although federal wildlife areas and migratory bird sanctuaries prohibit hunting or fishing, permits may be granted for activities that contribute to the conservation of wildlife, which can mean hunting if deemed necessary. Nature Canada reported in December 2011 that a loose permitting system had meant that only 14 per cent of Environment Canada's protected areas were immune to subsurface resource development threats.[37] For example, at the Kendall Island Migratory Bird Sanctuary in the Northwest Territories, subsurface natural gas extraction was permitted despite an environmental assessment.[38] Federal wildlife regulations also provide ministerial discretion to allow hunting or fishing in national wildlife areas.[39] Migratory game birds are hunted in Cap Tourmente National Wildlife Area.[40] Northern habitat and wildlife management plans allow for hunting by nonresidents.[41] Intrusive ecotourism and sport fishing are encouraged in some marine protected areas.[42]

Provincial protected areas afford limited protection for wildlife. In Duck Mountain Provincial Park in Manitoba, 61 per cent of the park is given over to logging.[43] Logging also occurs in British Columbia's wildlife habitat areas. In 2014 the Canadian Parks and Wilderness Society expressed fears over the long-range implications of legislation in the province that allowed industrial research in parks.[44] Proposed pipelines for liquefied natural gas will traverse at least two protected areas in northern

British Columbia, and another twenty-eight parks and protected areas are located within 10 kilometres of their route.[45] Hunting is allowed in provincial parks, and grizzly bears have been killed in sixty of them, including 231 in three parks alone.[46] In the province's southeast, two provincial parks, Height of the Rockies and Elk Lakes, allow hunters to kill mountain goats, bighorn sheep, elk, moose, mule, white-tailed deer, and grizzly bears as part of their attractions. Sport fishing is allowed in Nova Scotia's wilderness areas. Trapping is allowed in provincial parks in Saskatchewan "as a resource management tool."[47] Oil and gas development is undertaken in Moose Mountain Park in Saskatchewan, and mining activity is present in protected regions in the Yukon and Quebec.

Alberta allows oil and gas exploration and development in most of its protected areas. The province lists 419 protected areas in eight categories totalling around 2.7 million hectares, over 2 million of which are in thirty-three wildland parks where off-highway vehicles disturb mountain goats and other wildlife and where big game hunting, fishing, trapping, and other recreational uses are allowed. Another 300,000 hectares are given over to sixty-nine provincial parks and 248 recreational areas where a human presence and infrastructure are encouraged and where some hunting and trapping are allowed. Only two areas restrict human intrusion. These sixteen ecological reserves and two wilderness areas comprise only 130,000 hectares, or about 5 per cent of the total. Trapping is common in Alberta's protected areas. A government directive in 2003 instructed managers in wildland parks, provincial parks, provincial recreation areas, natural areas, and heritage rangelands to permit trapping if all or part of a registered fur management area lay within their boundaries.[48] A paper published in 2002 contended that forestry roads and clear-cutting activities in Alberta's boreal forests would impact the province's ability to design a protected areas network.[49]

The Province of Ontario classifies its protected areas broadly into 654 regulated provincial parks, conservation reserves, and wilderness areas totalling over 9 million hectares. All are amenable to human activities. Only 22 per cent of Algonquin Provincial Park's 7,851 square kilometres is actually protected. Forestry management activities are allowed there as well as in certain other parks.[50] Hunting occurs in 433 protected designations, including in all 292 conservation areas and in all 11 wilderness areas.[51] Trapping is allowed in 532 of the 654 protected areas and ranges across 7.8 million hectares, or 80 per cent, of all areas under protection.[52] Sport fishing occurs in provincial parks and conservation areas, and concern is being expressed over its pressure on almost 40 per cent of lakes under protection. Additionally, surveys have shown that camping, hiking, all-terrain vehicles, and boating are undermining ecological integrity.[53] Newfoundland and Labrador has about 6,500 square kilometres under provincial protection, of which wilderness and wildlife reserves take up over 5,200 square kilometres. Hunting and fishing are allowed in both. They are also conditionally permitted in ecological reserves. Mineral exploration is allowed in the province's 1,350 square kilometres of wildlife and public reserves.[54]

Most provincial and federal protected areas recognize Aboriginal rights to hunt and fish. Aboriginals have the same privileges in most federal areas, including twenty national parks established after 1982, and in northern areas under comprehensive land claims. In July 2013 Saskatchewan designated a new protected area in the provincial boreal forest. The Pink Lake Representative Area Ecological Reserve, at 3,660 square kilometres, is Saskatchewan's largest provincially designated protected area and was proposed as part of the Misinipiy Integrated Land Use Plan (2012),[55] which was developed in partnership with the Lac La Ronge Indian Band and with extensive public and stakeholder involvement. In addition to allowing hunting and trapping by First Nations and Métis people, recreational hunting and angling will be encouraged.[56]

In the Yukon, Northwest Territories, and Nunavut, although protected area strategies are completed or underway, there is no doubt that wildlife will continue to be exploited. For example, the Committee on the Status of Endangered Wildlife in Canada has noted that in Nunavut vulnerable narwhals are hunted even in protected areas.[57] Although whale hunting is prohibited in Canadian waters, Inuit in Nunavut are allowed an annual take of three bowhead whales, a species listed by the committee. When Fisheries and Oceans Canada consulted Aboriginal groups in 2009 about marine protected areas, Inuit expressed concerns about retaining their right to hunt, fish, and trap wildlife, including polar bears and whales, in proposed marine sanctuaries.[58] A series of case studies conducted by the Canadian Parks Council on protected areas showed that Aboriginals perceived them as both cultural resources and opportunities for tourism.[59] The link between protected areas, Aboriginal cultural survival, and the economic use of wildlife was also noted in a 2003 research report: "Ensuring that these areas are protected for ecological, educational, scientific, economic, cultural and spiritual benefits continues to be of paramount importance to Aboriginal Peoples."[60]

Ironically, the most fundamental problem with protected areas lies in their isolation. Surrounding land use affects protected areas through the flow of polluted waters and through air-borne toxic contaminants from industry, urbanization, and agriculture. When these impacts are combined with further fragmentation in protected areas occasioned by roads and other infrastructure, wildlife health is severely compromised and even more so in the 10-kilometre buffers that surround them.[61] According to Harris, "The use of lands surrounding nature reserves has typically been inimical to conservation, since it has usually involved heavy use of pesticides, industrial development, and the presence of human settlements in which fire, hunting, and firewood gathering feature as elements of the local economy."[62] A 2004 study on Canadian national parks concluded that a lack of suitable habitat area within a 50-kilometre radius from park boundaries was a factor in the loss of disturbance-sensitive mammals.[63]

THE REWILDING MOVEMENT

Surrounded and nurtured by human activity, protected areas appear as fragmented patchworks where the parts do not complement the whole and where the effectiveness of ecological processes is inevitably undermined. The modern rewilding movement represents a holistic view of protected areas and a revisionary view of wilderness.[64] Sometimes referred to as the "shifting baseline" syndrome, this view suggests that any historic visual or descriptive record of landscape is but a snapshot in time. Because there is no fixed state of nature and because humans have always been active or passive change agents, the true wilderness condition is closest to evolutionary unfolding. The original definition of "rewilding" in the 1990s referred to "large-scale conservation committed [to] restoring and protecting natural processes and states in core wilderness areas, providing

effective connectivity between such areas, and protecting or reintroducing apex predators and other keystone species."[65] Despite the different
approaches to rewilding, a common feature is the belief that natural processes are superior to active human management in meeting conservation
goals and objectives and in adjusting to environmental change.

Rewilding is a novel, bold, modern conservation approach that is
slowly gaining in popularity and acceptance. However, as with other
new approaches, its application is open to many variables and schools
of ecological thought. As viewed by author J.B. MacKinnon, "Rewilding
really can be as straightforward as putting up a birdhouse" and can mean
any activity that involves a perceived respect for restoring natural forces.[66]
For example, rewilding has been used to describe rooftop gardens, bringing nature into cities, drawing salmon back to Burrard Inlet estuaries in
British Columbia, and the stabilization of shoreline areas in Lake Simcoe
in Ontario.[67] On a larger, more focused level, several global initiatives are
underway. The Rewilding Europe project aims to create ten rewilded areas
totalling 1 million hectares by 2022. In Pleistocene Park in Russia, five
large herbivores – bison, musk ox, moose, horses, and reindeer – have
been reintroduced to turn 160 square kilometres of the Siberian taiga
into the grassy meadows that existed there 10,000 years ago. Plans are to
reintroduce the Siberian tiger once the herds have become established.[68]
Oostvaardersplassen in the Netherlands is a former drainage area of 60
square kilometres now stocked with animals similar to long-extirpated
originals.[69] These replacements – Heck cattle, red deer, and wild horses
– have attracted foxes, buzzards, herons, eagles, and migratory birds.[70]

The most topical application of rewilding is trophic rewilding, which
involves the reintroduction of apex predators to a large area where they
have been extirpated. As indicated, trophic rewilding must meet three
demands: the presence of core areas, connectivity between them, and
mobile and wide-ranging apex carnivores. Research has demonstrated
how large carnivores as umbrella species exert disproportionate levels of
top-down regulation of other components in the ecosystem.[71] According
to conservation biologists Michael Soulé and Reed Noss, "Once large
predators are restored, many if not most of the other keystone and 'habitat-
creating' species (e.g., beavers, prairie dogs), 'keystone ecosystems,'
and natural regimes of disturbance and other processes will recover on

their own."[72] The best North American example is the reintroduction of the wolf to Yellowstone National Park, which achieved species balance while improving riparian areas, wetland and stream health, and tree and shrub growth. To achieve wider goals, at least in North America, human tolerance of these big predators is necessary, as is acceptance of unimpaired protected areas. The ongoing North American Yellowstone to Yukon Conservation Initiative, launched in 1993, is an ambitious multi-stakeholder and multi-layered project that is attempting to replicate the three demands of trophic rewilding in a corridor of more than 3,000 kilometres of protected areas that, unimpaired by human contact, link the Yukon with Yellowstone National Park.[73] If it succeeds as envisaged, this initiative will make North America's most powerful statement yet about the value of wildlife and the willingness to pay a significant price to sustain them.

Other variations include passive rewilding, which involves restoring natural ecosystem processes by reducing human control of landscapes.[74] Current interest in relocating the American bison to public lands is a good case in point. Pleistocene rewilding, which aims to restore some of the evolutionary and ecological potential that was lost 13,000 years ago, involves the reintroduction of relatives, or proxies, of long-extinct ancestors who once roamed the prairies of North America.[75] These might include large herbivores such as the elephant or a scavenger species like the spotted hyena.[76] In contrast, translocational rewilding seeks to restore missing or dysfunctional ecological processes by means of an extant species. The aforementioned wolves in Yellowstone qualify as an example, even though they were returned rather than introduced.

Trophic rewilding has not yet taken hold in Canada, possibly because at the present time enough wilderness landscapes exist in the West for apex predators to dominate – but for how long? Conversely, in areas where apex predators have been extirpated, there is simply not enough land or social will to sustain them. For example, if the federal government was willing to protect black-tailed prairie dogs on community pastures and if the rural hostility toward them could be allayed, the reintroduction of the black-footed ferret could re-create a predator-prey balance and result in a successful rewilding experiment. However, it appears that in an age of global warming, the greatest opportunity may exist in more northerly areas, where changing landscapes and ecological conditions are already encouraging a northward movement of grizzly bears and wolves.[77] In this context, experiments like those in Russia have real potential. Also, free-ranging, large herbivores will increase seed-dispersal distances for many plants, thereby increasing the ability of these plants and herbivores to adjust to climate change.[78]

But as several scholars have pointed out, there are many unknowns about the impacts of rewilding. One scientific article states, "The management outputs that rewilding aims to achieve lack quantitative evidence and the focus of rewilding on functions rather than on biological diversity is questionable. The relationship between biodiversity and the multiple functions ecosystems provide has rarely been assessed globally in natural ecosystems."[79] Furthermore, one of the fundamental problems with protected areas remains: rewilded areas will continue to be surrounded by anthropogenic influences. Thus, regardless of the representative nature of ecosystems in the rewilded areas, they will not flourish unless they possess the resilience associated with size, and even that might not be enough. And there is always the belief system to consider. As has been discussed, Canadians do not desire protected areas that are strictly off limits. Furthermore, those living in proximity to trophic rewilding might not be happy with free-roaming predators. As environmental scientists Erwin van Maanen and Ian Convery observe, "It is also important to note that rewilding is context-dependent and not absolute. There are degrees of rewilding, often depending on the natural heritage in place and common societal perceptions on nature, and the shared need to conserve it."[80]

PARKS CANADA AND NATIONAL PARKS

In 2010 the chief executive officer of Parks Canada, Alan Latourelle, commented that "Parks Canada's network of national parks, national historic sites and national marine conservation areas has become symbolic of our national identity and is recognized internationally as the greatest among the great."[81] At a very broad level, he has a point. For the most part, Parks Canada does bask in the warmth of public approval, or at least 85 per cent, if its surveys are accurate. It is also undeniable that Canada's network of national and provincial parks is among the most beautiful, diverse, and popular in the world. Yet in terms of commitment to ecological integrity and its implications for wildlife preservation, the situation is anything but "the greatest among the great."

As far as Canada's network of national parks is concerned, the reason has to do with their mandate. Indeed, it is their very grandeur, beauty, and wild richness that make them a fitting example of the inherent weakness of the Canadian Biodiversity Strategy. The impossibility of accommodating the human presence in biotic communities while preserving their ecological integrity is well illustrated in Canada's national parks. According to section 4 of the National Parks Act (1930), "The Parks of Canada are hereby dedicated to the people of Canada for their benefit, education and enjoyment, subject to this Act and Regulations, and such Parks shall be maintained and made use of so as to leave them unimpaired for the enjoyment of future generations."[82] Over the next eighty-five years, administrators dealt with this issue, opting in the main for the people side of their mandate. The end result is that wildlife are not being protected adequately in Canada's national parks. A 2004 study concluded that size limitations in many parks, when combined with high visitations and ecological isolation, have militated against the viability of populations of wolves, black bears, and grizzly bears. The study also determined that most of Canada's national parks will not be able to guarantee these animals' continued existence.[83] Worse, wildlife have become objects of consumerism and adjuncts to entertainment, much like a major ride at a theme park.

In 2000 the federal government released a damning report on the ecological integrity of Canada's national parks. All but one of the nation's thirty-nine national parks were under stress and suffering loss of ecological integrity. The report noted the disappearance of animal species and their habitats and warned that "if we continue on our current path, we risk losing, for all time, access to the experience of protected nature, the wilderness we so cherish."[84] Although ecological integrity became the first priority for Canadian national parks, a measure that was reflected both in subsequent amendments to the National Parks Act and in the development of a framework of policies, directives, and guidelines, the decline in ecological integrity continued.[85] A 2011 report by Parks Canada admitted that ecological integrity in 41 per cent of national park ecosystems had not been assessed and would not be for several years. The report also found negative trends in ecosystems that had been assessed. More than half were not in good condition, and 43 per cent of those assessed as fair were actually deteriorating. Parks Canada also found similar negative trends in the ecosystems assessed as both good and poor.[86] In 2013 an audit by the commissioner of the environment and sustainable development expressed concern that Parks Canada was failing to meet deadlines and targets, that information for decision making was often incomplete or absent, and that a significant risk existed for Parks Canada to fall further behind in its efforts to maintain or restore ecological integrity in Canada's national parks.[87] Environmentalist and author Jeff Gailus offered a dismal assessment when he described Banff National Park as "a very unsafe place to be a grizzly bear (or a wolf or a caribou) … So many bears die in Banff National Park that it has become something of a mortality sink [place where populations decline] for the regional population."[88] Currently, a program is underway to bring woodland caribou back to Banff National Park following their extirpation in 2009. One hopes that suitable habitat will be made available and that consideration will be given to the dynamics of isolated populations and to low gene variability, factors that contributed to their extirpation in the first place.[89]

Ecological integrity plays "second fiddle" to the human presence. In 2001 the Canadian Parks and Wilderness Society tested the new ecological integrity provisions in the National Parks Act (2000)[90] by challenging a Parks Canada decision to allow a road through Wood Buffalo National Park, a road that served no park purpose and that unnecessarily disturbed the ecology of the park. The case was dismissed on the grounds that the interests of the people benefited by the road should override ecological integrity concerns if the impact was limited. In upholding the decision in the Federal Court of Appeal, the judge added that it was not the court's role to decide on how Parks Canada weighs ecological integrity in its management decisions.[91] Three years later, the Mountain Parks Watershed Association challenged Parks Canada's right to issue a permit to Chateau Lake Louise that allowed it to divert water from Lake Louise to meet its expansionist needs. The judge rejected the argument that lowering the lake impacted ecological integrity and felt that a balance must be struck with human needs. University of Calgary law professor Shaun Fluker concludes that these decisions "provide Parks Canada with the legal authority to consider the maintenance or restoration of ecological integrity as just another factor in parks decision-making" and that "ecological integrity is a factor which can be overridden by human commercial or economic interests."[92]

A final point concerns Parks Canada's current Guiding Principles and Operational Policies.[93] Despite provisions in the National Parks Act, Parks Canada does not parade ecological integrity as a primary mandate. In the Parks Canada Charter (2002), the closest reference to wildlife, biodiversity, or ecological integrity comes in the following goal: "To protect, as a first priority, the natural and cultural heritage of our special places and ensure that they remain healthy and whole."[94] The charter's human-centred values and goals cast Parks Canada as a supra-agency for the promotion of Canada's natural and cultural heritage, not as a guardian of biodiversity and its component wildlife.

CULLING IN NATIONAL PARKS

Incredibly, killing healthy wildlife is still a favoured practice in many Canadian national parks. The culling of animals is controversial. As zoologist David Lavigne pointed out in his presentation to Canada's Standing Senate Committee on Fisheries and Oceans in 2012, culling policies are political, not scientific. They are not based on science but represent responses to attitudes, values, and societal objectives where "scientific data – the 'facts' as we currently understand them – often become misrepresented, misquoted, or fabricated."[95] Also, most people are uneasy with the idea of killing healthy animals for so-called management purposes. A study in the Netherlands linked public opinions on culling to individual moral values and found that when human health was not a factor, the approval rate for culling was less than 25 per cent.[96] The simplicity of culling is mocked by the complexity of ecosystem interactions, climatic variables, the implications of fractured habitat loss, the isolation of species, and changing trophic levels and species communities. In referring specifically to culling wolves, two senior Canadian biologists contend, "It is a slippery slope, where, when you start, you are doomed to increasing intervention with unknown consequences."[97]

Overall, the merits of culling as a management tool are being called into question. The reasons for culling are several. All are contestable from practical, scientific, and moral perspectives. The most common is linked to notions of hyper-abundance. According to Lavigne, the term "hyper-abundant" is a propaganda word that has become part of the mythology used almost universally to justify the culling of animals. Lavigne believes that science cannot assess the number of animals of a given species that should live in a given area at a specific time and that this basis for culling animals constitutes no more than a convenient rationalization.[98] Another reason has to do with the human-induced variables associated with the predator-prey imbalance. The wolf cull is an apt example. In response to perceived high numbers of fallow deer in the Gulf Islands, one resident noted, "We have said we don't want cougars and wolves and bears in our backyard and then people wonder where all the deer are coming from."[99] A related reason for culling is based on perceived ecological damage. Most deer culling is rationalized on these grounds. Municipal jurisdictions routinely cull smaller mammals and birds, and although not always explained as such, these culls are based on social perceptions. The rabbits in Canmore, Alberta, are a good example. Culling is also carried out as a fear response to the spread of disease.

Culling practices for population control are unnecessary and cruel. Other nonlethal methods are available and have been successfully tested. A program in Baltimore, Maryland, uses radio-transmitter-equipped tranquilizer darts to capture does for sterilization surgery. Vaccination with the contraceptive PZP is also effective in controlling deer populations. For example, a study on elk in Colorado found that year-long contraception was an acceptable alternative to culling.[100] At the present time, expense factors are the main obstacles to widespread deployment of sterilization and contraception to control deer populations, but already there are indications that these can be reduced.[101] More natural forest management can reduce deer numbers by leaving smaller open spaces for them to browse.[102] For some animals like coyotes, skunks, and raccoons, culling does not work. Neither, apparently, given the current lack of interest, will trophic rewilding.

The fear of disease often spurs culling in the absence of forethought or scientific knowledge about how the disease is actually spread or the number of healthy lives to be forfeited.[103] A 2013 study concluded that culling might actually aid disease spread. It projected that host mortality – deaths of those with the disease – may select for less virulent strains able to grow and become established in the rest of the culled population.[104] The failure of badger culls in England to eliminate bovine tuberculosis was attributed in part to the breakdown of social organizations, which led surviving badgers to range farther and thus increase the risk of disease transmission.[105] Others are cautionary about the "alluring" thresholds, or population numbers, that are used to validate culling, noting several complicating factors, such as inadequate information or limited well-replicated data sets, complex population structures, disease dynamics, and alternative host species.[106]

Proponents who do not see culling as morally wrong rationalize it as necessary to secure broader benefits for both humans and animals. In contrast, opponents like evolutionary biologist Robert Lacy feel that culling desensitizes people to the value of animals. Lacy makes a relevant point by focusing on the often painful and unnecessary deaths of individuals rather than on "big picture" rationales. He concludes validly by emphasizing a crucial point not understood in the discourse of wildlife management: species can and do suffer unnecessary deaths, but a culled individual suffers a premature death unnecessarily.[107] Furthermore, in the context of this specific discussion, the idea of culling healthy wild creatures is bad enough, but somehow it seems a lot worse when it occurs in an area ostensibly set aside for their protection.

Culling is common practice in Canadian national parks. First, any encouragement of predators is a nonoption given real and imagined threats to human safety and equanimity. Ongoing culling for population control, primarily of ungulates, is factored into the perception that the parks are part of a socialized natural order and that they are operating in the interests of a traditional, even simplistic, viewpoint of ecosystem maintenance. It would also appear that Parks Canada might be hasty in its practices. In 2013 the commissioner of the environment and sustainable development, in assessing the ecological integrity of Canada's national parks, felt that Parks Canada's monitoring system for ecological integrity was lacking.[108] This lends credence to the notion that culling programs might be more a matter of policy than anything else. In fact, wildlife culling is not subject to regulatory oversight unless human health or economic issues are at stake.[109]

But regardless of whether or not their ecological assessments are being completed, many national parks choose to selectively kill their healthy residents. Elk numbers are being kept at 2,500 in Manitoba's Riding Mountain National Park on the grounds that they just might contract tuberculosis and spread it to domestic cattle.[110] Preparatory plans to reintroduce bison in Banff National Park contain provisions for annual culls.[111] The idea of returning animals to an environment and then selectively killing them when they thrive is an unhappy testament to the belief system. Over 1,000 licences are issued annually to kill moose in Gros Morne and Terra Nova National Parks in Newfoundland and Labrador.[112] The same fate awaits moose in Cape Breton Highlands National Park in Nova Scotia.[113] White-tailed deer populations are being reduced on an annual basis in Ontario's Point Pelee National Park by First Nations under agreement. Apparently, there were to be no more than thirty-two deer in Point Pelee National Park in 2016 according to scientific reckoning, which meant that over seventy deer had to be eliminated in the easiest and cheapest way. Dead deer are less expensive than relocated deer.[114] As of 2017, Parks Canada was considering eliminating 200 elk in Elk Island National Park in Alberta through an annual sport hunt.[115]

MIDDLE ISLAND CORMORANTS

A graphic example of Parks Canada's willingness to cull its own wildlife occurred in 2008 in Point Pelee National Park. Ongoing and controversial, the cull of double-crested cormorants on Middle Island has become the most damaging single indictment of Parks Canada's predilection to use the lethal problem-solving option on creatures under its protection.

Double-crested cormorants, one of several cormorant species in North America, are large, greenish-black, fish-eating water birds who nest in large colonies close to shore on islands and headlands. In addition to exhibiting strong social interactions, double-crested cormorants are doting parents, superb swimmers, and survivalists. They had almost been eradicated by the 1960s due to pesticide use and harassment. Disuse of persistent toxic chemicals in the Great Lakes led to an increase in cormorant numbers and reinforced their importance as an indicator species. Their return to healthy numbers by 2000 was also consistent with a recovered species in its natural environment.

According to conservation biologist Linda Wires, the double-crested cormorant is a historically persecuted and maligned species that has unfairly earned the reputation as a feathered pariah. She documents historic perceptions of the black-sheened birds as gluttonous, destructive agents of darkness and even as unclean harbingers of doom.[116] Negative opinions continue today about cormorants as dirty, messy, odoriferous, and socially distasteful creatures. Stakeholder groups like the Ontario Federation of Anglers and Hunters equate the cormorant's "voracious appetite" with a degradation of fishing stocks even though the cormorant presents no danger to fisheries and primarily eats small, noncommercial fish, including invasive species like the round goby and the alewife.[117] Reinforced by, and in large part complicit with, these perceptions, Parks Canada, with its simplistic baseline assessment of ecological integrity, viewed the increasing presence of cormorants on Middle Island with more than misgivings.

Located in the archipelago of the western Lake Erie basin, and part of the richest assemblage of nesting birds in Lake Erie, Middle Island is an 18.5-hectare, tadpole-shaped island just south of Point Pelee in Ontario and metres away from the US border. Thirty-three provincially significant species, including nine listed by the Committee on the Status of Endangered Wildlife in Canada, visit or inhabit the island.[118] In addition to the cormorants, at least five species of bird are present in numbers of national significance, including more than 1 per cent of the estimated North American herring gull population and about 500 pairs of great blue herons, black-crowned night herons, and great egrets. Although largely uninhabited for the past forty years, Middle Island has been subject to anthropogenic disturbance since the nineteenth century in the form of escaped slaves, a lighthouse, agriculture, rum-running activities during Prohibition, a later hotel, and an airstrip.

Middle Island was bought at auction in Cleveland, Ohio, in 1999 by the Nature Conservancy of Canada and partners for $1.3 million. The island was gifted to Canada in 2000 and became part of Point Pelee National

Park a year later. In announcing Middle Island's incorporation into the nation's national parks system, Minister of Heritage Sheila Copps called it "a glorious day for Canada" and proclaimed that the island's habitat – and, by implication, the creatures on it – would "be protected in perpetuity."[119] Unfortunately, this assurance did not last long. Only seven years later, Parks Canada initiated a culling program aimed at reducing the cormorant population on the island. Arguing that reductions were necessary to protect the island's ecosystem from irreversible damage, and amid bitter opposition from advocacy groups, Parks Canada launched its annual, ongoing cull of double-crested cormorants on Middle island in the late spring of 2008.

Parks Canada argued that the cull was necessary because the hyper-abundant cormorants were irreversibly damaging forest health and destroying the structure, composition, and function of Middle Island's ecosystem. The agency claimed that the cormorants' guano changed soil chemistry, that their nesting habits destroyed vegetation health, composition, and diversity, and that their hyper-abundance meant the end of other waterfowl since, once they had destroyed their own nesting trees, the cormorants would build ground nests and eventually displace all other nesting birds.[120] Parks Canada's environmental assessment warned that "without an immediate and maintained decrease in double-crested cormorant nest density on the island, there will be an almost complete loss of ecological integrity of the significant Carolinian ecosystem on Middle Island in less than a decade."[121]

Double-crested cormorants had already been subject to a cull in Ontario. In 2006 almost 3,000 were killed, many inhumanely, on High Bluff Island in Presqu'ile Provincial Park near Brighton on Lake Ontario by the Ontario Ministry of Natural Resources. Detailed onsite notes by Rob Laidlaw of Zoocheck Canada, who was in the company of observers from Cormorant Defenders International, documented the cruelty that accompanied the cull, making reference to wounded birds with wings or legs blown off and to the lack of care or compassion by Natural Resources personnel in retrieving them. In noting that the cull was poorly delivered, disruptive, wasteful, cruel, and out of the public eye, Laidlaw concluded, "There is little doubt that a cull conducted in this manner cannot be humane."[122]

Ostensibly, Parks Canada is committed to due process and to its own principles and guidelines respecting culling, and it is aware of the intent and context of the term "ecological integrity." If so, a lot was left unanswered when it resorted to its drastic step in 2008.

In early 2007 Parks Canada received a commissioned report by private consultants Aquila Applied Ecologists on the impact of cormorants on the biodiversity of islands in western Lake Erie, a report that was highly supportive of the need for culling.[123] According to Cormorant Defenders International (CDI), which decimated the report in a ninety-three-page critique, the report was highly selective in that it failed to provide balance and reflected "the Parks Canada bias that cormorant populations are unnaturally high and are destroying the ecological integrity of Middle Island and therefore some management actions must be taken."[124] CDI also claimed that Parks Canada was basing the cull on the misplaced concepts of ecological integrity as a fixed state in nature and biodiversity health as necessitating selective human interference through species removal.[125] The group further felt that Parks Canada was misinterpreting the literature and also relying on unscientific information. It was all for naught. A month later, on 6 March 2008, following fruitless discussion with CDI, Parks Canada released its conservation management plan for Middle Island, which proposed to cull cormorant colonies from over 4,000 nests to between 438 and 876 nests by 2012.[126]

Three weeks later, Zoocheck Canada and Animal Alliance of Canada, both members of CDI, filed for an injunction to stop the cull on the grounds that it was approved in the absence of the statutory management plan required every five years. In fact, the latest management plan for Point Pelee National Park had been filed in 1995, six years before Middle Island joined the park. Parks Canada admitted its lapse in meeting its requirements but quoted its own experts in contending that the situation was sufficiently dire to cause a "catastrophic ecosystem flip" on Middle Island.[127] The apocalyptic implications of this recently coined phrase were enough to convince the judge to refuse the injunction and allow the cull. Over 200 birds were subsequently shot during the cull, which took place between 30 April and 5 May 2008. According to one report, many more were killed in 2010.[128]

Aside from its failure to adhere to its statutory requirements, Parks Canada ignored the due consultation process, which showed overwhelming public sentiment against culling. It also mocked the intent of its own directives, which specified the use of lethal solutions only if more humane options were not feasible. Ineffectual solutions like egg oiling, nest destruction, artificial nesting platforms, predator introduction, and harassment were used to validate the cull.[129] However, not even considered were viable alternatives like washing the foliage of nest trees and landscape vegetation after the birds had migrated south, de-acidifying the soil with lime or another nontoxic substance, putting down liners and covering them with wood chips to be removed at the end of the nesting season, and mulching nesting areas for guano interception and removal.[130] The cull was far less expensive. Moreover, a 2009 research-based study on the herbaceous layers on Middle Island concluded that the negative impact of cormorants on the island was restricted to localized damage primarily on the perimeters.[131] It seems obvious that Parks Canada was committed to the lethal option from the outset.

There is no doubt that the cull was not only cruel but also distressing to other residents of the island. Highly sensitive wading birds like the great blue heron could not wait out the carnage by swimming offshore but had to circle the skies for long periods, leaving their nests untended. The disturbances have led the great egret to leave the island altogether. Although evidence of cruelty is scanty, the words of Cormorant Defenders International as an observer of the cull carry weight: "CDI asserts that birds with ruptured tissue from bullet wounds are in pain, that nestlings exposed to the elements, deprived of food or experiencing physical trauma, suffer accordingly. CDI also asserts that adult birds suffer when they are suddenly rendered flightless, are forced to drown, die of starvation, exposure or prolonged exsanguination."[132] Given the carnage documented at Presqu'ile Provincial Park two years earlier by CDI, one should not be surprised. Maintaining that the cull violates animal cruelty provisions, CDI referred to the guidelines of the Canadian Council on Animal Care, which call for the clear demonstration of benefit in instances of actions that result in severe discomfort, distress, and pain.[133]

More significant was Parks Canada's stand on ecological integrity. First, the "catastrophic ecosystem flip" argument was unsound. Although based primarily on theoretical modelling, the idea that dramatic ecosystem change can occur quite suddenly is scientifically accepted and subject to various models and interpretations.[134] Such change in ecosystems refers to a shift from one stable state to another, and although it might occur suddenly, it is due to a gradual loss of resilience.[135] To Linda Wires, any ecosystem shift involved the Great Lakes area and was the result of human disturbance through time. In any event, it could not be a confined event on a single small island occasioned over a short time by a species of bird native to the area.[136] Furthermore, Middle Island's ecosystem had withstood historic anthropogenic presence and prior cormorant presence. Wires and fellow conservation biologist Francesca Cuthbert have found records attesting to the presence of cormorants in the Great Lakes area in the first half of the nineteenth century.[137] However, they were absent for much of the twentieth century, and one could scarcely refer to their return to a nesting site in an area they had very likely inhabited in large numbers before their near extirpation as a "catastrophic ecosystem flip." Middle Island's ecosystem in 2001 was in a phase considered pleasing to the eye and framed by Parks Canada personnel as an ecological "museum piece" to be preserved as is. It is unfortunate that they resorted to crude, cruel, and simplistic lethal solutions rather than heeding the advice of Wires and Cuthbert that cormorant conservation strategies should "recognize humans, fish and cormorants as three components of a complex system driven by many species and dynamic interactions."[138]

The central ecological issue is Parks Canada's perception of a set-in-time pristine state of ecological integrity, or in this case, one that existed in 2001. Laidlaw refers to a "baseline culture" within Parks Canada where ecological conditions are culturally determined through human perceptions in a specific timeframe. One could go even further and suggest that the ecological integrity of Middle Island was measured in terms of change during individual administrative tenures.[139] This point is relevant in that a specific ecosystem's state in 2007 was assessed against a 2001 yardstick to reach conclusions about what was perceived as the sudden, catastrophic impact of a single species. Wires argues that on Middle Island ecological integrity was erroneously equated with conditions existing in the absence of cormorants and further that Parks Canada's definition of "hyperabundance" was a social construct in that it was closely tied to expectations about proper population size. Taken together, these perceptions linked the cormorant presence to a serious ecological problem.[140] The element of historic gradual change, especially on small islands, was ignored even though it is significant in terms of both the absence and the presence of species, vegetation loss and regeneration, and marine health. In that context, Wires writes, "Trying to manage cormorants in order to protect island change and to maintain particular communities in perpetuity is a little like building on a flood plain."[141]

The ongoing culling program on Middle Island is expensive, cruel, and ultimately fruitless. It stands outside science in abusing the meaning of "ecological integrity" and in reflecting negative popular attitudes. The "museum piece" view of ecosystem integrity as a static state to be held in place by selective humans is a biological absurdity. For example, the elimination of cormorants by humans would simply encourage similar species to take their place. Furthermore, what happened on Middle Island in 2008 should be a powerful reminder of where Parks Canada stands in protecting wildlife. That the whole issue of ecological integrity, or even the unwanted abundance of cormorants on Middle Island, has more to do with human-induced habitat degradation elsewhere in the Great Lakes ecosystem is just another example of the "blame the victim" syndrome. That Parks Canada buys into it is an added tragedy.

Parks Canada's treatment of the Middle Island cormorants worsened its already poor reputation among animal activists who simply do not trust it to consider the welfare of its wildlife as a high priority. In that context, the unresolved issue for wildlife in another parks area is a matter of some concern. Sable Island is a long, narrow, windswept, virtually uninhabited island southeast of Halifax, and in terms of wildlife it is noted for its feral ponies and colonies of grey seals. It also became a national park reserve in June 2013, and given Parks Canada's treatment of the cormorants, along with its mandate to sustain ecological integrity by maintaining the environmental conditions perceived as characteristic of the region, there are fears about the future of the Sable Island ponies, who are seen as an invasive species, and the grey seals, who are perceived as overabundant.

At present, both issues are in abeyance even though Parks Canada can claim enough scientific support to act against the ponies and seals. Some scientists attribute ecological degradation to the horses and worry about their possible impact on the freshwater wetlands, which support much of the island's rarer biodiversity.[142] Other concerns surround the horses' narrow genetic base and the possibility of extinction.[143] As for the seals, the federal government has been trying to reduce their population for years in order to save cod stocks.[144] According to a spokesperson for the Nova Scotia Fish Packers Association, "We would like to see, as an industry group, the grey seal herd on the Scotian Shelf, mainly the Sable Island breeding colony, reduced by 50 per cent."[145]

Evidence also exists to support opposing arguments. The horses have been on the island long enough to have been integrated into the island's ecosystem, which has stabilized in recent decades.[146] And a growing body of knowledge now suggests that the complexity of ocean ecosystems makes it impossible to directly correlate seal numbers with cod depletions.[147]

Parks Canada is saying little about its future plans for Sable Island, but it seems that, for the time being at least, the ponies and the seals are safe. Far more than the cormorants, the ponies have public support on their side, and opposition will be fierce if Parks Canada decides to move against them. The seals are in a more precarious position, and although the proposed cull is currently on hold, their fate is in the hands of Fisheries and Oceans Canada, leaving one to wonder what Parks Canada's reaction will be if the subject of a cull or harvest resurfaces. Finally, was Liz White of Animal Alliance of Canada right when she noted Parks Canada's "long and despicable record of killing off wildlife in its management programs and leaving places worse off than when they took control of them"?[148] If she was right, the future is anything but secure for Sable Island's iconic ponies and for its grey seal colonies.

With respect to culling, I leave the last word to an unnamed scientist with Fisheries and Oceans Canada who made the following comment in an official workshop on the future of the grey seals: "How certain do we have to be before asking other intelligent beings to die for our beliefs?"[149] It is unfortunate that Parks Canada and other wildlife management officials have little trouble rationalizing such decisions.

COMMERCIALIZATION OF PARKS

The increasing commercialization in Canada's national and other protected parks is a visible tribute to the place of tourism in national economies and an indication of the need to increase revenues and to pay down infrastructure debt.[150] It is also a response to scholarly literature suggesting that with proper management, protected areas can be accessed by tourists without ecological degradation while producing economic benefits nationally, regionally, and locally.[151] Canada's Federal Tourism Strategy (2011) reflected this philosophy. In announcing its intention to be an active player in making Canada a global tourist destination, the federal government put the national parks system front and centre.[152] Certainly, Canada's big parks are popular places. Over 20 million visitors flock to Canada's national parks annually. In 2009 over 64,000 full-time equivalent jobs were created in Canada's national, provincial, and territorial parks, resulting in $2.9 billion dollars in labour income and a $4.6 billion dollar contribution to the country's gross domestic product. More telling was that parks spending on accommodation, equipment, and other amenities was more than 5.7 times higher than the capital and operating costs of parks management.[153]

That national parks are for people is stipulated in the National Parks Act. The need to cultivate the human presence through amendable infrastructure and diversity of experience is critical to Canada's Federal Tourism Strategy, important to park administrators, and desirable from the visitor viewpoint. Snowmobiles, ski runs, golf courses, hiking trails, boats, campgrounds, restaurants, hotels, and other accommodation facilities catering to various wallet sizes are all part of the tourist experience in Canada's national and provincial parks. Although this has always been the case, the modern emphasis is on closer encounters with the more thrilling aspects of wilderness.

The point is not so much that our parks have become more likely to cater to human wants and recreational pleasures, although this trend should be a source of concern to anyone who takes the Canadian Biodiversity Strategy seriously. The most troubling issue goes deeper. In catering to a growing fixation on heightened and intrusive recreational encounters with nature, our national parks are moving further away from their first principle of placing ecological considerations front and centre. The opening of a via ferrata, or protected climbing route, in 2014 above the ski runs on Mount Norquay in Banff National Park is a prime example. The need to attract off-season visitors meant fixing cables, ladders, and bridges to the upper cliffs in order to allow comfortable but exciting climbing experiences. The needs of the grizzly bears and mountain sheep who use the area as a summer habitat were easily trumped by unnatural infrastructure in a natural setting.[154] In addition to the impact on wildlife, one senses a creeping violation that is both disturbing and disrespectful. Constructing a via ferrata above a ski run to put large numbers of people in wildlife habitat year-round is an act of violation. As protective areas for wild residents, our national parks should be places of restraint where the human footprint is made cautiously and respectfully.

TWO VIOLATIONS IN JASPER NATIONAL PARK

Jasper National Park, a world heritage site, is Canada's largest mountain national park. Its reputation for outstanding vistas and wildlife entices around 2 million visitors a year. Like Banff National Park, its sister to the south, Jasper National Park seems determined to push the natural experience intrusions as far as it is able. It also seems to be succeeding.

The Glacier Skywalk

In 2011 Brewster Travel Canada unveiled a $21 million proposal to mod- ify the Mount Kitchener–Sunwapta Canyon viewpoint on the Icefields Parkway in order to allow for a 300-metre interpretive boardwalk and a glass-floored observation platform extending 30 metres out and 280 metres above the Sunwapta Valley. Parks Canada reviewed the proposal and, after paying dubious tribute to the requisite public consultative pro- cess, approved the plan in 2012. It was unguarded about its reasons, which should tell us something about priorities in national parks management. Notably, it stated that "Parks Canada needs to become more relevant to more Canadians by providing services and activities that respond to a broader range of visitor needs and expectations."[155] It added that "Parks Canada seeks to offer experiences for different types of visitors who want to interact with nature in many different ways. Recent park survey results show that more than 90% of visitors come to the park for sightseeing and prefer a comfortable view from the edge."[156] The Glacier Skywalk opened to much fanfare in 2014.

Doubts about the merits of this new attraction on "the edge" were present from the start. With its usual proactivity, the Canadian Parks and Wilderness Society was front and centre, submitting a letter to the superintendent of Jasper National Park that took Parks Canada to task on several levels. The letter hammered Parks Canada for violating the ethos of its own legislative and policy framework and further criticized it for continuing to rely on grand infrastructure-based development, which failed to connect people with nature. It also claimed that the consultative process was skewed in favour of Brewster Travel and that the Glacier Skywalk set a dangerous precedent for further private commercial projects in national parks.[157] Another critic labelled the skywalk a "belligerent architectural stunt" and felt that it constituted an intrusive money-making contrivance to sell views that could be seen from the roadside.[158]

The Canadian Parks and Wilderness Society's most telling argument concerned the impact of the skywalk on wildlife. It contended that insufficient time, effort, and scope were given to the requisite study, resulting in flawed conclusions about long-term and short-term impacts on wildlife. Calling for the application of the precautionary principle, which advocates the avoidance of action-based risk in the absence of valid scientific consensus, it persuasively stressed that "given the shortcomings of the field work ... and given expert scientific opinion that impacts on goat populations will be difficult to predict, there would need to be more extensive scientific study of wildlife populations in the broader region as well as more study of wildlife (e.g. ungulate) behaviour in general in order to improve confidence in knowing what likely impacts may or may not be."[159]

However, it seems that whether or not Parks Canada and Brewster Travel followed due diligence in giving the public a visual extravaganza is beside the point. Predictably, both advanced the "have one's cake and eat it too" argument: the impact on wildlife would be minimal, with ecological integrity unaffected, all adding up to more fun being had by more people with negligible environmental harm. Yet the project did increase the human footprint in Jasper National Park. That it did not need to and that it invalidated its presence when a single mountain goat was terrorized were inconceivable to Parks Canada's human-centred mindset.

Maligne Lake

Maligne Lake, south of the Jasper town site, is the largest glacier-fed lake in the Canadian Rockies. Back-dropped by mountain peaks and three glaciers, with the contrasting green of Spirit Island set against its placid turquoise waters, Maligne Lake is one of the most beautiful and photographed lakes in the world. It also delineates habitat for an abundance of wildlife, including deer, black bears, wolves, moose, bighorn sheep, bald eagles, golden eagles, ospreys, and black swifts. Additionally, three species are important to Parks Canada, or at least they were in 2010. Woodland caribou, grizzly bears, and harlequin ducks are all listed by the Committee on the Status of Endangered Wildlife in Canada and are of "particular concern" to Parks Canada. The Jasper National Park Management Plan (2010) was well aware of its need for serious oversight when it specified that one of its major challenges in the Maligne Lake area was to maintain habitat security for its sensitive wildlife.[160] The management plan was also mindful of ecological integrity, stipulating unequivocally that "no new land will be released for overnight commercial accommodation outside the community," or town limits.[161] Yet three years later, Parks Canada, now fixated on increasing park attendance by 2 per cent a year in times of stiff competition for the tourist dollar, conveniently forgot its earlier statements about doing what national parks should do.

One impetus for change was provided by a private commercial operator. Maligne Tours Ltd (MTL) had a long-time presence at Maligne Lake, where it operated a day lodge, scenic boat cruises, boat rentals, and interpretive guided tours, as well as managing a historic chalet and boathouse. Faced with declining revenues, MTL approached Parks Canada in 2012 with a proposal to provide overnight accommodation facilities at Maligne Lake. Parks Canada was receptive to the idea and advised the company as to further action. MTL subsequently announced details of its project in July 2013.[162]

Regardless of MTL's suggestions, Parks Canada was also interested in upgrading the tourist presence in the Maligne Valley. In October 2013 it released its Situation Analysis for the Maligne Valley, a precursor document to its proposed implementation strategy, which was basically a spin-off management plan for the Maligne Valley.[163] Focusing on the need to increase visitors to the valley, the analysis had no hesitation in incorporating MTL's concepts into its vision for the valley, noting that the company was "uniquely positioned with their base of operations to contribute to enhancing visitor experience opportunities and park stewardship."[164] In a nonsensical rationalization that was devoid of scientific validity and in opposition to the intent of its own 2010 management plan, Parks Canada now proclaimed, "Resource protection and visitor experience objectives are inter-related and will benefit from a holistic approach that considers how initiatives to improve either area of mandate can support one another."[165] Its strategies for protecting wildlife were less than reassuring. Noting that "our understanding of wildlife movement in the valley is not perfect," Parks Canada believed that all it had to do in order to protect habitat was isolate and monitor wildlife-rich corridors.[166] Apparently, the sensitive at-risk wildlife using these corridors would not be impacted by the noisy trampling presence of an additional 400 semi-permanent visitors. Referring to the paucity of data on the extent of visitor use in protected areas, research scientist Ilona Rima Naujokaitis-Lewis argues that although park managers may recognize the importance of tracking and monitoring visitor movements, they are failing to do so.[167] Impossibly, Parks Canada also believed that protection for the endangered, minuscule caribou herd would be enhanced by "minimizing the effects of human activity on caribou while facilitating a high quality visitor experience."[168]

On 14 November 2013, MTL presented its detailed proposal to Parks Canada.[169] Among other amenities, it included plans for fifteen overnight, two-person tent-cabins with adjacent washroom and shower facilities and for a hotel with sixty-six double-occupancy units. The proposal sought justification by focusing on specific statements in the Jasper National Park Management Plan and commenting broadly on how it would honour them. Predictably, it omitted any reference to existing prohibitions on commercial accommodation. Although the proposal integrated wildlife into its education programs and included mitigations for potential wildlife-human conflicts, it downplayed the implications of the increased human presence by assuming that wildlife would be largely immune because the new facilities would be located within the footprint of previous development.[170] As the following comment attests, MTL was also on a par with Parks Canada when it came to overstatements: "Maligne Tours are responsible in many ways for environmental stewardship of the place they call home and for welcoming guests from around the world into a destination that is safe, secure and sustainable."[171]

During its subsequent obligatory public engagement process, MTL learned that neither its plans for accommodation at Maligne Lake nor its claims about environmental stewardship sat well with the general public and Aboriginal groups. The first serious volley against the proposal was fired by the Canadian Parks and Wilderness Society and the Jasper Environmental Association. In a letter on their behalf from Ecojustice to the superintendent of Jasper National Park, they contended that the proposed overnight accommodation was in clear violation of the 2010 management plan and was contrary to Parks Canada's Guiding Principles and Operational Policies and to its guidelines on commercial accommodation.[172] The letter also claimed that any additional development in the Maligne Valley severely jeopardized the survival of the woodland caribou and that grizzly bear and harlequin duck habitat would be disturbed by activities associated with increased and sustained human presence in the area.[173] The letter also maintained that the MTL had not carried out any market analysis to show the need for accommodation facilities at Maligne Lake.[174] It was a powerful, well-reasoned submission that was difficult to contradict.

Other criticisms followed. Of the 1,850 letters received by Parks Canada, only about 100 were not opposed to the project.[175] One long and informed critique discussed thirteen reasons why the accommodation proposal should be abandoned and emphasized what also should have been obvious to Parks Canada: "At the end of the day we must also recognize that we are at risk of destroying the very attractions we are selling."[176] No less convincing but more damning was an open letter to the federal environment minister by three senior former Parks Canada administrators. In addition to emphasizing the devastating impact of the accommodation facilities on endangered woodland caribou herds, the authors stressed the dangers of the ripple effect: "The incremental commercial development that would result from allowing this precedent-setting contravention of park policy would threaten the ecological integrity of all of our Rocky Mountain national parks by enabling more

development in sensitive ecosystems critical for the survival and movement of wildlife."[177] The significant public opposition was reflected in
roadside posters and picket signs and in an online petition initiated by
the Canadian Parks and Wilderness Society.[178]

MTL's final draft of the proposal went to Parks Canada on 21 April
2014. Three months later, on 27 July, Parks Canada rejected the hotel
but accepted the fifteen tent-cabins and every other proposal submitted
by MTL pending further consultation and approval of final submission
plans.[179] Jasper National Park's superintendent defended the decision with
the following delusional utterance: "Today's decision reflects our pledge
to ensure our protected natural and cultural heritage remain unimpaired
for future generations while facilitating ways for people to meaningfully
connect with and learn about nature."[180] Note the emphasis on people, not
wildlife, which shows what the whole issue was about and where Parks
Canada's priorities lay. A month later, Ecojustice filed an application for
judicial review on behalf of the Canadian Parks and Wilderness Society
and the Jasper Environment Association, arguing that the proposal was
in violation of the Jasper National Park Management Plan.[181] Although
the judicial review was denied in February 2016 on the grounds that the
management plan did not preclude the consideration of the proposal,
Justice James Russell went beyond Parks Canada's Guiding Principles and
Operational Policies, ruling that the plan needed to be amended by the
environment minister before the project could go ahead.[182]

National parks management plans are statutory documents prepared
through broad consultation with the public, stakeholders, and Aboriginal
groups, and their legal status has been recognized in several court challenges.[183] The 2010 Jasper National Park Management Plan was no different. Yet its stipulations were tossed aside in 2013–2014 like they never
existed, and an application for judicial review was necessary to put the
issue beyond Parks Canada's control. I am reminded of a statement by
Animal Alliance of Canada's outspoken director, Liz White. Although
she was not referring to Jasper National Park, she might have well been
when she said, "When dealing with Parks Canada and its 'management'
of animals, I've learned – from heartbreaking experience – neither to
believe nor trust anything it says, anything it does, nor anything it
promises."[184] With respect to Parks Canada's killing cormorants in Point

Pelee National Park and threatening at-risk species in Jasper National Park, she has a point.

White's negative perceptions of Parks Canada more than likely would be shared by internationally respected wolf behaviour expert Günther Bloch, who spent five years in Banff National Park observing, tracking, and documenting the behaviour of a new pack of wolves that appeared in the Pipestone area of the park in 2008–2009. His opinions of Banff National Park's wildlife management personnel were not positive. He found them to be ignorant of wolf behaviour and uneasy about their presence in the park. They bought into myths with respect to wolf habituation to humans, the dominant roles of alpha males, and uniform pack behaviour. His research demonstrated that the wolves tolerated the human presence but did not become habituated and that alpha wolves were communal family members who, for example, did not feast first at a kill but demurred to younger and weaker members. Using parks management's aversive-conditioning methods as an example, and arguing that there is no such thing as a uniform wolf, Bloch showed how responses differed in terms of individual wolf personalities.[185] If Banff National Park was any example, Bloch was of the opinion that wildlife managers in parks required intensive training in wildlife behaviour.

Most of all, Bloch felt that the failure of the Pipestone wolves to survive was linked to parks management's pursuit of commercialism over the welfare of the wolves, citing tolerance of overexuberant visitor disturbance and public announcement of the location of a den. A telling comment in the epilogue of his book on the Pipestone wolves hits at the heart at what is really going on in Banff National Park and in others with high visitor appeal and attendance: "Ostensibly protected, wild species live imperilled and impoverished lives, constantly exposed to hazardous road and rail traffic and displacement from development like hotels, ski hills and golf courses. Their livelihood and survival are threatened by excessive and ever increasing demands from people who are encouraged and enabled by a parks policy that unfailingly favours the destructive wants of humans over the integrity of the natural environment. An exemption from regulations that protect the environment is often given to activities incompatible with wildlife."[186] In the summer of 2016, two wolves were euthanized because in Parks Canada's opinion they posed threats to humans.[187]

In its mandatory and overdue (by three years) report on national parks in December 2016, Parks Canada admitted that ecological integrity in almost half of its 115 assessments in 41 national parks was rated as poor or fair.[188] It also acknowledged that its goals of increasing visitors' attendance and enhancing their experience would place stress on ecosystems in the most popular parks.[189] The word "wildlife" appeared only five times in the fifty-eight-page report, none of which referred to the necessity of curbing intrusive visitor engagements with wildlife or to specific actions that would address habitat degradation caused by commercial infrastructure.

Protected areas in Canada aim to shield ecosystems from degradation and species from extirpation or even extinction. Truly protected areas are the yardsticks of how serious humanity is about preserving wildlife and biodiversity. In the ideal environment, all wild beings contribute to ecological integrity. There is no waste, no imbalance that does not correct itself, and no deviation from rhythms inherent in the processes of birth, life, death, and regeneration. Humanity is not needed in this process, and its interference has created an artificial baseline of ecological integrity. One can imagine that any realization of this interdependence, as well as an awareness of humanity's negative input, might impel an emphasis on preserving life forms by removing humans from large tracts of pristine land and water still remaining in Canada in order to allow biodiversity to unfold as it should. One does not enhance biodiversity by infringement or small-scale manipulation. One does not help biodiversity by slaughtering its living components and damaging their habitats' health. Sadly, the belief system seems to demand that we do just that. The most we can hope for under this regime are baseline ecological enclaves and a species-degraded environment supported by captive breeding programs. A small hope for a place for wildlife unhindered by people might lie in the rewilding movement since, in theory at least, it does represent more than just a softening of the belief system.

CONCLUDING REMARKS

In 2010 the federal, provincial, and territorial governments worked together through 500 experts to produce a significant report on current trends in biodiversity status in Canada.[190] It was a succinct, no-nonsense document that reported on ecosystems and trends in habitat and wildlife. In addition to showing diagrammatically how all ecosystem measures involving wildlife and their habitat were trending downward, the report included twenty-two findings, of which the following are typical: shore-birds were down 50 per cent in the past decade; a decline in the numbers of a small shrimp in the Great Lakes was adversely affecting fish populations; the reduced number of big predators in eastern and southern Canada had led to unevenness among prey species and small predators; caribou populations were in serious decline, precipitously so in certain areas; amphibian numbers were down dramatically in the Great Lakes basin and the St Lawrence River corridor; and fluctuations in prey-herbivore numbers were impacting population cycles across northern Canada. Although the report gave valuable direction to policymakers, it was not heeded.

Four years later, in 2014, Canada released its 5th National Report to the Convention on Biological Diversity.[191] The 112-page document acknowledged its debt to the 2010 report and even duplicated its diagram on negative wildlife and habitat trends, a mystifying insertion since it amounted to an admission that nothing had been done in four years to deal with the issues raised in 2010. Furthermore, the report did not specifically address any of the above trends noted in 2010. It did not dwell on the implications of changes in population dynamics and ecosystem relationships raised in 2010, let alone include information on the specific ways they would be addressed. The report was in fact a narrative-based discussion of the scope of activities underway in Canada to promote biodiversity. For example, extensive space was given to the multiple inter-related initiatives of the jurisdictional and private sectors. By omitting analysis, conclusions, or policy specifics, the report essentially advised the convention that Canada was meeting its international obligations by paying attention to proper process.

The report also included Canada's new biodiversity goals, now set for 2020 as directed by the Secretariat of the Convention in 2010, which had concluded that many countries, including Canada, were not meeting their biodiversity targets.[192] In the four goals and nineteen supportive strategies, Canada set no specific targets beyond protected areas, opting instead to improve habitat generally, to hold the line with species at risk, to reduce contamination to the point where it was manageable, and to integrate the importance of biodiversity more securely into the national consciousness through education.[193] Interestingly, the government mirrored its 2010 predecessor by assessing its stewardship activities in positive terms while acknowledging that "the overall effectiveness of these activities in conserving and improving biodiversity and ecosystem health has not been fully assessed."[194] Neither report gave any assurance that positive results were to be achieved through detailed information-based strategies.

A few months before the 2014 report on biodiversity was released, the Office of the Auditor General of Canada produced a series of reports relevant to Canadian wildlife at risk. Their findings were damning with regard to vulnerable wildlife, their habitats, and designated protected areas. The commissioner of the environment and sustainable development found that 146 recovery strategies for species at risk, or over one-third, had not been completed and that 79 per cent of these were overdue by more than three years. In fact, it was estimated that Environment Canada would need at least ten years to complete recovery strategies due by 2014. Management plans for species of "special concern" had not been completed for almost 60 per cent of identified species, and 60 per cent of those were overdue by more than three years. Of the 97 species for which action plans were due, only 7 had been completed. The all-important critical habitat had not been identified in 43 per cent of all recovery strategies, including an appalling figure of 66 per cent for marine habitat.[195] Additionally, a 2012 academic article condemned Canada's protection of its oceans, referring to its global ranking of seventieth in terms of marine protected areas. The authors further noted that in order to meet its 2020 target, Canada would need to set aside 72,000 square kilometres of oceans a year in marine protected areas, an amount higher than the total area protected in 2011.[196]

Equally significant was the commissioner's conclusion that there seemed to be no link between spending on recovery plans and the results achieved. In other words, Environment Canada did not know precisely what it expected in a recovery plan, let alone when or how. Citing the example of the piping plover, the commissioner observed that although a recovery strategy had been in place since 2007, Environment Canada had not attempted to take stock of how its funding programs had actually aided recovery.[197] This might help to explain why the action plan for this endangered bird had still not been finalized by the end of 2015.

With regard to protected areas generally, the commissioner reported that more than 70 per cent of national wildlife areas and about 55 per cent of migratory bird sanctuaries were deficient in ecological integrity. Moreover, they were not being managed adequately. According to Environment Canada, in 2011 fully 90 per cent of Canada's national wildlife areas did not have adequate management plans. The management plans for thirty-one wildlife areas predated the Species at Risk Act (2002), and another eight had no plan at all. The commissioner was highly critical of Environment Canada's oversight: "Environment Canada has made little progress in monitoring activities, conditions, and threats for the protected areas it manages. The Department's own assessments show a lack of proper inventories and insufficient information on species at risk. Monitoring of sites is done sporadically. Without regular monitoring, the Department cannot track whether the ecological integrity in protected areas is changing, nor can it identify any new or potential threats to local species so that it can react in an appropriate and timely manner."[198]

Given Canada's mediocre track record thus far, it would be naive to think that major advances will be made by 2020. For example, the commissioner of the environment and sustainable development has expressed doubts about Environment Canada's capacity to provide the necessary leadership: "Without a clear and specific definition of how Environment Canada sees its role … it will be difficult to determine what the Department plans to achieve or what resources it will require. In a time of limited or reduced financial resources, we are concerned that this lack of clear planning means that it is not possible for Canadians to know how the Department intends to lead Canada's response to the Convention."[199]

Despite all its talk about moving forward to preserve biodiversity, ecosystems, and the wildlife represented by and in them, Canada is having very limited success in achieving its goals. Apathy, inefficiency, indifference, jurisdictional and funding constraints, and poor coordination all contribute to this dismal situation. However, even given the above, it would be wrong to claim that Canadian governments are totally indifferent to their wildlife. Admittedly, rhetoric is rhetoric, but a modicum of good intention is suggested by the fact that some recovery plans do get completed, that a few action plans are in place for the recovery of species, that a couple of species have been saved from extinction, that wetlands are being restored and some toxins banned, and that protected areas do offer some safeguards for wildlife and ecosystems.

But it is a modicum of good intention, and this is the whole point. One cannot expect tightly focused, well-funded, and deliberate policies that support, respect, and acknowledge the autonomy of wildlife and habitat integrity. The belief system will not allow it. Low-priority budgeting and the pressure from human interests in agriculture, resource extraction, and urban and other expansion undermine the effectiveness of the Species at Risk Act, protected areas policy, and supportive legislation, while endangering wildlife and their habitat generally. As Fisheries and Oceans Canada has noted about its marine protected areas, "The health of a marine ecosystem has real impacts on the amount of fish and other resources that can be sustainably harvested from it, which affects local economies and community well-being."[200] In short, human wants and needs are paramount, as every wildlife policy recognizes. Our sense of stewardship, the basic platform underlying our approach to wildlife and ecosystem management, assumes a benign human presence. Industrial agriculture, clear-cut forestry, toxic contaminants, marine pollution, energy infrastructure, pipelines, roads, urbanization, and hunters are anything but benign. Thus, the hardworking minority who labour on behalf of wildlife can do no better than blunt the raw use of power against wild creatures and try to modify wildlife policymaking's anthropocentric bias. Anything more demands a new belief system. If scientists Gerardo Ceballos, Paul Ehrlich, and Rodolfo Dirzo are right, humanity has just a tiny window of hope: "Thus, we emphasize that the sixth mass extinction is already here and the window for effective action is very short, probably two or three decades at most. All signs point to ever more powerful assaults on biodiversity in the next two decades, painting a dismal picture of the future of life, including human life."[201]

Conclusion

We cannot win this battle to save species and environments
without forging an emotional bond between ourselves and nature
as well – for we will not fight to save what we do not love.
STEPHEN JAY GOULD

The preceding discussion has argued that wildlife in Canada are managed according to a belief system that grants minimal moral worth and limited ethical standing to animals. Although the bases for this belief system are highly contestable, humans, certainly so in Canadian governments, accept the exploitation of animals as a right and a cultural norm. With respect to wildlife in Canada, this exploitation by right has stripped them of individuality and neutered them as a renewable resource. The arguments and evidence presented have tried to show that a belief system that privileges human entitlement and exploits wildlife as a minor resource in national and provincial management systems leads to ongoing species and habitat loss. It also argues that the belief system belies the current stewardship and sustainability principles, which suggest that rich wildlife diversity and biodiversity health can coexist with a benign and restrained human presence. Summarily, it predicts inevitable downward trajectories, or put more simply, nothing meaningful will change for wildlife until the belief system does.

Under the anthropocentric principles informing Canadian mainstream thought about animals, wildlife are managed as species, not individuals – as objects rather than living entities. Lethal options permeate management norms. Habitat is increasingly invaded, degraded, and constricted. Most significantly, the anthropogenic element is a constant in official attitudes, policies, and wildlife management regimes. Legislators, policymakers, and the bureaucracies that support them adhere to the dominant belief system about animals more narrowly than the general public, where a wider spectrum of values is evident. Moreover, the parliamentary system of government and a "first past the post" electoral system make it extremely difficult for attitudinal change – especially with respect to wildlife – to gain political traction.

Wildlife management in Canada rejects any argument that animals possess conscious states sufficient to warrant any moral equivalency with humans. Two management priorities flow from this anthropocentric assumption that has been acted out in human practices and attitudes through time and is embedded today as a cultural truth. The first concerns the priority accorded to human interests, needs, wants, and entitlements. Whether it be protected areas, agricultural lands, marine habitat in commercial shipping lanes, wildlife-human conflict situations in urban areas, habitat preservation in logging regimes, provincial management plans for game animals, rancher and farmer issues, cultural considerations, species at risk recovery, or recreational demands, the human dimension is dominant. Tourists, hunters, trappers, and motorized recreationists violate the integrity of protected areas. Agricultural lands are poisoned with chemicals. Whales are prejudiced by fishing and shipping interests. Paranoiac sentiment means death for any wild animal remotely perceived as a threat to human safety in urban areas. Birds and animals suffer from the advance of industry in the boreal forest. Management plans focus more on human dimensions than on the animals' ecological role. Wolves and coyotes are sacrificed to economic interests. The lives of polar bears and harp seals are less important than the need to protect human traditions. The survival of at-risk species is linked with socio-economic factors. And national parks value the tourist dollar and experience more than the welfare of the animals they are supposed to protect. Admittedly, these are very broad claims. They may be overstated and fail to recognize positive actions. They do, however, indicate an anthropogenic presence that bears badly on nonhuman lives, and they are predictive of a worsening trend.

The second assumption driving wildlife policies is that only the species counts. The lives of individual animals do not form part of the management process. This focus on species is ruinous because it banishes any human association with animals as kin. Wildlife policies reflect the abiding belief that humans stand outside nature and need to manage it like a department store by adjusting inventories, attracting customers, pushing big ticket items, and advertising its own merits. Management by species destroys empathy and replaces it with a discrete callousness. In the case of the mourning doves in Ontario, for instance, 20,000 individual deaths were deemed irrelevant because a few individuals wanted the right to kill them and because the overall number of mourning doves was not negatively impacted. Images of wounded creatures, the individual lives that were snuffed out as irrelevant, and the degradation of dove existence mattered not a whit. Management by species is not only desensitizing but has also led to the overarching error that humans have made in dealing with the wild creatures who share their biotic communities. The classification of wildlife as a renewable resource assured their minor place in the human calculus and predetermined their downward trajectory. Minor resources, those that do not heavily enrich government and private coffers or supply jobs and spin-off multiplier effects, are not heavily funded. As has been shown, the Species at Risk Act (2002) and the Canadian Biodiversity Strategy (1995) receive nowhere near the financial resources necessary to honour their intent. Even if they were imbued with a need to manage *for* wildlife rather than just managing wildlife, policymakers would still face an uphill battle with the meagre resources allocated to them.

It is difficult to believe that any major change can be expected in the dominant belief system about animals. Our species, which puts so much value on human life but so little on other life forms, is fixated on unique rights based on differences. As law professor Richard Epstein has noted, "The root of our discontent is that in the end we have to separate ourselves from (the rest of) nature from which we evolved. Unhappily but insistently, the collective *we* is prepared to do just that. Such is our lot, and perhaps our desire, as human beings."[1] It seems the price is too high to pay for humans to recognize animals as kindred souls, both in the case of domesticated animals and certainly so with regard to wildlife. In short, an alternate belief system about animals that accepts their moral standing and subsequent right to serious ethical treatment seems highly unlikely.

With respect to domesticated and captive animals, the belief system about their inferior status is a cultural truth. The price of change is simply too high and self-interest too compromised. Put more kindly, human dependence on domesticated animals is too deeply entrenched, too rooted in the social and economic orders, and too interwoven with human existence to change. It can however be significantly modified. The historical record shows that the sympathetic element in the current dominant belief system about animals drew its roots from the indirect duties argument and utilitarian philosophy. The former equated kindness toward animals with human betterment; the latter attributed sentient feelings to them, especially the capacity for pain. The classic welfare position can draw more deeply from both to ameliorate conditions and practices that animals must endure in order to achieve human satisfaction. This could be effected through highly enforceable, significantly protective legal regimes applicable to companion animals and to captive animals in zoos, theme parks and entertainment, factory farms, and cosmetic testing. It is possible for the dominant belief system to recognize that it owes domesticated and captive animals much more than it presently gives them while still preserving their instrumental status. The issue of property status or personhood seems less important than the urgent need to reform laws in order to bring the treatment of domesticated animals in line with the level of dignity we accord to human beings generally.

With wildlife, the situation is different. They remain for the most part shrouded in mystery and, as objects of curiosity, fear, and ignorance, stand outside the knowledge base and comfort zones of the vast majority of Canadians. In fact, Canada's urban society has distanced itself from the natural world more than at any time in history. English environmental scientist Norman Henderson has noted that the Canadian perception of wilderness is more a state of mind than a reality and that "only a tiny minority actually venture far away from their automobile into a wilderness situation."[2] Henderson is right. Only a small minority feel at one with pristine wilderness. For the majority of people, wildlife are enjoyed from a distance, superficially, and with as much curiosity as interest. If anything, natural wilderness imposes a fearful sense of alienation. Wildlife are an integral part of that fear and sense of not belonging. Unlike companion animals, wildlife are not of the human world. Wildlife are anonymous, easy sometimes to admire, difficult to love, and for almost everyone, impossible to identify in kinship terms.

Under such circumstances, ignorance and fear easily outpace knowledge and interest. Wildlife can have little relevance when they stand outside of, or are inimical to, human lifestyles.

I believe that we humans collectively lack the capacity to move away from long-held contentions about the instrumental status of all animals. I believe our attitude toward nonhumans is all about power and an allegiance to kin structured around exculpatory rationalizations. I think the sixteenth-century liberal thinker Michel de Montaigne described the situation accurately when he said, "Suppose beasts had all the virtue, the knowledge, the wisdom and sufficiency of the Stoics, they should still be beasts … For, when all is done, whatsoever is not as we are, is not of any worth."[3] However, if I was forced to see some hope for wildlife within a modified belief system, it would be on three levels, all interrelated and all, at the present time, equally implausible.

First, we need to banish our acceptance of wildlife as a renewable resource and instead see them as a trust to be guarded and honoured through a different, kinder, more compatible set of perceptions about living beings in an interdependent world. Management strategies would have to change. How and to what end are unknown, but at least if they acknowledged the moral worth of individual animals, it would mark an important first step in recognizing that wildlife diversity and health require more careful, thoughtful, and empathetic interventions.

Second, a recognition of wildlife's autonomous nature could modify the dominant belief system's underlying principles without appealing to arguments about equality, rights, or moral standing. Canadian philosophers Sue Donaldson and Will Kymlicka suggest that wildlife, like humans, are citizens and capable of exercising their own sovereignty in negotiating their own environments: "In general, when it comes to the day-to-day management of the risks of living in the wild, it is reasonable to view animals as competent actors in a division of labour in which they take responsibility for mutual assistance in their own communities, and indeed are much more competent to do so than we would be on their behalf."[4] Similarly, American philosopher Joel MacLellan advocates a hands-off approach to wild animals: "Perhaps what we owe wild animals in general is not, in a word, happiness, but something more like liberty and the pursuit of happiness."[5]

Australian philosopher John Hadley advocates property rights for animals and argues for specific and suitable ecological areas being set aside and given title as the property of the animals to be held in trust by a guardian. Harm in any way would be a legal violation of property rights. In this way, Hadley argues, "The nonhuman property regime ... strikes a balance between the naturalism explicit in environmentalism and a naturalistic orientation implicit in animal rights liberalism."[6] David Favre, a law professor and authority on animal legal issues, notes that wildlife must become part of humanity's ethical world. Acknowledging that all wildlife are living beings who share with humans the same needs, ecosystems, and interest in living, Favre sees a need for legal systems to grant wildlife status as juristic persons. "As juristic persons," he argues, "individual wildlife will be able to share the legal stage with humans," meaning that their right to be protected from intentional and unintentional harm would be legally enshrined in terms of human duties to create and protect habitat and to preserve species.[7] Essentially, Favre asks for a legal regime that will more ethically balance human threats and encroachment with opportunities for wildlife to exist independently in their own environments.

Third, we might rely on the very qualities we see as differentiating ourselves from nonhumans. We can resort to our higher levels of consciousness and ask ourselves what our rational responsibilities are toward those whom we are able to dominate? As philosopher Paul Taylor has so succinctly noted, "When rational, autonomous agents subscribe to the principles of moral consideration and intrinsic value and so conceive of wild living things as having that kind of worth, such agents are *adopting a certain ultimate moral attitude toward the natural world* [that] ... parallels the attitude of respect for persons in human ethics."[8] Similarly, philosopher Grace Clement refers to an ethic of justice capable of recognizing that although wildlife might not need humans to survive, they do require human restraint in order to do so.[9] In like vein, British animal ethicist Steve Cooke contends that wildlife's claim to habitat is basic and overrides secondary claims by humans.[10] To my mind, and from a rational perspective, humans can acknowledge wildlife's autonomy on a planet to which no one has exclusive claim. From a detached distance, and outside any personal interventions, humans can empathize with wildlife's individual travails and understand that, like themselves, they want to act out their subjective experiences, or simply to live. This rational empathetic position ignores rights, indirect duties, or obligations. Instead, it simply calls on humans to be the rational and moral creatures they claim to be and to recognize the autonomy of creatures who do not need them, who rarely violate human autonomy and never with purposeful ill intent, and who are caught up in experiencing the universal tasks of existence.

Chances are however that none of the above measures will transpire. They simply ask humans to give up too much: too much land and water, too many needs and wants, too many dollars, and too much of what is taken for granted. The changes I suggest call for humans to rethink views about themselves and their place in the world. They ask humans to re-evaluate and widen their notions about kinship. Most of all, they propose that humans delve into places they have never gone before, psychically, philosophically, socially, and culturally. For wildlife management, this means abandoning much of what is seen as standard and proper practice. It means creating management regimes whose foremost priority puts animals, not humans, front and centre. In terms of current thinking about wildlife, it means opening a Pandora's box and trying to live and cope with an enormous aggregate of unknowns.

Currently, a wide range of nonprofit environmental groups work tirelessly in support of wild creatures, and their growing membership is an indication of broader changing views about how animals should be treated. Collectively, they are working to modify the belief system and to pull speciesism away from what moral philosopher David DeGrazia describes as the last frontier of bigotry.[11] Unfortunately, these changing attitudes are not reflected in wildlife policymaking. It is worrying to find that wildlife management regimes, with their professional and scientific resources, continue to ignore the voices of change, the mounting evidence of higher animal cognitive faculties, and the presence of sophisticated levels of conscious behaviours, along with their moral and ethical implications. Likely, these professionals feel less inclined to move away from their human-centred policies because, in spite of the growing voice of the animal-activist groups, they know that they still enjoy the weight of public opinion.

But to end on a hopeful note, is it possible that as biodiversity health worsens, a newly elected reform-minded federal government, seeking an initial remedial step, just might take the rewilding concept seriously and proclaim that wildlife are no longer a renewable resource but vital ecological components whose overall health is an indicator of our own? Or as one author puts it, "The wild creatures of this earth are an essential part of the web of life and of our experience of it."[12] This first step taken, new streams of thought might help to arrest the biodiversity freefall that is imperilling the planet by recognizing that wildlife autonomy and ecological interdependence are inseparable. If wildlife were perceived as a trust to be honoured, as autonomous kindred souls who are physiologically, cognitively, socially, and morally more like us than different, we just might begin to move away from a power relationship to one of respect characterized by rational empathy that, once begun, could see Canada become a role model for the advancement of attitudes vital to preserving global biodiversity and ecosystem health.

Notes

INTRODUCTION

1 World Wildlife Fund, *Living Planet Report 2016*, 13.

2 Rowlands, *Philosopher and the Wolf*, 2.

3 For example, see Manfredo, Teel, and Zinn, "Understanding Global Values," 37.

4 Thomas, Carr, and Keller, "Animal-Totemic Clans," 347.

5 Ingold, *Perception of the Environment*, 67.

6 Hill, "Animals as Agents," 421.

7 Cited in Burkett, "Sacrificial Violence," 441.

8 Molyneaux, "Concepts of Humans and Animals," 194.

9 Preece, *Animals and Nature*, 233; Phelps, *Longest Struggle*, 8.

10 Soulé and Noss, "Rewilding and Biodiversity," 19.

11 Epstein, "Animals as Objects," 143.

12 See Livingston, *Rogue Primate*; Ingold, *Perception of the Environment*, 64; and Orton, "Both Subject and Object," 191.

13 Aristotle, "Politics," 2796.

14 Porphyry, *On Abstinence from Animal Food*, bk 1, para. 4.

15 See Bodson, "Zoological Knowledge."

16 For information, see Gilhus, *Animals, Gods and Humans*.

17 For examples of earlier Greek thought on animals, see Rosen, "Homer and Hesiod," 484; Heath, "Disentangling the Beast," 37; and Osborne, "On Nature and Providence."

18 Aristotle, "Politics," 2801–2.

19 Ibid., 2791.

20 Inwood, trans., *Seneca*, letter 124, para. 13, 101.

21 Steiner, *Anthropocentrism and Its Discontents*, 78.

22 Epictetus, "Of Providence."

23 Aurelius, *Meditations*, bk 6.

24 *R. v. Menard (1978), 43* CCC *(2d) 458 (Que.* CA*)*, 13–14, https://www.animallaw. info/sites/default/files/R%20v%20Menard.pdf. Antonio Lamer (1933–2007) was later appointed to the Supreme Court of Canada, where he became chief justice in 1990.

25 White Jr, "Historical Roots," 4.

26 The context refers to Moses's comment in Deuteronomy 25:4: "Thou shalt not muzzle the mouth of the ox that treadeth out the corn." The traditional meaning held that an ox who wore a muzzle during the process of tramping grain on the threshing floor would be unable to eat any of it. God, through Moses, is saying that this is wrong, that animals deserve proper consideration, and that the ox should be allowed to eat the corn while working. Paul, however, interpreted it differently, saying that God did not care at all for oxen and that what was really at stake in Moses's allegorical comment was an individual's right (in this case, Paul's) to be fully paid for his services.

27 Singer, *Animal Liberation*, 192.

28 Schaff, ed., "Of the Nature of the Human Soul."

29 Schaff, ed., "That Christians Have No Authority."

30 Second Vatican Council, "The Human Community."

31 Gilhus, *Animals, Gods and Humans*, 22.

32 Lucretius, *On the Nature of Things*, bk 5.

33 Cartmill, *View to a Death*, 48–51.

34 Hill, "Saints, Beasts," 66; Salisbury, *Beast Within*, 169–74.

35 For more examples, see Lysikatos, "Saints and the Animals."

36 Grant, *Early Christians and Animals*, 75.

37 Ibid., 96, 90, 82.

38 Ibid., 132, 133.

39 Freedman, "Representation of Mediaeval Peasants," 38. See also Midgley, *Animals and Why They Matter*, 112.

40 Sax, "Magic of Animals," 326.

41 Baxter, *Bestiaries and Their Users*; Sykes, "Human Drama, Animal Trials"; Conway, *Animal Magick*.

42 Steiner, *Anthropomorphism and Its Discontents*, 126, 131. See also Rickaby, trans., *Of God and His Creatures*, 448.

43 Rickaby, trans., *Of God and His Creatures*, 566.

44 Ibid., 490.

45 Government of Canada, Canada Revenue Agency, "Promotion of Animal Welfare," 2.

46 Hatfield, "René Descartes."

47 Smith, "Homo Sapiens and Human Being," 421.

48 Descartes, "Animals Are Machines."

49 Quoted in Nadler, *Cambridge Companion to Malebranche*, 42.

50 Francione and Garner, *Animal Rights Debate*, 106.

51 Steiner, *Anthropocentrism and Its Discontents*, 149.

52 Rousseau, *What Is the Origin?* preface.

53 Aristotle, "History of Animals."

54 Hume, *Treatise of Human Nature*, 300.

55 Ibid., 250.

56 Bentham, "Of the Limits of the Penal Branch," 17.6n122, original emphasis.

57 See Preece, "Role of Evolutionary Thought." For example, French naturalist Jean-Baptiste Lamarck (1744–1829) proposed that environmental factors were change agents in determining inheritable qualities in animals. According to Lamarck, changing environmental conditions impacted biological structures in certain animals and provided explanations for both the origin and transmission of new instinctual behaviours. The Lamarckian view continued to be an alternative to Darwinian thought.

58 Sorabji, *Animal Minds and Animal Morals*, 210; Steiner, *Anthropocentrism and Its Discontents*, 190–7.

59 For an excellent discussion of animal consciousness, see Rollin, "Animal Mind."

60 Thompson, "Many Perils." In that his method relied on both subjective and objective observation, Romanes used the word "ejective" to refer to the blending of the two.

61 Romanes, *Mental Evolution in Animals*, 342. Interestingly, Romanes's ideas were reflected in the turn-of-the-century writings of authors Ernest Thompson Seton and Charles Roberts in Canada and William Long in the United States. In books like Seton's *Wild Animals I Have Known* (1898), Roberts's *The Kindred of the Wild* (1902), and Long's *School of the Woods* (1902), wild animals took on personalities of their own in real-world narratives that highlighted their emotions, relationships, and significant abilities and behaviours. The Seton-Roberts-Long view of animals in the natural world was more psychological, or more attuned to their mental processes and what they might mean. Theodore Roosevelt, conservation guru, big game hunter, and American president, dubbed the trio the "Nature Fakers" for ignoring scientific accuracy in making assumptions about the natural world and animal mental capabilities and for violating the sanctity of nature. Roosevelt, "Nature Fakers." In line with early conservationism, Roosevelt was advocating the distinction between the natural world and the human, while ridiculing those who thought otherwise. See also Maclulich, "Animal Story."

62 Wynne, "Emperor's New Anthropomorphism," 152.

63 Quoted in Thomas, "Lloyd Morgan's Canon," 158.

64 Fitzpatrick, "Doing Away with Morgan's Canon," 224.

65 Quoted in ibid.

66 Wynne, "Emperor's New Anthropomorphism," 152; Allen-Hermanson, "Morgan's Canon Revisited," 612.

67 Ayer, *Language, Truth and Logic*, 13; Rollin, "Animal Mind," 269.

68 Thompson, "Many Perils," 70. See also Clark, "Good Dogs and Other Animals," 45.

69 Griffin, *Question of Animal Awareness*, 103–4.

70 Griffin, *Animal Minds*, 3.

71 Panksepp, "Affective Consciousness in Animals," 2907.

72 Barron and Klein, "What Insects Can Tell Us," 4901–3.

73 Cited in Boyle, "Neuroscience and Animal Sentience," 8.

74 Hof and Van der Gucht, "Structure of the Cerebral Cortex," 28. The authors particularly note "the presence of modular arrangements of specific groups of neurons over vast domains of cortex that in toothed whales are much more restricted, and the occurrence of large numbers of spindle cells, the latter making a case of parallel evolution with hominids."

75 Damasio and Meyer, "Behind the Looking-Glass."

76 *The Cambridge Declaration on Consciousness*, 7 July 2012, http://fcmconference.org/img/CambridgeDeclarationOnConsciousness.pdf. Included among the signatories were neuropharmacologists, neurophysiologists, neuroanatomists, and computational neuroscientists.

77 Reiss and Marino, "Mirror Self-Recognition."

78 Bekoff, *Emotional Lives of Animals*, xix.

79 Bekoff and Pierce, *Wild Justice*.

80 de Waal, *Age of Empathy*.

81 Duncan, "Changing Concept," 16; Barron and Klein, "What Insects Can Tell Us."

82 Liscovitch-Brauer et al., "Trade-Off." RNA (ribonucleic acid) is a nucleic acid present in all living cells. It functions like a messenger carrying instructions from DNA for controlling the synthesis of proteins.

83 Associated Press, "Bizarre Scene Caught on Video."

84 Bermúdez, "Thinking without Words." Although philosophy professor José Luis Bermúdez himself is positive toward the thinking process of animals, his overview discusses how and why various people are dismissive.

85 Dennett, *Brainchildren*, 347.

86 Griffin, *Question of Animal Awareness*, 69.

87 Nagel, "What Is It Like to Be a Bat?"

88 Ibid., 437.

89 Ibid.

90 Singer, *Animal Liberation*, 5. Although Singer is described as an animal rights philosopher, he uses the word "liberation" rather than "rights" as it applies to animals.

91 McGinn, "Animal Minds, Animal Morality," 746.

92 Regan, *Case for Animal Rights*, 18.

93 Francione, "Comparable Harm," 81.

94 See also Cavalieri and Singer, "Great Ape Project"; Wise, "Animal Rights"; and Fetissenko, "Beyond Morality."

95 Hughes, "Environmental Ethics," 195–6; Steiner, *Anthropocentrism and Its Discontents*, 46. Pythagoras was associated with vegetarianism to the degree that for centuries, and up to the modern era, a vegetarian was called a "Pythagorean."

96 Hughes, "Environmental Ethics," 195–6.

97 Quoted in ibid., 198.

98 Fortenbaugh and Sharples, "Theophrastus," 183–7.

99 Newmyer, *Animals, Rights and Reason*, 104.

100 Mates, trans., *Outlines of Pyrronism*, bk 1, ch. 14. As an example, Sextus recounted the story of a dog who lost his prey at a three-way intersection of trails. Sniffing two of the trails and detecting no trace of his quarry, the dog went helter-skelter down the third path without wasting time to detect a scent he knew had to be there.

101 Porphyry, "Rationality of Animals."

102 White Jr, "Historical Roots," 6.

103 Montaigne, "Apologie of Raymond Sebond."

104 Tryon, *Country-Man's Companion*, 146.

105 Garrett, "Francis Hutcheson."

106 See Ryder, "Primatt, Humphry."

107 Salt, *Animals' Rights*.

108 Donaldson and Kymlicka, *Zoopolis*, 32.

109 Hughes, "Scientific Experiments on Animals."

110 Sapontzis, "Evolution of Animals," 74.

CHAPTER ONE

1 Livingston, *Fallacy of Wildlife Conservation*, 11.

2 For the purposes of this discussion, wildlife are interpreted as including nondomesticated and indigenous mammals, birds, reptiles, fish, amphibians, and arthropods.

3 Rainer et al., *On Guard for Them*, 17–20.

4 Ryder, *Animal Revolution*, 295.

5 Wiken et al., "Habitat Integrity in Canada," 17.

6 Colpitts, *Game in the Garden*, 13.

7 Wetherell, *Wildlife, Land and People*, 73–4, 77–88.

8 Cited in Bloch, *Pipestone Wolves*, 208.

9 The conservation movement in Canada was formalized through the Commission of Conservation, established in 1909 to provide Canadian governments with scientific advice on the conservation of natural resources. Chaired by former minister of the interior Clifford Sifton and representative of federal

and provincial politicians as well as experts from Canadian universities, the commission produced much literature on Canadian resource problems and public health. By the time its work had ended in 1921, the commission had laid the foundation for twentieth-century wildlife conservation, including the need for tighter hunting regulations, the establishment of protected areas, the introduction of sport species, and the crucial concept of sustained yield.

10 Bavington, *Managed Annihilation*.

11 I owe much of the source material for this discussion to Canadian historian Tina Loo's insightful study of wildlife. See Loo, *States of Nature*, 63–92.

12 Government of Canada, Commission of Conservation, Committee on Fisheries, Game and Fur-Bearing Animals, *Conservation of Fish, Game and Birds*, 154. In the summer months, over 15,000 people a day visited the sanctuary, located outside of Kingsville between Lake Erie to the south and Lake Saint Clair to the north and within 16 kilometres of the well-known birding destination Point Pelee National Park.

13 Loo, *States of Nature*, 64.

14 H.R. Wade, quoted in ibid.

15 Sir Peter Scott, quoted in ibid., 66.

16 Ibid., 73.

17 The Isaiah comment is attributed to Wallace Stegner, author of the Canadian classic *Wolf Willow* (1955). See Callicott, "Conceptual Foundations," 438; and Schaefer and Beier, "Going Public," 431.

18 Quoted in Freyfogle, "Leopold's Last Talk," 244.

19 List, "Aldo Leopold," 3.

20 Leopold, *Sand County Almanac*, 224–5.

21 Quoted in Freyfogle, "Leopold's Last Talk," 281.

22 Leopold, *Game Management*, 3.

23 Ibid., 3, 422.

24 McCullough, "Of Paradigms and Philosophies," 6.

25 Quoted in Freyfogle, "Leopold's Last Talk," 246.

26 Leopold, *Game Management*, 391, 422; Wood Jr, *Delights and Dilemmas*, 124.

27 Leopold, *Sand County Almanac*, 182; Leopold, "On a Monument to a Pigeon."

28 Leopold, *Sand County Almanac*, 97, 121.

29 Ibid., 22, 145.

30 List, "Aldo Leopold," 4.

31 Cartmill, *View to a Death*, 224.

32 Kennedy and Donihee, *Wildlife and the Canadian Constitution*, 1.

33 Since wildlife are not mentioned in the British North America Act, provincial authority rests on an interpretation of section 109, which confers on provinces the ownership of public lands, waters, and natural resources such as timber and minerals. Under common law, wildlife are generally considered to be part of the

land and accordingly within the "property" that belongs to the provinces. See Wojciechowski et al., "SARA's Safety Net Provisions," 204.

34   Tina Loo contends that this process of centralized control occurred gradually and that initially wildlife control was exercised at the local level, or what she refers to as a "local commons." See Loo, *States of Nature*, ch. 2.

35   For instance, the courts ruled that wildlife violations on federal lands in Petawawa, Ontario, fell under provincial law. See Kennedy and Donihee, *Wildlife and the Canadian Constitution*, 8.

36   Ibid., 10–14.

37   For information on the history of the Canadian Wildlife Service, see Burnett, *Passion for Wildlife*.

38   Grainger, "B.C. First Nations Claim Right."

39   Elliott, "Commercial Trapping."

40   For details on these initiatives, see Canadian Parks and Wilderness Society, *Canadian Wilderness*.

41   McSheffrey, "Premier Clark Announces." Still, the agreement proposes to log 2.5 million cubic metres of old-growth forests every year for the next ten years and tends to undermine the overall merits of ending ancient-forest logging. See environmentalist Ian McAllister's comments quoted in Hunter, "Final Agreement Reached."

42   Bird and Bohr, "Views of a Swampy-Cree Elder," 92. For a broader view on the hunting traditions of hunter-gatherers, see Hughes, "Environmental Ethics."

43   Wenzel, *Animal Rights, Human Rights*, 138–9.

44   McNeely and Hunka, *Policy Critique*.

45   Wetherell, *Wildlife, Land and People*, 309.

46   Wildgen, "Canada's Government"; Government of Canada, Environment Canada, "Harper Government."

47   Livingston, "Prisoners of Prestige," 10.

48   Donihee, *Evolution of Wildlife Law*.

49   Livingston, *Fallacy of Wildlife Conservation*, 44.

50   Colpitts, *Game in the Garden*, 102, 124.

51   Taylor, "Ethics of Respect for Nature," 201.

52   Stibbe, "Counter-Discourses," 9.

53   Bath, "Role of Human Dimensions."

54   For two typical examples, see Schroeder et al., "Legitimization of Regulatory Norms," 235; and Urbanek et al., "Acceptability and Conflict," 401.

55   Leduc, "Fallacy of Environmental Studies?" 15.

56   Crichton, "Moose and Ecosystem Management," 469.

57   Quoted in Burnett, *Passion for Wildlife*, 7.

58   Quoted in Taber and Payne, *Wildlife Conservation*, 92.

59   Hart, *J.B. Harkin*.

60　Meredith and Radford, *Conservation, Pride and Passion*, 38.

61　Huestis, "Rabies Campaign," 4.

62　Bath, "Role of Human Dimensions," 349.

63　Bocking, *Nature's Experts*, 87.

64　Paehlke, "Democracy and Environmentalism," 38.

65　Meredith and Radford, *Conservation, Pride and Passion*, 269.

66　Cartmill, *A View to a Death*, 234.

67　Loo, "Making a Modern Wilderness."

68　Ibid., 95.

69　See Franklin, *Animals and Modern Cultures*, 105; Clarke, "Why I Hunt," 13; Reid, "Personal Expression"; Loo, "Of Moose and Men," 305; Loo, "Making a Modern Wilderness," 96, 99; Petersen, *Heartsblood*, 181; Atkinson, *Making Game*, 120–1; My Wild Alberta, "Hunter Harvest"; and *Western Sportsman*, "Hunting Forecast."

70　Colpitts, *Game in the Garden*, 86. With respect to the grouse, Colpitts suggests that under the regulations, an avid hunter could kill as many as 1,800 grouse over the hunting season.

71　Heffelfinger, Geist, and Wishart, "Role of Hunting," 400; Roosevelt, *Outdoor Pastimes*, 272.

72　Hewitt, *Conservation of the Wildlife*, 298–9.

73　Wetherell, *Wildlife, Land and People*, 191–5.

74　Quoted in ibid., 214.

75　Organ et al., *North American Model*, viii. The seven principles are (1) "Wildlife resources are a public trust," (2) "Markets for game are eliminated," (3) "Allocation of wildlife is by law," (4) "Wildlife can be killed only for a legitimate purpose," (5) "Wildlife is considered an international resource," (6) "Science is the proper tool to discharge wildlife policy," and (7) "Democracy of hunting is standard." Ibid., viii–ix.

76　Ibid., 24, 26–7.

77　Government of the Swiss Confederation, *Convention on International Trade*.

78　Quoted in Scully, *Dominion*, 189.

79　Ibid.

80　Meredith and Radford, *Conservation, Pride and Passion*, 61.

81　Lawson, "Wildlife Managers."

82　Ibid., 61.

83　Ibid., 54.

84　Ibid., 51–2.

85　Cutlac and Weber, "Economic Impact," 14.

86　Canada, Canadian Tourism Commission, *Sport Fishing and Game Hunting*, 3.

87　Government of Ontario, Ministry of Natural Resources, *2014 Hunting Regulations Summary*, 2.

88　About 80 per cent of Canadians refrained from hunting for nonethical reasons compared to the 14 per cent who refused to hunt on ethical grounds. Federal,

Provincial, and Territorial Governments of Canada, Canadian Councils of Resource Ministers, 2012 *Canadian Nature Survey*, table 11, 45.

89 Nelson et al., "Inadequate Construct?" 60.

90 Simard et al., "Is Hunting an Effective Tool?" 254.

91 Kuzyk, *Challenges to Increasing Mule Deer*, 14.

92 Treves, "Hunting for Large Carnivore Conservation," 1354.

93 Festa-Bianchet, "Exploitive Wildlife Management," 205, 203.

94 Stockwell, Hendry, and Kinnison, "Contemporary Evolution," 97.

95 Thompson, "Rapid Evolution," 329.

96 Darimont et al., "Unique Ecology."

97 Darimont et al., "Human Predators."

98 Steel, *How to Make a Human*, 21.

99 Ibid., 17.

100 Harris, "Achieving Sustainable Development," 15.

101 For a good discussion, see Manuel-Navarrete, Kay, and Dolderman, "Ecological Integrity Discourses."

102 Quoted in Woodley, "Planning and Managing," 115, emphasis added.

103 Vickerman and Kagan, "Assessing Ecological Integrity," 2.

104 Callicott, Crowder, and Mumford, "Current Normative Concepts," 30; Woodley, "Planning and Managing," 114.

105 Omernik, "Perspectives on the Nature," S28.

106 Government of Alberta, Alberta Environment and Parks, "Managing Alberta's Feral Horse."

107 Strategic Relations Inc., *Alberta's Feral Horses*, 12.

108 Ibid., 11.

109 Government of Alberta, Alberta Environment and Parks, "Feral Horses."

110 McCrory, *Preliminary Technical Review*, 11.

111 Ibid., 8.

112 Ibid., 4–5, 15.

113 Downer, *Report on Wild Horses*, 4.

114 Ibid., 5.

115 Bocking, *Nature's Experts*, 95.

116 Walters, *Adaptive Management*.

117 Arthur, Garaway, and Lorenzen, *Adaptive Learning*, 3.

118 Rist et al., "New Paradigm." The six stages are (1) defining and setting management objectives using system models that represent existing understandings, assumptions, and predictions for further knowledge gathering, (2) identifying uncertainty and the alternate hypotheses based on evidence and experience, (3) implementation of policies and actions to allow for continued management by learning, (4) monitoring the effect of these actions, (5) evaluation, and (6) revision based on learned outcomes.

119 Irwin and Mickett Kennedy, "Engaging Stakeholders."

120 Taylor, Kremsater, and Ellis, *Adaptive Management of Forests*, 3.

121 Rist et al., "New Paradigm."

122 Medema, McIntosh, and Jeffrey, "From Premise to Practice."

123 Runge, "Introduction to Adaptive Management," 226–7.

124 Peter Yodzis Colloquium in Fundamental Ecology, "Sustainability, Socio-Ecological Complexity."

125 United Nations, *Convention on Biological Diversity*.

126 Boutis and Weizenbluth, *"Species at Risk" Legislation*.

127 Theberge et al., "Pitfalls of Applying Adaptive Management."

128 Government of the Yukon, Environment Yukon, *Yukon Wolf Conservation*.

129 Government of Ontario, Ministry of Natural Resources and Forestry, "Wildlife Management."

130 Waithaka, "Policy on Management," 5–6.

131 Government of Canada, Canadian Environmental Assessment Agency, "Implementation of Hyperabundant Moose Management."

132 *CBC News*, "Hungry Moose."

133 Wilson and Shackleton, *Backcountry Research*, 19.

134 Ibid., 2–3.

135 Bocking, *Nature's Experts*, 94.

136 Quoted in Meissner, "B.C. to Increase Wolf Cull."

137 Wilson, *Recommendations for Predator-Prey Management*, 15.

138 Quoted in in Cartmill, *View to a Death*, 108.

139 Murphy and Noon, "Coping with Uncertainty," 778.

140 Beans, "British Columbia Expands."

141 Boyce, Derocher, and Garshelis, *Scientific Review*, 10.

142 Bocking, *Nature's Experts*, 39, 10.

143 Bruskotter, Vucetich, and Wilson, "Of Bears and Biases."

144 United Nations Educational, Scientific and Cultural Organization, *Ramsar Convention on Wetlands*.

145 Over 90 per cent of Canada's total designated Ramsar areas lie within national parks, national wildlife areas, migratory bird sanctuaries, and provincial parks and wildlife management areas. About 10 per cent of Canada's Ramsar areas lie on sites secured for conservation by nongovernment, Aboriginal, or other agencies.

146 See Government of Canada, Environment and Climate Change Canada, "Habitat Stewardship"; Government of Canada, Species at Risk Public Registry, "Aboriginal Fund"; Government of Canada, Environment and Climate Change Canada, "Great Lakes Sustainability Fund."

147 Federal, Provincial, and Territorial Governments of Canada, Canadian Councils of Resource Ministers, *2012 Canadian Nature Survey*, 2, 21, 40, 63.

148 Much of the information was secured from specific websites and from Grandy, *Environmental Charities in Canada.*

149 Wilson, "Green Lobbies," 111.

150 Rainer et al., *On Guard for Them,* 4.

151 Zoocheck, "About," https://www.zoocheck.com/about.

152 Government of Canada, Environment and Climate Change Canada, "Ecological Gifts Program."

153 The four conservation parcels – Gullchucks Estuary, Spider Island, Geldade, and Kiidiis – three of which were donated by a single family, "include old-growth trees, spawning rivers for all five kinds of Pacific salmon, breeding grounds for water and migratory birds, and feeding grounds for large carnivores and other marine mammals. They fall within traditional Heiltsuk Nation territory, a First Nation that has lived in the region for thousands of years." McSheffrey, "Conservationists Announce."

154 Grandy, *Environmental Charities in Canada,* 31, 40.

155 Ibid., 9.

156 Association for the Protection of Fur-Bearing Animals, email to members and sponsors, 28 April 2017.

157 Animal Alliance of Canada, circular to members and sponsors, April 2017. The Modernizing Animal Protections Act, a private members' bill, sought to introduce a gross negligence offence against animal cruelty in the Criminal Code, as well as to abolish the importation of shark fins and to ban the sale of dog and cat fur in Canada.

158 International Fund for Animal Welfare, *Falling Behind,* 5.

159 Ibid., 17–18.

160 Ibid., 18.

161 Francione, *Rain without Thunder,* 229–30.

162 Sorenson, ed., *Critical Animal Studies,* xvi.

163 Rollin, "Animal Mind," 274.

164 Livingston, *Fallacy of Wildlife Conservation,* 4, 14. Livingston has been described as one of Canada's greatest thinkers and by noted author Farley Mowat as Canada's "prime philosopher of the environmental movement." Mowat, *Rescue the Earth!* 266.

165 Livingston, *Fallacy of Wildlife Conservation,* 63.

166 Ibid., 75, original emphasis.

167 Ibid., 102–3.

168 Ibid., 61.

169 Ibid., 117.

170 Orton, with MacDonald and Whyte, "John Livingston," 3.

171 Paehlke, "Environmental Values and Public Policy," 78.

CHAPTER TWO

1 Taylor, "Ethics of Respect," 198.
2 Government of Alberta, Alberta Sustainable Resource Development, *Management Plan for Mountain Goats*, x, 61, 82, 83.
3 Ibid., 61.
4 Ibid., 63.
5 The term "grizzly bear" is used only in North America. Elsewhere, the traditional name "brown bear" is used.
6 Gailus, Moola, and Connolly, *Ensuring a Future*, 5.
7 Government of British Columbia, Ministry of Environment, Lands and Parks, "Use and Enjoyment of Grizzly Bears," 47.
8 Cited in Government of Canada, Species at Risk Public Registry, "Grizzly Bear Western Population."
9 Both cited in Griffiths, Wilson, and Anielski, *Alberta GPI Accounts*, appendix B, 24. Horejsi's assessment was 400. "GPI" refers to general performance indicators. In documenting the large number of fish stocks and wildlife species in decline, this report described its conclusions as "gloomy." Ibid., ii.
10 Government of British Columbia, Ministry of Environment, Lands and Parks, "Use and Enjoyment of Grizzly Bears," 8.
11 Government of British Columbia, Ministry of Environment, Lands and Parks, *Future for the Grizzly*, 3.
12 Ibid., 8.
13 Government of British Columbia, Ministry of Environment, Lands and Parks, "Use and Enjoyment of Grizzly Bears," 51–4.
14 McLoughlin, *Managing Risks of Decline*, v.
15 Gilbert et al., *Scientific Criteria*, 3. Declines exceeding 20 per cent over three generations, or thirty years for grizzly bears, meet the criteria of the International Union for the Conservation of Nature for a threatened species.
16 McLoughlin, *Managing Risks of Decline*, 57.
17 Peek et al., *Management of Grizzly Bears*, 5.
18 Ibid., 73.
19 Gilbert et al., *Scientific Criteria*, 3.
20 Ibid., 11.
21 Ibid., 12.
22 According to the background report, the harvest rate should be set at half the estimated mortality rate. Government of British Columbia, Ministry of Environment, Lands and Parks, "Use and Enjoyment of Grizzly Bears," 48.
23 Government of British Columbia, Ministry of Environment, *Grizzly Bear Hunting*, 8.
24 Ibid., 12. "Soft" means that there is significant enough immigration and emigration between the specific population unit and surrounding areas to justify hunting.

25 Government of British Columbia, Ministry of Forests, Lands and Natural Resource Operations, *Grizzly Bear Population Estimate*, 8.

26 Ibid., 2. The BC government tried to explain the drop by referring to more accurate assessment measures. It did not seem to realize that it was simply verifying what critics had always argued: population assessments are generally unreliable.

27 Garshelis and Hristienk, "State and Provincial Estimates," 1.

28 Kunkel, Mack, and Melquist, *Assessment of Current Methods*, 1.

29 Genovali, "Opinion: BC Government."

30 Harvey, "Bear Hunting Ban."

31 Center for Responsible Travel, *Economic Impact of Bear Viewing*, 12. The study also found that organized bear-viewing activities are generating over eleven times more direct revenue for the BC government than bear hunting carried out by guide outfitters; the gross domestic product for bear viewing was $7.3 million, and for nonresident and resident hunting combined, it was $660,500. Further, bear-viewing companies are estimated to employ 510 persons (or 133 full-time equivalent jobs) per year, whereas guide outfitters employ only 11 persons (or 4.8 full-time equivalent jobs) per year in the Great Bear Rainforest. In addition, bear viewing is attracting many more visitors to the Great Bear Rainforest than is bear hunting.

32 Vaske and Roemer, "Differences in Overall Satisfaction."

33 Center for Responsible Travel, *Economic Impact of Bear Viewing*, 14.

34 Harvey, "Bear Watching More Profitable."

35 Oliver, "Is B.C.'s Trophy Hunt?"

36 Julius Strauss, quoted in ibid.

37 Artelle et al., "Confronting Uncertainty."

38 Ibid., 5.

39 Beans, "British Columbia Expands."

40 Macdonald, "Grizzly Toll."

41 Gilbert et al., *Scientific Criteria*, 3.

42 Beans, "British Columbia Expands."

43 Government of British Columbia, *Debates of the Legislative Assembly*, 1984.

44 Mowat, Heard, and Schwartz, "Predicting Grizzly Bear Density."

45 Government of British Columbia, *Debates of the Legislative Assembly*, 1985.

46 CBC News, "Wolf Hunting in Peace Region."

47 Boyce, Derocher, and Garshelis, *Scientific Review*.

48 Ibid., 2.

49 Quoted in Government of British Columbia, Ministry of Forests, Lands and Natural Resource Operations, "Experts Find 'High Level.'"

50 Boyce, Derocher, and Garshelis, *Scientific Review*, 2, 39, 40.

51 Ibid., 10, 17.

52 Ibid., 27.

53 Insights West, "Rural British Columbians."

54 Hume, "Grizzly Bear Population."

55 Government of British Columbia, *Debates of the Legislative Assembly*, 1985; Hunter, "Trophy Hunting."

56 Genovali, "90% of B.C."

57 Russell and Enns, with Stenson, *Grizzly Heart*, 1–2.

58 Russell and Enns, *Grizzly Seasons*, 7.

59 Ibid.

60 Association for the Protection of Fur-Bearing Animals, "It's Time to Talk Conservation." The figures given were seventy-two killed and twenty-four relocated.

61 Russell and Enns, *Grizzly Seasons*, 7.

62 In August 2017 the newly installed New Democratic government announced a moratorium on grizzly bear trophy hunting in the province commencing 1 December. Although hailed as a major acknowledgment of the rising public antipathy to trophy hunting, the fact remains that hunting grizzly bears for meat will continue, leading one to wonder how much the moratorium will do to protect British Columbia's grizzlies from hunters. Kines, "Grizzly Bear Trophy Hunt."

63 McAllister, *Last Wild Wolves*, 27.

64 Ibid.

65 Paquet, "Introduction," 11.

66 Rowlands, *Philosopher and the Wolf*, 109. Rowlands argues that when the superficial trappings of ambition, connivance, and self-serving pursuits are stripped away, humans are redeemed only by their defiance or the way they maintain their place in the world. It is this defiance that defines the essence of the wolf. In realizing this, Rowlands concluded of his wolf companion, Brenin, "He taught me something that my formal extended education could not: that in some ancient part of my soul, there still lived a wolf." Ibid., 8.

67 Scarce, "What Do Wolves Mean?"

68 Coleman, *Vicious*. Historian Jon Coleman documents accounts of early settler experiences, including those of John James Audubon, a naturalist, wildlife painter, and hunter, that show extreme callousness in the torture of snared wolves: "The ingenious pit traps amazed him [Audubon], as did the fearsome predators' meek behavior and the childlike glee the farmer took in his work. The violence Audubon witnessed, however, did not shock him. Watching a pack of dogs rip apart terrified and defenseless animals was a 'sport' both he and the farmer found normal and enjoyable." Ibid., 1–2.

69 Slagle, Bruskotter, and Wilson, "Role of Affect."

70 Houston, Bruskotter, and Fan, "Attitudes toward Wolves."

71 Weber, "Scientists Criticize Alberta."

72 Government of British Columbia, Ministry of Environment, *Preliminary Wolf Management Plan*, iv, 14.

73 Government of British Columbia, Ministry of Forests, Lands and Natural
     Resource Operations, *Management Plan for the Grey Wolf*; Pynn, "Contest Offers
     Cash Prizes."

74 Government of British Columbia, Ministry of Forests, Lands and Natural
     Resource Operations, *Management Plan for the Grey Wolf*, 14–17.

75 Russell, *Review of Wolf Management*, 33–54.

76 Government of British Columbia, Ministry of Environment, *Preliminary Wolf
     Management Plan*, table 3, 30.

77 Allan and Hill, "BC's Wolf Killing Plan."

78 Hume, "Livestock Stats."

79 BC Agricultural Research and Development Corporation, Wild Predator Loss
     Prevention Pilot Project, *Economic Assessment*, 19, 22. The corporation is a
     private stakeholder group representing farmers and ranchers. The report was also
     financed by Agriculture and Agri-Food Canada.

80 Ibid., 42.

81 Ibid.

82 Government of Canada, Environment Canada, *Scientific Review*, 126. The affected
     caribou are the boreal (1,300 in 6 herds), the southern mountain (1,700 in 15
     herds), and the northern mountain (17,000 in 31 herds). All herds of the first two
     groups, as well as fifteen herds of the third group, are designated as "threatened"
     under Canada's Species at Risk Act.

83 Government of British Columbia, Ministry of Environment, Lands and Parks,
     Caribou in British Columbia.

84 Paquet, "Wolf and Caribou."

85 Wolf Awareness, "Wolf-Caribou Conservation Dilemma."

86 Wilson, *Recommendations for Predator-Prey Management*, 9. Wildlife consultant
     Steven Wilson recommended that the maximum number of wolves per
     1,000 square kilometres should be 6.5. Ibid., ii.

87 Ibid., 10. Wilson also referred to ongoing studies in the Quesnel area on chemical
     sterilization.

88 Chris Ritchie, cover letter, in Wilson, *Recommendations for Predator-Prey
     Management*.

89 Animal Alliance of Canada, "British Columbia Wolf Slaughter."

90 Hume, "Documents Indicate."

91 Quoted in Meissner, "B.C. to Increase Wolf Cull."

92 Paquet, "Wolf and Caribou."

93 Government of British Columbia, Ministry of Forests, Lands and Natural
     Resource Operations, *Management Plan for the Grey Wolf*.

94 Allan and Hill, "BC's Wolf Killing Plan"; McAllister, "British Columbia's
     War on Wolves"; Pynn, "B.C. Wolf Management Plan." The comments of
     environmentalist Ian McAllister and journalist Larry Pynn were directed at the

draft management plan released in 2012, which contained the same uncertainties reflected in the 2014 version and whose recommendations were less equivocal. See Government of British Columbia, Ministry of Forests, Lands and Natural Resource Operations, *Draft Management Plan*.

95 Government of British Columbia, Ministry of Forests, Lands and Natural Resource Operations, *Management Plan for the Grey Wolf*, 4–7.

96 Ibid., iv.

97 Base figures of 5 to 15 wolves per 1,000 square kilometres and 2 to 5 per 1,000 square kilometres were used in zones with high and low wolf density respectively. Neither figure was based on any specific BC study. Ibid., 5–6.

98 Cariappa et al., "Reappraisal of the Evidence," 729.

99 Government of British Columbia, Ministry of Forests, Lands and Natural Resource Operations, *Management Plan for the Grey Wolf*, 13.

100 Ibid., 25.

101 Ibid.

102 Ibid., 20.

103 Ibid., 21–2.

104 For critical comments, see MacLeod, "BC Keeps"; MacLeod, "BC Wolf Killing"; MacLeod, "Biologist Pokes Holes"; and Allan and Hill, "BC's Wolf Killing Plan."

105 Britten, "Limits on Wolf Hunting."

106 Pynn, "Contest Offers Cash Prizes." The entry fee for the "privately sponsored wolf-kill contest" was $50, "with winners receiving 10 to 40 per cent of the entry prize pool in addition to the guaranteed prizes of $150 to $1,000." Also included were "draws for prizes such as a rifle and free taxidermy work."

107 Pynn, "Permit Not Needed."

108 Pynn, "Controversial 'Wolf Kill' Contest."

109 See Bloch, *Pipestone Wolves*.

110 Lopez, *Of Wolves and Men*, 4.

111 Ibid., 196.

112 Government of Alberta, Alberta Environment and Sustainable Resource Development, *Management Plan for Cougars*, 48–9.

113 Ibid.

114 Ibid., 9–19.

115 Ibid., 51.

116 Ibid., 6.

117 Ibid., 48. It is a large figure with respect to cougars. The approximately 400 licences issued per year do not include private landowners, who can kill cougars on their land year-round. The implications are obvious when set against the estimated population of 2,000 cougars in the province.

118 Ibid., 58, 51.

119 Ibid., 32.

120 Double Diamond Outfitters, "Alberta's #1 Cougar Taken!" The joy was due to a
      client who had killed a cougar whose length of 7 feet and 9 inches and weight of
      218 pounds led him to be ranked fourth in the world by the gun-happy Boone
      and Crockett Club.
121 Derworiz, "Encounters with Cougars."
122 Government of Alberta, Alberta Environment and Sustainable Resource
      Development, *Management Plan for Cougars*, 8.
123 Ibid., 44–5.
124 Ibid., 61.
125 Quoted in Dedyna, "Island Cougars on Losing End." Conservation officers in
      British Columbia kill sixty offending cougars for every one they relocate. Pynn,
      "B.C. Conservation Officers Criticized."
126 Quoted in cbc *News*, "3 Alberta Cougars Killed."
127 Quoted in ctv *News Calgary*, "Cougars Killed." The second cougar was likely the
      dead female's child.
128 Ho, "Update: Fish and Wildlife." See also *National Post*, "Cougar 'Enjoying the
      Morning Sun.'"
129 Schmunk, "Mother and Trio."
130 Government of Alberta, Alberta Environment and Sustainable Resource
      Development, *Management Plan for Cougars*, 7, 60. The wording of the
      related objective reads, "Maximizing the recreational benefits and enjoyment
      to Albertans from the cougar resource through the provision of a variety of
      recreational opportunities, including viewing and hunting." Ibid., 7.
131 Ross, Jalkotzy, and Gunson, "Quota System," 490.
132 Ibid.
133 Government of Alberta, Alberta Environment and Sustainable Resource
      Development, *Management Plan for Cougars*, 44.
134 This is not quite accurate. A third study focused on the Cypress Hills area in
      2007 after cougars were unexpectedly found there. Knopff, Knopff, and Bacon,
      "North of 49."
135 From 1981 to 1986 this study was carried out by Arc Associated Resource
      Consultants Ltd and was funded and conducted by the Alberta Fish and Wildlife
      Division. From 1987 to 1989 Arc assumed operational responsibility. See Pall,
      Jalkotzy, and Ross, *Cougar in Alberta*.
136 Knopff, Knopff, and Bacon, "North of 49."
137 Pall, Jalkotzy, and Ross, *Cougar in Alberta*, 132.
138 Ibid., 85. Of the twenty-one kittens born in the study, eleven were alive two and a
      half years later.
139 Ross and Jalkotzy, "Characteristics of a Hunted Population," 424. The other
      leading investigator, Orval Pall, had passed away.
140 Ibid.

141 Knopff, Knopff, and Bacon, "North of 49," 27.
142 Government of Alberta, Alberta Environment and Sustainable Resource Development, *Management Plan for Cougars*, 16.
143 Cooley et al., "Does Hunting Regulate?" 2913.
144 Ibid., 2919.
145 Ibid., 2920. In fact, the plan referred to this article but simplistically assumed that in-migration of males was compensatory without considering the broader implications for female mortalities and kitten survival.
146 Ibid.
147 Wielgus, Robinson, and Cooley, "Effects of White-Tailed Deer," 214.
148 Carpenter, Decker, and Lipscomb, "Stakeholder Acceptance Capacity."
149 Riley and Decker, "Risk Perception."
150 Thornton and Quinn, "Risk Perceptions and Attitudes."
151 Ibid., 369; Kellert et al., "Human Culture."
152 Thornton and Quinn, "Risk Perceptions and Attitudes," 369.
153 Government of Alberta, Alberta Environment and Sustainable Resource Development, *Management Plan for Cougars*, 7.
154 Double Diamond Outfitters, "Alberta's #1 Cougar Taken!"
155 Adult male polar bears weigh 350 to 700 kilograms and measure 2.4 to 3 metres in length.
156 Of the thirteen population units, nine are found solely in Canada: Norwegian Bay, Lancaster Sound, Gulf of Boothia, Foxe Basin, Southern Hudson Bay, Western Hudson Bay, McClintock Channel, Viscount Melville Sound, and Northern Beaufort Sea. Three are shared with Greenland: Davis Strait, Baffin Bay, and Kane Basin. And one is shared with the United States: Southern Beaufort Sea. The four provinces are Newfoundland and Labrador, Quebec, Ontario, and Manitoba.
157 Wiig, Aars, and Born, "Effects of Climate Change," 153.
158 In all, there are several pieces of legislation, policies, or regulations relevant to polar bears spread across seven jurisdictions. Cooperative federal management bodies at the national level include the Canadian Wildlife Directors' Committee (representing federal, provincial, and territorial governments), which develops national policy frameworks and promotes cooperative management and sharing of information among the various wildlife agencies. The Polar Bear Administrative Committee (representing federal, provincial, and territorial governments, wildlife co-management boards, and Aboriginal groups) acts as an information and referral source. The Polar Bear Technical Committee (representing federal, provincial, and territorial governments and wildlife co-management boards) evaluates research and prepares annual information on population statistics.
159 Government of the United States, Department of the Interior, Fish and Wildlife Service, "Endangered and Threatened Wildlife," figure 1, 28216.
160 Maki, "How the Effects."

161 World Wildlife Fund, "Record Low Sea Ice."

162 Cited in Richards, "This Is How Polar Bears."

163 World Wildlife Fund, "Dramatic Polar Bear Population." .

164 Hunter et al., "Climate Change Threatens," 2894.

165 Ibid., 2895.

166 Regehr et al., "Survival and Breeding," 125.

167 Braun, "Interview with Polar Bears International."

168 Diet changes are already observable, but the long-range impacts are unknown. Porpoises have now become a favoured prey, and easier access to land has led to large predation on the nests of birds, especially snow geese. See Richards, "This Is How Polar Bears."

169 Cherry et al., "Migration Phenology," 919.

170 Maki, "How the Effects." The average weight loss was given as 65 kilograms, with a length loss of 5 centimetres.

171 Government of Nunavut, Draft Nunavut Polar Bear, 10.

172 Government of Nunavut, Nunavut Polar Bear Co-Management, 5.

173 Brazil and Goudle, 5 Year Management Plan, 7–8.

174 Government of Canada, Environment and Climate Change Canada, National Polar Bear Conservation, 4.

175 Ibid., 13.

176 Government of Canada, Aboriginal Affairs and Northern Development Canada, Canadian Arctic Contaminants Assessment, vi.

177 Kucklicka et al., "Persistent Organochlorine Pollutants."

178 Norstrom et al., "Contaminant Trends"; Letcher, Temporal and Spatial Trends, 3.

179 Horton et al., "Stable Isotope Food-Web."

180 Government of Canada, Environment and Climate Change Canada, "Northern Contaminants Program."

181 Government of Canada, Aboriginal Affairs and Northern Development Canada, Canadian Arctic Contaminants Assessment, 12.

182 Ibid., 343.

183 Ibid., 351.

184 Ibid., 393.

185 Government of Canada, Environment and Climate Change Canada, National Polar Bear Conservation, 4.

186 Government of the Northwest Territories, Species at Risk Committee, Species Status Report, 95.

187 Government of Nunavut, Draft Nunavut Polar Bear, 9.

188 Government of Canada, Aboriginal Affairs and Northern Development Canada, Canadian Arctic Contaminants Assessment, x.

189 World Wildlife Fund, "wwf-Canada Statement."

190 Vongraven and Peacock, Development of the Pan-Arctic Plan, 24.

191 Ibid., 24–30; Vongraven, "IUCN/SSC Polar Bear."

192 IUCN/SSC Polar Bear Specialist Group, "Summary of Polar Bear Population."

193 Government of Canada, Environment Canada, CITES Scientific Authority, *Ursus maritimus (Polar Bear)*, 2.

194 Gill, "Foreword."

195 Vongraven and Peacock, *Development of the Pan-Arctic Plan*, table 1, 20.

196 NBC News, "Fewer Polar Bear Cubs."

197 Wiig, Aars, and Born, "Effects of Climate Change," 155.

198 DeMaster and Stirling, "Estimation of Survival," 263.

199 Government of Canada, Environment Canada, CITES Scientific Authority, *Ursus maritimus (Polar Bear)*, 5.

200 Government of Nunavut, *Draft Nunavut Polar Bear*, 1.

201 Government of Nunavut, *Nunavut Polar Bear Co-Management*, 2.

202 Ibid., 6.

203 Government of Nunavut, *Draft Nunavut Polar Bear*, 3. In fact, the plan intimated that the bears were becoming habituated to humans, more aggressive, and more dangerous, resulting in increased defence kills.

204 Ibid., appendix A, 18.

205 Government of the Northwest Territories, Species at Risk Committee, *Species Status Report*, v–xxii.

206 Ibid., vii.

207 Sandlos, *Hunters at the Margins*.

208 Government of Canada, "Order Amending Schedule 1" (2011), 2292.

209 Canadian Press, "Canada Must Explain."

210 Cheadle, "NAFTA Tribunal Finds."

211 Canadian Press, "NAFTA Panel Won't Review."

212 Government of Canada, Environment and Climate Change Canada, *National Polar Bear Conservation*, 12.

213 Rainer et al., *On Guard for Them*, 27.

214 Government of Canada, Environment and Climate Change Canada, *Polar Bear SARA Management*.

215 Waters, Rose, and Todd, *Economics of Polar Bear Hunting*, 3.

216 Nuttall et al., "Hunting, Herding," 674.

217 I recall reading a magazine article in the 1960s featuring a Canadian hunter who had returned from Alaska, where he had shot a polar bear from a helicopter. Exulting in his experience and in Roosevelt-like fashion, he told his interviewer that the days of experiences like his were numbered.

218 Government of Canada, Environment and Climate Change Canada, "Agreement on the Conservation of Polar Bears."

219 Ibid., art. 3, 24.

220 Government of Canada, Environment and Climate Change Canada, "Canada's Letter of Interpretation."

221 Government of Canada, "Section 24: Hunting, Fishing and Trapping." Section 24.6.3c of the James Bay and Northern Quebec Agreement reads, "There shall always be some allocations for non-Native sport hunting."

222 Waters, Rose, and Todd, *Economics of Polar Bear Hunting*, 4–5.

223 Wenzel, *Animal Rights, Human Rights*, 60–1; Wenzel, "Inuit and Polar Bears," 94.

224 See Wenzel, *Sometimes Hunting*.

225 Wenzel, *Animal Rights, Human Rights*, 138–9.

226 The commercial nature of an Inuit-guided hunt, where the end result will be polar bear skins and body parts adorning the walls and floors of some foreign abode, stretches the concept of respect for the symbolic white icon.

227 Government of the Swiss Confederation, *Convention on International Trade*. The United States had banned the importation of polar bear products in 2008 following its designation of the species as "threatened." Unsurprisingly, the powerful US hunting lobby is doing its best to have the import ban overturned. In 2013 Canada and Inuit leaders were again successful in pleading their case before the convention following a US request for a ban on all international importation of polar bear parts.

228 Associated Press, "US Proposal to Ban."

229 Natural Resources Defense Council, *On the Precipice*.

230 O'Connor, "Canada's Fur Trade."

231 International Fund for Animal Welfare, "IFAW Newsletter," email to sponsors, November 2014.

232 Dowsley, "Value of a Polar Bear," 43; George, "Polar Bear Management."

233 Vongraven, "IUCN/SSC Polar Bear."

234 Vongraven, "Re: Written Hearing," point 11.

235 ÉcoRessources Consultants, *Evidence of the Socio-Economic Importance*, 30.

236 Nuttall et al., "Hunting, Herding," 674.

237 ÉcoRessources Consultants, *Evidence of the Socio-Economic Importance*, 12.

238 Government of the Northwest Territories, Species at Risk Committee, *Species Status Report*, xv.

CHAPTER THREE

1 Government of Alberta, Alberta Environment and Sustainable Resource Development, "Big Game Harvest Estimates 2013 – Mule Deer"; Government of Alberta, Alberta Environment and Sustainable Resource Development, "Big Game Harvest Estimates 2013 – White-Tailed Deer."

2 Pursell, Weldy, and White, "Too Many Deer."

3 Quoted in Ton That, "Cull or Harvest?"

4 Quoted in CBC News, "Too Many Deer."

5 For example, see Waller and Alverson, "White-Tailed Deer."

6   VerCauteren, "Deer Boom."

7   Ballard et al., "Deer-Predator Relationships," 110.

8   Government of British Columbia, Ministry of Forests, Lands and Natural Resource Operations, "Wildlife Health Fact Sheet."

9   Government of Alberta, Alberta Forestry, Lands and Wildlife, *Management Plan for Mule Deer*, iii.

10 Ibid., 42–53, 54.

11 Ibid., 86.

12 Alberta Fish and Game Association, *Overview of Alberta Hunting Statistics*.

13 Tocker, "Fewer Hunting Licences."

14 Ibid.

15 Government of British Columbia, Ministry of Forest, Lands and Natural Resource Operations, "Cariboo-Chilcotin," 1.

16 Quoted in Madson, "Mule Deer Decline."

17 Alberta Conservation Association, *Delegated Big Game Surveys*, 30, 44, 46, 50, tables 11, 12, 13. One of the four blocks was in the southeast Prairies, two were in central Alberta, and one was in the far northwest.

18 Ibid., 50, 52.

19 Findholt et al., "Diet Composition."

20 Mule Deer Working Group, Western Association of Fish and Wildlife Agencies, *Mule Deer*, 5.

21 Wielgus, Robinson, and Cooley, "Effects of White-Tailed Deer."

22 Geist, *Mule Deer Country*, 163.

23 Mule Deer Working Group, Western Association of Fish and Wildlife Agencies, "Range-Wide Status."

24 Herrero et al., "Fatal Attacks," 596. The City of Toronto reported 79 homicides in 2013, and New York City reported 328 in 2014.

25 Siemer et al., "Factors That Influence," 194–5. See also Slagle, "Building Tolerance for Bears." Environmentalist Kristina Slagle emphasizes programs that stress the positive qualities and ecological value of black bears.

26 Ecojustice, *Failure to Protect*, 14.

27 Williamson, *In the Black*, 11, 23.

28 Government of Ontario, Ministry of Natural Resources, *Framework for Enhanced Black Bear*, 1.

29 Government of Ontario, Ministry of Natural Resources, *Backgrounder on Black Bears*, 28.

30 Quoted in Diebel, "Ontario Spring Bear Hunt."

31 See Government of Ontario, *Heritage Hunting and Fishing Act*.

32 Quoted in Reidner, "Bear Wise Program Cuts."

33 Ibid.

34 Government of Ontario, Ministry of Natural Resources and Forestry, "Ontario Proposing."

35 Cited in Taylor, "Shooting Back."

36 Harries, "Re: Safety First."

37 Zoocheck Canada, "Spring Bear Hunt."

38 Lemelin, "Impacts of the Cancellation," 148. Major lobbyists for the return of the spring bear hunt included the Ontario Federation of Anglers and Hunters, Canadian Outdoor Heritage Alliance, Northern Ontario Tourist Outfitters, and Northwestern Sportsmen's Alliance.

39 Quoted in Diebel, "Ontario Spring Bear Hunt."

40 Government of Ontario, Environmental Registry, "Amendment to Two Regulations" (2014).

41 Reeves, "Controversial Spring Bear Hunt."

42 "Applicant's Factum: Part 1 – Introduction," 1–2, in *Animal Alliance of Canada v. Ontario (Minister of Natural Resources), 2014, ONSC 2826*, in possession of author (hereafter *Animal Alliance v. OMNR*).

43 "Decision," 2, in *Animal Alliance v. OMNR*.

44 Ibid., 6–11.

45 Hodgins, "Spring Bear Hunt Back."

46 Government of Ontario, Ministry of Natural Resources, *Backgrounder on Black Bears*, 12.

47 "Respondent's Application Record: Exhibit F," 41, in *Animal Alliance v. OMNR*.

48 "Decision," 8–9, in *Animal Alliance v. OMNR*.

49 "Respondent's Application Record: Exhibit F," 42, in *Animal Alliance v. OMNR*.

50 The applicants further maintained that the minister of environment had ignored the basis on which the hunt had been cancelled in 1999, that he had not considered the established science, and that there was nothing to indicate that he had weighed the potential enhancement of public safety expected from a spring bear hunt against the number of cubs who would die as a result. "Decision," 6, in *Animal Alliance v. OMNR*.

51 Two of the four submitted criteria referred to the accumulation of knowledge that would result from the hunt and to stakeholder and public communication. The explanation of how the hunt integrated into "a sound understanding of natural and ecological systems" was meaningless rhetoric: "The regulatory changes under the Fish and Wildlife Conservation Act emphasize the continued protection and sustainable management of Black Bears. Ontario is home to a healthy and sustainable bear population." "Respondent's Application Record: Exhibit C," 26, in *Animal Alliance v. OMNR*.

52 Ibid., 27.

53 Government of Ontario, Environmental Registry, "Amendment to Two Regulations" (2015).

54 Ibid.

55 Ibid.

56 Quoted in Csanady, "'Political Killing'?"

57 Any moose I have encountered, and I have seen many, have either ignored me, gazed at me with little interest, or just taken off. However, I would not recommend confronting a mother moose with a calf or a bull moose during mating season.

58 McLaren et al., "Effects of Overabundant Moose," 47.

59 Byrne, "Introduction of Moose," 4.

60 Loo, "Making a Modern Wilderness."

61 McLaren et al., "Effects of Overabundant Moose," 48.

62 Lohr, Ballard, and Bath, "Attitudes toward Gray Wolf."

63 McLaren et al., "Effects of Overabundant Moose," 48–50. Balsam fir, yellow birch, and red maple trees are popular food sources for moose.

64 Ibid., 48–52.

65 Quoted in *The Packet*, "Terra Nova to Start."

66 *CBC News*, "Moose Cull in Gros Morne."

67 McLaren and Mercer, "How Management Unit."

68 Crichton, "Moose and Ecosystem Management."

69 Mathisen et al., "Moose Density and Habitat," 713.

70 *CBC News*, "Moose Population Declining."

71 Byrne, "Introduction of Moose," 9.

72 Government of Newfoundland and Labrador, Department of Environment and Conservation, "Hunting and Trapping Guide."

73 Clevenger, "Moose-Vehicle Collisions."

74 According to official provincial documents, the cost of fencing 9,000 kilometres at $150,000 per kilometre plus bridges and other infrastructure and activities exceeded well over $1 billion. *George v. Newfoundland and Labrador*, 2016, NLCA 24, 12, records.court.nl.ca/public/supremecourt/decisiondownload/?decision-id=2261.

75 Clevenger, "Moose-Vehicle Collisions," 2.

76 Robert Stack, cited in *CBC News*, "Moose Class-Action Lawsuit."

77 Ches Crosbie, cited in ibid.

78 Government of Newfoundland and Labrador, Department of Environment and Conservation, *2015–2020 Newfoundland and Labrador Moose Management Plan*, 17.

79 Ibid., 3, 19.

80 Hatler, Poole, and Beal, *Furbearer Management Guidelines*.

81 Brisbane, "Coyotes Survivors Despite Humans."

82 Government of Alberta, Alberta Agriculture and Forestry, *Coyote Predation Control*, 7.

83 Quoted in Canadian Press, "Saskatchewan Defends Coyote Bounty."

84 Wildlife biologist and coyote expert Dianne Wittner told the *Rocky Mountain Outlook* that she had "received word from a veterinarian in Nova Scotia that the animals that killed the young woman had less than 20 per cent coyote DNA." Cited in Brisbane, "Coyotes Survivors Despite Humans."

85 Canadian Press, "Saskatchewan Defends Coyote Bounty."

86 Quoted in Gartner, "Comeback Coyote."

87 Fox and Valastro, "Coyote Bounties Are Futile." The authors of this *Toronto Star* article, Camilla Fox and AnnaMaria Valastro, are respectively the executive director of Project Coyote and the executive director of the Peaceful Parks Coalition.

88 Canadian Press, "Saskatchewan Defends Coyote Bounty."

89 Quoted in ibid.

90 Quoted in Project Coyote, "Nature Saskatchewan Passes Resolution."

91 Quoted in Biber, "Coyote Bounty."

92 Brisbane, "Coyotes Survivors Despite Humans."

93 Quoted in ibid.

94 Gartner, "Comeback Coyote."

95 Government of Saskatchewan, Ministry of Agriculture, "Crop Insurance's Wildlife Damage." This press release stated, "Producers will be compensated for 100 per cent of the market value of their livestock killed by predators and up to 80 per cent of the market value for injured livestock requiring veterinary services." Eligible for compensation were predations by any wild animals that caused injury or death to specified livestock. Government of Saskatchewan, *Wildlife Damage*.

96 Quoted in Government of Saskatchewan, Ministry of Agriculture, "Crop Insurance's Wildlife Damage."

97 Lesley Sampson, executive director of Coyote Watch Canada, cited in CBC *News*, "Coyote Hunt with Cash Prizes."

98 Government of Alberta, Alberta Agriculture and Forestry, *Coyote Predation Control*, 25.

99 Biber, "Coyote Bounty."

100 Hayslette, Armstrong, and Mirarchi, "Mourning Dove Hunting."

101 Humane Society of the United States, "Dove Shooting."

102 Duda and Jones, "Public Opinion," figure 3, 188.

103 Barney et al., "Mourning Dove," 4–5.

104 Long Point Waterfowl, "About Us," http://www.longpointwaterfowl.org/about-us.

105 Ontario Federation of Anglers and Hunters, "Simcoe Area Waterfowl Expert."

106 MacKay, "Stop Dove Hunting."

107 Government of Canada, Canadian Wildlife Service – Ontario Region, "Assessment on the Feasibility," 13.

108 Ibid., 11–12.

109 Ibid., 13.

110 Government of Canada, Canadian Wildlife Service, *Proposals to Amend*, 8.

111 Christensen, "Ontario Province-Wide." A copy of the questionnaire is contained as an appendix in Barney et al., "Mourning Dove," 36–7.

112 In the thesis, the survey respondent was asked the following: "If it is determined that Mourning dove populations are increasing in Ontario, I would agree to the

opening of a season to hunt this species within the province." In response to this question, 25 per cent were neutral, 58 per cent agreed (of which only 18 per cent strongly agreed), and 17 per cent disagreed. Christensen, "Ontario Province-Wide," 6, 8.

113 Ibid., 9. The 5 per cent figure was attributed to the cws and dated 2005.

114 Daubs, "It's Open Season."

115 Dietsche, "Mourning Dove Hunt."

116 Quoted in Galloway, "Controversy Greets Mourning-Dove."

117 MacKay, "Stop Dove Hunting."

118 Animal Alliance of Canada, "Help Us Fight."

119 Animal Liberation Front, "Opposing Recreational Hunting."

120 Burnett, *Passion for Wildlife*, 296. In 2016 the cws approved a mourning dove hunting season in southern Quebec.

121 Other areas of seal concentration are off the coast of Labrador and in Quebec around Montreal's North Shore, the Gaspe Peninsula, and the Magdalen Islands in the Gulf of Saint Lawrence.

122 The yearly kill topped 400,000 in 1956, and in the subsequent years before 1970 the number of seals who died annually on the ice floes was rarely below 250,000. Fink, *Canada's Commercial Seal Slaughter*, 24.

123 The term "whitecoats" refers to the pristine white fur of pre-moulted harp seals under two weeks of age. In the mid-1970s whitecoats amounted to almost 80 per cent of the total seal catch. Dauvergne, *Shadows of Consumption*, 188. The European Union's ban also applied to pre-moulted hooded seals, or bluebacks. European Union, Council of the European Communities, "Council Directive 83/129/EEC."

124 Government of Canada, Fisheries and Oceans Canada, *2011–2015 Integrated Fisheries Management*, sec. 3.1.6.

125 Fink, *Canada's Commercial Seal Slaughter*, 24. In fact, the boycott was so successful that the International Fund for Animal Welfare discontinued it in 1985 because of its negative impact on fishermen and their families. Best, *Influencing Canadian Seal Hunt*, 10–11.

126 Royal Commission on Seals and the Sealing Industry in Canada, *Seals and Sealing in Canada*, vol. 1. In addition to recommending against the use of nets and advocating for the deployment of smaller boats, the commission stressed the need for effective population monitoring and for definitive research to assess the impact of seals on fish stocks. Most significant, the commission upheld the European Union's ban on the killing of infant seals, a recommendation that the government adopted in 1987. Ethical or moral considerations were rationalized away through reference to personal choice. The practice of clubbing moulted seals, however young, was acceptable as long their deaths involved no unnecessary pain, but no rigid oversight procedures were included to ensure that this impossible condition was rendered possible. Culling was sound practice if the situation warranted.

The commissioners were adamant on the hunt's viability and crucial economic importance to Atlantic communities. Subsidies were recommended for sealing interests and Inuit hurt by the ban. The commission also posited that opponents of the seal hunt had been more successful in presenting their views to an ill-informed public than had the pro-seal hunt coalitions, and it urged the government to become proactive on the side of the latter.

127 Through direct and indirect subsidies, loans, and other assistance measures, the government spent millions of dollars annually to keep the seal hunt afloat. A study conducted by the Canadian Institute for Business and the Environment documented thirty-eight separate subsidies totalling over $20 million paid by the federal and provincial governments to support the seal industry between 1995 and 2001. Although the federal government has ended direct subsidies, it still allocates millions of dollars annually for the hunt by way of icebreakers and aircraft, for lobbying the European Union, and for the substantial costs of monitoring, enforcement, and management. One estimate set a figure of $6.9 million a year. Canadian Institute for Business and the Environment, *Economics of the Canadian Sealing Industry*, 6; Livernois, "Economics of Ending," 49. John Livernois is an economics professor at the University of Guelph.

128 European Union, Council on Trade in Seal Products, "Regulation (EC) No. 1007/2009," para. 1.

129 For Canada's written submission to the World Trade Organization (WTO), see World Trade Organization, *European Communities*. The WTO found that the ban was contrary to free trade rules but felt that it should continue because it "fulfils the objective of addressing the EU public moral concerns on seal welfare." Quoted in Vaughan, "Seal Product Ban." On appeal, the federal government contended that the WTO position was "hypocritical" in that it discriminated against "one way of killing animals." Cited in CBC News, "Seal Product Ban Upheld."

130 Canadian Sealers Association, "Important Notice: CSA Operations."

131 Government of Canada, Minister of Finance, *Strong Leadership*, 18.

132 The hakapik is used on seals under one year old. Following refinement recommendations, its use now involves a three-step killing process: stunning, checking (palpation of the skull), and bleeding. Other refinements over the years include the adoption of an objective-based management system using variable reference points and control measures to set annual quotas and the implementation of what is termed a "precautionary approach."

133 Quoted in MacDonald, "East Coast Seal Hunt."

134 Millar, "Skinned Alive."

135 Smith, *Improving Humane Practice*, 12. Prepared on request by sealing groups, it was this report that recommended the three-phase killing method later adopted as standard practice.

136 Daoust and Craguel, "Canadian Harp Seal Hunt," 453.

137   Ibid.

138   Ibid.

139   Butterworth and Richardson, "Review of Animal Welfare Implications," 466.

140   Canadian Press, "Court Upholds Restriction."

141   Government of Canada, Minister of Justice, *Marine Mammal Regulations (SOR/93–56)*, sec. 32(1).

142   Government of Canada, Minister of Fisheries and Oceans, "Regulations Amending," sec. 33(2)(e). Licensed observation helicopters must stay above 150 metres (500 feet) from the hunt. Humane Society International/Canada, "Sealing Industry Tries."

143   Quoted in Reichel, "Animal Rights Groups."

144   These inside workers are primarily undercover investigative journalists. Cronin, "Bill Will Block Observers."

145   According to the International Fund for Animal Welfare, as many as 150,000 seals have been killed over a two-day period. International Fund for Animal Welfare, "Why Commercial Sealing."

146   MacDonald, "Commercial Seal Hunt."

147   MacDonald, "Sale of Seal Meat."

148   Government of Canada, Fisheries and Oceans Canada, *2011–2015 Integrated Fisheries Management*, sec. 3.3.

149   Government of Canada, *European Communities*, 21.

150   Korski, "Newfoundland Sealers?"

151   Canadian Institute for Business and the Environment, *Economics of the Canadian Sealing Industry*, 20.

152   Humane Society International/Canada, "Canadian Commercial Seal Slaughter."

153   Fink, *Canada's Commercial Seal Slaughter*, 18.

154   Livernois, "Economics of Ending," 47.

155   Humane Society International/Canada, *Newfoundlanders' Views*, 4.

156   Crosbie, "Foreword," ix.

157   Furlong, "Are the Animal Rights Groups?"

158   Government of Canada, Fisheries and Oceans Canada, *2011–2015 Integrated Fisheries Management*, sec. 3.5.1.5.

159   European Union, Council on Trade in Seal Products, "Regulation (EC) No. 1007/2009," para. 14. In 2014, following the dismissal of Canada's appeal to the WTO, the European Union agreed to allow the importation and sale of any seal products harvested by Indigenous people, not just Inuit, in Canada. *Nunatsiaq News*, "Canada, EU Strike Deal."

160   International Fund for Animal Welfare, "Indigenous Seal Hunts."

161   Government of Canada, Fisheries and Oceans Canada, *Impacts of Grey Seals*, 2.

162   Government of Canada, Fisheries and Oceans Canada, "Grey Seals and Cod."

163   Emery, *Northern Cod Crisis*, 2.

164 Bavington, *Managed Annihilation*, 156–70.

165 McLaren et al., *Report of the Eminent Panel*, 71.

166 See Pannozzo, *Devil and the Deep Blue Sea*; and Whitehead et al., "Independent Marine Scientists Respond."

167 Pannozzo, "Sealfall, Licence to Cull."

168 Government of Canada, Fisheries and Oceans Canada, *Impacts of Grey Seals*, 46.

169 Following pubic opposition from animal-support groups, including Animal Alliance of Canada, the grey seal hunt was suspended by the Conservative government of Prime Minister Stephen Harper in 2010 because of low pelt prices.

170 Hervieux-Payette, "News Release"; *CTV News*, "Seal Meat Lunch."

171 Government of Newfoundland and Labrador, "Statements by Ministers."

172 Quoted in Dekel, "Fisheries Minister."

173 See Wenzel, *Animal Rights, Human Rights*. Under article 3 of the European Union's ban, the Inuit were exempted. European Union, Council on Trade in Seal Products, "Regulation (EC) No. 1007/2009," art. 3(1).

174 Winter, "Sealing: A Rightful Occupation."

175 Ibid.

176 Barry, *Icy Battleground*, 150.

177 In its guiding principles, the IFAW, the most powerful lobby in the campaign to secure the European Union's ban, stresses value and the need to treat animals with sensitivity and respect. In the case of wild animals, this means ensuring "the minimization, prevention or elimination of harm." Nowhere are "rights" mentioned. For example, Indigenous hunting is permissible, and culling is endorsed, albeit under extreme need. International Fund for Animal Welfare, "Glossary and Statements of Principle," art. 1.3.

178 Calvert et al., "Synthesis of Human-Related," table 1.

179 Shochat et al., "Invasion, Competition," 203–5.

180 Ditchkoff, Saalfeld, and Gibson, "Animal Behavior," 6–10.

181 Lefebvre, *Wildlife Management Responses*, 7–8.

182 Wittmann et al., "Standards for Lethal Response," 33.

183 Morgan, "We Need to Cull."

184 City of Calgary, Parks and Recreation, "Common Pests in Calgary."

185 For example, see Dubois and Harshaw, "Exploring 'Humane' Dimensions"; and Manfredo, Teel, and Bright, "Why Are Public Values?"

CHAPTER FOUR

1 Childs, *Apocalyptic Planet*, xvi.

2 Wilson, *In Search of Nature*, 178.

3 Ibid., 179.

4 Burnett, *Passion for Wildlife*, 264–5.

5 Bocking, *Nature's Experts*, 87.

6 Burnett, *Passion for Wildlife*, 264–5. The federal Wildlife Act introduced the process of cooperative federalism to the management of wildlife.

7 Aird, "Tory Cuts."

8 Government of Canada, Environment Canada, *Canadian Biodiversity Strategy*, 3.

9 Armenteras and Finlayson, "Biodiversity," figure 5.16, 158.

10 Cited in Boyd, *Unnatural Law*, 165.

11 World Commission on Environment and Development, *Our Common Future*.

12 Livingston, *Rogue Primate*, 59.

13 United Nations, *Convention on Biological Diversity*.

14 A flurry of legislation and accords followed, including the Canadian Environmental Assessment Act (1995), the Wild Animal and Plant Protection and Regulation of International and Interprovincial Trade Act (1996), and the Canada Oceans Act (1997).

15 Government of Canada, Species at Risk Public Registry, *Accord for the Protection of Species.*

16 Government of Canada, Species at Risk Public Registry, "Backgrounder."

17 Government of Canada, Environment Canada, *Canadian Biodiversity Strategy,* 16–17.

18 Ibid.7

19 Suzuki, "Beyond the Species at Risk Act," 205.

20 McNeely and Hunka, *Policy Critique*, 1.

21 Canada was growing its first genetically modified crops in 1995, the year that the Biodiversity Strategy was introduced, so it is doubly surprising that reference to these crops was absent, even more so given that one of the strategy's goals was to protect biodiversity from the adverse effects of "living modified organisms." Government of Canada, Environment Canada, *Canadian Biodiversity Strategy*, 17.

22 Ibid., 41.

23 Ibid., 19, 20, 21.

24 Harris, *Fragmented Forest*, 107.

25 Government of Canada, Environment and Climate Change Canada, "Status of Wild Species."

26 Rainer et al., *On Guard for Them*, 17, 18, 20.

27 Smith, "Canada's Incredible."

28 Government of Canada, *Species at Risk Act*.

29 Smith, "Canada's Incredible."

30 Ibid.

31 Interviewed in Waldick, "Noteworthy – Legislation."

32 The Committee on the Status of Endangered Wildlife in Canada (COSEWIC) dates to 1977 and arose from the need for a single, official, scientifically sound,

national classification of wildlife species at risk. It was given legal status by SARA in 2003 as the authority for assessing the conservation status of wildlife species that may be at risk of extinction in Canada. Members of COSEWIC include academics, independent specialists, Aboriginal knowledge-holders, government biologists, museum staff, and independent biologists. Members have considerable experience with wildlife and biological science, including Aboriginal traditional knowledge, ecology, genetics, wildlife and fisheries management, systematics, and risk assessment, coupled with years of field experience. Among the thirty-one voting members of COSEWIC are a co-chair from each of the ten Species Specialist Subcommittees (Vascular Plants, Mosses and Lichens, Molluscs, Arthropods, Marine Fishes, Freshwater Fishes, Amphibians and Reptiles, Birds, Marine Mammals, and Terrestrial Mammals), a co-chair from the Aboriginal Traditional Knowledge Subcommittee, one representative from each of the thirteen provincial and territorial governments, one representative from each of the four federal agencies (Canadian Wildlife Service, Parks Canada, Fisheries and Oceans Canada, and the Canadian Museum of Nature), and three nongovernment scientists. All members must demonstrate that they possess the required expertise to serve on the committee. Once appointed, they act as independent experts, not as representatives of any government or organization.

33 Government of Canada, Environment Canada, *Canadian Biodiversity Strategy*, 13.
34 Smallwood, *Guide*, 7.
35 Government of the United States and Government of Great Britain, *Convention between the United States and Great Britain*.
36 Government of Canada, Species at Risk Public Registry, *Accord for the Protection of Species*.
37 The Canadian Endangered Species Conservation Council is comprised of the federal ministers of environment, fisheries and oceans, and heritage and the provincial and territorial ministers with responsibilities for wildlife species. The council also provides general direction on the activities of COSEWIC. The Canadian Wildlife Directors Committee is comprised of federal, provincial, and territorial wildlife directors, plus representatives from Environment Canada, Fisheries and Oceans Canada, and Parks Canada. The National General Status Working Group is comprised of representatives from each of the Canadian provinces and territories and from the federal government.
38 These provinces are Quebec, Ontario, Saskatchewan, and British Columbia. For an example of an agreement, see Government of Canada and Government of British Columbia, *Canada-British Columbia Agreement*.
39 Government of Canada, Environment Canada, *Evaluation of Programs and Activities*, 17, 24, 28, 56, 58.
40 Ibid., 43.
41 Jones, "Groups Challenge."

42 Quoted in ibid.

43 Casey, "'Terrible Day.'"

44 Ecojustice, *Failure to Protect*, 11; Government of Alberta, Alberta Environment and Parks, "Alberta's Species at Risk Strategies," strategies 4 and 6.

45 Moola et al., "Waiting for the Ark," 7.

46 Ibid., 12; Government of Saskatchewan, *Wildlife Act*, part 5.

47 Ecojustice, *Failure to Protect*, 13, 14; Government of Ontario, *Endangered Species Act*, sec. 11.

48 Ecojustice, *Failure to Protect*, 15–17, 20–1.

49 Wojciechowski et al., "sara's Safety Net Provisions," 210.

50 Ecojustice, "Endangered Species Protection."

51 Wojciechowski et al., "sara's Safety Net Provisions," 214.

52 Extrapolated from the Species at Risk Public Registry and from the various provincial species at risk websites.

53 Wojciechowski et al., "sara's Safety Net Provisions," 214.

54 Ibid.

55 Cited in *cbc News*, "Canada's Process to Protect."

56 Government of Canada, Environment Canada, Fisheries and Oceans Canada, and Parks Canada, *Formative Evaluation*, 15. The species affected are the red crossbill, horned grebe, roseate tern, Banff Springs snail, and Ontario's piping plover.

57 Hoberg, "What's behind the Woeful Implementation?"

58 Parliament of Canada, House of Commons, Standing Committee on Environment and Sustainable Development, "Evidence – Dr. C. Scott Findlay."

59 Government of Canada, Species at Risk Public Registry, "Red-Headed Woodpecker."

60 Government of Canada, Species at Risk Public Registry, "Response Statement – Red-Headed Woodpecker"; Government of Canada, Parks Canada, *Multi-Species Action Plan for Bruce Peninsula*; Government of Canada, Parks Canada, *Multi-Species Action Plan for Point Pelee*.

61 Government of Canada, Species at Risk Public Registry, "Action Plans."

62 See Clark and Harvey, "Assessing Multi-Species Recovery," 661.

63 McDevitt-Irwin et al., "Missing the Safety Net," 1603.

64 Government of Canada, Environment Canada, *Recovery Strategy for the Wolverine* (2014), iii.

65 Government of Canada, Environment Canada, *Recovery Strategy for the Burrowing Owl*, 28.

66 Government of Canada, Fisheries and Oceans Canada, *Recovery Strategy for the Leatherback Turtle*.

67 Cited in Cheadle, "Environment, Fisheries Ministers Failed."

68 Government of Canada, Fisheries and Oceans Canada, "Recovery Strategies, Action Plans."

69 VanderZwaag, Engler-Palma, and Hutchings, "Canada's *Species at Risk Act*," 282.

70 Ibid., 305.

71 Smith, "Canada's Incredible."

72 Ecojustice, *Failure to Protect*, 7. The grades were C+ for Ontario, C for Nova Scotia, C- for Canada (i.e., SARA itself), Manitoba, Quebec, Newfoundland and Labrador, and Nunavut, D+ for the Northwest Territories and New Brunswick, D for Prince Edward Island, and F for British Columbia, Alberta, Saskatchewan, and the Yukon.

73 Ibid., 23.

74 McNeely and Hunka, *Policy Critique*, 74.

75 Quoted in Ball, "Feds Removal of Humpback."

76 Findlay et al., "Species Listing," 1610.

77 Mooers et al., "Biases in Legal Listing."

78 Ibid., 574.

79 Ibid., 573. Fifteen years was the window given for the survival of the beluga whale in the eastern Hudson Bay.

80 Findlay et al., "Species Listing," 1612.

81 Green Party of Canada, "Species at Risk."

82 Government of Canada, Environment Canada, *Evaluation of Programs and Activities*, 56.

83 COSEWIC, *Assessment and Status Report on the Porbeagle*, iv, v.

84 Ibid., vi.

85 Rudd, "National Values," 240.

86 COSEWIC, *Assessment and Status Report on the Atlantic Bluefin Tuna*, iii, 25.

87 Government of Canada, Species at Risk Public Registry, "List of Wildlife Species at Risk."

88 Ibid.

89 COSEWIC, *Assessment and Status Report on the Wolverine*, ix.

90 Ibid., vi.

91 Stewart et al., "Wolverine Behavior."

92 COSEWIC, *Assessment and Status Report on the Wolverine*, viii, 37.

93 Ibid., 29–36.

94 Government of Canada, Environment Canada, *Recovery Strategy for the Wolverine* (2016), iv.

95 Ibid., vi, x.

96 COSEWIC, *Assessment and Status Report on the Wolverine*, 36.

97 CBC News, "Canada's Process to Protect."

98 Government of Canada, Environment Canada, *Evaluation of Programs and Activities*, 62.

99 See Environmental Law Centre, "Re: Proposed Partial Identification."

100 Government of Canada, Environment Canada, *Species at Risk Act and You*. This guide to SARA states, "Under SARA, permits may be issued or agreements may be entered into to authorize certain activities that would otherwise contravene

the general or critical habitat prohibitions, if certain conditions are met. These authorizations are sometimes called 'Section 73 Permits,' referring to the section of the Act that deals with authorizations." Ibid., 2.

101   Suzuki, "Beyond the Species at Risk Act," 250.

102   Olive, "Can Stewardship Work?" 235, 231.

103   Henderson, Reed, and Davis, "Voluntary Stewardship," 29.

104   Government of Canada, Environment Canada, *Evaluation of Programs and Activities*, 57.

105   Henderson, Reed, and Davis, "Voluntary Stewardship," 24, 29.

106   COSEWIC, *Assessment and Status Report on the Black-Tailed Prairie Dog*, v.

107   Government of Canada, Parks Canada, *Management Plan for the Black-Tailed Prairie Dog*, 4.

108   For excellent general information on the black-footed ferret, particularly the reintroduction program in the United States, see Jachowski, *Wild Again*.

109   Ibid., 166.

110   Ibid., 39.

111   Government of Canada, Parks Canada, *Management Plan for the Black-Tailed Prairie Dog*, v.

112   Ibid., 14.

113   Ibid.

114   Government of Canada, Parks Canada, *Recovery Strategy for the Black-footed Ferret*, 15.

115   Jachowski, *Wild Again*, 178–93.

116   However, there have been enzootic outbreaks, which are far less deadly.

117   COSEWIC, *Assessment and Status Report on the Black-Tailed Prairie Dog*, 38.

118   Wojciechowski et al., "SARA's Safety Net Provisions," 215.

119   Federal programs in support of species at risk include the Habitat Stewardship Program for Species at Risk, Aboriginal Fund for Species at Risk, and Interdepartmental Recovery Fund.

120   Government of Canada, Environment Canada, *Evaluation of Programs and Activities*, 16. This funding went primarily to the Habitat Stewardship Program for Species at Risk, Aboriginal Fund for Species at Risk, Interdepartmental Recovery Fund, Natural Areas Conservation Program, and Ecological Gifts Program.

121   Government of Canada, Treasury Board of Canada, *2015–2016 Estimates*, part 1, 1.

122   Government of Canada, Minister of Finance, *Strong Leadership*, 368, 310. It is unclear whether this $25 million is an addition to or a replacement of an earlier commitment of $44.6 million a year for the next three years. Either way, the amount would still be low even compared to spending between 2007 and 2011.

123   Government of Ontario, Ministry of Natural Resources and Forestry, *Estimates, 2015–16*, 9.

124   Government of Newfoundland and Labrador, Department of Finance, *Estimates of the Program Expenditure*, x, 11.11.

125 Government of Alberta, Alberta Environment and Sustainable Resource Development, *Annual Report, 2014–2015*, 67.

126 Government of British Columbia, Ministry of Environment and Environmental Assessment Office, *2015/16–2017/18 Service Plan*, 15.

127 See Government of Canada, Environment and Climate Change Canada, *Recovery Strategy for the Blue Racer*, part 2, 10. The federal recovery strategy is blended with the provincial strategy, allowable under section 44 of the Species at Risk Act.

128 Ibid., part 2, 25.

129 Government of Canada, Environment Canada, *Canadian Biodiversity Strategy*, 20.

130 Fitzpatrick, "Environment Canada Job Cuts."

131 Nikiforuk, "Facing Millions in Cuts."

132 Payton, "Parks Canada Hit."

133 Boutilier, "Parks Canada Services."

134 De Souza, "Harper Government Cutting."

135 Government of Canada, Treasury Board of Canada, *2015–2016 Estimates*, part 2, 113.

136 Ellis, "Parks Canada Conservation Spending."

137 Government of Canada, Environment and Climate Change Canada, "Habitat Stewardship."

138 Government of Canada, Fisheries and Oceans Canada, *Partial Action Plan*, 17–18.

139 Carson, Flores, and Meade, "Contingent Valuation," 173.

140 Willingness to pay is often associated with contingency value research, which is the research tool used in developing the survey information.

141 Loomis, Edwards, and Richardson, "Total Economic Valuation."

142 Entem, Adamowicz, and Boxall, "Habitat Conservation."

143 Carson, Flores, and Meade, "Contingent Valuation."

144 Edwards, "Ethical Preferences," 149.

145 Fluker, "Curious Case."

146 Government of Canada, *Species at Risk Act*, preamble and sec. 49(1)(e).

147 Filion, Jacquemot, and Reid, *Importance of Wildlife to Canadians*, 5.

148 Ibid., 18. See also Adamowicz et al., "Components of the Economic Value."

149 Government of Canada, Fisheries and Oceans Canada, "Health of the Oceans," under "Environment Canada – Biodiversity and Corporate Services – Marine Wildlife Areas Establishment."

150 Government of Canada, Species at Risk Public Registry, "Emergency Order ... Greater Sage-Grouse."

151 ÉcoRessources Consultants, *Evidence of the Socio-Economic Importance*, vi. See also Richardson and Loomis, "Total Economic Value," which gives WTP figures for several at-risk species based on US dollars.

152 Government of Canada, "Order Amending Schedule 1" (2017).

153 Giraud and Valcic, "Willingness-to-Pay," 71.

154 Rudd, "National Values," 248.

155 Gilbert and Halsted, "Economic Considerations."

156 Christie, "Triage in the Wild."

157 Cited in Boyd, *Unnatural Law*, 185.

158 Canadian Bar Association, National Environmental Law Section, *Submission on Bill C-33*, 5. The three legal precedents were *R. v. Crown Zellerbach Ltd* (1988), *Friends of the Oldman River Society v. Canada* (1992), and *Canada v. Hydro-Québec* (1997).

159 Ibid.

160 Of course, the federal reluctance to intrude on areas of provincial constitutional authority is a consideration. However, defenders of wildlife would contend that it is warranted since wildlife protection is essentially a national issue.

161 Government of Canada, *Species at Risk Act*, sec. 80.

162 Smallwood, *Guide*, 8.

163 Freeman, "Ontario's New Species Law."

164 Fundira, "Ottawa Issues Emergency Protection."

165 *Western Canadian Wilderness Committee v. Fisheries and Oceans Canada, 2014 FC 148*, http://decisions.fct-cf.gc.ca/fc-cf/decisions/en/item/66803/index.do. The four species were the endangered Nechako white sturgeon and the threatened Pacific humpback whale, marbled murrelet, and southern mountain caribou. The other four nongovernmental organizations were the David Suzuki Foundation, Greenpeace Canada, the Sierra Club of British Columbia Foundation, and the Wildsight Society.

166 Ibid., arts 96, 100. Even though section 42 of SARA stipulates that recovery plans must be prepared within a year for endangered and two years for threatened species, the respondents tried to argue that in an "administrative law sense," these provisions were not mandatory but directory only.

167 Ibid., arts 101, 102, original emphasis.

168 Ibid., art. 92.

169 Ibid., arts 85, 86.

170 Ecojustice, "Defending Ontario's Endangered Species."

171 Aldridge and Brigham, "Distribution, Abundance, and Status," 28.

172 Government of Canada, Environment Canada, *Amended Recovery Strategy for the Greater Sage-Grouse*, iii.

173 Alberta has 1,533 wells in sage-grouse country, of which 411 are active.

174 James, "Imminent Extinction of Sage-Grouse."

175 Government of Alberta, Alberta Sustainable Resource Development, *Alberta Greater Sage-Grouse Recovery Plan 2005–2010*, 14, 15, 28.

176 Government of Canada, Parks Canada, *Recovery Strategy for the Greater Sage-Grouse*, 27–8.

177 *Alberta Wilderness Association v. Canada (Environment), 2009 FC 710*, http://www.canlii.org/en/ca/fct/doc/2009/2009fc710/2009fc710.html.

178 Briere, "Ecojustice Files Lawsuit."

179 Hume, "Court Weighs."

180 James, "Feds Must Disclose."

181 Government of Canada, Species at Risk Public Registry, "Emergency Order … Greater Sage-Grouse."

182 Ibid.

183 Ibid.

184 Quoted in McKenzie, "Greater Sage-Grouse."

185 Fluker, "Curious Case."

186 McClure, "Sage Grouse Protections." The main impact concerned limitations on fencing.

187 Quoted in ibid.

188 Glen, "Energy Industry Challenges Efforts."

189 Haydu, "Medicine Hat Suing Feds."

190 Government of Alberta, Alberta Environment and Sustainable Resource Development, *Alberta Greater Sage-Grouse Recovery Plan 2013–2018*, 21.

191 Ibid., 23.

192 Rubec and Stover, *New Listing*, 7.

193 Government of Saskatchewan, Ministry of Environment, *Conservation Plan for Greater Sage-Grouse*, 14.

194 Government of Canada, Environment Canada, *Amended Recovery Strategy for the Greater Sage-Grouse*, 22–30.

195 Ibid., 18, 14.

196 Ibid., 8–9, 14, 32.

197 Ibid., 14.

198 Ibid.

199 Government of Canada, Species at Risk Public Registry, "Emergency Order … Greater Sage-Grouse."

200 Kerr and Cihlar, "Patterns and Causes," 743.

201 Anthony, "Trail Hazards," 7.

202 Government of British Columbia, Conservation Data Centre, *Conservation Status Report*.

203 Government of Canada, Environment Canada, *Recovery Strategy for the Oregon Spotted Frog*, part 1, 6, 10.

204 Ibid., part 2, vi, 14, 21.

205 COSEWIC, "Assessing Wildlife Species-Theory," question 1.

206 Cranshaw and Redak, *Bugs Rule!* 2–3.

207 Finnamore, *Advantages of Using Arthropods*, 4.

208 Government of Canada and Government of Alberta, *Report of the Joint Review Panel*, 51.

209 Cranshaw and Redak, *Bugs Rule!* 3–5.

210　Langor and Spence, "Arthropods as Ecological Indicators," 346.

211　Finnamore, *Advantages of Using Arthropods*, 1.

212　Langor and Spence, "Arthropods as Ecological Indicators," 347, 348.

213　Cited in Government of Canada and Government of Alberta, *Report of the Joint Review Panel*, 52.

214　Biological Survey of Canada, "Arthropods of Canadian Grasslands."

215　Government of Canada, Environment Canada, *Evaluation of Programs and Activities*, 64.

216　McNeely and Hunka, *Policy Critique*, 74.

217　Lambeck, "Focal Species."

218　Beazley and Cardinal, "Systematic Approach."

219　*Species at Risk Act*, sec. 77(1) and amendment in sec. 77(1.1). See also Government of Canada, *Bill C-38*, sec. 165.

220　Green Budget Coalition, *Protecting Canada's Species*, 1.

221　Ibid., 3.

222　Rainer et al., *On Guard for Them*, appendix B.

CHAPTER FIVE

1　Government of Canada, Canadian Wildlife Service, *How Much Habitat?* 1.

2　Boyd, *Unnatural Law*, 165.

3　Government of Canada, Office of the Auditor General, *2013 Fall Report*, "The Commissioner's Perspective," exhibit 1.

4　Venter et al., "Threats to Endangered Species," 904.

5　Nature Conservancy Canada, correspondence to contributors, 30 March 2015.

6　Bloom et al., "Relationships between Grazing."

7　Javorek and Grant, *Trends in Wildlife Habitat*.

8　Nature Canada, *Wildlife in Crisis*, 6.

9　Calvert et al., "Synthesis of Human-Related."

10　Ceballos, Ehrlich, and Dirzo, "Biological Annihilation," E6089.

11　Gauthier and Wiken, "Monitoring the Conservation," 343.

12　Hobson, Bayne, and Van Wilgenburg, "Large-Scale Conversion," 1530.

13　Garcia and Altieri, "Transgenic Crops," 340.

14　Glen, "Fewer Birds Sing." Although it is true that these depletions are also due to habitat loss in southern wintering areas, the loss of perennial birds indicates severe habitat depletion north of the border as well.

15　Nature Conservancy Canada, correspondence to contributors, 30 March 2015.

16　Government of Canada, Species at Risk Public Registry, "Burrowing Owl."

17　Government of Alberta, Alberta Environment and Sustainable Resource Development, *Alberta Burrowing Owl Recovery Plan 2012–2017*, 16.

18 Government of Canada, Environment Canada, *Management Plan for the McCown's Longspur*, 8. In contrast to source habitats, sink habitats are those where death rates exceed birth rates.

19 Ibid., 13.

20 Badiou, *Conserve First, Restore Later*, 3, 9.

21 Government of Canada, Environment Canada, *Status and Trends*, 6.

22 Main and Morrissey, "Distribution and Impact."

23 Bartzen et al., "Trends in Agricultural Impact," 534–6.

24 Cortus et al., "Impacts of Agriculture Support."

25 Altieri and Nicholls, *Agroecology and the Search*, 29–39.

26 Pal et al., "Degradation and Effects," 252.

27 Stark and Banks, "Population-Level Effects of Pesticides," 508.

28 Cloyd, "Indirect Effects of Pesticides," 138.

29 Other GM plants produce rice, potatoes, tomatoes, lentils, squash, sugar cane, and papaya. Others increase biofuel efficiency. The development of GM heat-tolerant yeast, for example, might have implications for the pharmaceutical and chemical industries as well as for biofuels.

30 Cited in Gillam, "U.S. GMO Crops."

31 Gertsberg, "Loss of Biodiversity."

32 Garcia and Altieri, "Transgenic Crops," 339.

33 Ibid., 342.

34 Childs, *Apocalyptic Planet*, 187.

35 Garcia and Altieri, "Transgenic Crops," 344; Murnaghan, "Are GM Foods?"

36 Gertsberg, "Loss of Biodiversity."

37 Morandin and Winston, "Wild Bee Abundance," 872.

38 University of Guelph, "Bee Flower Choices Altered."

39 Ibid. A pollination deficit is the difference between potential and actual pollination.

40 Amos, "Death of the Bees."

41 GM Watch, "Fish and Wildlife." The GM crops were for feeding wildlife.

42 Maguire, "Ecosystem Effects," 33, 34.

43 Canadian Biotechnology Action Network, *Are GM Crops Better?* 35.

44 Canola Council of Canada, "Industry Overview."

45 Garcia and Altieri, "Transgenic Crops," 340.

46 Johnson, "Genetically Modified Crops," 135.

47 Carpenter, "Impact of GM Crops," 7.

48 Ibid., table 3, 14.

49 Sanvido et al., *Valuating Environmental Impacts*, 138–9.

50 Statistics Canada, "Table 6: Pesticide Use."

51 Canadian Press, "Chemical Industry Powers."

52 Institute of Science in Society, "Why Glyphosate," sec. 5.3.

53 Ibid.

54 Friends of the Earth Europe, *Environmental Impacts of Glyphosate.*

55 Hendrickson, "How Neonicotinoid Pesticides."

56 Quoted in Canadian Biotechnology Action Network, *Are GM Crops Better?* 17.

57 Hallmann et al., "Declines in Insectivorous Birds."

58 Goulson, "Ecology," 295.

59 Hendrickson, "Toxic Plants, Poisoned Ecosystems."

60 Cited in ibid.

61 Hendrickson, "How Neonicotinoid Pesticides."

62 Atkins, "Ontario Grain Farmers."

63 Gurian-Sherman, "Genetically Engineered Crops."

64 Cited in Patterson, "Health Canada Fails."

65 Government of Ontario, Ministry of the Environment and Climate Change, "Regulating Neonicotinoids."

66 *CBC News*, "Law to Reduce Use."

67 Quoted in RealAgriculture, "Standing on Principle."

68 Government of Canada, Health Canada, *Re-evaluation of Imidacloprid.*

69 Ecojustice, "Challenge of Neonicotinoid."

70 *CTV News Calgary*, "Poll Question."

71 Bakx, "Castle Area Logging Halted."

72 Canadian Press, "Castle Wilderness Area Plan."

73 Government of Alberta, Alberta Environment and Parks, *Castle Management Plan*, viii.

74 Ibid., 97–107.

75 Nikiforuk, "Schindle's Warning."

76 Blancher, *Importance of Canada's Boreal Forest*, 1.

77 In a culture that assesses pretty well everything in financial terms, it might be worthwhile to note that an economic study on monetary benefits of predation by birds estimated that their impact on the western spruce budworm translated into US$1,820 of positive economic benefit per year per square kilometre. Niemi et al., "Ecological Sustainability of Birds."

78 Marsden, "Report Says Canada Leads."

79 Cited in Blancher, *Importance of Canada's Boreal Forest*, 26–7.

80 Thompson et al., "Forest Birds," 247.

81 Ibid., 248.

82 International Boreal Conservation Science Panel, "Threats to the Boreal."

83 See Reid, "Canadian Boreal Forest Agreement."

84 Anielski and Wilson, *Counting Canada's Natural Capital*, 35.

85 Both studies cited in Stutchbury, "Boreal Songbird Declines," 5.

86 Alberta Biodiversity Monitoring Institute, *Boreal Chickadee.*

87 See Imbeau, Monkkonen, and Desrochers, "Long-Term Effects of Forestry," 1151.

88 Edworthy and Martin, "Persistence of Tree Cavities," 770.

89 Schmiegelow and Monkkonen, "Habitat Loss and Fragmentation," 382.

90 Cited in Stutchbury, "Boreal Songbird Declines," 5.

91 St-Laurent et al., "Planning Timber Harvest," 261.

92 Mining Watch Canada and Northwatch, *Boreal Below*, 2.

93 Wells et al., *Danger in the Nursery*, iv.

94 Ibid., 3. These breeding waterfowl include "as many as 20,000 Mallards, over 15,000 Lesser Scaup, nearly 10,000 Canvasbacks, 7,000 Common Goldeneye, and 5,000 Bufflehead."

95 Government of Canada, Canadian Wildlife Service, *Canadian Shorebird Conservation Plan*, appendix 1, 20.

96 Wells et al., *Danger in the Nursery*, iv.

97 Ibid., 24.

98 Greenberg et al., "Understanding Declines in Rusty Blackbirds," 114.

99 Government of Canada, Environment Canada, *Bird Conservation Strategy*, 1.

100 See North America Bird Conservation Initiative, *State of Canada's Birds*, 10–13, 24.

101 Greenberg et al., "Understanding Declines in Rusty Blackbirds," 107.

102 Government of Canada, Environment Canada, *Management Plan for the Rusty Blackbird*.

103 COSEWIC, *Assessment and Status Report on the Rusty Blackbird*, v.

104 Government of Canada, Environment Canada, *Management Plan for the Rusty Blackbird*, 7.

105 Ibid., 12.

106 Alberta Biodiversity Monitoring Institute, *Boreal Chickadee*, 5.

107 Hadley, "Winter Habitat Use."

108 Bolgiano, "Cause and Effect," 29.

109 Lait, Lauff, and Burg, "Genetic Evidence," 146.

110 Hadley, "Winter Habitat Use."

111 Boreal Avian Modelling Project, "Boreal Chickadee."

112 Partners in Flight, *North American Landbird Conservation*, part 1, 22.

113 BirdLife International, "Boreal Chickadee (*Parus hudsonicus*)."

114 Hadley and Desrochers, "Winter Habitat Use," 144.

115 Government of Canada, Environment and Climate Change Canada, "Boreal Chickadee (*Poecile hudsonicus*)."

116 COSEWIC, "Candidate Wildlife Species."

117 The federal recovery strategy refers to two other species of caribou: Dawson's caribou, which is extinct; and Grant's caribou, which is usually included with the barren-ground caribou.

118 COSEWIC lists the southern and central populations as "endangered," the boreal population as "threatened," and the northern population as a "special concern." The Species at Risk Act lists the southern mountain and boreal populations as

"threatened" and the northern mountain population as a "special concern." The central mountain population is not mentioned. It is estimated that southern mountain caribou numbers in British Columbia have dwindled to around 1,500. Government of British Columbia, "Southern Mountain Caribou."

119   Government of Canada, Environment Canada, "Public Notice."

120   Government of Canada, Environment Canada, *Scientific Review*, 67–8.

121   Government of Alberta, Alberta Environment and Alberta Conservation Association, *Status of the Woodland Caribou* (2001), 23, 21, 24. As discussed earlier, wolves also become scapegoats, taking the blame for caribou declines when in fact the fundamental cause is anthropogenic disturbance.

122   Government of Canada, Environment Canada, *Recovery Strategy for the Woodland Caribou*, table F-1, 67–8. The Alberta range is Little Smoky, where only seventy-eight caribou remain.

123   Canadian Parks and Wilderness Society and David Suzuki Foundation, *Population Critical*, 10.

124   For information on the recommendations, see ibid.

125   Government of British Columbia, Ministry of Environment, *Implementation Plan*, v.

126   Ibid., iv.

127   Canadian Parks and Wilderness Society, *Ten Years After*, 4.

128   Ibid., 2; Linnitt, "Alberta to Sell."

129   Government of Alberta, Alberta Environment and Alberta Conservation Association, *Status of the Woodland Caribou* (2010), v.

130   Cited in Ecojustice, "Woodland Caribou Battle."

131   Government of Canada, Environment Canada, *Recovery Strategy for the Woodland Caribou*.

132   Ibid., 16, 57.

133   Ibid., 62.

134   Government of Canada, Environment Canada, *Scientific Assessment*, 91.

135   Melissa Gorrie, quoted in Ecojustice, "Proposed Caribou Recovery Strategy."

136   Government of Canada, Environment Canada, *Recovery Strategy for the Woodland Caribou*, 38. Federal oversight was linked primarily to these range plans, which were to be developed under the authority of the appropriate jurisdictions and which operated at arm's length from Environment Canada.

137   Ibid., 63.

138   Government of Alberta, Alberta Environment and Alberta Conservation Association, *Status of the Woodland Caribou* (2001), 13.

139   Government of Canada, Environment Canada, *Scientific Assessment*, 8.

140   Government of Canada, Environment Canada, *Recovery Strategy for the Woodland Caribou*, 23.

141   Ibid., 20.

142 Ibid., 14.

143 Government of Canada, Environment Canada, *Scientific Review*, 90.

144 Government of Canada, Environment Canada, *Recovery Strategy for the Woodland Caribou*, 34.

145 Extrapolated from ibid., table F-1, 67–9.

146 Ibid., 64.

147 Government of Canada, Environment Canada, "Appendix 7.2," 168–9.

148 Extrapolated from Government of Canada, Environment Canada, *Recovery Strategy for the Woodland Caribou*, table F-1, 67–9.

149 Ibid., 67.

150 Government of Canada, Environment Canada, *Scientific Assessment*, 70.

151 Government of Alberta, Alberta Environment and Sustainable Resource Development, *Alberta Caribou Action*, 1.

152 Ibid., 8.

153 Canadian Press, "Alberta to Sell Off Land." Impacted is the Narraway herd, whose numbers are estimated at fewer than 100.

154 Canadian Parks and Wilderness Society, *2015 Update*.

155 Government of Manitoba, Manitoba Conservation and Water Stewardship, *Conserving a Boreal Icon*.

156 Ibid., 20, 15. The upward figure is 80 per cent, well beyond the federal guideline of 65 per cent.

157 Canadian Parks and Wilderness Society, *Looking for Action*.

158 Canadian Boreal Initiative et al., *Canadian Boreal Forest Agreement*, 25–6. The signatories were the Canadian Boreal Initiative, the Canadian Parks and Wilderness Society, the David Suzuki Foundation, ForestEthics, the Nature Conservancy, the Pew Environment Group International Boreal Conservation Campaign, the Ivey Foundation, and the Forest Products Association of Canada, whose signing members were Alberta-Pacific Forest Industries Inc., AV Group, Canfor Corporation, Canfor Pulp Limited Partnership, Cariboo Pulp and Paper Company, Cascades Inc., Conifex Timber Inc., Daishowa-Marubeni International Ltd, F.F. Soucy Inc., Howe Sound Pulp and Paper Ltd, Kruger Inc., Louisiana-Pacific Canada Ltd, Mercer International, Mill and Timber Products Ltd, Millar Western, NewPage Corporation, Resolute Forest Products, Tembec, Tolko Industries Ltd, West Fraser Timber Company Ltd, and Weyerhaeuser Company Ltd.

159 Ibid., 4.

160 Marowits, "Boreal Forest Agreement."

161 Cited in Crawford, "Forest Conservation Group Withdraws."

162 Los, "Boreal Truce."

163 Grech, "Mills to Lose $100 Million."

164 Hubert, "Canadian Boreal Forest Agreement."

165 For information on marginal impacts, see Whitaker, Taylor, and Warkentin, "Survival of Adult Songbirds." For negative impacts on birds due to deterioration in migratory habitat farther south, see Stutchbury, "Boreal Songbird Declines." And for Canadian-European comparisons, see Schmiegelow and Monkkonen, "Habitat Loss and Fragmentation."

166 Partners in Flight, *North American Landbird Conservation*, part 1, 26.

167 Government of Canada, Office of the Auditor General, *2013 Fall Report*, ch. 1, 1.31.

168 Anielski and Wilson, *Counting Canada's Natural Capital*, 6; Wilderness Committee, "Canada's Boreal Region."

169 Venter, "Threats to Endangered Species," 909.

170 Royal Society of Canada Expert Panel, *Sustaining Canada's Marine Biodiversity*, 39. According to the panel, only 16 per cent of Canadian researchers with taxonomic expertise worked in marine areas. Ibid., 44.

171 Sabine Jessen, director, Oceans Program, Canadian Parks and Wilderness Society, circular to members, 16 September 2016.

172 Government of Canada, Office of the Auditor General, *2005 September Report*, ch. 1, 1.74.

173 Mooers et al., "Biases in Legal Listing," 573.

174 Royal Society of Canada Expert Panel, *Sustaining Canada's Marine Biodiversity*, 13.

175 Ibid., 18.

176 Ibid., 13.

177 Bonamis, "Utilization of Two-Stage," 31, 38.

178 Parliament of Canada, House of Commons, Standing Committee on Environment and Sustainable Development, "Evidence – Dr. Michael Pearson."

179 Government of Canada, Fisheries and Oceans Canada, *Recovery Strategy for the Nooksack Dace* (2007), iv.

180 Ibid., 12.

181 Hume, "Future of Tiny Fish." One of those to file an affidavit, Mike Pearson, a world authority on the Nooksack dace, did not receive his customary research grant for 2010.

182 Hume, "Ottawa Asks Court"; Government of Canada, Species at Risk Public Registry, "Nooksack Dace in Canada."

183 Government of Canada, Fisheries and Oceans Canada, *Recovery Strategy for the Nooksack Dace* (2008), 18.

184 *Environmental Defence Canada v. Minister of Fisheries and Oceans, 2009 FC 878*, 56–9. https://stephenrees.files.wordpress.com/2009/09/nooksack-dace-court-decision.pdf. Ecojustice acted as counsel for the applicants, which were Environmental Defence Canada, the Georgia Strait Alliance, the Western Canada Wilderness Committee, and the David Suzuki Foundation. Ibid., 43, 2.

185 Ibid., 42–4.

186 Ibid., 2, 43.
187 Government of Canada, Fisheries and Oceans Canada, *Action Plan for the Nooksack Dace … and the Salish Sucker.*
188 Ibid., 4, 15.
189 Government of Canada, Fisheries and Oceans Canada, *Recovery Strategy for the Northern and Southern Resident Killer Whales* (2008), 35–40, 42–3.
190 Government of Canada, Species at Risk Public Registry, "Northern and Southern Resident Killer Whales."
191 Government of Canada, Species at Risk Public Registry, "Critical Habitats of the Northeast Pacific."
192 *David Suzuki Foundation v. Minister of Fisheries and Oceans, 2010 FC 1233*, 4–5. http://raincoast.org/wp-content/uploads/Killer-Whale-Judgement-Dec-20101.pdf. The other appellants were the Dogwood Initiative, Environmental Defence Canada, Greenpeace Canada, the International Fund for Animal Welfare, the Raincoast Conservation Society, Sierra Club of Canada, and the Western Canada Wilderness Committee. The minister of environment was also a respondent.
193 Ibid., 124–25.
194 Ibid., 125.
195 Government of Canada, Fisheries and Oceans Canada, *Recovery Strategy for the Northern and Southern Resident Killer Whales* (2011), 42, 35n6.
196 Ibid., 40.
197 *Minister of Fisheries and Oceans v. David Suzuki Foundation et al., 2012 FCA 40*, 3–4, https://www.canlii.org/en/ca/fca/doc/2012/2012fca40/2012fca40.pdf. The other respondents were the Dogwood Initiative, Environmental Defence Canada, the Georgia Strait Alliance, Greenpeace Canada, the International Fund for Animal Welfare, the Raincoast Conservation Society, Sierra Club of Canada, and the Western Canada Wilderness Committee.
198 Ibid., 58.
199 Government of Canada, Fisheries and Oceans Canada, *Action Plan for the Northern and Southern Resident Killer Whales*, 16.
200 Ibid., 6, 12.
201 David Suzuki Foundation et al., "Re: March 2014 Draft," 3, 5.
202 Ibid., 25.
203 West Coast Environmental Law, "Fisheries Act Amendments." The four former ministers were John Fraser, Tom Siddon, David Anderson, and Herb Dhaliwal.
204 Government of Canada, *Bill C-38.*
205 Government of Canada, *Fisheries Act*, 35(1).
206 Ashfield, "Federal Government Committed."
207 Cited in Lowey, "Study: Changes to Fisheries."

208 Government of Canada, *Fisheries Act*, sec. 35(2), 35(3).
209 Ashfield, "Letter from Minister," 1, cited in De Souza, "Harper Minister Ducks Questions." The letter was addressed to Todd Panas, national president of the Union of Environment Workers.
210 Galloway, "Controversial Changes to Fisheries Act."
211 Quoted in ibid.
212 Quoted in ibid.
213 Quoted in Casselman, "Changes to Canada's Fisheries Law."
214 Quoted in Nikiforuk, "Don't Gut Fisheries Act."
215 Hutchings and Post, "Gutting Canada's Fisheries Act," 498.
216 Ibid., 501.
217 Humpback whales are fascinating creatures renowned for their "bubble-netting, a form of social hunting, in which several whales encircle a school of fish and blow bubbles that form a 'net' around the fish. The fish cluster tightly inside these nets," and the whales get all they can eat by swimming "through the net with their mouths open." Another unique aspect of humpbacks is the singing of the males, who perform "the longest and most complex songs in the animal kingdom." Sung by every male, these songs are unique to a population and always evolving. Government of Canada, Species at Risk Public Registry, "Humpback Whale."
218 COSEWIC, *Assessment and Update Status Report on the Humpback Whale* (2003), iii.
219 Government of Canada, Species at Risk Public Registry, "Response Statement – Humpback Whale."
220 COSEWIC, *Assessment and Status Report on the Humpback Whale* (2011).
221 Ibid., iii, 17, 8, 20.
222 COSEWIC, "Wildlife Species Assessment," table 2.
223 The four locations are Gil Island, Langara Island, southeast Moresby Island, and southwest Vancouver Island. The first three are directly in major shipping lanes.
224 North Coast Cetacean Society, *Occurrence of Humpback Whales*, part 3, 30.
225 Government of Canada, Fisheries and Oceans Canada, *Recovery Strategy for the North Pacific Humpback Whale*.
226 Ibid., 13.
227 Ibid., 11, 27.
228 Ibid., 41–2.
229 Government of Canada, "Order Amending Schedule 1" (2014).
230 Government of Canada, *Species at Risk Act*, sec. 60(1); Government of Canada, National Energy Board, *Report of the Joint Review Panel*, vol. 2, 233.
231 MacDonald, "Why Is Downgraded Protection?"
232 Raincoast Conservation Foundation, "Re: Comments on the Proposed Down-Listing."
233 COSEWIC, *Assessment and Status Report on the Humpback Whale* (2011), 9.
234 Ibid.

235 Both cited in Ball, "Critics Say Canada."

236 Ecojustice, "Challenging Kinder Morgan's Pipeline."

237 Canadian Press, "Panel Should Have Considered." The organizations that filed the court challenge were ForestEthics Advocacy, the Living Oceans Society, the Raincoast Conservation Foundation, and B.C. Nature. The federal appeal court overturned the approval of the pipeline. It did not, however, accept these organizations' argument on the contentious grounds that under the Canadian Environmental Assessment Act (1995), the findings of the Joint Review Panel for the Enbridge Northern Gateway Project could not be directly challenged legally. As reported by lawyer Barry Robinson of Ecojustice, "The precedent ties our hands when it comes to challenging environmental assessments in court. We need these avenues to make sure [judges], not government officials, are the final decision-makers on whether an assessment meets the requirements of law." Robinson, "Why We're Asking."

238 Northern Gateway Pipelines Incorporated proposed implementing specific vessel speed restrictions. It also proposed using a dedicated whale-monitoring vessel to survey the area before tanker passage. As part of an adaptive management approach, the boundaries of the core humpback area could change as a result of future monitoring results.

239 Allen, "Why Are These Humpback?"

240 Trevor Swerdfager, quoted in Ball, "Feds Removal of Humpback."

241 Wristen, "Letter from the Executive Director"; Trites, "Attacks on Whale Science."

242 Much of the assessment was based on its author's 2008 master's thesis. See Rambeau, "Determining Abundance and Stock Structure."

243 For a good discussion on habitat, see Ashe et al., "Abundance and Survival."

244 Federal, Provincial, and Territorial Governments of Canada, Canadian Councils of Resource Ministers, *Canadian Biodiversity*, 84.

245 Government of Canada, Fisheries and Oceans Canada, "Mission, Vision and Values." 2017. http://www.dfo-mpo.gc.ca/about-notre-sujet/org/vision-eng.htm.

CHAPTER SIX

1 United Nations, *Convention on Biological Diversity*.

2 Government of Canada, Environment Canada, *Environment Canada Protected Areas Strategy*, 8, 5.

3 Government of Canada, Environment Canada, *Canadian Biodiversity Strategy*.

4 Government of Canada, Fisheries and Oceans Canada, *National Framework*.

5 Government of Canada, Fisheries and Oceans Canada, *Canada's Federal Marine Protected Areas Strategy*.

6 Government of Canada, Fisheries and Oceans Canada, *National Framework*, sec. 1.

7 Ibid., sec. 5.1

8 Ibid., sec. 7.1

9 Ibid., sec. 7.2.

10 Ibid.

11 Government of Canada and Government of British Columbia, *Canada–British Columbia Marine Protected Area*, 11.

12 United Nations, *Convention on Biological Diversity*, art. 8(a).

13 Government of Canada, Environment Canada, *Canadian Biodiversity Strategy*, 23.

14 Government of Canada, Fisheries and Oceans Canada, *Canada's Federal Marine Protected Areas Strategy*.

15 Government of Canada, Environment Canada, *Environment Canada Protected Areas Strategy*, 5.

16 Ibid., 9.

17 Government of Canada, Environment and Climate Change Canada, *2020 Biodiversity Goals*, goal A, target 1.

18 Government of Canada, Environment Canada, "Canada's Protected Areas."

19 Harris, *Fragmented Forest*, xii.

20 Government of Canada, Environment Canada, *Environment Canada Protected Areas Strategy*, ii.

21 Ibid., 10.

22 Ibid., 5–6, 9.

23 Government of Canada, Environment and Climate Change Canada, *2020 Biodiversity Goals*.

24 Cited in Government of Canada, Environment Canada, *Status and Trends*, 21.

25 Canadian Press, "Canadian Protected Areas."

26 Statistics Canada, *Human Activity and the Environment*, 34.

27 Galloway, "Canada Lags."

28 Lee and Cheng, *Canada's Terrestrial Protected Areas*, 26. The figures given were 84.54 million hectares under protection, of which 37.53 million hectares were under interim protection.

29 Deguise and Kerr, "Protected Areas."

30 Government of Canada, Environment Canada, *Status and Trends*, 21.

31 Lee and Cheng, *Canada's Terrestrial Protected Areas*, 8.

32 Government of Canada, Environment Canada, "Canada's Protected Areas."

33 Lee and Cheng, *Canada's Terrestrial Protected Areas*, 40; Government of Canada, Environment Canada, "Canada's Protected Areas."

34 Government of Canada, Environment and Climate Change Canada, "National Wildlife Areas across Canada."

35 Lee and Cheng, *Canada's Terrestrial Protected Areas*, table 8, 46.

36 Canadian Parks and Wilderness Society, Southern Alberta Chapter, "Help Protect Castle Wildland and Provincial Parks," email memo to members, 7 February 2017.

37 Nature Canada, *Underlying Threat*, 25.

38 Ibid., 28.

39 Government of Canada, Environment and Climate Change Canada, "Management Plans and Activities."

40 Government of Canada, *Wildlife Area Regulations*, sec. 8.1(1).

41 For example, see Government of the Yukon, Environment Yukon, *Horseshoe Slough*, 5–6.

42 Murgatroyd, "Managing Tourism and Recreational Activities," sec. 3.3.3.

43 Wilderness Committee, "End Logging."

44 Cited in Galloway, "National Parks under Threat."

45 Canadian Parks and Wilderness Society, BC Chapter, *Gas Gone Wild*, 4.

46 Hume, "Hunting in B.C. Provincial Parks."

47 Government of Saskatchewan, Ministry of Environment, *Saskatchewan Fur Program*, 3.

48 Government of Alberta, Community Development – Parks and Protected Areas Division, *Program Policy for Managing Fur*, 3.

49 Ross, *Legal and Institutional Responses*, 6.

50 Lee and Cheng, *Canada's Terrestrial Protected Areas*, 16.

51 Government of Ontario, Ministry of Natural Resources, *State of Ontario's Protected Areas*, 56.

52 Ibid., 57.

53 Ibid., 59.

54 Government of Newfoundland and Labrador, Department of Environment and Conservation, "Protected Areas in Newfoundland and Labrador."

55 Government of Saskatchewan, Ministry of Environment, *Misinipiy Integrated Land Use Plan*. February 2012. http://publications.gov.sk.ca/documents/66/86730-English.pdf.

56 Government of Canada, *Canada's 5th National Report*, 55.

57 COSEWIC, *Assessment and Update Status Report on the Narwhal*.

58 Fast and Healy, *Federal Marine Protected Area*, 5.

59 Canadian Parks Council, *Aboriginal Peoples and Canada's Parks*, "Introduction," 3–4.

60 National Aboriginal Forestry Association and Wildlands League, *Honouring the Promise*, 6.

61 Ibid.

62 Harris, *Fragmented Forest*, xii.

63 Wiersma, Nudds, and Rivard, "Models to Distinguish Effects," 780.

64 MacKinnon, *Once and Future World*, 7–9.

65 Quoted in van Maanen and Convery, "Rewilding," 305.

66 Cited in Bailey, "Author J.B. MacKinnon."

67 Berg, "Bringing Nature Back"; Lindsay, "Rewilding a Salmon Stream"; Ontario Water Centre, "Communities and Shorelines."

68 Chrulew, "Reversing Extinction."

69   van Maanen and Convery, "Rewilding," 307.

70   Canadian Broadcasting Corporation (cbc), "Top Spots."

71   van Maanen and Convery, "Rewilding," 305–6.

72   Soulé and Noss, "Rewilding and Biodiversity," 24.

73   van Maanen and Convery, "Rewilding," 306.

74   Nogués-Bravo et al., "Rewilding," R88.

75   Chrulew, "Reversing Extinction."

76   van Maanen and Convery, "Rewilding," 308.

77   Montgomery, "More Grizzlies and Wolves."

78   Svenning et al., "Science for a Wilder Anthropocene," 903.

79   Nogués-Bravo et al., "Rewilding," R91.

80   van Maanen and Convery, "Rewilding," 313–14.

81   Government of Canada, Parks Canada, *2010–2011 Parks Canada Agency Corporate Plan*, "Chief Executive Officer's Message," 1.

82   Government of Canada, *National Parks Act* (1930), sec. 4. For the 2000 consolidation of the act, see Government of Canada, *Canada National Parks Act* (2000), sec. 4(1).

83   Dearden and Dempsey, "Protected Areas in Canada."

84   Government of Canada, Parks Canada, *"Unimpaired for Future Generations?"* vol. 1, 9.

85   Government of Canada, *Canada National Parks Act* (2000), sec. 8(2): "Maintenance or restoration of ecological integrity, through the protection of natural resources and natural processes, shall be the first priority of the Minister when considering all aspects of the management of parks."

86   Cited in Government of Canada, Office of the Auditor General, *2013 Fall Report*, ch. 7, sec. 7.66.

87   Ibid.

88   Gailus, "All Sizzle, No Stake."

89   Foubert, "Banff to See Caribou Return."

90   Government of Canada, *Canada National Parks Act* (2000).

91   Cited in Fluker, "How Legal Design," 4–5. See also Fluker, "Ecological Integrity."

92   Fluker, "How Legal Design," 6.

93   Government of Canada, Parks Canada, "Guiding Principles and Operational Policies."

94   Government of Canada, Parks Canada, *Parks Canada Charter*.

95   Lavigne, *Grey Seals, Cod and Culling*, 2.

96   Cohen, Brom, and Stassen, "Moral Convictions," 361.

97   Theberge and Theberge, "Opinion: Ecologists Oppose."

98   Cited in Liz White, director, Animal Alliance of Canada, letter to sponsors, June 2017.

99   Quoted in Lavoie, "Fallow Deer."

100 Bradford and Hobbes, "Regulating Overabundant Ungulate," 526.
101 Lange, "Out of Season."
102 European Commission, "Deer Culls Are Not Effective."
103 Wesserberg et al., "Host Culling." The authors of this article focus on the differences in transmission rates between host density dependence and host frequency dependence.
104 Bolzoni and De Leo, "Unexpected Consequences," 301.
105 Wildlife Trusts, "Bovine TB," 2.
106 Lloyd-Smith et al., "Should We Expect?" 518.
107 Lacy, "Culling Surplus Animals," 190.
108 Government of Canada, Office of the Auditor General, 2013 Fall Report, ch. 7.
109 Farnese, "Searching for Wildlife," 508.
110 Parliament of Canada, House of Commons, "Proposed Government Response," recommendation 2.
111 Government of Canada, Parks Canada, Reintroduction Plan, 5, 8.
112 CBC News, "Moose Cull in Gros Morne."
113 Grant, "Moose Population Threatens Health."
114 CBC News, "Point Pelee National Park."
115 Liz White, director, Animal Alliance of Canada, letter to sponsors, June 2017.
116 Wires, Double-Crested Cormorant, 56–9.
117 Ontario Federation of Anglers and Hunters, "Cormorant Control Needed Now"; Glendenning, "Bridge Too Farr."
118 Woodley, Engaging Visitors.
119 Quoted in Government of Canada, Parks Canada, "Middle Island."
120 Government of Canada, Parks Canada, Project Description and Scope, 7.
121 Ibid.
122 Laidlaw, Cormorant Monitoring, 1–13, 11.
123 Aquila Applied Ecologists, Impacts of Double-Crested Cormorant.
124 MacKay and White, Critical Analysis of Point Pelee, 53.
125 Ibid., 90, 58.
126 Government of Canada, Parks Canada, Project Description and Scope, 8.
127 Cormorant Defenders International, Observations of the 2008 Cormorant Cull, 4.
128 Schmidt, "For Sale."
129 Government of Canada, Parks Canada, Project Description and Scope, 13–16.
130 Cormorant Defenders International, Observations of the 2008 Cormorant Cull, 12.
131 McGrath, "Testing the Existence."
132 MacKay and White, Critical Analysis of Point Pelee, 8.
133 Ibid., 42.
134 Scheffer et al., "Catastrophic Shifts in Ecosystems."
135 Ibid., 591.
136 Wires, Double-Crested Cormorant, 257.

137   Wires and Cuthbert, "Historic Populations," 16.
138   Ibid., 32.
139   Rob Laidlaw, Zoocheck Canada, interview with author, 26 May 2015.
140   Wires, *Double-Crested Cormorant*, 260–1.
141   Ibid., 263–4.
142   Freedman, Catling, and Lucas, "Effects of Feral Horses," 209.
143   Beeby, "Sable Island Horses."
144   See Senate of Canada, Standing Senate Committee on Fisheries and Oceans, *Sustainable Management of Grey Seal*, 1–2.
145   Quoted in ibid., 24.
146   Freedman, Catling, and Lucas, "Effects of Feral Horses," 209; MacKay, "Should They Kill the Horses?"
147   Pannozzo, *Devil and the Deep Blue Sea*; Whitehead et al., "Independent Marine Scientists Respond."
148   Liz White, director, Animal Alliance of Canada, letter to donors and supporters, January 2015.
149   Quoted in Lavigne, *Grey Seals, Cod and Culling*, 13.
150   According to one report, Parks Canada has a backlog of $2.8 billion in maintenance and repair work. Boutilier, "Parks Canada Services."
151   For example, see Eagles, McCool, and Haynes, *Sustainable Tourism*.
152   Government of Canada, Industry Canada, *Canada's Federal Tourism Strategy*, 33–4.
153   Interprovincial Sport and Recreation Council and Canadian Parks and Recreation Association, *Pathways to Wellbeing*, 11.
154   Derworiz, "Controversial Cabled Path Approved."
155   Government of Canada, Parks Canada, "Questions and Answers," 1.
156   Quoted in glacierdiscoverywalkjasper, "Parks Canada 'Heard.'" Parks Canada currently uses the term "the edge" to describe safe but more titillating encounters with nature.
157   Canadian Parks and Wilderness Society, "RE: CPAWS Response to Environmental Assessment," 1–2.
158   Angry Architect, "Skywalk Scandal."
159   Canadian Parks and Wilderness Society, "RE: CPAWS Response to Environmental Assessment," 4.
160   Government of Canada, Parks Canada, *Jasper National Park*, 68.
161   Ibid., 41.
162   Maligne Tours Ltd, "Maligne Tours in Jasper."
163   Government of Canada, Parks Canada, *Situation Analysis for the Maligne Valley*, 6.
164   Ibid., 6.
165   Ibid., 4.
166   Ibid., 65.
167   Naujokaitis-Lewis, "Assessing Potential Resource Use," 3–4.
168   Government of Canada, Parks Canada, *Situation Analysis for the Maligne Valley*, 64.

169 Maligne Tours Ltd, *Imagination, Innovation and Commitment.*

170 Ibid., 98.

171 Ibid., 40.

172 Robinson, "Re: Maligne Tours Ltd.," 2.

173 Ibid., 15–22.

174 Ibid., 21.

175 Robb, "Park Development Proposal."

176 McClure, "Maligne Valley Conceptual Proposal," 12.

177 Lopoukhine, Woodley, and Van Tighem, "Re: Maligne Tours Proposal," 2.

178 Jasper Environmental Association, "Day of Protest."

179 Canadian Press, "Parks Canada Turns Down."

180 Quoted in ibid.

181 Lilwall, "Jasper National Park."

182 Veerman, "Judge Dismisses Maligne." See Government of Canada, Parks Canada, "Guiding Principles and Operational Policies," part 2, ch. 1, sec. 2.1.5.

183 For legal examples, see Robinson, "Re: Maligne Tours Ltd."

184 Liz White, director, Animal Alliance of Canada, letter to donors and supporters, January 2015.

185 Bloch, *Pipestone Wolves*, 38, 45, 136, 138.

186 Ibid., 207.

187 Derworiz, "Wolf Deaths."

188 Government of Canada, Parks Canada, *State of Canada's*, 32.

189 Lunn, "Nearly Half."

190 Federal, Provincial, and Territorial Governments of Canada, Canadian Councils of Resource Ministers, *Canadian Biodiversity*, 10–17.

191 Government of Canada, *Canada's 5th National Report.*

192 Government of Canada, Office of the Auditor General, *2013 Fall Report*, ch. 2, sec. 2.5.

193 See also Government of Canada, Environment and Climate Change Canada, *2020 Biodiversity Goals.*

194 Government of Canada, *Canada's 5th National Report*, 12.

195 Government of Canada, Office of the Auditor General, *2013 Fall Report*, ch. 6, sec. 6.26.

196 Hutchings et al., "Is Canada Fulfilling?" 356.

197 Government of Canada, Office of the Auditor General, *2013 Fall Report*, ch. 5, sec. 5.18.

198 Ibid., ch. 4, "Main Points."

199 Ibid., ch. 2, sec. 2.35.

200 Government of Canada, Fisheries and Oceans Canada, *Spotlight on Marine Protected Areas*, 7.

201 Ceballos, Ehrlich, and Dirzo, "Biological Annihilation," E6095.

CONCLUSION

1 Epstein, "Animals as Objects," 158.
2 Henderson, "Wilderness and the Nature," 395.
3 Montaigne, "Apologie of Raymond Sebond," 491.
4 Donaldson and Kymlicka, *Zoopolis*, 176.
5 MacLellan, "What the Wild Things Are," 65.
6 Hadley, "Nonhuman Animal Property," 467, 473.
7 Favre, "Wildlife Jurisprudence," 476, 509.
8 Taylor, "Ethics of Respect for Nature," 202, original emphasis.
9 Clement, "Ethic of Care," 3–4.
10 Cooke, "Animal Kingdoms." Cooke does concede that in some cases basic human claims will compete with those of wildlife. However, he argues that any resolution should not deprive wildlife of habitat.
11 DeGrazia, "Regarding the Last Frontier."
12 Fiedeldey, "Wild Animals," 122.

Bibliography

Adamowicz, W.L., J. Asafu-Adjayei, P.C. Boxall, and W.E. Phillips. "Components of the Economic Value of Wildlife: An Alberta Case Study." *Canadian Field-Naturalist* 105, no. 3 (1991): 423–9.

Aird, Paul. "Tory Cuts to the Canadian Wildlife Service." *Forestry Chronicle*, February 1985. http://pubs.cif-ifc.org/doi/pdf/10.5558/tfc61002-1.

Alberta Biodiversity Monitoring Institute. *Boreal Chickadee [Poecile hudsonicus] Distribution and Habitat Associations in Alberta*. 2007. http://ftp.public.abmi.ca/ home/publications/documents/359_ABMI_BorealChickadeeHabitatAnd Distribution_ABMI.pdf.

Alberta Conservation Association. *Delegated Big Game Surveys, 2012/2013 Survey Season*. 2013. http://www.ab-conservation.com/downloads/big_game_surveys/ Big_Game_Survey_2012-2013.pdf.

Alberta Fish and Game Association. *Overview of Alberta Hunting Statistics by wmu Zone and User Group*. 2014. http://www.afga.org/pdf/Hunting/Hunting-Demographics-Harvest-Rates-Allocations-2014.pdf.

Aldridge, Cameron L., and R. Mark Brigham. "Distribution, Abundance, and Status of the Greater Sage-Grouse, *Centrocercus urophasianus*, in Canada." *Canadian Field-Naturalist* 117, no. 1 (2003): 25–34.

Allan, Gary R., and Brad Hill. "bc's Wolf Killing Plan a Big Step Backwards." *The Tyee*, 25 July 2014. http://thetyee.ca/Opinion/2014/07/25/BC-Wolf-Killing-Plan.

Allen, Colin, and Marc Bekoff. "Animal Minds, Cognitive Ethology and Ethics." *Journal of Ethics* 11, no. 3 (2007): 299–317.

Allen, Kate. "Why Are These Humpback Whale Conservationists Applauding the Harper Government?" *Toronto Star*, 26 April 2014. https://www.thestar.com/news/ insight/2014/04/26/why_are_these_humpback_whale_conservationists_ applauding_the_harper_government.html.

Allen-Hermanson, Sean. "Morgan's Canon Revisited." *Philosophy of Science* 72, no. 4 (2005): 608–31.

Altieri, Miguel A., and Clara I. Nicholls. *Agroecology and the Search for a Truly Sustainable Agriculture*. Mexico: United Nations Environment Program, 2005.

Amos, Brit. "Death of the Bees: Genetically Modified Crops and the Decline of Bee Colonies in North America." *Global Research*, 9 August 2011. http://www. globalresearch.ca/death-of-the-bees-genetically-modified-crops-and-the-decline-of-bee-colonies-in-north-america/25950.

Angry Architect. "The Skywalk Scandal: Jasper's Bridge of Glass Exposes the Perverse Nature of Tourism Architecture." *Architizer Blog*, 12 May 2014. http://architizer. com/blog/the-skywalk-scandal-jaspers-bridge-of-glass-exposes-the-perverse-nature-of-tourism-architecture.

Anielski, Mark, and Sara Wilson. *Counting Canada's Natural Capital: Assessing the Real Value of Canada's Boreal Ecosystems*. Pembina Institute, 2009. http://www.anielski. com/wp-content/uploads/2011/11/BorealBook_CCNC_09_enFINAL.pdf.

Animal Alliance of Canada. "British Columbia Wolf Slaughter." Circular to sponsors, March 2015.

– "Help Us Fight to Protect Mourning Doves." Brochure, 2013. https://www.animalalliance. ca/wp-content/uploads/2016/04/Folder-mourning_doves_September-2013.pdf.

Animal Liberation Front. "Opposing Recreational Hunting of Mourning Doves." October 2013. http://www.animalliberationfront.com/ALFront/Actions-Canada/CanadiansVsKillingDoves.htm.

Anthony, Leslie. "Trail Hazards: Outdoor Recreators and the Seasonal Movements of Reptiles and Amphibians." *Canadian Herpetologist* 4, no. 1 (2014): 6–8.

Aquila Applied Ecologists. *Impacts of Double-Crested Cormorant (Phalacrocorax auritus) Populations on the Biodiversity of Islands in Western Lake Erie: Management Recommendations*. Unpublished report, Parks Canada, January 2007.

Aristotle. "History of Animals." In *Works*, ed. W.D. Ross, 1389–1790. Oxford: Clarendon, 1908. http://www.constitution.org/ari/aristotle-organon+physics.pdf.

– "Politics." In *Works*, ed. W.D. Ross, 2788–3049. Oxford: Clarendon, 1908. http://www. constitution.org/ari/aristotle-organon+physics.pdf.

Armenteras, Dolors, and C. Max Finlayson. "Biodiversity." In United Nations Environment Program, *Global Environment Outlook (GEO-5): Environment for the Future We Want*, 133–66. United Nations Environment Program, 2014. https://www. researchgate.net/publication/236211399_Chapter_5_Biodiversity.

Artelle, K.A., S.C. Anderson, A.B. Cooper, P.C. Paquet, J.D. Reynolds, and C.D. Darimont. "Confronting Uncertainty in Wildlife Management: Performance of Grizzly Bear Management." *PLOS ONE* 8, no. 11 (2013): 1–9. http://www.web.uvic. ca/~darimont/wp-content/uploads/2013/11/Artelle-et-al-2013-BC-grizz-hunt.pdf.

Arthur, Robert, Caroline Garaway, and Kai Lorenzen. *Adaptive Learning: A Broadening of the Concept of Adaptive Management and Implications for Its Implementation*. Renewable Resources Assessment Group, Huxley School of Environment, Earth Science and Engineering, Imperial College, London, n.d. https://assets.publishing. service.gov.uk/media/57a08d34ed915d3cfd0018aa/R7335d.pdf.

Ashe, Erin, Janie Wray, Christopher R. Picard, and Rob Williams. "Abundance and Survival of Pacific Humpback Whales in a Proposed Critical Habitat Area." *PLOS ONE* 8, no. 9 (2013): 1–7. https://www.ncbi.nlm.nih.gov/pmc/articles/PMC3772752/pdf/pone.0075228.pdf.

Ashfield, Keith. "Letter from Minister of Fisheries and Oceans Canada to Todd Panas, National President, Union of Environment Workers." 13 June 2012. https://www.scribd.com/document/98213162/Fisheries-Pollution.

– "Federal Government Committed to Protecting Vast, and Abundant Resource." *The Hill Times*, 1 June 2012. http://www.hilltimes.com/policy-briefing/2012/06/04/federal-government-committed-to-protecting-vast-and-abundant-resource/30967.

Associated Press. "Bizarre Scene Caught on Video: Wild Turkeys Circle Dead Cat." *CBS News*, 2 March 2017. http://www.cbsnews.com/news/bizarre-scene-caught-on-video-wild-turkeys-circle-dead-cat.

– "US Proposal to Ban Cross-Border Polar Bear Trade Fails." *CBC News*, 7 March 2013. http://www.cbc.ca/news/canada/u-s-proposal-to-ban-cross-border-polar-bear-trade-fails-1.1332495.

Association for the Protection of Fur-Bearing Animals. "It's Time to Talk Conservation in B.C." *Wild and Free Press*, no. 161, August 2015, 7. http://thefurbearers.com/downloads/newsletters/FBD161(email).pdf.

Atkins, Eric. "Ontario Grain Farmers Seek Legal Stay on 'Unworkable' Neonics Cap." *Globe and Mail*, 29 June 2015. http://www.theglobeandmail.com/report-on-business/industry-news/energy-and-resources/ontario-grain-farmers-seek-stay-on-unworkable-neonics-cap/article25187737.

Atkinson, Peter L. *Making Game: An Essay on the Hunting of Familiar Things, and the Strangeness of Being Who One Is*. Edmonton: Athabasca University Press, 2009.

Aurelius, Marcus. *The Meditations*. Bk 6. Trans. George Long. http://classics.mit.edu/Antoninus/meditations.6.six.html.

Ayer, Alfred. *Language, Truth and Logic*. London: Penguin, 1936.

Badiou, Pascal H.J. *Conserve First, Restore Later: A Summary of Wetland Loss in the Canadian Prairies and Implications for Water Quality*. Institute for Wetland and Waterfowl Research, Ducks Unlimited Canada, n.d. http://www.yorkton.ca/news/2013/waterseminar/pdf/conserve_first_restore_later.pdf.

Bailey, Ian. "Author J.B. MacKinnon Argues for 'Rewilding': Helping Nature Revive." *Globe and Mail*, 4 October 2013. https://beta.theglobeandmail.com/news/british-columbia/author-jb-mackinnon-argues-for-rewilding-helping-nature-revive/article14693790/.

Bakx, Kyle. "Castle Area Logging Halted by Alberta Government." *CBC News*, 4 September 2015. http://www.cbc.ca/news/canada/calgary/alberta-protects-castle-wilderness-1.3215448.

Ball, David P. "Critics Say Canada Shouldn't Have Taken Humpback Whales off the Endangered Species List." *Vice*, 28 April 2014. http://www.vice.com/en_ca/read/critics-say-canada-shouldnt-have-taken-humpback-whales-off-the-endangered-species-list.

– "Feds Removal of Humpback Whales from At-Risk List Questioned."
    24 Hours Vancouver, 22 April 2014. http://vancouver.24hrs.ca/2014/04/22/
    feds-removal-of-humpback-whales-from-at-risk-list-questioned.

Ballard, Warren B., Daryl Lutz, Thomas W. Keegan, Len H. Carpenter, and James
    C. deVos Jr. "Deer-Predator Relationships: A Review of Recent North American
    Studies with Emphasis on Mule and Black-Tailed Deer." *Wildlife Society Bulletin* 29,
    no. 1 (2001): 99–115.

Barney, Ted, Scott Petrie, Shannon Badzinski, John Paul Leblanc, and Amanda
    Christensen. "Mourning Dove (*Zenaida macroura*) Population Dynamics
    and Societal Assessment towards a Proposed Hunting Season in Ontario."
    Long Point Waterfowl, 2007. https://www.scribd.com/doc/276873748/
    barney-et-al-2007-modo-technical-report.

Barron, Andrew B., and Colin Klein. "What Insects Can Tell Us about the Origins of
    Consciousness." *Proceedings of the National Academy of Sciences* 113, no. 18 (2016):
    4900–8.

Barry, Donald. *Icy Battleground: Canada, the International Fund for Animal Welfare
    and the Seal Hunt*. St John's, NL: Breakwater Books, 2005.

Bartzen, Blake A., Kevin W. Dufour, Robert G. Clark, and F. Dale Caswell. "Trends
    in Agricultural Impact and Recovery of Wetlands in Prairie Canada." *Ecological
    Applications* 20, no. 2 (2010): 525–38.

Bath, Alistair J. "The Role of Human Dimensions in Wildlife Resource Research in
    Wildlife Management." *Ursus* 10 (1998): 349–55.

Bavington, Dean. *Managed Annihilation: An Unnatural History of the Newfoundland
    Cod Collapse*. Vancouver: UBC Press, 2010.

Baxter, Ron. *Bestiaries and Their Users in the Middle Ages*. Stroud, UK: Sutton, 1998.

BC Agricultural Research and Development Corporation, Wild Predator Loss Prevention
    Pilot Project. *An Economic Assessment of Wildlife Predation in British Columbia:
    Main Report*. November 2011. http://www.bcac.bc.ca/sites/bcac.localhost/files/An%20
    Economic%20Assessment%20of%20Predation%20in%20BC.pdf.

Beans, Laura. "British Columbia Expands Controversial Grizzly Bear Trophy
    Hunt." *EcoWatch*, 11 April 2014. http://ecowatch.com/2014/04/11/bc-expands-
    grizzly-bear-trophy-hunt.

Beazley, Karen, and Nathan Cardinal. "A Systematic Approach for Selecting Focal
    Species for Conservation in the Forests of Nova Scotia and Maine." *Environmental
    Conservation* 31, no. 2 (2004): 91–101.

Beeby, Dean. "Sable Island Horses May Face Extinction, Parks Canada Report Warns."
    CBC News, 28 November 2014. http://www.cbc.ca/news/politics/sable-
    island-horses-may-face-extinction-parks-canada-report-warns-1.2852442.

Bekoff, Marc. *The Emotional Lives of Animals*. Novato, CA: New World Library, 2007.

Bekoff, Marc, and Jessica Pierce. *Wild Justice: The Moral Lives of Animals*. Chicago:
    University of Chicago Press, 2009.

Bentham, Jeremy. "Of the Limits of the Penal Branch of Jurisprudence: Limits between Private Ethics and the Art of Legislation." In *An Introduction to the Principles of Morals and Legislation*, ch. 17. Oxford: Clarendon, 1907. http://www.econlib.org/library/Bentham/bnthPML18.html#.

Berg, Nate. "Bringing Nature Back to Cities Is Good for Plants, Animals and Humans." *Ensia*, 19 October 2016. https://ensia.com/features/nature-cities.

Bermúdez, José Luis. "Thinking without Words: An Overview for Animal Ethics." *Journal of Ethics* 11, no. 3 (2007): 319–35.

Best, Stephen. *Influencing Canadian Seal Hunt Policy with a Consumer Boycott of Canadian Seafood*. Animal Alliance of Canada and Environmental Voters, August 2004. http://stephenbest.ca/Seafood_Boycott.pdf.

Beston, Henry. *The Outermost House: A Year of Life on the Great Beach of Cape Cod*. New York: Doubleday and Company, 1928.

Biber, Francois. "Coyote Bounty Will Not Control Population: Experts." *paNOW*, 26 November 2012. http://panow.com/article/270359/coyote-bounty-will-not-control-population-experts.

Biological Survey of Canada. "Arthropods of Canadian Grasslands." 2012. http://www.biology.ualberta.ca/bsc/english/grasslands.htm.

Bird, Louis, and Roland Bohr. "Views of a Swampy-Cree Elder on the Spiritual Relationship between Hunters and Animals." In *The Culture of Hunting in Canada*, ed. Jean L. Manore and Dale G. Miner, 89–104. Vancouver: UBC Press, 2007.

BirdLife International. "Boreal Chickadee (*Parus hudsonicus*)." 2017. http://www.birdlife.org/datazone/speciesfactsheet.php?id=7025.

Blancher, Peter. *The Importance of Canada's Boreal Forest to Landbirds*. Canadian Boreal Initiative and Boreal Songbird Initiative, May 2003. http://www.borealbirds.org/sites/default/files/publications/blancher_report_FINAL.pdf.

Bloch, Günter. *The Pipestone Wolves: The Rise and Fall of a Wolf Family*. Victoria, BC: Rocky Mountain Books, 2016.

Bloom, Pauline M., David W. Howerter, Robert B. Emery, and Llwellyn M. Armstrong. "Relationships between Grazing and Waterfowl Production in the Canadian Prairies." *Journal of Wildlife Management* 77, no. 3 (2013): 534–44.

Bocking, Stephen. *Nature's Experts: Science, Politics, and the Environment*. New Brunswick, NJ: Rutgers University Press, 2004.

Bodson, Liliane. "Zoological Knowledge in Ancient Greece and Rome." In *The Oxford Handbook of Animals in Classical Thought and Life*, ed. G.L. Campbell, 566–78. Oxford: Oxford University Press, 2014. http://promethee.philo.ulg.ac.be/Zoologica/lbodson/bibl/BODSON_Zool_Kn_2014.pdf.

Bolgiano, Nicholas C. "Cause and Effect: Changes in Boreal Bird Irruptions in Eastern North America Relative to the 1970s Spruce Budworm Infestation." *American Birds* 58 (2004): 26–33. http://www.audubon.org/sites/default/files/documents/104_026-33BUDWORMfeature.pdf.

Bolzoni, Lucia, and Giulio A. De Leo. "Unexpected Consequences of Culling on the Eradication of Wildlife Diseases: The Role of Virulence Evolution." *American Naturalist* 181, no. 3 (2013): 301–13.

Bonamis, Alston. "Utilization of Two-Stage Single-Pass Electrofishing to Estimate Abundance and Develop Recovery-Monitoring Protocols for the Endangered Nooksack Dace (*Rhinichthys cataractae*) in Canada." Master's thesis, Simon Fraser University, 2011. http://rem-main.rem.sfu.ca/theses/BonamisAlston_2011_MRM523.pdf.

Boreal Avian Modelling Project. "Boreal Chickadee (*Poecile hudsonicus*): Conservation Status." 8 March 2012. http://www.borealbirds.ca/avian_db/accounts.php/Poecile+hudsonicus/status.

Botelho, Luís Miguel, and Helder Coelho. "Agents That Rationalize Their Decisions." *Proceedings of the Second International conference on Multiagent Systems* (1996): 3–10. https://www.aaai.org/Papers/ICMAS/1996/ICMAS96-001.pdf.

Boutilier, Alex. "Parks Canada Services Take Hit in Budget Cuts." *Toronto Star*, 13 July 2014. http://www.thestar.com/news/canada/2014/07/13/parks_canada_services_take_hit_in_budget_cuts.html.

Boutis, Paula, and Jessica Weizenbluth. *"Species at Risk" Legislation in Ontario and Canada*. Law Society of Upper Canada, 17 October 2012. https://www.ilercampbell.com/blog/wp-content/uploads/Species-at-Risk-6-Minute-Environmental-Lawer-Paula-Boutis.pdf.

Bowman, Jeffrey. "Theophrastus." *Hutchinson Dictionary of Scientific Biography*. 2005. http://connection.ebscohost.com/c/biographies/19932658/theophrastus-c-372-c-287-bc.

Boyce, Mark S., Andrew E. Derocher, and David L. Garshelis. *Scientific Review of Grizzly Bear Harvest Management System in British Columbia*. BC Ministry of Forests, Lands and Natural Resource Operations, August 2015. http://www.env.gov.bc.ca/fw/wildlife/management-issues/docs/grizzly-bear-harvest-management-2016.pdf.

Boyd, David R. *Unnatural Law: Rethinking Canadian Environmental Law and Policy*. Vancouver: UBC Press, 2003.

Boyle, Deborah. "Hume on Animal Reason." *Hume Studies* 29, no. 1 (2003): 3–28.

Boyle, Eleanor. "Neuroscience and Animal Sentience." Compassion in World Farming, March 2009. https://www.ciwf.org.uk/includes/documents/cm_docs/2009/b/boyle_2009_neuroscience_and_animal_sentience.pdf.

Boxall, P., W. Adamowicz, M. Olar, G.E. West, and G. Cantin. "Analysis of the Economic Benefits Associated with the Recovery of Threatened Marine Mammal Species in the Canadian St. Lawrence Estuary." *Marine Policy* 36, no. 1 (2012): 189–97.

Bradford, John B., and N. Thompson Hobbes. "Regulating Overabundant Ungulate Populations: An Example for Elk in Rocky Mountain National Park, Colorado." *Journal of Environmental Management* 86 (2008): 520–8. https://profile.usgs.gov/myscience/upload_folder/ci2011Mar1715265871597Bradford_JEM_2008.pdf.

Braun, David Maxwell. "Interview with Polar Bears International Chief Scientist Steven Amstrup." *National Geographic*, 7 October 2010. http://newswatch. nationalgeographic.com/2010/10/07/steven_amstrup_polar_bears_international.

Brazil, Joe, and Jim Goudle. *A 5 Year Management Plan (2006–2011) for the Polar Bear/Nanuk (Ursus maritimus) in Newfoundland and Labrador.* Government of Nunatsiavut, Department of Lands and Natural Resources, and Government of Newfoundland and Labrador, Environment and Conservation, July 2006. http://www. env.gov.nl.ca/env/wildlife/endangeredspecies/polar_bear_mgmnt_plan.pdf.

Briere, Karen. "Ecojustice Files Lawsuit Seeking Sage-Grouse's Protection." *Western Producer*, 29 May 2012. http://www.producer.com/2012/05/ecojustice-files-lawsuit-seeking-sage-grouses-protection%E2%80%A9.

Brisbane, Justin. "Coyotes Survivors Despite Humans." *Rocky Mountain Outlook*, 5 May 2011. http://www.rmoutlook.com/article/20110505/RMO0801/305059985/-1/rmo/coyotes-survivors-despite-humans.

Britten, Liam. "Limits on Wolf Hunting Removed in Large Areas of Thompson Region." cbc *News*, 16 June 2016. http://www.cbc.ca/news/canada/british-columbia/wolf-hunting-limits-1.3634020.

Bruskotter, Jeremy T., John A. Vucetich, and Robyn S. Wilson. "Of Bears and Biases: Scientific Judgment and the Fate of Yellowstone's Grizzlies." *The Conversation*, 21 June 2016. https://theconversation.com/of-bears-and-biases-scientific-judgment-and-the-fate-of-yellowstones-grizzlies-59570.

Burkett, Walter. "Sacrificial Violence: A Problem in Ancient Religions." In *The Oxford Handbook of Religion and Violence*, ed. Mark Juergensmeyer, Margo Kitts, and Michael Jerryson, 437–54. Oxford: Oxford University Press, 2013.

Burnett, J. Alexander. *A Passion for Wildlife: The History of the Canadian Wildlife Service.* Vancouver: ubc Press, 2003.

Butterworth, Andrew, and Mary Richardson. "A Review of Animal Welfare Implications of the Canadian Commercial Seal Hunt." *Marine Policy* 38 (2013): 457–69.

Byrne, Alan. "The Introduction of Moose to the Island of Newfoundland." Newfoundland and Labrador Provincial Historic Commemorations Program, 15 September 2012. http://www.seethesites.ca/media/48059/introduction%20of%20 moose.pdf.

Callicott, J. Baird. "Conceptual Foundations of the Land Ethic." In *Technology and Values: Essential Readings*, ed. Craig Hanks, 438–53. Chichester, uk: John Wiley and Sons, 2009.

Callicott, J. Baird, Larry B. Crowder, and Karen Mumford. "Current Normative Concepts in Conservation." *Conservation Biology* 13, no. 1 (1999): 22–35.

Calvert, A.M., C.A. Bishop, R.D. Elliot, E.A. Krebs, T.M. Kydd, C.S. Machtans, and G.J. Robertson. "A Synthesis of Human-Related Avian Mortality in Canada." *Avian Conservation and Ecology* 8, no. 2 (2013). http://dx.doi.org/10.5751/ ACE-00581-080211.

Canadian Bar Association, National Environmental Law Section. *Submission on Bill C-33: Species at Risk Act*. May 2002. http://www.cba.org/CMSPages/GetFile. aspx?guid=0d6e5bad-f4fc-4ea8-9a92-c1537d4eb01c.

Canadian Biotechnology Action Network. *Are GM Crops Better for the Environment?* May 2015. http://gmoinquiry.ca/wp-content/uploads/2015/05/Are-GM-crops-better-for-the-environment_-E-web.pdf.

Canadian Boreal Initiative et al. *The Canadian Boreal Forest Agreement: An Historic Agreement Signifying a New Era in the Boreal Forest*. May 2010. cbfa-efbc.ca/wp-content/uploads/2014/12/CBFAAgreement_Full_NewLook.pdf.

Canadian Broadcasting Corporation (CBC). "Top Spots: Rewilding around the World." *The Nature of Things with David Suzuki*, 3 September 2017. http://www.cbc.ca/natureofthings/features/top-spots-rewilding-around-the-world.

Canadian Institute for Business and the Environment. *The Economics of the Canadian Sealing Industry*. 11 June 2001. http://www.ifaw.org/sites/default/files/2001_The%20economics%20of%20the%20Canadian%20sealing%20industry.pdf.

Canadian Parks Council. *Aboriginal Peoples and Canada's Parks and Protected Areas*. 2011. http://www.parks-parcs.ca/english/cpc/aboriginal.php.

Canadian Parks and Wilderness Society. *Canadian Wilderness*, Fall 2015/Winter 2016. http://cpaws.org/uploads/CanadianWilderness-Fall15Winter16-web.pdf.

– *Looking for Action: Caribou Losing Ground*. December 2014. http://cpaws.org/uploads/CPAWS_Caribou_Report_2014.pdf.

– "RE: CPAWS Response to Environmental Assessment for Brewster Glacier Discovery Walk in Jasper National Park, CEAA Registry Reference Number 11-01-59982." Letter to Greg Fenton, superintendent, Jasper National Park, 16 December 2011. http://cpawssouthernalberta.org/upload/CPAWS_response_to_Glacier_Discover_Walk_Final_Dec_16_2011.pdf.

– *Ten Years after the Alberta Caribou Recovery Plan Was Drafted, Alberta's Caribou Are Declining Faster Than Ever: What Needs to Be Done Differently?* 2014. http://cpaws.org/uploads/Ten_Years_after_the_AB_Reocvery_Plan.pdf.

– *2015 Update: Boreal Woodland Caribou Conservation in Canada*. December 2015. http://cpaws.org/uploads/CPAWS-Caribou_Report_EN-2015.pdf.

Canadian Parks and Wilderness Society, BC Chapter. *Gas Gone Wild – LNG in BC: Impacts on Parks, Wilderness and Wildlife*. December 2014. http://www.cpawsbc.org/upload/lng-report-2014.pdf.

Canadian Parks and Wilderness Society and David Suzuki Foundation. *Population Critical: How Are Caribou Faring?* December 2013. http://cpaws.org/uploads/BorealCaribouReport-CPAWS_DSF.pdf.

Canadian Press. "Alberta to Sell Off Land That Serves as Crucial Caribou Habitat." *CTV News*, 13 May 2014. http://www.ctvnews.ca/canada/alberta-to-sell-off-land-that-serves-as-crucial-caribou-habitat-1.1819926.

– "Canada Must Explain Polar Bear Policies to NAFTA Group." *CBC News*, 1 December 2012. http://www.cbc.ca/news/canada/north/canada-must-explain-polar-bear-policies-to-nafta-group-1.1129372.

– "Canadian Protected Areas below Global Average: Report." *CTV News*, 29 June 2011. http://www.ctvnews.ca/canadian-protected-areas-below-global-average-report-1.663575.

– "Castle Wilderness Area Plan Will Create 'Watered-Down' Park, Critics Worry." *CBC News*, 2 October 2015. http://www.cbc.ca/news/canada/calgary/castle-wilderness-watered-down-park-1.3254333.

– "Chemical Industry Powers Hike in Manufacturing Sales – Data." *Chronicle Herald*, 15 August 2014. http://thechronicleherald.ca/business/1229808-chemical-industry-powers-hike-in-manufacturing-sales-data.

– "Court Upholds Restriction on Animal Rights Activists Pursuing Seal Hunt." *Vancouver Sun*, 10 December 2005. https://www.pressreader.com/canada/vancouver-sun/20051210/textview.

– "NAFTA Panel Won't Review Canada's Polar Bear Policy." *CBC News*, 6 June 2014. http://www.cbc.ca/news/canada/manitoba/nafta-panel-won-t-review-canada-s-polar-bear-policy-1.2667925.

– "Panel Should Have Considered Whales When It Reviewed Pipeline Proposal: Lawyer." *Vancouver Observer*, 5 October 2015, http://www.vancouverobserver.com/news/panel-should-have-considered-whales-when-it-reviewed-pipeline-proposal-lawyer.

– "Parks Canada Turns Down New Hotel for Jasper National Park." *Travelweek News*, 27 July 2014. http://www.travelweek.ca/news/parks-canada-turns-new-hotel-jasper-national-park.

– "Saskatchewan Defends Coyote Bounty That Saw 71,000 Animals Killed." *The News* (New Glasgow, Nova Scotia), 26 May 2010. http://www.ngnews.ca/News/Canada---World/2010-05-26/article-1166564/Saskatchewan-defends-coyote-bounty-that-saw-71,000-animals-killed/1. ·

Canadian Sealers Association. "Important Notice: CSA Operations." Press release, 17 April 2015. https://www.sealharvest.ca/?p=3821.

Canola Council of Canada. "Industry Overview." 2014. http://www.canolacouncil.org/markets-stats/industry-overview.

Cariappa, C.A., John K. Oakleaf, Warren B. Ballard, and Stewart W. Breck. "A Reappraisal of the Evidence for Regulation of Wolf Populations." *Journal of Wildlife Management* 75, no. 3 (2011): 726–30.

Carpenter, Janet E. "Impact of GM Crops on Biodiversity." *GM Crops* 2, no. 1 (2011): 7–23.

Carpenter, Len H., Daniel J. Decker, and James F. Lipscomb. "Stakeholder Acceptance Capacity in Wildlife Management." *Human Dimensions of Wildlife* 5, no. 3 (2000): 5–19.

Carson, Richard T., Nicholas E. Flores, and Norman F. Meade. "Contingent Valuation: Controversies and Evidence." *Environmental and Resource Economics* 19, no. 2 (2001): 173–210.

Cartmill, Matt. *A View to a Death in the Morning: Hunting and Nature through History.* Cambridge, MA: Harvard University Press, 1993.

Casey, Liam. "'A Terrible Day for Endangered Species': Ontario Court Dismisses Legal Challenge." *Waterloo Region Record*, 11 October 2016. http://www.therecord. com/news-story/6905481--a-terrible-day-for-endangered-species-ontario-court-dismisses-legal-challenge.

Casselman, Anne. "Changes to Canada's Fisheries Law Alarm Biologists." *Nature*, 25 November 2013. http://www.nature.com/news/changes-to-canada-s-fisheries-law-alarm-biologists-1.14234.

Cavalieri, Paola, and Peter Singer. "The Great Ape Project – and Beyond." In *The Great Ape Project: Equality beyond Humanity*, ed. Paola Cavalieri and Peter Singer, 304–12. New York: St Martin's Press, 1993.

CBC *News*. "Canada's Process to Protect Endangered Species Is Failing, Study Finds." 28 November 2014. http://www.cbc.ca/news/technology/canada-s-process-to-protect-endangered-species-is-failing-study-finds-1.2853444.

– "Coyote Hunt with Cash Prizes Draws Controversy, Threats in Alberta." 8 January 2015. http://www.cbc.ca/news/canada/edmonton/coyote-hunt-with-cash-prizes-draws-controversy-threats-in-alberta-1.2894093.

– "Hungry Moose Upsetting Gros Morne Habitat." 13 October 2013. http://www.cbc.ca/ news/canada/newfoundland-labrador/hungry-moose-upsetting-gros-morne-habitat-1.1991540.

– "Law to Reduce Use of Bee-Killing Pesticides Upheld in Court." 26 October 2015. http://www.cbc.ca/news/business/grain-farmers-neonics-1.3289326.

– "Moose Class-Action Lawsuit Dismissed, Province Found Not Liable." 19 September 2014. http://www.cbc.ca/news/canada/newfoundland-labrador/ moose-class-action-lawsuit-dismissed-province-found-not-liable-1.2771971.

– "Moose Cull in Gros Morne Expanded to Save Habitat." 6 November 2013. http:// www.cbc.ca/news/canada/newfoundland-labrador/moose-cull-in-gros-morne-expanded-to-save-habitat-1.2416887.

– "Moose Population Declining, French Says." 26 March 2012. http://www.cbc.ca/news/ canada/newfoundland-labrador/moose-population-declining-french-says-1.1231302.

– "Point Pelee National Park to Close for 2 Weeks for Deer Cull." 5 January 2016. http:// www.cbc.ca/news/canada/windsor/point-pelee-national-park-to-close-for-2-weeks-for-deer-cull-1.3390570.

– "Seal Product Ban Upheld on 'Ethical' Grounds." 25 November 2013. http://www. cbc.ca/news/canada/newfoundland-labrador/seal-product-ban-upheld-on-ethical-grounds-1.2438904.

– "3 Alberta Cougars Killed after 'Unusual' Behaviour." 4 January 2014. http://www.cbc.ca/news/canada/calgary/3-alberta-cougars-killed-after-unusual-behaviour-1.2484295.

– "Too Many Deer on Gulf Islands: B.C. Biologist." 18 January 2011. http://www.cbc.ca/news/canada/british-columbia/too-many-deer-on-gulf-islands-b-c-biologist-1.1035047.

– "Wolf Hunting in Peace Region Could Have No Limits, Province Proposes." 10 December 2015. http://www.cbc.ca/news/canada/british-columbia/wolf-hunting-peace-region-1.3360160.

Ceballos, Gerardo, Paul R. Ehrlich, and Rodolfo Dirzo. "Biological Annihilation via the Ongoing Sixth Mass Extinction Signaled by Vertebrate Population Losses and Declines." *Proceedings of the National Academy of Sciences of the United States of America* 114, no. 30 (2017): E6089–96. http://www.pnas.org/content/114/30/E6089.full.pdf.

Center for Responsible Travel. *Economic Impact of Bear Viewing and Bear Hunting in the Great Bear Rainforest of British Columbia.* 2014. http://www.responsibletravel.org/projects/documents/Economic_Impact_of_Bear_Viewing_and_Bear_Hunting_in_GBR_of_BC.pdf.

Cheadle, Bruce. "Environment, Fisheries Ministers Failed to Enforce Species at Risk Act, Court Rules." *Toronto Star,* 14 February 2014. http://www.thestar.com/news/canada/2014/02/14/environment_fisheries_ministers_failed_to_enforce_species_at_risk_act_court_rules.html.

– "NAFTA Tribunal Finds 'Open Questions' about Canada's Polar Bear Protections." *Vancouver Sun,* 12 December 2013. http://www.biologicaldiversity.org/news/media-archive/a2014/PolarBear_vancouversun_12-12-13.pdf.

Cherry, Seth G., Andrew E. Derocher, Gregory W. Thiemann, and Nicholas J. Lunn. "Migration Phenology and Seasonal Fidelity of an Arctic Marine Predator in Relation to Sea Ice Dynamics." *Journal of Animal Ecology* 82, no. 4 (2013): 912–21.

Childs, Craig. *Apocalyptic Planet: Field Guide to the Future of the Earth.* 2012. Reprint, New York: Vintage Books, 2013.

Christensen, Amanda. "Ontario Province-Wide Societal Assessment of Attitudes towards Wildlife, Hunting and a Potential Mourning Dove (*Zenaida macroura*) Harvest." BSc honour's thesis, University of Western Ontario, 2006. Accessed 18 December 2014. http://longpointwaterfowl.org/wp-content/uploads/2011/05/Christiansen-BSc-Thesis-2006.pdf (site discontinued).

Christie, Peter. "Triage in the Wild: Is It Time to Choose Which Species Live and Which Die Out?" *National Post,* 31 October 2015. http://news.nationalpost.com/news/canada/triage-in-the-wild-is-it-time-to-choose-which-species-live-and-which-die-out.

Chrulew, Matthew. "Reversing Extinction: Restoration and Resurrection in the Pleistocene Rewilding Projects." *Humanimalia: A Journal of Human/Animal Interface Studies* 2, no. 2 (2011): 4–27. https://www.depauw.edu/humanimalia/issue%2004/pdfs/chrulew.pdf.

City of Calgary, Parks and Recreation. "Common Pests in Calgary: Beavers."
    http://www.calgary.ca/CSPS/Parks/Pages/Planning-and-Operations/Pest-
    Management/Beavers.aspx.

Clark, J.A., and Harvey E. "Assessing Multi-Species Recovery Plans under the
    Endangered Species Act." *Ecological Applications* 12, no. 3 (2002): 655–62.

Clark, Stephen R.L. "Good Dogs and Other Animals." In *Defense of Animals*, ed. Peter
    Singer, 41–51. New York: Basil Blackwell, 1985. http://www.animal-rights-library.
    com/texts-m/clark02.htm.

Clarke, Leigh. "Why I Hunt." In *The Culture of Hunting in Canada*, ed. Jean L. Manore
    and Dale G. Miner, 11–13. Vancouver: UBC Press, 2007.

Clement, Grace. "The Ethic of Care and the Problem of Wild Animals." *Between the
    Species* 13, no. 3 (2003): 1–12. http://webs.wofford.edu/williamsnm/animal%20
    ethics%20articles/ethic%20of%20care%20wild%20animals.pdf.

Clevenger, Anthony P. "Moose-Vehicle Collisions and Their Mitigation in
    Newfoundland." February 2011. http://sopacnl.com/sopac/wp-content/uploads/2011
    /05/Moose-vehicle-collisions-and-their-mitigation-in-Newfoundland.pdf.

Cloyd, Raymond. "Indirect Effects of Pesticides on Natural Enemies." In *Pesticides –
    Advances in Chemical and Botanical Pesticides*, ed. R.P. Soundararajan, 127–50.
    Rijeka, Croatia: InTech, 2012. https://www.intechopen.com/books/pesticides-
    advances-in-chemical-and-botanical-pesticides/indirect-effects-of-pesticides-
    on-natural-enemies.

Cohen, Nina E., Frans W.A. Brom, and Elsbeth N. Stassen. "Moral Convictions and
    Culling Animals: A Survey in the Netherlands." *Anthrozoös: A Multidisciplinary
    Journal of the Interactions of People and Animals* 25, no. 3 (2012): 353–67.

Conway, D.G. *Animal Magick: The Art of Recognizing and Working with Familiars.*
    St Paul, MN: Llewellyn, 1997.

Cooke, Steve. "Animal Kingdoms: On Habitat Rights for Wild Animals." *Environmental
    Values* 26, no. 1 (2017): 53–72.

Coleman, Jon T. *Vicious: Wolves and Men in America.* New Haven, CT: Yale University
    Press, 2004.

Colpitts, George. *Game in the Garden: A Human History of Wildlife in Western Canada
    to 1940.* Vancouver: UBC Press, 2002.

Committee on the Status of Endangered Wildlife in Canada (COSEWIC). "Assessing
    Wildlife Species-Theory." 4 January 2017. http://www.cosewic.gc.ca/default.
    asp?lang=en&n=A3B2015B-1#wsCD595DD2.

– *Assessment and Status Report on the Atlantic Bluefin Tuna (Thunnus tynnus) in
    Canada.* 2011. http://www.registrelep-sararegistry.gc.ca/virtual_sara/files/cosewic/
    sr_atlantic_bluefin_tuna_0911_eng.pdf.

– *Assessment and Status Report on the Black-Tailed Prairie Dog (Cynomys ludovicianus)
    in Canada.* 2011. http://www.registrelep-sararegistry.gc.ca/virtual_sara/files/
    cosewic/sr_chien_prairie_black_tailed_prairie_dog%20_0912_e.pdf.

– *Assessment and Status Report on the Humpback Whale (Megaptera novaeangliae) North Pacific Population in Canada.* 2011. https://www.registrelep-sararegistry.gc.ca/virtual_sara/files/cosewic/sr_humpback_whale_0911_eng1.pdf.

– *Assessment and Status Report on the Porbeagle (Lamna nasus) in Canada.* 2014. http://www.registrelep-sararegistry.gc.ca/virtual_sara/files/cosewic/sr_Porbeagle_2014_e.pdf.

– *Assessment and Status Report on the Rusty Blackbird (Euphagus carolinus) in Canada.* 2006. http://www.sararegistry.gc.ca/virtual_sara/files/cosewic/sr_rusty_blackbird_0806_e.pdf.

– *Assessment and Status Report on the Wolverine (Gulo gulo) in Canada.* 2014. http://www.registrelep-sararegistry.gc.ca/virtual_sara/files/cosewic/sr_Wolverine_2014_e.pdf.

– *Assessment and Update Status Report on the Humpback Whale (Megaptera novaeangliae) in Canada: North Pacific Population and Western North Atlantic Population.* 2003. http://www.sararegistry.gc.ca/virtual_sara/files/cosewic/sr_humpback_whale_e.pdf.

– *Assessment and Update Status Report on the Narwhal (Monodon monoceros) in Canada.* 2004. http://www.sararegistry.gc.ca/virtual_sara/files/cosewic/sr_narwhal_e.pdf.

– "Candidate Wildlife Species." 30 March 2015. http://www.cosewic.gc.ca/default.asp?lang=en&n=258BE9F5-1.

– "Wildlife Species Assessment." November 2015. http://www.cosewic.gc.ca/default.asp?lang=En&n=ED199D3B-1&printfullpage=true#fnb1.

Cooley, Hillary S., Robert B. Wielgus, Gary M. Koehler, Hugh S. Robinson, and Benjamin T. Maletzke. "Does Hunting Regulate Cougar Populations? A Test of the Compensatory Mortality Hypothesis." *Ecology* 90, no. 10 (2009): 2913–21.

Cormorant Defenders International. *Observations of the 2008 Cormorant Cull on Middle Island in Point Pelee National Park.* 30 September 2008. http://www.zoocheck.com/wp-content/uploads/2015/06/2008MiddleIslandReport.pdf.

Cortus, Brett G., James R. Unterschultz, Scott R. Jeffrey, and Peter C. Boxall. "The Impacts of Agriculture Support Programs on Wetland Retention on Grain Farms in the Prairie Pothole Region." *Canadian Water Resources Journal* 34, no. 3 (2009): 245–54.

Cranshaw, Whitney, and Richard Redak. *Bugs Rule! Introduction to the World of Insects.* Princeton, NJ: Princeton University Press, 2013.

Crawford, Emma. "Forest Conservation Group Withdraws from Canadian Boreal Forest Agreement." *Business Vancouver,* 16 April 2013. https://www.biv.com/article/2013/4/forest-conservation-group-withdraws-from-canadian-.

Crichton, Vince. "Moose and Ecosystem Management in the 21st Century: Does the King Have a Place? A Canadian Perspective." *Alces* 34 (1998): 467–77.

Cronin, Melissa. "Bill Will Block Observers from Reporting Canada's Appalling Seal Hunt." *The Dodo,* 13 March 2014. https://www.thedodo.com/bill-will-block-observers-from-463495120.html.

Crosbie, John C. "Foreword." In Donald Barry, *Icy Battleground: Canada, the International Fund for Animal Welfare and the Seal Hunt*, viii–ix. St Johns: Breakwater Books, 2005.

Csanady, Ashley. "'Political Killing' or 'Economic Opportunity'? Ontario Spring Black Bear Hunt Extended amid Cheers and Jeers." *National Post*, 3 November 2015. http://news.nationalpost.com/news/canada/political-killing-or-economic-opportunity-ontario-spring-black-bear-hunt-extended-amid-cheers-and-jeers.

CTV News. "Seal Meat Lunch Offered at Parliamentary Restaurant." 10 March 2010. http://www.ctvnews.ca/seal-meat-lunch-offered-at-parliamentary-restaurant-1.490900.

CTV News Calgary. "Cougars Killed by Wildlife Officer in Canmore." 16 December 2013. http://calgary.ctvnews.ca/cougars-killed-by-wildlife-officer-in-canmore-1.1595540.

– "Poll Question." 11 June 2015.

Cutlac, Marius, and Marian Weber. *The Economic Impact of Outfitted Hunting in Alberta*. Alberta Innovate – Technology Futures, December 2014. https://www.apos.ab.ca/media/13785/the-economic-impact-of-outfitted-hunting-in-alberta.pdf.

Damasio, Antonio, and Kaspar Meyer. "Behind the Looking-Glass." *Nature* 454 (2008): 167–8.

Daoust P.Y., and C. Craguel. "The Canadian Harp Seal Hunt: Observations on the Effectiveness of Procedures to Avoid Poor Animal Welfare Outcomes." *Animal Welfare* 21 (2012): 445–55. https://www.sealharvest.ca/wp-content/uploads/2015/04/Canadian-harp-seal-hunt-Animal-Welfare-2012.pdf.

Darimont, Chris T., Stephanie M. Carlson, Michael T. Kinnison, Paul C. Paquet, Thomas E. Reimchen, Christopher C. Wilmers, and Gretchen C. Daily. "Human Predators Outpace Other Agents of Trait Change in the Wild." *Proceedings of the National Academy of Sciences of the United States of America* 106, no. 3 (2009): 952–4.

Darimont, Chris T., Caroline H. Fox, Heather M. Bryan, and Thomas E. Reimchen. "The Unique Ecology of Human Predators." *Science* 349, no. 6250 (2015): 858–60.

Daubs, Katie. "It's Open Season on Mourning Doves in Parts of Ontario." *Toronto Star*, 4 October 2013. http://www.thestar.com/news/gta/2013/10/04/its_open_season_on_mourning_doves_in_parts_of_ontario.html.

Dauvergne Peter. *Shadows of Consumption: Consequences for the Global Environment*. Cambridge, MA: MIT Press, 2010.

David Suzuki Foundation, Georgia Strait Alliance, Raincoast Conservation Foundation, Wilderness Committee, and Ecojustice. "Re: March 2014 Draft Action Plan for the Northern and Southern Resident Killer Whales (*Orcinus orca*) in Canada." Letter to Fisheries and Oceans Canada, 15 April 2014. https://www.raincoast.org/wp-content/uploads/Comments-on-DFO-Draft-Action-Plan-for-Resident-killer-whales-April-2014.pdf.

Dearden, Philip, and Jessica Dempsey. "Protected Areas in Canada: Decade of Change." *Canadian Geographer* 48, no. 2 (2004): 225–39.

Dedyna, Katherine. "Island Cougars on Losing End of Interactions with Humans." *Victoria Times Colonist*, 23 January 2015. http://www.timescolonist.com/ island-cougars-on-losing-end-of-interactions-with-humans-1.1741261.

DeGrazia, David. "Regarding the Last Frontier of Bigotry." *Logos* 4, no. 2 (2005). http:// www.logosjournal.com/issue_4.2/degrazia.htm.

Deguise, Isabelle E., and Jeremy T. Kerr. "Protected Areas and Prospects for Endangered Species Conservation in Canada." *Conservation Biology* 7, no. 1 (2006): 48–55. http://mysite.science.uottawa.ca/jkerr/pdf/consbiol2006.pdf.

Dekel, Jon. "Fisheries Minister Says Morrissey 'Brainwashed by Decades of Propaganda.'" *Canada.com*, 22 April 2014. http://o.canada.com/news/ fisheries-minister-says-morrissey-brainwashed-about-seal-hunt.

DeMaster, Donald, and Ian Stirling. "The Estimation of Survival and Litter Size of Polar Bear Cubs." Paper presented at the 5th International Conference on Bear Research and Management, Madison, Wisconsin, February, 1980. http://www.bearbiology.com/ fileadmin/tpl/Downloads/URSUS/Vol_5/Demaster___Stirling_Vol_5.pdf.

Dennett, Daniel C. *Brainchildren: Essays on Designing Minds.* Cambridge, MA: MIT Press, 1998.

Derworiz, Colette. "Controversial Cabled Path Approved for Summer Use at Mount Norquay." *Calgary Herald*, 21 May 2013. http://www.calgaryherald.com/technology/ Controversial+cabled+path+approved+summer+Mount+Norquay/8415543/story.html.

– "Encounters with Cougars on the Rise across Alberta." *Calgary Herald*, 5 April 2015. http://calgaryherald.com/news/local-news/ encounters-with-cougars-on-the-rise-across-alberta.

– "Wolf Deaths Called a Symbol of Bigger Problems in Banff National Park." *Calgary Herald*, 13 August 2016. http://calgaryherald.com/news/local-news/ wolf-deaths-called-a-symbol-of-bigger-problems-in-banff-national-park.

Descartes, René. "Animals Are Machines." Reprinted from *Passions of the Soul* (1649). *Journal of Cosmology* 14 (2011). http://journalofcosmology.com/ Consciousness136.html.

De Souza, Mike. "Harper Government Cutting More Than $100 million Related to Protection of Water." *Canada.com*, 27 December 2013. http://o.canada.com/news/ harper-government-cutting-more-than-100-million-related-to-protection-of-water.

– "Harper Minister Ducks Questions on Plan to 'Authorize' Water Pollution." *Canada. com*, 29 June 2012. http://o.canada.com/news/politics-and-the-nation/parliament/ harper-minister-ducks-questions-on-plan-to-authorize-water-pollution.

de Waal, Frans. *The Age of Empathy: Nature's Lessons for a Kinder Society.* Toronto: McClelland and Stewart, 2009.

Diebel, Linda. "Ontario Spring Bear Hunt to Resume, Wynne's Office Confirms." *Toronto Star*, 6 April 2014. http://www.thestar.com/news/canada/2014/04/06/ ontario_spring_bear_hunt_to_resume_wynnes_office_confirms.html.

Dietsche, Deborah. "Mourning Dove Hunt Should Be Stopped." Letter to the
    editor, *Guelph Mercury*, 6 September 2013. http://www.guelphmercury.com/
    opinion-story/4063849-mourning-dove-hunt-should-be-stopped.

Ditchkoff, Stephen S., Sarah T. Saalfeld, and Charles J. Gibson. "Animal Behavior
    in Urban Ecosystems: Modifications due to Human-Induced Stress." *Urban
    Ecosystems* 9, no. 1 (2006): 5–12.

Donaldson, Sue, and Will Kymlicka. *Zoopolis: A Political Theory of Animal Rights.*
    Oxford: Oxford University Press, 2011.

Donihee, John. *The Evolution of Wildlife Law in Canada.* Canadian Institute of
    Research Law, May 2000. https://dspace.ucalgary.ca/bitstream/1880/47200/1/
    OP09Wildlife.pdf.

Double Diamond Outfitters. "Alberta's #1 Cougar Taken with Diamond Outfitters!"
    2013. http://www.albertahunt.com/cougar.htm.

Downer, Craig C. *Report on Wild Horses and Ecosystem in Rocky Mountain Foothills
    East of Banff National Park and West of Sundre, Alberta, Canada (Red Deer River,
    James River and Vicinity).* Zoocheck, 11 December 2015. https://www.zoocheck.
    com/wp-content/uploads/2015/04/Downer-Report-2015.pdf.

Dowsley, Martha. "The Value of a Polar Bear: Evaluating the Role of a Multiple-Use
    Resource in the Nunavut Mixed Economy." *Arctic Anthropology* 47, no. 1 (2010):
    39–56.

Dubois, Sara, and H.W. Harshaw. "Exploring 'Humane' Dimensions of Wildlife."
    Human Dimensions of Wildlife: An International Journal 18, no. 1 (2013): 1–19.

Duda, Mark Damian, and Martin F. Jones. "Public Opinion on and Attitudes toward
    Hunting." In *Transactions of the 73rd North American Wildlife and Natural
    Resources Conference*, ed. Jennifer Rahm, 180–98. Washington, DC: Wildlife
    Management Institute, 2009. http://s3.amazonaws.com/zanran_storage/www-lib.
    uwyo.edu/ContentPages/453379225.pdf.

Duncan, J.H. "The Changing Concept of Animal Sentience." *Applied Animal Behaviour
    Science* 100, nos 1–2 (2006): 11–19.

Eagles, Paul F.J., Stephen F. McCool, and Christopher D. Haynes. *Sustainable
    Tourism in Protected Areas: Guidelines for Planning and Management.* United
    Nations Environment Program, World Tourism Organization, and International
    Union for Conservation of Nature (IUCN), 2002. http://cmsdata.iucn.org/
    downloads/pag_008.pdf.

Ecojustice. "Challenge of Neonicotinoid Pesticide Registrations." Case update, April
    2017. In possession of author.

– "Challenging Kinder Morgan's Pipeline Expansion Project." Case update, April 2017.
    In possession of author.

– "Defending Ontario's Endangered Species Act and the Species It Protects." *Ecojustice*,
    no. 75 (Winter 2015): 3. http://www.ecojustice.ca/wp-content/uploads/2015/02/
    Winter-2015-newsletter.pdf.

- "Endangered Species Protection." Case update, April 2017. In possession of author.
- *Failure to Protect: Grading Canada's Species at Risk Laws*. October 2012. https://www.ecojustice.ca/wp-content/uploads/2014/08/Failure-to-protect_Grading-Canadas-Species-at-Risk-Laws.pdf.
- "Proposed Caribou Recovery Strategy Violates SARA." Press release, 1 October 2012. http://www.ecojustice.ca/pressrelease/proposed-caribou-recovery-strategy-violates-sara.
- "Woodland Caribou Battle Goes to Federal Court." Press release, 1 October 2012. http://www.ecojustice.ca/pressrelease/woodland-caribou-battle-goes-to-federal-court.
ÉcoRessources Consultants. *Evidence of the Socio-Economic Importance of Polar Bears for Canada*. Environment Canada, June 2011. http://www.motherjones.com/files/value_of_polar_bears_in_canada.pdf.
Edwards, Steven F. "Ethical Preferences and the Assessment of Existence Values: Does the Neoclassical Model Fit?" *Northeastern Journal of Agricultural and Resource Economics* 15, no. 2 (1986): 145–50. http://ageconsearch.umn.edu/bitstream/29059/1/15020145.pdf.
Edworthy, Amanda B., and Kathy Martin. "Persistence of Tree Cavities Used by Cavity-Nesting Vertebrates Declines in Harvested Forests." *Journal of Wildlife Management* 77, no. 4 (2013): 770–6.
Elliott, Cam. "Commercial Trapping – a Foundation of Wapusk National Park." *Wapusk News*, no. 7 (2014). https://www.pc.gc.ca/en/pn-np/mb/wapusk/decouvrir-discover/ne1/ne1_2014/ne1_2014_8.
Ellis, Cathy. "Parks Canada Conservation Spending $31.4 Million under Budget." *Rocky Mountain Outlook*, 19 February 2015. http://www.rmoutlook.com/Parks-Canada-conservation-spending-31.4-million-under-budget-20150219.
Elton, Charles. *Animal Ecology*. London: Sidgwick and Jackson, 1927.
Emery, Claude. *The Northern Cod Crisis*. Parliamentary Research Branch, Canadian Library of Parliament, 1992. https://lop.parl.ca/Content/LOP/ResearchPublicationsArchive/pdf/bp1000/bp313-e.pdf.
Entem, A., W.L. Adamowicz, and P.C. Boxall. "Habitat Conservation for Grassland Species-at-Risk: A Multi-Species Benefit-Cost Analysis." In *Engaging People in Conservation: Proceedings of the 10th Prairie Conservation and Endangered Species Conference, February 19 to 22 2013 – Red Deer, Alberta*, ed. G.L. Holroyd. A.J. Trefry, and B. Crockett, 52–6. Lethbridge, AB: Alberta Prairie Conservation Forum, 2014. http://www.pcesc.ca/media/8212/pcesc_proceedings_2014-09-19_for_web.pdf.
Environmental Law Centre. "Re: Proposed Partial Identification of Sprague's Pipit Critical Habitat in Alberta and Saskatchewan." Letter to Recovery Planning, Environment Canada, 4 May 2011. http://elc.ab.ca/Content_Files/Files/SpraguespipitELC2011FINAL.pdf.
Epictetus. "Of Providence." In *The Discourses*. http://classics.mit.edu/Epictetus/discourses.mb.txt.

Epstein, Richard A. "Animals as Objects, or Subjects, of Rights." In *Animal Rights: Current Debates and New Directions*, ed. Cass R. Sunstein and Martha C. Nussbaum, 142–61. Oxford: Oxford University Press, 2004.

European Commission. "Deer Culls Are Not Effective for Forest Protection." *Science for Environment Policy*, March 2012. http://ec.europa.eu/environment/integration/research/newsalert/pdf/275na4_en.pdf.

European Union, Council of the European Communities. "Council Directive 83/129/EEC." 28 March 1983. http://eur-lex.europa.eu/legal-content/EN/TXT/?uri=CELEX:31983L0129.

European Union, Council on Trade in Seal Products. "Regulation (EC) No. 1007/2009." 16 September 2009. http://eur-lex.europa.eu/legal-content/EN/TXT/?uri=CELEX:32009R1007.

Farnese, Patricia L. "Searching for Wildlife: A Critique of Canada's Regulatory Response to Emerging Zoonotic Diseases." *Queens Law Journal* 39, no. 2 (2014): 471–509.

Fast, Helen, and Maria Healy. *Federal Marine Protected Area Network Plan and Community Perspectives: Baffin and Kitikmeot Regions – Nunavut 2009*. Fisheries and Oceans Canada, January 2010. http://www.dfo-mpo.gc.ca/Library/339408.pdf.

Favre, David. "Wildlife Jurisprudence." *Journal of Environmental Law and Litigation* 25 (2010): 459–510. https://www.animallaw.info/sites/default/files/Wildlife%20Jurisprudence.compressed.pdf.

Federal, Provincial, and Territorial Governments of Canada, Canadian Councils of Resource Ministers. *Canadian Biodiversity: Ecosystem Status and Trends 2010*. 2010. http://www.biodivcanada.ca/A519F000-8427-4F8C-9521-8A95AE287753/EN_CanadianBiodiversity_FULL.pdf.

– *2012 Canadian Nature Survey: Awareness, Participation, and Expenditures in Nature-Based Recreation, Conservation, and Subsistence Activities*. 2014. http://publications.gc.ca/collections/collection_2014/ec/En4-243-2014-eng.pdf.

Festa-Bianchet, Marco. "Exploitive Wildlife Management as a Selective Pressure for Life-History Evolution of Large Mammals." In *Animal Behavior and Wildlife Conservation*, ed. Marco Festa-Bianchet and Marco Apollonia, 191–207. London: Island, 2003.

Fetissenko, Maxim. "Beyond Morality: Developing a New Rhetorical Strategy for the Animal Rights Movement." *Journal of Animal Ethics* 1, no. 2 (2011): 150–75.

Fiedeldey, André C. "Wild Animals in a Wilderness Setting: An Ecosystemic Experience?" *Anthrozoös: A Multidisciplinary Journal of the Interactions of People and Animals* 7, no. 2 (1994): 113–23.

Filion, F.L., A. Jacquemot, and R. Reid. *The Importance of Wildlife to Canadians: An Executive Overview of the Recreational Economic Significance of Wildlife*. Canadian Wildlife Service, 1985. http://publications.gc.ca/collections/collection_2011/ec/CW66-76-1985-eng.pdf.

Findholt, S.L., B.K. Johnson, D. Damiran, T. DelCurto, and J.G. Kie. "Diet Composition, Dry Matter Intake, and Diet Overlap of Mule Deer, Elk, and

Cattle." In *The Starkey Project: A Synthesis of Long-Term Studies of Elk and Mule Deer*, ed. M.J. Wisdom, 159–68. Lawrence, KS: Alliance Communications Group, 2005. http://oregonstate.edu/dept/eoarcunion/sites/default/files/publications/Dietcompositiondrymatterintakeanddietoverlapofmuledeerelkandcattle.pdf.

Findlay, J. Scott, Stewart Elgie, Brian Giles, and Linda Burr. "Species Listing under Canada's Species at Risk Act." *Conservation Biology* 23, no. 8 (2009): 1609–17.

Fink, Sheryl. *Canada's Commercial Seal Slaughter 2009*. International Fund for Animal Welfare, 2009. http://www.ifaw.org/sites/default/files/2009%20seal%20sealing.pdf.

Finnamore, Albert T. *The Advantages of Using Arthropods in Ecosystem Management*. Biological Survey of Canada, 1996. http://www.biology.ualberta.ca/bsc/pdf/advantages.pdf.

Fitzpatrick, Meagan. "Environment Canada Job Cuts Raise Concerns." *CBC News*, 4 August 2011. http://www.cbc.ca/news/politics/environment-canada-job-cuts-raise-concerns-1.998346.

Fitzpatrick, Simon. "Doing Away with Morgan's Canon." *Mind and Language* 23, no. 2 (2008): 224–46.

Fluker, Shaun. "The Curious Case of the Greater Sage Grouse in Alberta." Faculty of Law, University of Calgary, 17 January 2014. http://ablawg.ca/2014/01/17/the-curious-case-of-the-greater-sage-grouse-in-alberta.

– "Ecological Integrity in Canada's Parks: The False Promise of Law." *Windsor Review of Legal and Social Issues* 29 (2010): 89–124.

– "How Legal Design May Constrain the Power of Law to Implement Environmental Norms: The Case of Ecological Integrity in Canada's National Parks." Paper presented at the conference "A Symposium on Environment in the Courtroom: Key Environmental Concepts and the Unique Nature of Environmental Damage," University of Calgary, 23–24 March 2012. cirl.ca/files/cirl/shaun_fluker-en.pdf.

Fortenbaugh, William F., and Robert W. Sharples, eds. "Theophrastus: Piety, Justice and Animals." In *Theophrastean Studies: On Natural Science, Physics and Metaphysics, Ethics, Religion and Rhetoric*, ed. William F. Fortenbaugh and Robert W. Sharples, 173–89. New Brunswick, NJ: Transaction Books, 1988.

Foubert, Tanya. "Banff to See Caribou Return through Captive Breeding Program." *Rocky Mountain Outlook*, 1 December 2011. http://www.rmoutlook.com/apps/pbcs.dll/article?AID=/20111201/RMO0801/312019982/banff-to-see-caribou-return-through-captive-breeding-program.

Fox, Camilla, and AnnaMaria Valastro. "Coyote Bounties Are Futile." *Toronto Star*, 11 March 2012. https://www.thestar.com/opinion/editorialopinion/2012/03/11/coyote_bounties_are_futile.html.

Francione, Gary L. "Comparable Harm and Equal Inherent Value: The Problem of the Dog in the Lifeboat." *Between the Species* 11, no. 3 (1995): 81–9.

– *Rain without Thunder: The Ideology of the Animal Rights Movement*. Philadelphia: Temple University Press, 1996.

– "Taking Sentience Seriously." In *Animal Rights*, ed. Clare Palmer, 425–44. Aldershot, UK: Ashgate, 2008.

Francione, Gary L., and Robert Garner. *Animal Rights Debate: Abolition or Regulation?* New York: Columbia University Press, 2010.

Franklin, Adrian. *Animals and Modern Cultures: A Sociology of Human-Animal Relations in Modernity*. London: Sage, 1999.

Freedman, Bill, Paul M. Catling, and Zoe Lucas. "Effects of Feral Horses on Vegetation of Sable Island, Nova Scotia." *Canadian Field-Naturalist* 125, no. 3 (2011): 200–12.

Freedman, Paul H. "The Representation of Mediaeval Peasants as Bestial and as Human." In *The Animal/Human Boundary: Historical Perspectives*, ed. Andrea N.H. Creager and William Chester Jordon, 29–49. New York: University of Rochester Press, 2002.

Freeman, Aaron. "Ontario's New Species Law Puts Feds to Shame." *The Hill Times*, 28 May 2007. http://www.hilltimes.com/columns/2007/05/28/ontarios-new-species-law-puts-feds-to-shame/18432.

Freyfogle, Eric T. "Leopold's Last Talk." *Washington Journal of Environmental Law and Policy* 2, no. 2 (2012): 236–81. https://digital.law.washington.edu/dspace-law/bitstream/handle/1773.1/1191/2WJELP236.pdf?sequence=1&isAllowed=y.

Friends of the Earth Europe. *The Environmental Impacts of Glyphosate*. June 2013. http://www.foeeurope.org/sites/default/files/press_releases/foee_5_environmental_impacts_glyphosate.pdf.

Fundira, Melissa. "Ottawa Issues Emergency Protection Order for Rare Quebec Frog." *CBC News*, 22 June 2016. http://www.cbc.ca/news/canada/montreal/quebec-western-chorus-frog-emergency-protection-order-1.3647624.

Furlong, John. "Are the Animal Rights Groups on to Something?" *CBC News*, 19 January 2013. http://www.cbc.ca/news/canada/newfoundland-labrador/furlong-are-the-animal-rights-groups-on-to-something-1.1395864.

Gailus, Jeff. "All Sizzle, No Stake." *Alternatives Journal*, January 2012. http://www.alternativesjournal.ca/policy-and-politics/all-sizzle-no-stake.

Gailus, Jeff, Faisal Moola, and Michelle Connolly. *Ensuring a Future for Canada's Grizzly Bears: A Report on the Sustainability of the Trophy Hunt in B.C.* David Suzuki Foundation and Natural Resources Defense Council, April 2010. http://www.davidsuzuki.org/publications/downloads/2010/Ensuring-a-future-for-Canadas-grizzly-bears.pdf.

Galloway, Gloria. "Canada Lags in Protecting Oceans: Report." *Globe and Mail*, 2 June 2014. http://www.theglobeandmail.com/news/politics/canada-lags-in-protecting-oceans-report/article18942166.

– "Controversial Changes to Fisheries Act Guided by Industry Demands." *Globe and Mail*, 5 August 2013. http://www.theglobeandmail.com/news/politics/fisheries-act-change-guided-by-industry/article13606358.

– "Controversy Greets Mourning-Dove Hunt's Return to Ontario." *Globe and Mail*, 1 October 2013. https://beta.theglobeandmail.com/news/

national/controversy-greets-mourning-dove-hunts-return-to-ontario/
article14648781/?ref=http://www.theglobeandmail.com&.

– "National Parks under Threat, Report Says." *Globe and Mail*, 14 July 2014. http://
www.theglobeandmail.com/news/politics/national-parks-under-threat-report-says/
article19582932.

Garcia, Maria Alice, and Miguel A. Altieri. "Transgenic Crops: Implications for Biodiversity and Sustainable Agriculture." *Bulletin of Science, Technology and Society* 25,
no. 4 (2005): 335–53. https://www.biosafety-info.net/file_dir/10978488599ca487c1.pdf.

Garrett, Aaron. "Francis Hutcheson and the Origin of Animal Rights." *Journal of the
History of Philosophy* 45, no. 2 (2007): 251–61.

Garshelis, David L., and Hank Hristienk. "State and Provincial Estimates of American
Black Bear Numbers versus Assessments of Population Trend." *Ursus* 17, no. 1
(2006): 1–7.

Gartner, Ken. "The Comeback Coyote." *Fur Is Green*, 12 January 2012. http://www.
furisgreen.com/afficherevenement.aspx?id=628andlangue=enandunite=001.

Gauthier, David A., and E.B. Wiken. "Monitoring the Conservation of Grassland
Habitats, Prairie Ecozone, Canada." *Environmental Monitoring and Assessment* 88,
nos 1–3 (2003): 343–64.

Geist, Valerius. *Mule Deer Country*. Minocqua, WI: Northwood, 1990.

Genovali, Chris. "90% of B.C. Hates the Grizzly Hunt, So Why Are We Still Doing It?"
DeSmog Canada, 15 April 2014. https://www.desmog.ca/2014/04/15/90-b-c-hates-
grizzly-hunt-so-why-are-we-still-doing-it.

– "Opinion: BC Government Wants Grizzly Bears Dead." *Vancouver Sun*, 14 April
2014. http://www.vancouversun.com/opinion/op-ed/Opinion+government+wants
+grizzly+bears+dead/9737955/story.html.

George, Jane. "Polar Bear Management in Nunavut: A Conservation Tight-Rope."
Nunatsiaq News, 19 November 1999. http://www.nunatsiaqonline.ca/archives/
nunavut991130/nvt91119_07.html.

Gertsberg, Deniza. "Loss of Biodiversity and Genetically Modified Crops." GMO
Journal, 17 June 2011. http://gmo-journal.com/2011/06/17/loss-of-biodiversity-
and-genetically-modified-crops.

Gilbert, Barry, Lance Craighead, Brian L. Horejsi, Paul Paquet, and Wayne McCrory.
*Scientific Criteria for Evaluation and Establishment of Grizzly Bear Management
Areas in British Columbia*. Environmental Investigation Agency and Raincoast
Conservation Foundation, February 2004. http://www.raincoast.org/files/
publications/reports/GBMA.pdf.

Gilbert, Laura A., and John M. Halsted. "Economic Considerations in the Endangered
Species Debate: The Case of the Piping Plover." *Human Dimensions of Wildlife* 2, no.
3 (1997): 1–15.

Gilhus, Ingvild Saelid. *Animals, Gods and Humans: Changing Attitudes to Animals in
Greek, Roman and Early Christian Ideas*. London: Routledge, 2006.

Gill, Mike. "Foreword." In Dag Vongraven and Elizabeth Peacock, *Development of a Pan-Arctic Monitoring Plan for Polar Bears: Background Paper*. Akureyri, Iceland: Circumpolar Biodiversity Monitoring Program, CAFF International Secretariat, 2011. https://www.caff.is/monitoring-series/22-development-of-a-pan-arctic-monitoring-plan-for-polar-bears-background-paper.

Gillam, Carey. "U.S. GMO Crops Show Mix of Benefits, Concerns – USDA Report." *Reuters*, 24 February 2014. http://www.reuters.com/article/usda-gmo-report-idUSL1N0LT16M20140224.

Giraud, Kelly, and Branka Valcic. "Willingness-to-Pay and Geographic Embedded Samples: Case Study of the Alaska Stellar Sea Lion." *Journal of International Wildlife Law and Policy* 7, nos 1–2 (2004): 57–72.

glacierdiscoverywalkjasper. "Parks Canada 'Heard' but Did Not 'Heed.'" Blog, 16 February 2012. https://glacierdiscoverywalkjasper.wordpress.com/2012/03/07/parks-canada-reason-for-ignoring-public-input.

Glen, Barb. "Energy Industry Challenges Efforts to Protect Grouse." *Western Producer*, 17 January 2014. http://www.producer.com/2014/01/energy-industry-challenges-efforts-to-protect-grouse.

– "Fewer Birds Sing on Canadian Prairies." *Western Producer*, 16 July 2012. http://www.producer.com/2012/07/fewer-birds-sing-on-canadian-prairies%E2%80%A9.

Glendenning, Paul. "A Bridge Too Farr: Questioning the Campaign against Cormorants." *Raise the Hammer*, 22 September 2010. http://raisethehammer.org/article/1178/a_bridge_too_farr:_questioning_the_campaign_against_cormorants.

GM Watch. "Fish and Wildlife Will Phase-Out GM Crops and Ban Bee-Killing Pesticides on National Refuges." 1 August 2014. http://gmwatch.org/index.php/news/archive/2014/15561-fish-and-wildlife-will-phase-out-gm-crops-and-ban-bee-killing-pesticides-on-national-refuges.

Goulson, Dave. "Ecology: Pesticides Linked to Bird Declines." *Nature* 511 (2014): 295–6.

Government of Alberta, Alberta Agriculture and Forestry. *Coyote Predation Control Manual and Study Guide*. March 2016. http://www1.agric.gov.ab.ca/general/progserv.nsf/all/pgmsrv403/$FILE/coyote_manual.pdf.

Government of Alberta, Alberta Environment and Alberta Conservation Association. *Status of the Woodland Caribou (Rangifer tarandus caribou) in Alberta*. January 2001. http://aep.alberta.ca/fish-wildlife/species-at-risk/species-at-risk-publications-web-resources/mammals/documents/SAR-StatusWoodlandCaribouAlberta-Jan2001.pdf.

– *Status of the Woodland Caribou (Rangifer tarandus caribou) in Alberta: Update*. 2010. http://www.ab-conservation.com/downloads/AWSR/Mammal%20Reports/Status%20of%20Woodland%20Caribou%20in%20Alberta_update%202010.pdf.

Government of Alberta, Alberta Environment and Parks. "Alberta's Species at Risk Strategies." 2017. http://aep.alberta.ca/fish-wildlife/species-at-risk/

albertas-species-at-risk-strategy/default.aspx.

– *Castle Management Plan: Castle Provincial Park and Castle Wildland Provincial Park: Revised Draft.* March 2017. https://talkaep.alberta.ca/2864/documents/5326.

– "Feral Horses." 2 February 2016. http://aep.alberta.ca/land/land-management/feral-horses/default.aspx.

– "Managing Alberta's Feral Horse Population: The Rules and Regulations of a Capture Season." 22 January 2014. https://albertaep.wordpress.com/2014/01/22/managing-albertas-feral-horse-population-the-rules-and-regulations-of-a-capture-season.

Government of Alberta, Alberta Environment and Sustainable Resource Development. *Alberta Burrowing Owl Recovery Plan 2012–2017.* October 2012. http://aep.alberta.ca/fish-wildlife/species-at-risk/species-at-risk-publications-web-resources/birds/documents/SAR-BurrowingOwlAlberta-RecoveryPlan-Oct2012.pdf.

– *Alberta Caribou Action and Range Planning Project.* 30 July 2013. http://www.aenweb.ca/files/caribou_planning_charter_2013-07-30.pdf.

– *Alberta Greater Sage-Grouse Recovery Plan 2013–2018.* September 2013. http://aep.alberta.ca/fish-wildlife/species-at-risk/species-at-risk-publications-web-resources/birds/documents/SAR-AlbertaGreaterSageGrouseRecoveryPlan-2013-2018.pdf.

– *Annual Report, 2014–2015.* 2015. http://aep.alberta.ca/about-us/corporate-documents/documents/ESRD-AnnualReport-2014-2015.pdf.

– "Big Game Harvest Estimates 2013 – Mule Deer." https://mywildalberta.ca/hunting/documents/MuleDeerHunterHarvest-2013.pdf.

– "Big Game Harvest Estimates 2013 – White-Tailed Deer." https://mywildalberta.ca/hunting/documents/WhiteTailedDeerHunterHarvest-2013.pdf.

– *Management Plan for Cougars in Alberta.* November 2012. http://aep.alberta.ca/fish-wildlife/wildlife-management/documents/WildlifeMgmtPlan-Cougars-Nov2012B.pdf.

Government of Alberta, Alberta Forestry, Lands and Wildlife. *Management Plan for Mule Deer in Alberta.* November 1989. http://aep.alberta.ca/fish-wildlife/wildlife-management/documents/WildlifeMgmtPlan-MuleDeer-Nov1989.pdf.

Government of Alberta, Alberta Sustainable Resource Development. *Alberta Greater Sage-Grouse Recovery Plan 2005–2010.* December 2005. http://www.assembly.ab.ca/lao/library/egovdocs/2005/alsrd/153512.pdf.

– *Management Plan for Mountain Goats in Alberta.* July 2003. http://aep.alberta.ca/fish-wildlife/wildlife-management/documents/WildlifeMgmtPlan-MountainGoats-Jul2003.pdf.

Government of Alberta, Community Development – Parks and Protected Areas Division. *Program Policy for Managing Fur Trapping in Alberta's Parks and Protected Areas.* September 2003. https://open.alberta.ca/dataset/31f07e38-7020-41ed-8c78-3d864a7f02e5/resource/99e82642-90ae-47b5-8db2-3b50a34b2fe2/download/2003-approved-policy-trapping-in-parks.pdf.

Government of British Columbia. *Debates of the Legislative Assembly.* 6 March 2014. https://www.leg.bc.ca/content/Hansard/40th2nd/20140306pm-Hansard-v7n7.htm.

– "Southern Mountain Caribou." 2017. https://www2.gov.bc.ca/gov/content/
environment/plants-animals-ecosystems/wildlife/wildlife-conservation/caribou/
southern-mountain-caribou.

Government of British Columbia, Conservation Data Centre. *Conservation Status
Report: Rana pretiosa, Oregon Spotted Frog*. Ministry of Environment, 15 December
2010. http://a100.gov.bc.ca/pub/eswp/esr.do;jsessionid=5ab94849e6dfa3abae
85c34ffa9d25eaa79775c4b2c0f6b44c495e44ba8da3ab.e3uMah8KbhmLe3aOchq
KaNuOci1ynknvrkLOlQzNp65Ino?id=15352.

Government of British Columbia, Ministry of Environment. *Grizzly Bear Hunting:
Frequently Asked Questions*. 7 October 2010. http://www.env.gov.bc.ca/fw/wildlife/
management-issues/docs/grizzly_bear_faq.pdf.

– *Implementation Plan for the Ongoing Management of Boreal Caribou (Rangifer
tarandus caribou pop. 14) in British Columbia*. 2011. http://www2.gov.bc.ca/assets/
gov/environment/plants-animals-and-ecosystems/species-ecosystems-at-risk/
recovery-planning/boreal_caribou_implementation_plan_final_12aug2011.pdf.

– *Preliminary Wolf Management Plan for British Columbia*. October 1979. http://www.
naturalart.ca/voice/pdf/Prel_Wolf_ManagementPlan_1979_OCR.pdf.

Government of British Columbia, Ministry of Environment and Environmental
Assessment Office. *2015/16–2017/18 Service Plan*. February 2015. http://bcbudget.gov.
bc.ca/2015/sp/pdf/ministry/env.pdf.

Government of British Columbia, Ministry of Environment, Lands and Parks. *Caribou
in British Columbia: Ecology, Conservation and Management*. Brochure, 2000.
http://www.env.gov.bc.ca/wld/documents/caribou_fs.pdf.

– *A Future for the Grizzly: British Columbia Grizzly Bear Conservation Strategy*.
June 1995. https://www2.gov.bc.ca/assets/gov/environment/plants-animals-and-
ecosystems/wildlife-wildlife-habitat/grizzly-bears/futureforgrizzly1995.pdf.

– "Use and Enjoyment of Grizzly Bears." In *Conservation of Grizzly Bears in British
Columbia: Background Report*, 47–59. May 1995. http://www.env.gov.bc.ca/wld/
documents/techpub/grizzly/grizzly_3.pdf.

Government of British Columbia, Ministry of Forests, Lands and Natural Resource
Operations. "Cariboo-Chilcotin (Region 5) Mule Deer: Frequently Asked
Questions." http://www.env.gov.bc.ca/fw/wildlife/management-issues/docs/
WMIMuleDeer.pdf.

– *Draft Management Plan for the Grey Wolf (Canis lupus) in British Columbia*.
November 2012. http://www.env.gov.bc.ca/fw/public-consultation/grey-wolf/docs/
PublicConsultation-WolfManagementPlan.pdf.

– "Experts Find 'High Level of Rigour' in Grizzly Management." *BC Gov News*, 18
October 2016. https://news.gov.bc.ca/releases/2016FLNR0263-002022.

– *Grizzly Bear Population Estimate for 2012*. April 2012. http://www.env.gov.bc.ca/fw/
wildlife/docs/Grizzly_Bear_Pop_Est_Report_Final_2012.pdf.

– *Management Plan for the Grey Wolf (Canis lupus) in British Columbia.* April 2014. http://www.env.gov.bc.ca/fw/wildlife/management-issues/docs/grey_wolf_ management_plan.pdf.

– "Wildlife Health Fact Sheet: Translocation of Deer." n.d. https://www2.gov.bc.ca/ assets/gov/environment/plants-animals-and-ecosystems/wildlife-wildlife-habitat/ wildlife-health/wildlife-health-documents/translocation_fact_sheet.pdf.

Government of Canada. *Bill C-38: An Act to Implement Certain Provisions of the Budget Tabled in Parliament on March 29, 2012 and Other Measures, SC 2012, c. 19.* 29 June 2012. http://www.parl.ca/Content/Bills/411/Government/C-38/C-38_4/C-38_4.PDF.

– *Canada National Parks Act, SC 2000, c. 32.* http://laws-lois.justice.gc.ca/PDF/N-14.01.pdf.

– *Canada's 5th National Report to the Convention on Biological Diversity.* March 2014. https://www.cbd.int/doc/world/ca/ca-nr-05-en.pdf.

– *European Communities – Measures Prohibiting the Importation and Marketing of Seal Products: First Written Submission of Canada.* World Trade Organization, 9 November 2012. http://lawsociety.nu.ca/wp-content/uploads/2011/08/DS400-Canadas-FWS-9-Nov-2012-3.pdf.

– *Fisheries Act, RSC 1985, c. F-14.* http://laws-lois.justice.gc.ca/PDF/F-14.pdf.

– *National Parks Act, SC 1930, 20–21 George V, c. 33.* http://parkscanadahistory.com/ publications/national-parks-act-1930.htm.

– "Order Amending Schedule 1 to the Species at Risk Act." *Canada Gazette,* part 2, vol. 145, no. 23, 9 November 2011, 2282–311. http://publications.gc.ca/collections/ collection_2011/gazette/SP2-2-145-23.pdf.

– "Order Amending Schedule 1 to the Species at Risk Act." *Canada Gazette,* vol. 148, no. 16, 19 April 2014. http://www.gazette.gc.ca/rp-pr/p1/2014/2014-04-19/html/regi-eng.php.

– "Order Amending Schedule 1 to the Species at Risk Act." *Canada Gazette,* vol. 151, no. 9, 3 May 2017. http://www.gazette.gc.ca/rp-pr/p2/2017/2017-05-03/html/sor-dors59-eng.php.

– "Section 24: Hunting, Fishing and Trapping." In *James Bay and Northern Quebec Agreement.* 11 November 1975. http://www.gcc.ca/pdf/LEG000000006.pdf.

– *Species at Risk Act, SC 2002, c. 29.* http://laws-lois.justice.gc.ca/eng/acts/S-15.3/ page-1.html.

– *Wildlife Area Regulations, CRC, c. 1609.* 2010. http://laws.justice.gc.ca/PDF/ C.R.C.,_c._1609.pdf.

Government of Canada, Aboriginal Affairs and Northern Development Canada. *Canadian Arctic Contaminants Assessment Report III, 2013: Persistent Organic Pollutants in Canada's North.* Ed. Derek Muir, Perihan Kurt-Karakus, and Jason Stow. 2013. http://publications.gc.ca/collections/collection_2014/aadnc-aandc/R74-2-2-2013-eng.pdf.

Government of Canada, Canada Revenue Agency. "Promotion of Animal Welfare and
    Charitable Registration." 19 August 2011. http://www.cra-arc.gc.ca/chrts-gvng/chrts/
    plcy/cgd/nmlwlfr-eng.html.
Government of Canada, Canadian Environmental Assessment Agency.
    "Implementation of Hyperabundant Moose Management Plan for Gros Morne
    National Park." March–April 2011. http://www.ceaa.gc.ca/052/details-eng.
    cfm?pid=61090.
Government of Canada, Canadian Tourism Commission. *Sport Fishing and Game
    Hunting in Canada: An Assessment on the Potential International Tourism
    Opportunity.* October 2012. http://publications.gc.ca/collections/collection_2013/ic/
    Iu86-49-2012-eng.pdf.
Government of Canada, Canadian Wildlife Service. *Canadian Shorebird Conservation
    Plan.* 2000. http://publications.gc.ca/collections/collection_2011/ec/CW69-15-5-
    2000-eng.pdf.
– *How Much Habitat Is Enough?* 3rd ed. 2013. http://www.ec.gc.ca/nature/E33B007C-
    5C69-4980-8F7B-3AD02B030D8C/894_How_much_habitat_is_enough_E_
    WEB_05.pdf.
– *Proposals to Amend the Canadian Migratory Birds Regulations (Including Regulation
    Proposals for Overabundant Species).* December 2011. http://publications.gc.ca/
    collections/collection_2012/ec/CW69-16-35-2011-eng.pdf.
Government of Canada, Canadian Wildlife Service – Ontario Region. "An Assessment
    on the Feasibility of Reinstatement of a Mourning Dove Hunting Season in
    Ontario." 17 September 2011. Accessed 4 December 2014. http://longpointwaterfowl.
    org/wp-content/uploads/2013/09/CWS-ON-MODO-Popn-Assessment-Sept-2011.
    pdf (site discontinued).
Government of Canada, Commission of Conservation, Committee on Fisheries,
    Game and Fur-Bearing Animals. *Conservation of Fish, Game and Birds.* Ottawa:
    Government of Canada, 1915.
Government of Canada, Environment and Climate Change Canada. "The Agreement
    on the Conservation of Polar Bears." In *National Polar Bear Conservation Strategy
    for Canada,* appendix 1, 24–6. August 2011. http://www.cec.org/sites/default/files/
    submissions/2011_2015/16904_11-3-annex_13-national_polar_bear_conservation_
    strategy.pdf.
– "Boreal Chickadee (*Poecile hudsonicus*)." 2014. https://wildlife-species.canada.ca/
    bird-status/oiseau-bird-eng.aspx?sY=2014&sL=e&sM=a&sB=BOCH.
– "Canada's Letter of Interpretation" (1974). In *National Polar Bear Conservation
    Strategy for Canada,* appendix 2, 27–8. August 2011. http://www.cec.org/sites/
    default/files/submissions/2011_2015/16904_11-3-annex_13-national_polar_bear_
    conservation_strategy.pdf.
– "Ecological Gifts Program." 2 August 2017. http://www.ec.gc.ca/pde-egp.
– "The Great Lakes Sustainability Fund." 2013. http://www.ec.gc.ca/default.
    asp?lang=En&n=E586C83E-1&news=04D0493F-0289-4E22-9407-986AD4A84820.

– "Habitat Stewardship for Species at Risk." 2017. https://www.canada.ca/en/
environment-climate-change/services/environmental-funding/programs/habitat-
stewardship-species-at-risk.html.

– "Management Plans and Activities for National Wildlife Areas." 2017. https://www.
canada.ca/en/environment-climate-change/services/national-wildlife-areas/site-
selection/management-plans-activities.html.

– *National Polar Bear Conservation Strategy for Canada*. August 2011. http://www.cec.
org/sites/default/files/submissions/2011_2015/16904_11-3-annex_13-national_polar_
bear_conservation_strategy.pdf.

– "National Wildlife Areas across Canada." 2017. https://www.ec.gc.ca/ap-pa/default.
asp?lang=En&n=2BD71B33-1.

– "Northern Contaminants Program." 2016. http://www.science.gc.ca/eic/site/063.nsf/
eng/h_7A463DBA.html.

– *Polar Bear SARA Management Plan Progress Report*. 15 September 2016. https://
www.registrelep-sararegistry.gc.ca/virtual_sara/files/plans/MpPr-PolarBear-v00-
2016Sep21-Eng.pdf.

– *Recovery Strategy for the Blue Racer (Coluber constrictor foxii) in Canada [Proposed]*.
2017. http://www.registrelep-sararegistry.gc.ca/virtual_sara/files/plans/rs_blue_
racer_e_proposed.pdf.

– "Status of Wild Species." 2010. https://www.canada.ca/en/environment-climate-
change/services/environmental-indicators/status-species.html.

– *2020 Biodiversity Goals and Targets for Canada*. 2016. http://publications.gc.ca/
collections/collection_2016/eccc/CW66-524-2016-eng.pdf.

Government of Canada, Environment Canada. *Action Plan for the Kirtland's
Warbler (Setophaga kirtlandii) in Canada [Proposed]*. 2014. http://www.
registrelep-sararegistry.gc.ca/virtual_sara/files/plans/ap_kirtlands_warbler_
e_proposed.pdf.

– *Amended Recovery Strategy for the Greater Sage-Grouse (Centrocercus
urophasianus urophasianus) in Canada [Proposed]*. 2013. https://www.registrelep-
sararegistry.gc.ca/virtual_sara/files/plans/amended_rs_sage_grouse_e_
proposed.pdf.

– "Appendix 7.2: Anthropogenic Disturbance Mapping across Boreal Caribou (*Rangifer
tarandus caribou*) in Canada – Mapping Process Documentation." In *Scientific
Assessment to Inform the Identification of Critical Habitat for Woodland Caribou
(Rangifer tarandus caribou), Boreal Population, in Canada: Update*, 124–77. 2011.
http://ec.gc.ca/data_donnees/STB-DGST/001/Anthropogeneic_Disturbance_
Mapping_Methods_Appendix_-_ENGLISH.pdf.

– *Bird Conservation Strategy for Bird Conservation Region 6: Boreal Taiga Plains*.
October 2013. http://publications.gc.ca/collections/collection_2014/ec/CW66-317-
2-2014-eng.pdf.

– "Canada's Protected Areas." 2017. https://www.ec.gc.ca/indicateurs-indicators/default.
asp?lang=en&n=478A1D3D-1.

– *Canadian Biodiversity Strategy: Canada's Response to the Convention on Biological Diversity*. 1995. http://www.biodivcanada.ca/560ED58E-0A7A-43D8-8754-C7DD12761EFA/CBS_e.pdf.

– *Environment Canada Protected Areas Strategy*. 2011. http://publications.gc.ca/collections/collection_2012/ec/En14-44-2011-eng.pdf.

– *Evaluation of Programs and Activities in Support of the Species at Risk Act*. 24 September 2012. https://www.ec.gc.ca/ae-ve/6AE7146E-0991-4C2F-BE2F-E89DF4F8ED1E/13-018_EC_ID_1568_PDF_accessible_ANG.pdf.

– "Harper Government Supports Fur Industry with New Investment for Humane Trapping." News release, 31 July 2015. http://www.newswire.ca/fr/news-releases/harper-government-supports-fur-industry-with-new-investment-for-humane-trapping-520286221.html.

– *Management Plan for the McCown's Longspur (Rhynchophanes mccownii) in Canada*. 2014. http://www.sararegistry.gc.ca/virtual_sara/files/plans/mp_mccown's%20longspur_e_final.pdf.

– *Management Plan for the Rusty Blackbird (Euphagus carolinus) in Canada*. 2015. http://www.sararegistry.gc.ca/virtual_sara/files/plans/mp_rusty_blackbird_e_final.pdf.

– "Public Notice on the Minister of the Environment's Reconsideration of the Emergency Order for Boreal Caribou." 13 January 2012. https://www.registrelep-sararegistry.gc.ca/default.asp?lang=En&n=F9B73960-1.

– *Recovery Strategy for the Burrowing Owl (Athene cunicularia) in Canada*. 2012. http://www.registrelep-sararegistry.gc.ca/virtual_sara/files/plans/rs_cheveche_terriers_burrowing_owl_final_0512_e.pdf.

– *Recovery Strategy for the Oregon Spotted Frog (Rana pretiosa) in Canada*. 2015. http://www.registrelep-sararegistry.gc.ca/virtual_sara/files/plans/rs_oregon_spotted_frog_e_final.pdf.

– *Recovery Strategy for the Wolverine (Gulo gulo), Eastern Population, in Canada [Proposed]*. 2014. https://www.registrelep-sararegistry.gc.ca/virtual_sara/files/plans/rs_wolverine_eastern_population_e_proposed.pdf.

– *Recovery Strategy for the Wolverine (Gulo, gulo), Eastern Population, in Canada*. 2016. http://www.registrelep-sararegistry.gc.ca/virtual_sara/files/plans/rs_wolverine_eastern_population_e_final.pdf.

– *Recovery Strategy for the Woodland Caribou (Rangifer tarandus caribou), Boreal Population, in Canada*. 2012. https://ca.fsc.org/preview.canadian-federal-recovery-strategy.a-499.pdf.

– *Scientific Assessment to Inform the Identification of Critical Habitat for Woodland Caribou (Rangifer tarandus caribou), Boreal Population, in Canada: Update*. 2011. http://www.registrelep-sararegistry.gc.ca/virtual_sara/files/ri_boreal_caribou_science_0811_eng.pdf.

– *Scientific Review for the Identification of Critical Habitat for Woodland Caribou (Rangifer tarandus caribou), Boreal Population, in Canada*. 2008. http://www.

sararegistry.gc.ca/virtual_sara/files/Caribou_Full_0409_e.pdf.

– *The Species at Risk Act and You: A Guide to the Species at Risk Act (SARA):* *Information for Private Landowners.* 2007. https://www.registrelep-sararegistry. gc.ca/6AC53F6B-550E-473D-9BDB-1CCBF661F521/privland-eng.pdf.

– *Status and Trends in Fish and Wildlife Habitat on the Canadian Side of Lake Ontario.* 2001. http://publications.gc.ca/site/eng/98784/publication.html.

Government of Canada, Environment Canada, CITES Scientific Authority. *Ursus maritimus (Polar Bear) Non-Detriment Finding for Canada.* 11 December 2009. http://assembly.nu.ca/library/Edocs/2009/001150-e.pdf.

Government of Canada, Environment Canada, Fisheries and Oceans Canada, and Parks Canada. *Formative Evaluation of Federal Species at Risk Programs: Final Report.* July 2006. http://publications.gc.ca/collections/collection_2013/ec/En4-220-2006-eng.pdf.

Government of Canada, Fisheries and Oceans Canada. *Action Plan for the Nooksack Dace (Rhinichthys cataractae) and the Salish Sucker (Catostomus sp. cf. catostomus) in Canada [Proposed].* 2016. http://www.registrelep-sararegistry.gc.ca/virtual_sara/ files/plans/Ap-NooksackDace-v00a-2016Sept06-Eng.pdf.

– *Action Plan for the Northern and Southern Resident Killer Whales (Orcinus orca) in Canada [Draft].* March 2014. http://www.raincoast.org/wp-content/uploads/ 2009/07/DFO_Resident_Killer_Whale_Action_Plan_-.pdf.

– *Canada's Federal Marine Protected Areas Strategy.* 2005. http://www.dfo-mpo.gc.ca/ Library/315822e.pdf.

– "Grey Seals and Cod." 2016. http://www.dfo-mpo.gc.ca/fm-gp/seal-phoque/cod-morue-eng.htm.

– "Health of the Oceans." Table. In *Departmental Performance Report 2011–12.* http://www.dfo-mpo.gc.ca/dpr-rmr/2011-12/SupplementaryTables/hi-ih-eng.html.

– *Impacts of Grey Seals on Fish Populations in Eastern Canada.* March 2011. http://waves-vagues.dfo-mpo.gc.ca/Library/343116.pdf.

– "Mission, Vision and Values." 2017. http://www.dfo-mpo.gc.ca/about-notre-sujet/org/ vision-eng.htm.

– *National Framework for Canada's Network of Marine Protected Areas.* 2011. http://waves-vagues.dfo-mpo.gc.ca/Library/345207.pdf.

– *Partial Action Plan for the Blue, Fin, Sei and Pacific Right Whales (Balaenoptera musculus, B. physalus, B. borealis, and Eubalaena japonica) in Pacific Canadian Waters.* 2016. http://www.sararegistry.gc.ca/virtual_sara/files/plans/Ap-BlueFinSei Whales-v00-2016Jun13-Eng.pdf.

– "Recovery Strategies, Action Plans and Management Plans for Aquatic Species at Risk." 5 December 2015. http://www.qc.dfo-mpo.gc.ca/peril-risk/retablissement-restoration-eng.html.

– *Recovery Strategy for the Leatherback Turtle (Dermochelys coriacea) in Atlantic Canada.* 2006. http://www.sararegistry.gc.ca/virtual_sara/files/plans/rs_ Leatherback_turtle_Atlantic_population_0207_e.pdf.

– *Recovery Strategy for the Nooksack Dace (Rhinichthys cataractae) in Canada.*
   July 2007. http://www.registrelep-sararegistry.gc.ca/virtual_sara/files/plans/
   rs_nooksack_dace_0707_e.pdf.

– *Recovery Strategy for the Nooksack Dace (Rhinichthys cataractae) in Canada.*
   June 2008. http://www.registrelep-sararegistry.gc.ca/virtual_sara/files/plans/
   rs_nooksack_dace_0608_e.pdf.

– *Recovery Strategy for the Northern and Southern Resident Killer Whales (Orcinus
   orca) in Canada.* March 2008. http://www.cbc.ca/bc/news/bc-081009-killer-whale-
   recovery-strategy.pdf.

– *Recovery Strategy for the Northern and Southern Resident Killer Whales (Orcinus
   orca) in Canada.* August 2011. http://www.sararegistry.gc.ca/virtual_sara/files/plans/
   rs_epaulard_killer_whale_1011_eng.pdf.

– *Recovery Strategy for the North Pacific Humpback Whale (Megaptera novaeangliae)
   in Canada.* 2013. https://www.sararegistry.gc.ca/virtual_sara/files/plans/rs_rb_pac_
   nord_hbw_1013_e.pdf.

– *Spotlight on Marine Protected Areas in Canada.* 2010. http://waves-vagues.dfo-mpo.
   gc.ca/Library/341100e.pdf.

– *2011–2015 Integrated Fisheries Management Plan for Atlantic Seals.* 16 March 2011.
   http://www.dfo-mpo.gc.ca/fm-gp/seal-phoque/reports-rapports/mgtplan-planges
   20112015/mgtplan-planges20112015-eng.htm.

Government of Canada, Health Canada. *Re-evaluation of Imidacloprid – Preliminary
   Pollinator Assessment.* 18 January 2016. http://www.hc-sc.gc.ca/cps-spc/pest/part/
   consultations/_rev2016-05/rev2016-05-eng.php.

Government of Canada, Industry Canada. *Canada's Federal Tourism Strategy: Welcoming
   the World.* 2011. https://www.ic.gc.ca/eic/site/034.nsf/vwapj/Canadas_Federal_
   Tourism_Strategy-eng.pdf/$file/Canadas_Federal_Tourism_Strategy-eng.pdf.

Government of Canada, Minister of Finance. *Strong Leadership: A Balanced-Budget,
   Low-Tax Plan for Jobs, Growth and Security.* 21 April 2015. http://www.budget.
   gc.ca/2015/docs/plan/budget2015-eng.pdf.

Government of Canada, Minister of Fisheries and Oceans. "Regulations Amending
   the Marine Mammal Regulations." *Canada Gazette* 149, no. 15 (2015). http://www.
   gazette.gc.ca/rp-pr/p2/2015/2015-07-29/html/sor-dors188-eng.php.

Government of Canada, Minister of Justice. *Marine Mammal Regulations (SOR/93-56).*
   16 July 2015. http://laws-lois.justice.gc.ca/PDF/SOR-93-56.pdf.

Government of Canada, National Energy Board. *Report of the Joint Review Panel
   for the Enbridge Northern Gateway Project.* Vol. 2, *Considerations.* 2013. http://
   publications.gc.ca/collections/collection_2014/one-neb/NE23-176-2013-2-eng.pdf.

Government of Canada, Office of the Auditor General. *2005 September Report of the
   Commissioner of the Environment and Sustainable Development.* 2005. http://www.
   oag-bvg.gc.ca/internet/English/parl_cesd_200509_e_1122.html.

– *2013 Fall Report of the Commissioner of the Environment and Sustainable Development.*
   2013. http://www.oag-bvg.gc.ca/internet/English/parl_cesd_201311_e_38658.html.

Government of Canada, Parks Canada. "Guiding Principles and Operational Policies."
2017. http://www.pc.gc.ca/en/docs/pc/poli/princip.

– *Jasper National Park of Canada Management Plan.* June 2010. http://publications.
gc.ca/collections/collection_2010/pc/R61-36-2010-eng.pdf.

– *Management Plan for the Black-Tailed Prairie Dog (Cynomys ludovicianus) in Canada*
[Proposed]. March 2009. http://www.registrelep-sararegistry.gc.ca/virtual_sara/
files/plans/mp_blacktailed_prairie_dog_0309_e.pdf.

– "Middle Island Joins Point Pelee National Park of Canada." Press release, 19 July
2001. http://web.archive.org/web/20160111082410/http://www.pc.gc.ca/apps/cp-nr/
release_e.asp?id=525&andor1=nr.

– *Multi-Species Action Plan for Bruce Peninsula National Park and Fathom Five*
National Marine Park of Canada. 2016. http://www.registrelep-sararegistry.gc.ca/
virtual_sara/files/plans/Ap-BpnPark-v00-2016Nov21-Eng.pdf.

– *Multi-Species Action Plan for Point Pelee National Park of Canada and Niagara*
National Historic Sites of Canada. 2016. http://www.registrelep-sararegistry.gc.ca/
virtual_sara/files/plans/Ap-PpnpFinal-v00-2016Jul5-Eng.pdf.

– *Parks Canada Charter.* 2002. https://www.pc.gc.ca/en/agence-agency/mandat-mandate.

– *Project Description and Scope of Environmental Assessment for Implementation of the*
Proposed Middle Island Conservation Plan Point Pelee National Park. 7 March 2008.
http://www.torontobirding.ca/toc-docs/ProjectDescriptionDraft.pdf.

– "Questions and Answers – The Proposed Brewster Glacier Discovery Walk."
12 December 2011. http://cpaws-southernalberta.org/upload/Parks_Canada_
Questions__Answers_-_proposed_Brewter_Glacier_Discovery_Walk__12Dec2011.pdf.

– *Recovery Strategy for the Black-Footed Ferret (Mustela nigripes) in Canada.* March 2009.
https://www.registrelep-sararegistry.gc.ca/virtual_sara/files/plans/rs_blackfooted_
ferret_0309_e.pdf.

– *Recovery Strategy for the Greater Sage-Grouse (Centrocercus urophasianus urophasianus)*
in Canada. January 2008. http://www.sararegistry.gc.ca/virtual_sara/files/plans/
rs_sagegrouse_0108_e.pdf.

– *Reintroduction Plan: Plains Bison in Banff National Park.* March 2015. http://www.
bisonbelong.ca/docs/2015_Reintroduction-Plan-Plains-Bison_Banff-National-Park.pdf.

– *Situation Analysis for the Maligne Valley [Draft].* October 2013. http://www.
jasperenvironmental.org/wp-content/uploads/2013/10/Maligne-Valley-Situation-
Analysis-FINAL-October-29-2013-1.pdf.

– *State of Canada's Natural and Cultural Heritage Places 2016.* 2016. https://www.pc.gc.
ca/en/docs/pc/rpts/elnhc-scnhp/2016/index.

– *2010–2011 Parks Canada Agency Corporate Plan.* 2010. http://www.pc.gc.ca/eng/docs/
pc/plans/plan2010-2011/sec02/index.aspx.

– *"Unimpaired for Future Generations?" Conserving Ecological Integrity with Canada's*
National Parks. Vol. 1, *A Call to Action.* Report of the Panel on the Ecological
Integrity of Canada's National Parks, 2000. http://publications.gc.ca/collections/
Collection/R62-323-2000-1E.pdf.

Government of Canada, Species at Risk Public Registry. "Aboriginal Fund for Species at Risk." 2017. http://www.registrelep-sararegistry.gc.ca/default.asp?lang=En&n =100965FB-1.

– *Accord for the Protection of Species at Risk*. 1996. https://www.registrelep-sararegistry. gc.ca/default.asp?lang=En&n=92D90833-1.

– "Action Plans." 2017. http://www.registrelep-sararegistry.gc.ca/sar/recovery/action PlansTimelines_e.cfm.

– "Backgrounder: The Accord for the Protection of Species at Risk." 1996. https://www. registrelep-sararegistry.gc.ca/default.asp?lang=En&n=EDA4979C-1.

– "Burrowing Owl." 2017. http://www.registrelep-sararegistry.gc.ca/species/species Details_e.cfm?sid=20.

– "Critical Habitats of the Northeast Pacific Northern and Southern Resident Populations of the Killer Whale (*Orcinus orca*) Order." 23 February 2009. http://www.sararegistry.gc.ca/document/default_e.cfm?documentID=1756.

– "Emergency Order for the Protection of the Greater Sage-Grouse." 20 November 2013. http://www.registrelep-sararegistry.gc.ca/default.asp?lang=En&n=F25868B7-1.

– "Grizzly Bear Western Population." 2017. http://www.registrelep-sararegistry.gc.ca/ species/speciesDetails_e.cfm?sid=1195.

– "Humpback Whale North Pacific Population." 2017. http://www.sararegistry.gc.ca/ species/speciesDetails_e.cfm?sid=148.

– "List of Wildlife Species at Risk (Decisions Not to Add Certain Species) Order." 13 April 2017. https://www.registrelep-sararegistry.gc.ca/default.asp?lang=En&n =5E40E592-1.

– "Nooksack Dace in Canada: Critical Habitat Protection Statement." 29 July 2010. http:// www.registrelep-sararegistry.gc.ca/document/default_e.cfm?documentID=1958.

– "Northern and Southern Resident Killer Whales (*Orcinus orca*) in Canada: Critical Habitat Protection Statement." 10 September 2008. http://www.registrelep-sararegistry.gc.ca/document/default_e.cfm?documentID=1664.

– "Red-Headed Woodpecker." 2017. http://www.sararegistry.gc.ca/species/species Details_e.cfm?sid=57.

– "Response Statement – Humpback Whale, North Pacific Population." 8 December 2011. http://www.registrelep-sararegistry.gc.ca/document/dspHTML_e.cfm?ocid=8949.

– "Response Statement – Red-Headed Woodpecker." 4 December 2007. https://www. sararegistry.gc.ca/virtual_sara/files/statements/rs57_187_2007-8_e.pdf.

Government of Canada, Treasury Board of Canada. *2015–2016 Estimates*. Parts 1 and 2, *The Government Expenditure Plan and Main Estimates*. 2016. https://www.tbs-sct. gc.ca/ems-sgd/me-bpd/20152016/me-bpd-eng.pdf.

Government of Canada and Government of Alberta. *Report of the Joint Review Panel: EnCana Shallow Gas Infill Development Project*. 27 January 2009. https://www.aer. ca/documents/decisions/2009/2009-008.pdf.

Government of Canada and Government of British Columbia. *Canada–British Columbia Agreement on Species at Risk*. 2005. http://www.sararegistry.gc.ca/

virtual_sara/files/agreements/aa_Canada-British_Columbia_agreement_on_
species_at_risk_0805_e.pdf.

– *Canada–British Columbia Marine Protected Area Network Strategy.* 2014. https://
www.for.gov.bc.ca/tasb/slrp/pdf/ENG_BC_MPA_LOWRES.PDF.

Government of Manitoba, Manitoba Conservation and Water Stewardship. *Conserving
a Boreal Icon: Manitoba's Boreal Woodland Caribou Recovery Strategy.* 2015. http://
www.gov.mb.ca/conservation/wildlife/sar/pdf/cariboustrategy_octfall2015.pdf.

Government of Newfoundland and Labrador. "Statements by Ministers." *House of
Assembly Proceedings* 43, no. 18 (4 May 1998). http://www.assembly.nl.ca/business/
hansard/ga43session3/98-05-04.htm.

Government of Newfoundland and Labrador, Department of Environment and
Conservation. "Hunting and Trapping Guide and Big Game Licence Applications."
18 April 2012. http://www.releases.gov.nl.ca/releases/2012/env/0418n07.htm.

– "Protected Areas in Newfoundland and Labrador." 2017. http://www.env.gov.nl.ca/
env/parks/apa/panl/index.html.

– *2015–2020 Newfoundland and Labrador Moose Management Plan.* April 2015. http://
www.flr.gov.nl.ca/wildlife/wildlife/pdf/Moose_Plan_2015_2020.pdf.

Government of Newfoundland and Labrador, Department of Finance. *Estimates of the
Program Expenditure and Revenue of the Consolidated Revenue Fund, 2015–16.* 30
April 2015. http://www.budget.gov.nl.ca/budget2015/estimates/estimates_2015_16.pdf.

Government of the Northwest Territories, Species at Risk Committee. *Species Status
Report: Polar Bear in the Northwest Territories.* December 2012. http://www.
nwtspeciesatrisk.ca/sites/default/files/polar_bear_nwt_status_report_dec_2012_0.pdf.

Government of Nunavut. *Draft Nunavut Polar Bear Management Plan.* 16 January
2014. http://www.gov.nu.ca/sites/default/files/files/consultation_draft_polar_bear_
management_plan.pdf.

– *Nunavut Polar Bear Co-Management Plan.* July 2015. https://www.scribd.com/
document/303417856/Draft-Polar-Bear-Management-Plan-July-2015.

Government of Ontario. *Endangered Species Act, 2007, so 2007, c. 6.* https://www.canlii.
org/en/on/laws/stat/so-2007-c-6/latest/so-2007-c-6.html.

– *Heritage Hunting and Fishing Act, 2002.* http://www.ontla.on.ca/web/bills/bills_detail.
do?locale=en&BillID=904&isCurrent=false&detailPage=bills_detail_the_bill.

Government of Ontario, Environmental Registry. "Amendment to Two
Regulations under the Fish and Wildlife Conservation Act to Establish a
2 Year Black Bear Pilot Project in Parts of Northern Ontario." 5 February
2014. http://www.ebr.gov.on.ca/ERS-WEB-External/displaynoticecontent.
do?noticeId=MTIxNTE3&statusId=MTgxOTg4.

– "Amendment to Two Regulations under the Fish and Wildlife Conservation Act,
1997, to Extend and Expand the Black Bear Pilot Project in Parts of Northern
and Central Ontario for an Additional Five Years and to Regulate the Baiting of
Black Bears." 30 October 2015. http://www.ebr.gov.on.ca/ERS-WEB-External/
displaynoticecontent.do?noticeId=MTI2MzQ1&statusId=MTkwNjk4.

Government of Ontario, Ministry of the Environment and Climate Change. "Regulating Neonicotinoids." *Newsroom*, 9 June 2015. http://news.ontario.ca/ene/en/2015/06/regulating-neonicotinoids.html.

Government of Ontario, Ministry of Natural Resources. *Backgrounder on Black Bears in Ontario*. June 2009. https://dr6j45jk9xcmk.cloudfront.net/documents/3088/274503.pdf.

– *Framework for Enhanced Black Bear Management in Ontario*. June 2009. https://dr6j45jk9xcmk.cloudfront.net/documents/3087/274504.pdf.

– *State of Ontario's Protected Areas Report*. 2011. https://dr6j45jk9xcmk.cloudfront.net/documents/2713/stdprod-085564.pdf.

– *2014 Hunting Regulations Summary*. Fall 2014 to Spring 2015. https://snnf.ca/wp-content/uploads/2014-ontario-hunting-regulations.pdf.

Government of Ontario, Ministry of Natural Resources and Forestry. *The Estimates, 2015–16*. http://www.fin.gov.on.ca/en/budget/estimates/2015-16/volume1/MNRF.pdf.

– "Ontario Proposing a Black Bear Management Pilot in North." Press release, 14 November 2013. http://news.ontario.ca/mnr/en/2013/11/ontario-proposing-a-black-bear-management-pilot-in-north.html.

– "Wildlife Management: How Ontario Manages Wildlife to Support Healthy Ecosystems." 17 July 2014. https://www.ontario.ca/page/wildlife-management.

Government of Saskatchewan. *The Wildlife Act, 1998, W-13.12*. http://www.qp.gov.sk.ca/documents/English/Statutes/Statutes/W13-12.pdf.

– *The Wildlife Damage and Livestock Predation Regulations*. 2010. http://www.qp.gov.sk.ca/documents/english/Regulations/Regulations/F8-001r41.pdf.

Government of Saskatchewan, Ministry of Agriculture. "Crop Insurance's Wildlife Damage Compensation Program Further Enhanced." Press release, 11 March 2010. http://www.saskatchewan.ca/government/news-and-media/2010/march/11/producer-compensation-for-livestock-predation.

Government of Saskatchewan, Ministry of Environment. *A Conservation Plan for Greater Sage-Grouse in Saskatchewan*. June 2014. http://www.environment.gov.sk.ca/Default.aspx?DN=4744637b-4ae7-44df-b466-97d278de7b6a.

– *Misinipiy Integrated Land Use Plan*. February 2012. http://publications.gov.sk.ca/documents/66/86730-English.pdf.

– *Saskatchewan Fur Program: Summary of Regulations, Policy and Associated Programs*. 18 June 2012. http://publications.gov.sk.ca/documents/66/76577-Saskatchewan%20Fur%20Program.pdf.

Government of the Swiss Confederation. *Convention on International Trade in Endangered Species of Wild Fauna and Flora*. 1975. https://www.fws.gov/le/pdf/CITESTreaty.pdf.

Government of the United States, Department of the Interior, Fish and Wildlife Service. "Endangered and Threatened Wildlife and Plants: Determination of

Threatened Status for the Polar Bear (*Ursus maritimus*) throughout Its Range: Final Rule." *Federal Register* 73, no. 5 (2008): 28212–303. http://www.fws.gov/alaska/fisheries/mmm/polarbear/pdf/Polar_Bear_Final_Rule.pdf.

Government of the United States and Government of Great Britain. *Convention between the United States and Great Britain for the Protection of Migratory Birds*. 1916. https://www.fws.gov/migratorybirds/pdf/Treaties-Legislation/Treaty-Canada.pdf.

Government of the Yukon, Environment Yukon. *Horseshoe Slough Nuna Kʼóhonete Yédäk Tahʼé Habitat Protection Area Management Plan*. 2007. http://www.env.gov.yk.ca/animals-habitat/documents/HorseshoeSloughPlan2007.pdf.

– *Yukon Wolf Conservation and Management Plan*. 2012. http://www.env.gov.yk.ca/publications-maps/documents/yukon_wolf_conservation_and_management_plan.pdf.

Grainger, Peter. "B.C. First Nations Claim Right to Hunt Bald Eagles." CTV *News*, 24 June 2010. http://bc.ctvnews.ca/b-c-first-nations-claim-right-to-hunt-bald-eagles-1.526002.

Grandy, John. *Environmental Charities in Canada*. Charity Intelligence Canada, June 2013. https://www.charityintelligence.ca/images/environmental_charities_in_canada.pdf.

Grant, Laura Jean. "Moose Population Threatens Health of Cape Breton Highlands National Park Forest." *Cape Breton Post*, 4 November 2014. http://www.capebretonpost.com/News/Local/2014-11-04/article-3928731/Moose-population-threatens-health-of-Cape-Breton-Highlands-National-Park-forest/1.

Grant, Robert M. *Early Christians and Animals*. London: Routledge, 1999.

Grech, Ron. "Mills to Lose $100 Million over Caribou Plan." *Timmins Daily Express*, 7 February 2013. http://www.timminspress.com/2013/02/06/mills-to-lose-100-million-over-caribou-plan.

Greenberg, R., D.W. Demarest, S.M. Matsuoka, C. Mettke-Hofmann, D. Evers, P.B. Hamel, J. Luscier, L.L. Powell, D. Shaw, M.L. Avery, K.A. Hobson, P.J. Blancher, and D.K. Niven. "Understanding Declines in Rusty Blackbirds." In *Boreal Birds of North America: A Hemispheric View of Their Conservation Links and Significance*, ed. J.V. Wells, 107–26. Berkeley: University of California Press, 2011. https://www.aphis.usda.gov/wildlife_damage/nwrc/publications/11pubs/avery114.pdf.

Green Budget Coalition. *Protecting Canada's Species at Risk: Proper Species at Risk Act (SARA) Implementation Funding*. 2016. http://greenbudget.ca/wp-content/uploads/2016/01/GBC-SARA.pdf.

Green Party of Canada. "Species at Risk." n.d. http://www.greenparty.ca/en/policy/vision-green/environment/species-at-risk.

Griffin, Donald R. *Animal Minds: Beyond Cognition to Consciousness*. Chicago: University of Chicago Press, 2001.

– *The Question of Animal Awareness: Evolutionary Continuity of Mental Experience*. New York: Rockefeller University Press, 1976.

Griffiths, Mary, Sara Wilson, and Mark Anielski. *The Alberta GPI Accounts: Fish and Wildlife*. Pembina Institute, September 2001. https://www.pembina.org/reports/22_fish_and_wildlife.pdf.

Gurian-Sherman, Doug. "Genetically Engineered Crops in the Real World: Bt Corn, Insecticide Use, and Honey Bees." Union of Concerned Scientists, 10 January 2012. http://blog.ucsusa.org/doug-gurian-sherman/genetically-engineered-crops-in-the-real-world-bt-corn-insecticide-use-and-honeybee.

Hadley, Adam. "Winter Habitat Use by Boreal Chickadee Flocks within a Managed Forest Landscape." Master's thesis, Laval University, 2006. http://theses.ulaval.ca/archimede/fichiers/23847/23847.html.

Hadley, Adam, and André Desrochers. "Winter Habitat Use by Boreal Chickadee Flocks in a Managed Forest." *Wilson Journal of Ornithology* 120, no. 1 (2008): 139–45.

Hadley, John. "Nonhuman Animal Property: Reconciling Environmentalism and Animal Rights." In *Animal Rights*, ed. Clare Palmer, 465–75. Aldershot, UK: Ashgate, 2008.

Hallmann, Caspar A., Ruud P.B. Foppen, Chris A.M. van Turnhout, Hans de Kroon, and Eelke Jongejans. "Declines in Insectivorous Birds Are Associated with High Neonicotinoid Concentrations." *Nature* 521 (2014): 341–3.

Harries, Kate. "Re: Safety First on Bears, Editorial March 10." Letter to the editor, *Toronto Star*, 15 March 2014. http://www.thestar.com/opinion/letters_to_the_editors/2014/03/15/restoring_the_spring_bear_hunt.html.

Harris, Ken. "Achieving Sustainable Development: Organizing to Focus on Systems." In *Implementing Ecosystem-Based Management Approaches in Canada's Forests*, ed. Brenda McAfee and Christian Malouin, 13–16. Ottawa: Natural Resources Canada, 2008. http://www.cfs.nrcan.gc.ca/pubwarehouse/pdfs/28282.pdf.

Harris, Larry D. *The Fragmented Forest: Island Biogeography Theory and the Preservation of Biotic Diversity*. Chicago: University of Chicago Press, 1984.

Hart, E.J. (Ted). *J.B. Harkin: Founder of Canada's National Parks*. Edmonton: University of Alberta Press, 2010.

Harvey, Marissa. "Bear Hunting Ban Declared by 10 B.C. First Nations." *CBC News*, 13 September 2012. http://www.cbc.ca/news/canada/british-columbia/bear-hunting-ban-declared-by-10-b-c-first-nations-1.1180591.

– "Bear Watching More Profitable Than Bear Hunting, Says Study." *CBC News*, 8 January 2014. http://www.cbc.ca/news/canada/british-columbia/bear-watching-more-profitable-than-bear-hunting-says-study-1.2488311.

Hatfield, Gary. "René Descartes." *Stanford Encyclopedia of Philosophy*. 2014. http://plato.stanford.edu/entries/descartes.

Hatler, David F., Kim G. Poole, and Alison M.M. Beal. *Furbearer Management Guidelines: Coyote (Canis latrans)*. BC Ministry of Environment, May 2003. http://www.env.gov.bc.ca/fw/wildlife/trapping/docs/coyote.pdf.

Haydu, Carter. "Medicine Hat Suing Feds for $42 Million in Ongoing Manyberries Oilfield Sage-Grouse Saga." *Daily Oil Bulletin*, 16 October 2014. http://www.

dailyoilbulletin.com/article/2014/10/16/medicine-hat-suing-feds-42-million-ongoing-manyber.

Hayslette, Steven, James B. Armstrong, and Ralph E. Mirarchi. "Mourning Dove Hunting in Alabama: Motivations, Satisfactions, and Sociocultural Influences." *Human Dimensions of Wildlife* 6, no. 2 (2001): 81–95.

Heath, John. "Disentangling the Beast: Humans and Other Animals in Aeschylus' *Oresteia.*" *Journal of Hellenic Studies* 119 (1999): 17–47.

Heffelfinger, James R., Valerius Geist, and William Wishart. "The Role of Hunting in North American Wildlife Conservation." *International Journal of Environmental Studies* 70, no. 3 (2013): 399–413.

Henderson, Alice E., Maureen Reed, and Stephen K. Davis. "Voluntary Stewardship and the Canadian Species at Risk Act: Exploring Rancher Willingness to Support Species at Risk in the Canadian Prairies." *Human Dimensions of Wildlife* 19, no. 1 (2014): 17–32.

Henderson, Norman. "Wilderness and the Nature Conservation Ideal: Britain, Canada, and the United States Contrasted." *Ambio* 21, no. 6 (1992): 394–9.

Hendrickson, Ole. "How Neonicotinoid Pesticides Are Poisoning Canada's Agriculture." *Rabble.ca*, 18 August 2014. http://rabble.ca/columnists/2014/08/how-neonicotinoid-pesticides-are-poisoning-canadas-agriculture.

– "Toxic Plants, Poisoned Ecosystems: The Battle over Neonicotinoids in Canada." *Rabble.ca*, 4 December 2013. http://rabble.ca/columnists/2013/12/toxic-plants-poisoned-ecosystems-battle-over-neonicotinoids-canada.

Herrero, Stephen, Andrew Higgins, James E. Cardoza, Laura I. Hajduk, and Tom S. Smith. "Fatal Attacks by American Black Bears on People: 1900–2009." *Journal of Wildlife Management* 75, no. 3 (2011): 596–603.

Hervieux-Payette, Céline. "News Release." Senate of Canada, 1 December 2009. Accessed 16 January 2015. http://www.sealsonline.org/universal-declaration-newsroom.php (site discontinued).

Hewitt, C. Gordon. *The Conservation of the Wildlife of Canada.* New York: Charles Scribner's Sons, 1921.

Hill, Erica. "Animals as Agents: Hunting Ritual and Relational Ontologies in Prehistoric Alaska and Chukotka." *Cambridge Archaeological Journal* 21, no. 3 (2011): 407–26.

Hill, Rosalind. "Saints, Beasts, and Legal Order in the Middle Ages." *Anthrozoös: A Multidisciplinary Journal of the Interactions of People and Animals* 1, no. 2 (1987): 65–70.

Ho, Clara. "Update: Fish and Wildlife Defends Decision to Kill Cougar at South Health Campus." *Calgary Herald*, 18 September 2014. http://www.calgaryherald.com/update+fish+wildlife+defends+decision+kill+cougar+south+health+campus/10214393/story.html.

Hoberg, George. "What's behind the Woeful Implementation of Canada's Species at Risk Act?" *GreenPolicyProf*, 23 July 2010. http://greenpolicyprof.org/wordpress/?p=445.

Hobson, Keith, Erin M. Bayne, and Steve L. Van Wilgenburg. "Large-Scale Conversion of Forest to Agriculture in the Boreal Plains of Saskatchewan." *Conservation Biology* 16, no. 6 (2002): 1530–41.

Hodgins, Bill. "Spring Bear Hunt Back for 2015." *Ontario Out of Doors*, 30 April 2015. http://www.oodmag.com/hunting/big-game/spring-bear-hunt-back-for-2015.

Hof, Patrick R., and Estel Van der Gucht. "Structure of the Cerebral Cortex of the Humpback Whale, *Megaptera novaeangliae* (Cetacea, Mysticeti, Balaenopteridae)." *Anatomical Record* 290, no. 1 (2007): 1–31.

Horton, Travis W., Joel D. Blum, Zhouqing Xie, Michael Hren, and C. Page Chamberlain. "Stable Isotope Food-Web Analysis and Mercury Biomagnification in Polar Bears (*Ursus maritimus*)." *Polar Research* 28, no. 3 (2009): 443–54. http://www.tandfonline.com/doi/pdf/10.1111/j.1751-8369.2009.00114.x?needAccess=true.

Houston, Melanie J., Jeremy T. Bruskotter, and David Fan. "Attitudes toward Wolves in the United States and Canada: A Content Analysis of the Print News Media, 1999–2008." *Human Dimensions of Wildlife* 15, no. 5 (2010): 389–403.

Hubert, Mark. "The Canadian Boreal Forest Agreement: Protecting Caribou and Jobs." *Business.2020* 9, no. 1 (2014): 13–14. https://www.cbd.int/doc/newsletters/news-biz-2014-06-en.pdf.

Huestis, E.S. "Rabies Campaign Will Help to Kill off Predators." *Within Our Borders*, 15 March 1953, 4. https://archive.org/stream/withinourborders519albe#page/no/mode/2up.

Hughes, Donald. "The Environmental Ethics of the Pythagoreans." *Environmental Ethics* 3, no. 2 (1980): 195–213.

Hughes, Elaine L. "Scientific Experiments on Animals and Constitutional Principle." *Forum Constitutionel* 21, no. 3 (2003): 69–76. https://ejournals.library.ualberta.ca/index.php/constitutional_forum/article/viewFile/11075/8513.

Humane Society International/Canada. "Canadian Commercial Seal Slaughter." 15 December 2010. http://www.hsi.org/world/canada/work/protect_seals/facts/canada_seals.html.

– *Newfoundlanders' Views on the Canadian Seal Hunt: Research Report*. May 2010. http://www.hsi.org/assets/pdfs/hsi_newfoundland_report_052411.pdf.

– "Sealing Industry Tries to Conceal Seal Hunt Cruelty." 26 November 2014. http://www.hsi.org/world/canada/news/releases/2014/11/sealing-observation-bill-112614.html?referrer=https://www.google.ca.

Humane Society of the United States. "Dove Shooting." n.d. http://www.humanesociety.org/issues/dove_shoot.

Hume, Claire. "Grizzly Bear Population at Risk as B.C. Liberal Government Aligns with Trophy Hunters." *Vancouver Observer*, 27 January 2015. http://www.vancouverobserver.com/news/grizzly-bear-population-risk-bc-liberal-government-aligns-trophy-hunters.

Hume, David. *A Treatise of Human Nature* (1739). Ed. L.A. Selby-Bigge. Oxford: Clarendon, 1896. https://people.rit.edu/wlrgsh/HumeTreatise.pdf.

Hume, Mark. "Court Weighs Peter Kent's Right to Silence on Endangered Sage Grouse." *Globe and Mail*, 19 March 2013. http://www.theglobeandmail.com/news/british-columbia/court-weighs-peter-kents-right-to-silence-on-endangered-sage-grouse/article9980813.

– "Documents Indicate B.C. Wolf Cull Linked to Forest Industry Concerns." *Globe and Mail*, 25 October 2015. http://www.theglobeandmail.com/news/british-columbia/documents-indicate-bc-wolf-cull-linked-to-forest-industry-concerns/article26968437.

– "Future of Tiny Fish Caught in Web of Politics." *Globe and Mail*, 9 October 2011. http://www.theglobeandmail.com/news/british-columbia/future-of-tiny-fish-caught-in-web-of-politics/article4199413.

– "Hunting in B.C. Provincial Parks Puts Grizzlies at Risk, Study Finds." *Globe and Mail*, 26 February 2010. http://www.theglobeandmail.com/news/national/hunting-in-bc-provincial-parks-puts-grizzlies-at-risk-study-finds/article4311867.

– "Ottawa Asks Court to Ignore Experts' Affidavits." *Globe and Mail*, 9 January 2008. http://www.theglobeandmail.com/news/national/ottawa-asks-court-to-ignore-experts-affidavits/article666068.

Hume, Stephen. "Livestock Stats Don't Justify Wolf Cull." *Vancouver Sun*, 9 October 2012. http://www.timberwolfinformation.org/ca-bc-livestock-stats-dont-justify-wolf-cull.

Hunter, Christine M., Hal Caswell, Michael C. Runge, Eric V. Regehr, Steve C. Amstrup, and Ian Stirling. "Climate Change Threatens Polar Bear Populations: A Stochastic Demographic Analysis." *Ecology* 91, no. 10 (2010): 2883–97.

Hunter, Justine. "Final Agreement Reached to Protect B.C.'s Great Bear Rainforest." *Globe and Mail*, 1 February 2016. https://www.theglobeandmail.com/news/british-columbia/final-agreement-reached-to-protect-bcs-great-bear-rainforest/article28475362.

– "Trophy Hunting of Grizzly Bears to Continue in British Columbia." *Globe and Mail*, 13 June 2016. http://www.theglobeandmail.com/news/british-columbia/trophy-hunting-of-grizzly-bears-to-continue-in-british-columbia/article30440707.

Hutchings, Jeffrey A., Isabelle M. Côté, Julian J. Dodson, Ian A. Fleming, S. Jennings, Nathan J. Mantua, Randall M. Peterman, Brian E. Riddell, Andrew J. Weaver, and David L. VanderZwaag. "Is Canada Fulfilling Its Obligations to Sustain Marine Biodiversity? A Summary Review, Conclusions, and Recommendations." *Environmental Reviews* 20, no. 4 (2012): 353–61.

Hutchings, Jeffrey A., and John R. Post. "Gutting Canada's Fisheries Act: No Fishery, No Fish Habitat Protection." *Fisheries* 38, no. 11 (2013): 497–501.

Imbeau, Louis, Mikko Monkkonen, and Andre Desrochers. "Long-Term Effects of Forestry on Birds of the Eastern Canadian Boreal Forests: A Comparison with Fennoscandia." *Conservation Biology* 15, no. 4 (2001): 1151–62.

Ingold, Tim. *The Perception of the Environment: Essays on Livelihood, Dwelling and Skill*. London: Routledge, 2000.

Insights West. "Rural British Columbians Oppose Hunting of Grizzly Bears." 30 March 2017. http://www.insightswest.com/news/rural-british-columbians-oppose-trophy-hunting-of-grizzly-bears.

Institute of Science in Society. "Why Glyphosate Should Be Banned." 10 October 2012. http://www.i-sis.org.uk/Why_Glyphosate_Should_be_Banned.php.

International Boreal Conservation Science Panel. "Threats to the Boreal." 2010. http://www.borealscience.org/boreal/threats.

International Fund for Animal Welfare. *Falling Behind: An International Comparison of Canada's Animal Cruelty Legislation*. 2008. http://www.ifaw.org/sites/default/files/Falling%20behind%202008%20an%20international%20comparison%20of%20Canadas%20animal%20cruelty%20legislation.pdf.

– "Glossary and Statements of Principle." 4 April 2013. http://www.ifaw.org/canada/our-work/glossary-and-statements-principle.

– "Indigenous Seal Hunts." n.d. http://www.ifaw.org/united-states/our-work/seals/indigenous-seal-hunts.

– "Why Commercial Sealing Is Cruel." n.d. http://www.ifaw.org/united-states/our-work/seals/why-commercial-sealing-cruel.

Interprovincial Sport and Recreation Council and Canadian Parks and Recreation Association. *Pathways to Wellbeing: A National Framework for Recreation in Canada [Draft]*. April 2014. http://www.activecircle.ca/images/files/resources/recreation-framework-april2014.pdf.

Inwood, Brad, trans. *Seneca: Selected Philosophical Texts*. Ed. Jonathan Barnes and A.A. Long. Oxford: Oxford University Press, 2007. https://archive.org/stream/Seneca/Seneca_djvu.txt.

Irwin, Elise R., and Kathryn D. Mickett Kennedy. "Engaging Stakeholders for Adaptive Management Using Structured Decision Analysis." Paper presented at the Third Interagency Conference on Research in the Watersheds, Estes Park, Colorado, 8–11 September 2008. https://pubs.usgs.gov/sir/2009/5049/pdf/Irwin.pdf.

IUCN/SSC Polar Bear Specialist Group. "Summary of Polar Bear Population Status per 2017." 30 March 2017. http://pbsg.npolar.no/en/status/status-table.html.

Jachowski, David. *Wild Again: The Struggle to Save the Black-Footed Ferret*. Berkeley: University of California Press, 2014.

James, Meredith. "Feds Must Disclose: Will They Save the Endangered Sage Grouse?" Siskinds Environmental Group, 13 August 2013. https://www.siskinds.com/envirolaw/feds-disclose-save-endangered-sage-grouse.

– "Imminent Extinction of Sage-Grouse a Red Flag; Oil Wins in Canada, Not Environment." Siskinds Environmental Group, 10 April 2013. https://www.siskinds.com/envirolaw/imminent-extinction-sagegrouse-red-flag-oil-wins-environment.

Jasper Environmental Association. "Day of Protest in the Maligne Valley." 30 June 2014. http://www.jasperenvironmental.org/day-of-protest-in-the-maligne-valley.

Javorek, S.K., and M.C. Grant. *Trends in Wildlife Habitat Capacity on Agricultural Land in Canada, 1986–2006.* Canadian Councils of Resource Ministers, 2011. http://publications.gc.ca/collections/collection_2012/ec/En14-43-14-2011-eng.pdf.

Johnson, Brian. "Genetically Modified Crops and Other Organisms: Implications for Agricultural Sustainability and Biodiversity." In *Agricultural Biotechnology and the Poor: Proceedings of an International Conference, Washington, D.C., 21–22 October 1999,* ed. G.J. Persley and M.M. Lantin, 131–8. Washington, DC: Consultative Group on International Agricultural Research and US National Academy of Sciences, 2000. http://documents.worldbank.org/curated/en/978101468766220594/pdf/multiopage.pdf.

Jones, Allison. "Groups Challenge Ontario's Endangered Species Rule in Court." CTV *News,* 14 January 2015. http://www.ctvnews.ca/politics/groups-challenge-ontario-endangered-species-rules-in-court-1.2188578#ixzz3OuATQLWB.

Kellert, S.R., M. Black, C.R. Rush, and A.J. Bath. "Human Culture and Large Carnivore Conservation in North America." *Conservation Biology* 10, no. 4 (1996): 977–90.

Kennedy, Priscilla, and John Donihee. *Wildlife and the Canadian Constitution.* Canadian Institute of Resources Law, August 2006. https://dspace.ucalgary.ca/bitstream/1880/47560/1/CIRL-WL-KennedyDonihee-Report-4w.pdf.

Kerr, Jeremy T., and Josef Cihlar. "Patterns and Causes of Species Endangerment in Canada." *Ecological Applications* 14, no. 3 (2004): 743–53.

Kines, Lindsay. "Grizzly Bear Trophy Hunt to Be Banned in B.C." *Victoria Times Colonist,* 14 August 2017. http://www.timescolonist.com/news/local/grizzly-bear-trophy-hunt-to-be-banned-in-b-c-1.21876304.

Knopff, Kyle, Aliah Knopff, and Michelle Bacon. "North of 49: Ongoing Cougar Research in Alberta, Canada." *Wild Cat News* 5 (2009): 26–41. http://www.cougarnet.org/sites/original/Assets/S09north.pdf.

Korski, Tom. "Newfoundland Sealers Get Mostly Positive Media Coverage, Eh?" *The Hill Times,* 8 May 2006. https://www.hilltimes.com/2006/05/08/newfoundland-sealers-get-mostly-positive-media-coverage-eh/6750.

Kucklicka, John R., William D.J. Struntz, Paul R. Becker, Geoff W. York, Todd M. O'Hara, and Jessica E. Bohonowych. "Persistent Organochlorine Pollutants in Ringed Seals and Polar Bears Collected from Northern Alaska." *Science of the Total Environment* 287, nos 1–2 (2002): 45–59. http://www.nativescience.org/assets/Documents/PDF%20Documents/TSTE.pdf.

Kunkel, Kyran, Curt Mack, and Wayne Melquist. *An Assessment of Current Methods for Surveying and Monitoring Wolves.* Lapwai, ID: Nez Perce Tribe, 2005. http://www.nezperce.org/programs/wolf%20project.pdf.

Kuzyk, Gerry. *Challenges to Increasing Mule Deer Populations.* Victoria, BC: Wildlife Management Section, Government of British Columbia, 2012. http://peachlandsportsmens.ca/wp-content/uploads/2012/05/Kuzyk_Mule-Deer-BCWF-April-26-2012.pdf.

Lacy, Robert. "Culling Surplus Animals for Population Management." In *Ethics on the Ark: Conservation and Animal Welfare*, ed. B. Morton, T. Maple, and M. Hutchins, 187–94. Washington, DC: Smithsonian Institution Press, 1995.

Laidlaw, Rob. *Cormorant Monitoring, Presqu'ile Provincial Park, Brighton, Ontario, May 8–30, 2006*. Cormorant Defenders International and Zoocheck Canada, 2006. In possession of author.

Lait, Linda A., Randy F. Lauff, and Theresa M. Burg. "Genetic Evidence Supports Boreal Chickadee (*Poecile hudsonicus*) × Black-Capped Chickadee (*Poecile atricapillus*) Hybridization in Atlantic Canada." *Canadian Field-Naturalist* 126, no. 2 (2012): 143–7. http://journals.sfu.ca/cfn/index.php/cfn/article/view/1330/1323.

Lambeck, Robert J. "Focal Species: A Multi-Species Umbrella for Nature Conservation." *Conservation Biology* 11, no. 4 (1997): 849–56.

Lange, Karen E. "Out of Season." *All Animals Magazine*, May–June 2014. http://www.humanesociety.org/news/magazines/2014/05-06/out-of-season-alternatives-to-deer-culls.html.

Langor, David W., and John R. Spence. "Arthropods as Ecological Indicators of Sustainability in Canadian Forests." *Forestry Chronicle* 82, no. 3 (2006): 344–50. http://www.cfs.nrcan.gc.ca/bookstore_pdfs/26238.pdf.

Lavigne, David M. *Grey Seals, Cod and Culling: Notes for a Presentation to the Standing Senate Committee on Fisheries and Oceans, Ottawa*. 14 February 2012. http://www.chasseursdephoques.com/sites/default/files/PDF/lavigne.pdf.

Lavoie, Judith. "Fallow Deer Eating Their Way across Gulf Islands." *Victoria Times Colonist*, 18 January 2013. http://www.timescolonist.com/news/local/fallow-deer-eating-their-way-across-gulf-islands-1.51352.

Lawson, Helene M. "Wildlife Managers: Boundary Workers between the Human Community and the Wilderness." *International Review of Modern Sociology* 30, no. 1 (2002): 46–65.

Leduc, Timothy B. "The Fallacy of Environmental Studies? Critiques of Canadian Interdisciplinary Programs." *Environments* 37, no. 2 (2009): 1–28.

Lee, Peter, and Ryan Cheng. *Canada's Terrestrial Protected Areas Status Report 2010: Number, Area and Naturalness*. Global Forest Watch Canada, 2011. http://www.globalforestwatch.ca/files/publications/20110629A_Canada_Protected_Areas_2010.pdf.

Lefebvre, Julie. *Wildlife Management Responses within the City of Calgary*. Faculty of Environmental Design, University of Calgary, c. 2002. http://www.ucalgary.ca/ev/designresearch/projects/EVDS663/wildlifemanagement.pdf.

Lemelin, Raynald Harvey. "Impacts of the Cancellation of the Spring Bear Hunt in Ontario, Canada." *Human-Wildlife Interactions*, no. 52 (2008): 148–50. http://digitalcommons.unl.edu/cgi/viewcontent.cgi?article=1051&context=hwi.

Leopold, Aldo. *Game Management*. New York: Charles Scribner's Sons, 1933.

– "On a Monument to a Pigeon" (1947). In *Sand County Almanac*. Oxford: Oxford University Press, 1953. http://faculty.fortlewis.edu/dott_c/bio%20250-swecol/ Activities/On%20a%20Monument%20to%20the%20Pigeon.pdf.

– *A Sand County Almanac and Sketches Here and There*. London: Oxford University Press, 1949.

Letcher, Robert. *Temporal and Spatial Trends in Organic and Metal Contaminants in Canadian Polar Bears: 2006–2007 NCP Project Summary Report*. Nunavut Department of Environment, 2007. http://www.gov.nu.ca/sites/default/files/temporal_and_spatial_ trends_in_organic_and_metal_contaminants_in_canadian_polar_bears_-_2006- 2007_ncp_project_summary_report._interim_wildlife_report_no.14_2007.pdf.

Lilwall, Scott. "Jasper National Park Cabin Plan Goes to Federal Court." CBC *News*, 28 August 2014. http://www.cbc.ca/news/canada/edmonton/jasper-national- park-cabin-plan-goes-to-federal-court-1.2749816.

Lindsay, Bethany. "Rewilding a Salmon Stream." *Vancouver Sun*, 19 August 2015. http:// www.vancouversun.com/news/Rewilding+salmon+stream/11302506/story.html.

Linnitt, Carol. "Alberta to Sell More Oil and Gas Leases in Endangered Caribou Habitat." DeSmog Canada, 11 June 2014. http://www.desmog.ca/2014/06/09/ alberta-sell-more-oil-and-gas-leases-endangered-caribou-habitat.

Linzey, Andrew. *Why Animal Suffering Matters: Philosophy, Theology and Practical Ethics*. Oxford: Oxford University Press, 2008.

Liscovitch-Brauer, Noa, Shahar Alon, Hagit T. Porath, Boaz Elstein, Ron Unger, Tamar Ziv, Arie Admon, Erez Y. Levanon, Joshua J.C. Rosenthal, and Eli Eisenberg. "Trade-Off between Transcriptome Plasticity and Genome Evolution in Cephalopods." *Cell* 169, no. 2 (2017): 191–202.

List, Peter. "Aldo Leopold: His Career and His Land Ethic." Paper presented in the lecture series "The Ethical Legacy of Aldo Leopold," Oregon State University, 1998. http://liberalarts.oregonstate.edu/sites/liberalarts.oregonstate.edu/files/history/ ideas/list_aldoleopold.pdf.

Livernois, John. "The Economics of Ending Canada's Commercial Harp Seal Hunt." *Marine Policy* 34, no. 1 (2009): 41–53.

Livingston, John. *The Fallacy of Wildlife Conservation*. Toronto: McClelland and Stewart, 2007.

– "Prisoners of Prestige: Of Status Seekers, Aboriginals and Animals." In *Skinned: Activists Condemn the Horrors of the Fur Trade*, ed. Anne Doncaster, 1–11. North Falmouth, MA: International Wildlife Coalition, 1988.

– *Rogue Primate: An Exploration of Human Domestication*. Toronto: Key Porter Books, 1994.

Lloyd-Smith, James O., Paul C. Cross, Cheryl J. Briggs, Matt Daugherty, Wayne M. Getz, John Latto, Maria S. Sanchez, Adam B. Smith, and Andrea Swei. "Should We Expect Population Thresholds for Wildlife Disease?" *Trends in Ecology and Evolution* 20, no. 9 (2005): 511–19.

Lohr, Christine, Warren B. Ballard, and Alistair Bath. "Attitudes toward Gray Wolf Reintroduction to New Brunswick." *Wildlife Society Bulletin* 24, no. 2 (1996): 414–20.

Loo, Tina. "Making a Modern Wilderness: Conserving Wildlife in Twentieth-Century Canada." *Canadian Historical Review* 82, no. 1 (2001): 91–121.

– "Of Moose and Men: Hunting for Masculinities in British Columbia, 1880–1939." *Western Historical Quarterly* 32, no. 3 (2001): 296–319.

– *States of Nature: Conserving Canada's Wildlife in the Twentieth Century.* Vancouver: UBC Press, 2006.

Loomis, John, Arthur Edwards, and Leslie Richardson. "Total Economic Valuation of Threatened and Endangered Species." *The Encyclopedia of Earth*, 28 June 2014. http://editors.eol.org/eoearth/wiki/Total_economic_valuation_of_threatened _and_endangered_species.

Lopez, Barry Holstun. *Of Wolves and Men.* London: J.M. Dent and Sons, 1978.

Lopoukhine, Nikita, Stephen Woodley, and Kevin Van Tighem. "Re: Maligne Tours Proposal for Overnight Accommodation at Maligne Lake, Jasper National Park." Letter to Leona Aglukkaq, minister of the environment, 9 April 2014. http://cpaws.org/uploads/MaligneLetter_Apr2014.pdf.

Lorblanchet, Michel. "From Man to Animal and Sign in Palaeolithic Art." In *Animals into Art*, ed. Howard Morphy, 109–43. London: Unwin Hyman, 1989.

Los, Fraser. "Boreal Truce." *National Geographic*, 1 January 2014. https://www. canadiangeographic.ca/article/boreal-truce.

Lowey, Mark. "Study: Changes to Fisheries Legislation Have Removed Habitat Protection for Most Species in Canada." *UToday*, 7 November 2013. https://www. ucalgary.ca/utoday/issue/2013-11-07/study-changes-fisheries-legislation-have-removed-habitat-protection-most-species.

Lucas, Philip, and Anne Sheeran. "Asperger's Syndrome and the Eccentricity and Genius of Jeremy Bentham." *Journal of Bentham Studies* 8 (2006): 1–37.

Lucretius. *On the Nature of Things.* Bk 5. Trans. William Ellery Leonard. http://classics. mit.edu/Carus/nature_things.html.

Lunn, Susan. "Nearly Half of National Park Ecosystems Rate as 'Fair' or 'Poor' in Parks Canada Report." *CBC News*, 26 January 2017. http://www.cbc.ca/news/politics/ parks-canada-report-condition-1.3952144.

Lysikatos, Soterios. "The Saints and the Animals." n.d. http://www.impantokratoros.gr/ saints-animals.en.aspx.

MacDonald, Alex. "Why Is Downgraded Protection for BC's Humpback Whales an Extra Special Concern?" *Nature Canada*, 29 April 2014. http://naturecanada.ca/ news/new-status-of-north-pacific-humpback-whale-an-extra-special-concern.

MacDonald, Michael. "Commercial Seal Hunt off Canada's East Coast One of the Worst on Record." *Global News*, 14 June 2011. http://globalnews.ca/news/123359/ commercial-seal-hunt-off-canadas-east-coast-one-of-the-worst-on-record.

– "East Coast Seal Hunt Continues amid Legal Wrangling over European Ban." *Maclean's*, 24 April 2013. http://www.macleans.ca/news/east-coast-seal-hunt-continues-amid-legal-wrangling-over-european-ban.

– "Sale of Seal Meat to China Thwarted by Anti-Hunt Activists: Fisheries Minister." CTV *News*, 14 April 2014. http://www.ctvnews.ca/canada/sale-of-seal-meat-to-china-thwarted-by-anti-hunt-activists-fisheries-minister-1.1775111.

Macdonald, Nancy. "Grizzly Toll: B.C.'s Controversial Trophy Bear Hunt." *Maclean's*, 24 October 2014. http://www.macleans.ca/society/grizzly-toll-b-cs-controversial-trophy-bear-hunt.

MacEwan, Grant. *Entrusted to My Care*. Saskatoon: Modern Press, 1966.

MacKay, Barry Kent. "Should They Kill the Horses on Sable Island?" *Zoocheck Perspectives*, 25 September 2014. http://zoocheckperspectives.blogspot.mx/2014/09/should-they-kill-horses-of-sable-island.html.

– "Stop Dove Hunting in Ontario Canada." All-Creatures.org, September 2013. http://www.all-creatures.org/articles/ar-kill-a-dove.html.

MacKay, Barry Kent, and Liz White. *A Critical Analysis of Point Pelee National Park's Rationale for Killing the Middle Island Cormorants*. Cormorant Defenders International, February 2008. https://www.zoocheck.com/wp-content/uploads/2015/11/CDI-Middle-Island-Cormorant-Report-PDF.pdf.

MacKinnon, J.B. *The Once and Future World: Nature As It Was, As It Is, As It Could Be*. Toronto: Random House Canada, 2013.

MacLellan, Joel P. "What the Wild Things Are: A Critique on Clare Palmer's 'What (If Anything) Do We Owe Animals?'" *Between the Species* 16, no. 1 (2013): 53–67. http://digitalcommons.calpoly.edu/cgi/viewcontent.cgi?article=2013&context=bts.

MacLeod, Andrew. "BC Keeps Wolf Killing Plans Secret." *The Tyee*, 10 March 2014. https://thetyee.ca/News/2014/03/10/BC-Wolf-Killing-Plans.

– "BC Wolf Killing Plan Based on 'Unreliable Data': Advocate." *The Tyee*, 18 April 2014. https://thetyee.ca/News/2014/04/18/BC-Wolf-Killing-Plan.

– "Biologist Pokes Holes in BC's Wolf Killing Plan." *The Tyee*, 6 June 2014. https://thetyee.ca/News/2014/06/06/BC-Wolf-Killing-Plan.

Maclulich, T.D. "The Animal Story and the 'Nature Faker' Controversy." *Essays on Canadian Writing* 33 (1986): 112–26.

Madson, Chris. "Mule Deer Decline: A Treasured Icon of the West, the Mule Deer Nevertheless Is a Species in Crisis." *National Wildlife*, 24 November 2014. http://www.nwf.org/News-and-Magazines/National-Wildlife/Animals/Archives/2015/Mule-Deer.aspx.

Maguire, R.J. "Ecosystem Effects of Genetically Modified Organisms." In Environment Canada, National Water Research Institute, *Threats to Sources of Drinking Water and Aquatic Ecosystem Health in Canada*, 33–5. 2001. http://belsp.uqtr.ca/1229/1/National%20water%20reaserch%20institue_2001_Threats_drinking_water.pdf.

Main, Anson, and Christy Morrissey. "Distribution and Impact of Neonicotinoid
    Insecticides on Wetland Ecosystems in Prairie Canada." Paper presented at
    "Risk Assessment in Northern Ecosystems: Opportunities and Challenges," 3rd
    Annual Meeting of the Prairie Northern Chapter of the Society of Environmental
    Toxicology and Chemistry (SETAC), University of Saskatchewan, 15 June 2012.

Maki, Alan. "How the Effects of Climate Change in Arctic Canada Are Shrinking Polar
    Bears." *Globe and Mail*, 2 October 2014. https://beta.theglobeandmail.com/
    technology/science/shrinking-polar-bears-a-barometer-for-the-climate-
    sensitive-north/article20904215/

Maligne Tours Ltd. *Imagination, Innovation and Commitment: The Next Generation
    of Visitor Services and Operations at Maligne Lake: A Conceptual Proposal for
    Responsible Experiential Enhancement at Maligne Lake Submitted to Jasper National
    Park*. 14 November 2013. http://parkscanadahistory.com/publications/jasper/
    maligne-conceptual-proposal.pdf.

– "Maligne Tours in Jasper National Park Invests in Sustainable Tourism Strategy."
    Press release, 10 July 2013. http://amppe.org/2013/07/10/maligne-tours-invests-
    in-sustainable-tourism-strategy.

Manfredo, Michael J., Tara L. Teel, and Alan D. Bright. "Why Are Public Values toward
    Wildlife Changing? *Human Dimensions of Wildlife* 8, no. 4 (2003): 287–306.

Manfredo, Michael J., Tara L. Teel, and Harry C. Zinn. "Understanding Global Values
    towards Wildlife." In *Wildlife and Society: The Science of Human Dimensions*, ed.
    Michael J. Manfredo, Jerry J. Vaske, Perry J. Brown, Daniel J. Decker, and Esther A.
    Duke, 32–43. Washington, DC: Island, 2009.

Manore, Jean L., and Dale G. Miner, eds. *The Culture of Hunting in Canada*.
    Vancouver: UBC Press, 2007.

Manser, A.R. "The Concept of Evolution." *Philosophy* 40, no. 151 (1965): 18–34.

Manuel-Navarrete, David, James J. Kay, and Dan Dolderman. "Ecological Integrity
    Discourses: Linking Ecology with Cultural Transformation." *Human Ecology
    Review* 11, no. 3 (2004): 215–29.

Manuel-Navarrete, David, Dan Dolderman, and James J. Kay. "An Ecosystem Approach
    for Sustaining Ecological Integrity – But Which Ecological Integrity?" In *The
    Ecosystem Approach: Complexity, Uncertainty, and Managing for Sustainability*, ed.
    David Waltner-Toews, James J. Kay, and Nina-Marie E. Lister, 335–44. New York:
    Columbia University Press, 2008.

Markic, Olga. "Rationality and Emotions in Decision Making." *Interdisciplinary
    Descriptions of Complex Systems* 7, no. 2 (2009): 54–64.

Marowits, Ross. "Boreal Forest Agreement to Protect Caribou Fails after 3 Years
    of Negotiations." *Huffington Post*, 21 May 2013. http://www.huffingtonpost.
    ca/2013/05/21/boreal-forest-agreement-fails-caribou_n_3312738.html.

Marsden, William. "Report Says Canada Leads World in Forest Decline." *Regina
    Leader Post*, 5 September 2014. https://www.wildernesscommittee.org/ontario/

news/report_says_canada_leads_world_forest_decline.

Mates, Benson, trans. *Outlines of Pyrronism*, by Sextus Empiricus. Oxford: Oxford University Press, 1996. http://www.sciacchitano.it/pensatori%20epistemici/scettici/outlines%20of%20pyrronism.pdf.

Mathisen, K.M., F. Buhtz, K. Danell, R. Bergstrom, C. Skarpe, O. Suominen, and I.L. Persson. "Moose Density and Habitat Productivity Affects Reproduction, Growth and Species Composition in Field Layer Vegetation." *Journal of Vegetation Science* 21, no. 4 (2010): 705–16.

McAllister, Ian. "British Columbia's War on Wolves Continues with Newly Released Draft Management Plan." Pacific Wild, 15 November 2012. https://pacificwild.org/news-and-resources/great-bear-blog/british-columbia%E2%80%99s-war-on-wolves-continues-with-newly-released.

– *The Last Wild Wolves: Ghosts of the Great Bear Rainforest*. Vancouver: Greystone Books, 2007.

McClure, Matt. "Sage Grouse Protections Anger Ranchers." *Calgary Herald*, 24 March 2014. http://www.calgaryherald.com/news/alberta/Sage+grouse+protections+anger+ranchers/9652695/story.html.

McClure, Peter. "Maligne Valley Conceptual Proposal." Open letter, 27 November 2013. http://www.abhiking.ca/pdf/files/a6517336b78ac97ec1c22f5d2054f356.pdf.

McCrory, Wayne. *Preliminary Technical Review of Management of Free-Roaming ("Feral") Horses in Alberta's Six Foothills Equine Zones*. Zoocheck, 12 November 2015. https://www.zoocheck.com/wp-content/uploads/2016/01/McCrory-report-with-stamp-for-web-site.pdf.

McCullough, Dale R. "Of Paradigms and Philosophies: Aldo Leopold and the Search for a Sustainable Future." Paper presented in the lecture series "The Ethical Legacy of Aldo Leopold," Oregon State University, 1998. http://liberalarts.oregonstate.edu/sites/liberalarts.oregonstate.edu/files/history/ideas/mccullough.pdf.

McDevitt-Irwin, Jamie Marie, Susanna Drake Fuller, Catharine Grant, and Julia Kathleen Baum. "Missing the Safety Net: Evidence for Inconsistent and Insufficient Management of At-Risk Marine Fishes in Canada." *Canadian Journal of Fisheries and Aquatic Sciences* 72, no. 10 (2015): 1596–1608.

McGinn, Colin. "Animal Minds, Animal Morality." *Social Research* 62, no. 3 (1995): 731–47.

McGrath, Darby. "Testing the Existence and Extent of Impacts of Double-Crested Cormorant (*Phalacrocorax auritus*) Nesting on Three Islands in Lake Erie." Master's thesis, University of Waterloo, 2009. https://uwspace.uwaterloo.ca/handle/10012/4508.

McKenzie, Marika. "Greater Sage-Grouse Faces Grim Future, Say Scientists." *Canadian Geographic*, 1 December 2013. https://www.canadiangeographic.ca/article/greater-sage-grouse-faces-grim-future-say-scientists.

McLaren, Brian E., and W.E. Mercer. "How Management Unit Licence Quotas Relate to Population Size, Density, and Hunter Access in Newfoundland." *Alces* 41 (2005): 75–84.

McLaren, Brian E., Bruce A. Roberts, Nathalie Djan-Chékar, and Keith P. Lewis. "Effects of Overabundant Moose on the Newfoundland Landscape." *Alces* 40 (2004): 34–59.

McLaren, Ian, Solange Brault, John Harwood, and David Vardy. *Report of the Eminent Panel on Seal Management*. Fisheries and Oceans Canada, 2001. http://publications. gc.ca/collections/Collection/Fs23-405-2001E.pdf.

McLoughlin, Philip D. *Managing Risks of Decline for Hunted Populations of Grizzly Bears Given Uncertainty in Population Parameters*. British Columbia Independent Scientific Panel on Grizzly Bears, 5 March 2003. http://www.env.gov.bc.ca/wld/ documents/gbear_mcl.pdf.

McNeely, Joshua E., and Roger J. Hunka. *Policy Critique of the Draft Species at Risk Overarching Policy Framework: Perspectives for the Improvement of the Government of Canada's Implementation of the Species at Risk Act*. Maritime Aboriginal Peoples Council – IKANAWTIKET, January 2011. http://mapcorg.ca/home/wp-media/ SARAPolicy11.pdf.

McSheffrey, Elizabeth. "Conservationists Announce New Protected Areas for Great Bear Rainforest." *National Observer*, 15 September 2016. http://www. nationalobserver.com/2016/09/15/news/conservationists-announce-new-protected-areas-great-bear-rainforest.

– "Premier Clark Announces Landmark Great Bear Rainforest Agreement." *National Observer*, 1 February 2016. http://www.nationalobserver.com/2016/02/01/news/ premier-clark-announces-landmark-great-bear-rainforest-agreement.

Medema, Wietske, Brian S. McIntosh, and Paul J. Jeffrey. "From Premise to Practice: A Critical Assessment of Integrated Water Resources Management and Adaptive Management Approaches in the Water Sector." *Ecology and Society* 13, no. 2 (2008). https://www.ecologyandsociety.org/vol13/iss2/art29.

Meissner, Dirk. "B.C. to Increase Wolf Cull, Says It's the Best Plan to Save Endangered Caribou." *City News*, 20 September 2015. http://www.citynews.ca/2015/09/20/b-c-to-increase-wolf-cull-says-its-the-best-plan-to-save-endangered-caribou.

Mendelson, Michael. "Saint Augustine." *Stanford Encyclopedia of Philosophy*. 2010. http://plato.stanford.edu/entries/augustine.

Meredith, Don, and Duane Radford. *Conservation, Pride and Passion: The Alberta Fish and Game Association, 1908–2008*. Edmonton: Edmonton Journal, 2008.

Midgley, Mary. *Animals and Why They Matter*. Athens: University of Georgia Press, 1984.

Millar, Stuart. "Skinned Alive: Seal Cull Shocks Vets." *Guardian* (London), 7 April 2001. http://www.theguardian.com/world/2001/apr/07/stuartmillar.

Mining Watch Canada and Northwatch. *The Boreal Below: Mining Issues and Activities in Canada's Boreal Forest*. May 2008. https://miningwatch.ca/sites/default/files/ Boreal_Below_2008_ES_web.pdf.

Mithen, Steven. "The Hunter-Gatherer Prehistory of Human-Animal Interactions." *Anthrozoös: A Multidisciplinary Journal of the Interactions of People and Animals* 12, no. 4 (1999): 195–204.

Molyneaux, Brian. "Concepts of Humans and Animals in Post-Contact Micmac Rock Art." In *Animals into Art*, ed. Howard Morphy, 193–214. London: Unwin Hyman, 1989.

Montaigne, Michel de. "An Apologie of Raymond Sebond." In *Montaigne's Essays* (1603), trans. John Florio, bk 2, ch. 12, 449–596. Renascence Editions, University of Oregon, 1998. http://www.mises.ch/library/Montaigne_Essays_Florio_Translation.pdf.

Montgomery, Marc. "More Grizzlies and Wolves Moving North to High Arctic." *Radio Canada International*, 9 October 2013. http://www.rcinet.ca/en/2013/10/09/more-grizzlies-and-wolves-moving-north-to-high-arctic.

Mooers, A.O., L.R. Prugh, M. Festa-Bianchet, and J.A. Hutchings. "Biases in Legal Listing under Canadian Endangered Species Legislation." *Conservation Biology* 21, no. 3 (2007): 572–5.

Moola, Faisal, Devon Page, Michelle Connolly, and Lindsay Coulter. "Waiting for the Ark: The Biodiversity Crisis in British Columbia, Canada, and the Need for a Strong Endangered Species Law." *Biodiversity* 8, no. 1 (2007): 3–11.

Morandin, Lora A., and Mark L. Winston. "Wild Bee Abundance and Seed Production in Conventional, Organic and Genetically Modified Canola." *Ecological Applications* 15, no. 3 (2005): 871–81.

Morgan, Gwyn. "We Need to Cull the Urban Beasts among Us." *Globe and Mail*, 24 September 2012. https://www.theglobeandmail.com/opinion/we-need-to-cull-the-urban-beasts-among-us/article4560914/?arc404=true.

Mowat, Farley. *Rescue the Earth! Conversations with the Green Crusaders*. Toronto: McClelland and Stewart, 1990.

Mowat, G., D.C. Heard, and C.J. Schwartz. "Predicting Grizzly Bear Density in Western North America." *PLOS ONE* 8, no. 12 (2013). http://www.plosone.org/article/info:doi/10.1371/journal.pone.0082757.

Mule Deer Working Group, Western Association of Fish and Wildlife Agencies. *Mule Deer: Changing Landscapes, Changing Perspectives*. 2003. https://wildlife.utah.gov/pdf/mule_deer_wafwa.pdf.

– "Range-Wide Status of Mule Deer and Black-Tailed Deer in 2013." In *Proceedings of the Tenth Biennial Western States and Provinces Deer and Elk Workshop, 2013*, ed. Michael Mitchell, Jay Newell, Justin A. Gude, Kelly M. Proffitt, and Kristina Skogen, 102–21. Helena: Montana Fish, Wildlife and Parks, 2014. fwp.mt.gov/fwpDoc.html?id=65707.

Murgatroyd, Louise V. "Managing Tourism and Recreational Activities in Canada's Marine Protected Areas: The Pilot Project at Race Rocks, British Columbia." Master's thesis, Dalhousie University, 1999. http://www.racerocks.com/racerock/rreo/tourism/louise.htm.

Murnaghan, Ian. "Are GM Foods Destroying Biodiversity?" *Genetically Modified Foods*,
    31 May 2017. http://www.geneticallymodifiedfoods.co.uk/are-gm-foods-destroying-
    biodiversity.html.

Murphy Dennis D., and Barry D. Noon. "Coping with Uncertainty in Wildlife Biology."
    Journal of Wildlife Management 55, no. 4 (1991): 773–82.

My Wild Alberta. "Hunter Harvest: 2013." n.d. https://mywildalberta.ca/hunting/
    hunters-harvest.aspx.

Nadler, Steven. *The Cambridge Companion to Malebranche*. Cambridge, UK:
    Cambridge University Press, 2000.

Nagel, Thomas. "What Is It Like to Be a Bat?" *Philosophical Review* 83, no. 4 (1974):
    435–50.

Nance, Susan. "Animal History: The Final Frontier." *American Historian* 6 (2015): 28–32.

National Aboriginal Forestry Association and Wildlands League. *Honouring the
    Promise: Aboriginal Values in Protected Areas in Canada*. September 2003.
    https://www.ontarionature.org/discover/resources/PDFs/toolkits/PAToolkit/12_
    HonourPromise_2003.pdf.

National Post. "Cougar 'Enjoying the Morning Sun' Has Hospital in Southeast Calgary on
    Full Lockdown – Until It's Shot Dead." 18 September 2014. http://news.nationalpost.
    com/2014/09/18/calgary-hospital-under-lockdown-after-two-cougars-spotted-in-area.

Natural Resources Defense Council. *On the Precipice: Why International Commercial
    Trade in Polar Bears Should Be Eliminated*. 2012. http://www.nrdc.org/wildlife/cites/
    polar-bear/files/polar-bear-OV.pdf.

Nature Canada. *The Underlying Threat: Addressing Subsurface Threats to Environment
    Canada's Protected Areas*. December 2011. http://naturecanada.ca/wp-content/
    uploads/2016/02/PUBLIC-The-Underlying-Threat-Full-length-Report-February-
    2012.pdf.

– *Wildlife in Crisis*. 2004. Accessed 28 June 2013. http://naturecanada.ca/pdf/nwa_
    crisis.pdf (site discontinued).

Naujokaitis-Lewis, Ilona Rima. "Assessing Potential Resource Use Conflicts between
    Wildlife and Recreationists in Gwaii Haanas National Park Reserve, British
    Columbia." Master's thesis, Simon Fraser University, 2004. summit.sfu.ca/system/
    files/iritems1/6495/etd0416.pdf.

NBC News. "Fewer Polar Bear Cubs Surviving, Study Finds." 16 November 2006. http://
    www.nbcnews.com/id/15747502/ns/us_news-environment/t/fewer-polar-bear-cubs-
    surviving-study-finds/#.Vf27Xd9Viko.

Nelson, Michael P., John A. Vucetich, Paul C. Paquet, and Joseph K. Bump. "An
    Inadequate Construct? North American Model: What's Flawed, What's Missing,
    What's Needed." *Wildlife Professional*, Summer 2011, 58–60. http://www.
    isleroyalewolf.org/sites/default/files/Nelson%20et%20al%202011-An%20
    Inadequate%20Construct.pdf.

Newmyer, Stephen T. *Animals, Rights and Reason in Plutarch and Modern Ethics*. New York: Routledge, 2006.

– "Being the One and Becoming the Other: Animals in Ancient Philosophical Schools." In *The Oxford Handbook of Animals in Classical Thought and Life*, ed. G.L. Campbell, 505–35. Oxford: Oxford University Press, 2014.

Niemi, G., J. Hanowski, P. Helle, R. Howe, M. Mönkkönen, L. Venier, and D. Welsh. "Ecological Sustainability of Birds in Boreal Forests." *Conservation Ecology* 2, no. 2 (1998). http://www.consecol.org/vol2/iss2/art17.

Nikiforuk, Andrew. "Don't Gut Fisheries Act, Plead 625 Scientists." *The Tyee*, 24 March 2012. http://thetyee.ca/News/2012/03/24/Fisheries-Act-Gutting.

– "Facing Millions in Cuts, Environment Canada Prepares to Get Lean." *The Tyee*, 15 March 2014. http://thetyee.ca/News/2014/03/15/Environment-Canada-Cuts.

– "Schindle's Warning: Will It Be Heard?" *Globe and Mail*, 24 February 2000. https://beta.theglobeandmail.com/technology/science/schindlers-warning-will-it-be-heard/article4160594/

Nogués-Bravo, David, Daniel Simberloff, Carsten Rahbek, and Nathan James Sanders. "Rewilding Is the New Pandora's Box in Conservation." *Current Biology* 26, no. 3 (2016): R87–91.

Norstrom, R.J., M. Taylor, M. Ramsay, I. Stirling, S. Schliebe, O. Wiig, E. Born, S. Belikov, J.L. Murray, and R.G. Shearer. "Contaminant Trends in Polar Bears." In *Synopsis of Research Conducted under the 1991/92 Northern Contaminants Program*, ed. J.L. Murray and R.G. Shearer, 126–34. Ottawa: Department of Indian Affairs and Northern Development, 1992.

North America Bird Conservation Initiative. *The State of Canada's Birds*. Environment Canada, 2012. http://www.stateofcanadasbirds.org/State_of_Canada's_birds_2012.pdf.

North Coast Cetacean Society. *Occurrence of Humpback Whales (Megaptera novaeangliae) in the Confined Channel Assessment Area between Wright Sound and Caamano Sound from North Coast Cetacean Society Observations for the period 2004 to 2011*. Part 3. 9 January 2011. http://www.ceaa-acee.gc.ca/050/documents/54935/54935E.pdf.

Noske, Barbara. "Deconstructing the Animal Image: Toward an Anthropology of Animals." *Anthrozoös: A Multidisciplinary Journal of the Interactions of People and Animals* 5, no. 4 (1992): 226–30.

Nunatsiaq News. "Canada, EU Strike Deal on Indigenous-Hunted Seal Products." 10 October 2014. http://www.nunatsiaqonline.ca/stories/article/65674canada_eu_strike_deal_on_indigenous-hunted_seal_products.

Nuttall, Mark, Fikret Berkes, Bruce Forbes, Gary Kofinas, Tatiana Vlassova, and George Wenzel. "Hunting, Herding, Fishing and Gathering: Indigenous Peoples and Renewable Resource Use in the Arctic." In Arctic Climate Impact Assessment, *Scientific Report*, 649–90. Cambridge, UK: Cambridge University Press, 2005. http://www.acia.uaf.edu/PDFs/ACIA_Science_Chapters_Final/ACIA_Ch12_Final.pdf.

O'Connor, Joe. "Canada's Fur Trade Is Booming Again – Thanks to Demand from China's New Capitalists." *National Post*, 25 June 2013. http://news.nationalpost.com/news/canada/canadas-fur-trade-is-booming-again-thanks-to-demand-from-chinas-new-capitalists.

Olive, Andrea. "Can Stewardship Work for Species at Risk? A Pelee Island Case Study." *Journal of Environmental Law and Practice* 22, no. 3 (2011): 223–38.

Oliver, Cassidy. "Is B.C.'s Trophy Hunt for Grizzly Bears Bad Business?" *Vancouver Province*, 7 November 2015. http://www.theprovince.com/travel/bear+hunt+business/11501635/story.html.

Oma, Kristin Armstrong. "Between Trust and Domination: Social Contracts between Humans and Animals." *World Archaeology* 42, no. 2 (2010): 175–87.

Omernik, James M. "Perspectives on the Nature and Definition of Ecological Regions." *Environmental Management* 34, suppl. 1 (2004): S27–38. https://insideclimatenews.org/sites/default/files/assets/2012-03/Ecoregions_Omernik2004.pdf.

Ontario Federation of Anglers and Hunters. "Cormorant Control Needed Now." 9 April 2008. https://www.ofah.org/2008/04/cormorant-control-needed-now.

– "Simcoe Area Waterfowl Expert Wins Prestigious Conservation Leadership Award." 17 March 2014. https://www.ofah.org/2014/03/simcoe-area-waterfowl-expert-wins-prestigious-conservation-leadership-award.

Ontario Water Centre. "Communities and Shorelines." 2015. http://www.ontariowatercentre.ca/projects/rewilding-lake-simcoe.

Organ, J.F., V. Geist, S.P. Mahoney, S. Williams, P.R. Krausman, G.R. Batcheller, T.A. Decker, R. Carmichael, P. Nanjappa, R. Regan, R.A. Medellin, R. Cantu, R.E. McCabe, S. Craven, G.M. Vecellio, and D.J. Decker. *The North American Model of Wildlife Conservation: The Wildlife Society Technical Review 12-04*. Bethesda, MD: Wildlife Society, 2012. http://conservationvisions.com/sites/default/files/tws_north_american_model_of_wildlife_conservation.pdf.

Orton, David. "Both Subject and Object: Herding, Inalienability and Sentient Property in Prehistory." *World Archaeology* 42, no. 2 (2010): 188–200.

Orton, David, with Billy MacDonald and Ian Whyte. "John Livingston: An Appreciation." *Green Web Bulletin*, no. 79 (2010). http://home.ca.inter.net/~greenweb/GW79-John_Livingston.pdf.

Osborne, Catherine. "On Nature and Providence: Readings in Herodotus, Protagoras, and Democritus." In *Dumb Beasts and Dead Philosophers: Humanity and the Humane in Ancient Philosophy and Literature*, 25–42. New York: Oxford University Press, 2007.

– "On the Transmigration of Souls: Reincarnation into Animal Bodies in Pythagoras, Empedocles, and Plato." In *Dumb Beasts and Dead Philosophers: Humanity and the Humane in Ancient Philosophy and Literature*, 45–64. New York: Oxford University Press, 2007.

The Packet. "Terra Nova to Start Moose Reduction Program." 8 October 2014. http://www.thepacket.ca/news/local/2014/10/8/terra-nova-to-start-moose-reduction-prog-3896888.html.

Paehlke, Robert C. "Democracy and Environmentalism: Opening a Door to the Administrative State?" In *Managing Leviathan: Environmental Politics and the Administrative State*, ed. Robert Paehlke and Douglas Torgerson, 35–55. Peterborough, ON: Broadview, 1990.

– "Environmental Values and Public Policy." In *Environmental Policy: New Directions for the Twenty-First Century*, ed. Michael E. Kraft and Norman J. Vig, 77–97. Washington, DC: CQ Press, 2000.

Pal, R., K. Chakrabarti, A. Chakraborty, and A. Chowdhury. "Degradation and Effects of Pesticides on Soil Microbiological Parameters: A Review." *International Journal of Agricultural Research* 1, no. 3 (2006): 240–58. http://docsdrive.com/pdfs/academicjournals/ijar/2006/240-258.pdf.

Pall, Orval, Martin Jalkotzy, and Ian Ross. *The Cougar in Alberta*. Calgary: Arc Associated Resource Consultants Ltd, 1988.

Panksepp, Jaak. "Affective Consciousness in Animals: Perspectives on Dimensional and Primary Process Emotion Approaches." *Proceedings of the Royal Society B* 277, no. 1696 (2010): 2905–7. http://rspb.royalsocietypublishing.org/content/277/1696/2905.full.pdf+html.

Pannozzo, Linda. *The Devil and the Deep Blue Sea: An Investigation into the Scapegoating of Canada's Grey Seal*. Halifax: Fernwood Books, 2013.

– "Sealfall, Licence to Cull." *Halifax Coast*, 15 November 2012. http://www.thecoast.ca/halifax/sealfall-license-to-cull/Content?oid=3482101.

Paquet, Paul. "Introduction." In Ian McAllister, *The Last Wild Wolves: Ghosts of the Great Bear Rainforest*, 6–12. Vancouver: Greystone Books, 2007.

– "Wolf and Caribou Management Backgrounder." Raincoast Conservation Foundation, 7 February 2015. https://www.raincoast.org/2015/02/wolf-and-caribou-management-backgrounder.

Parliament of Canada, House of Commons. "Proposed Government Response to the First Report of the Standing Committee on Agriculture and Agri-Food on Bovine Tuberculosis in the Immediate Vicinity of Riding Mountain National Park in Manitoba." 2003. http://www.parl.gc.ca/HousePublications/Publication.aspx?DocId=1031105andMode=1andParl=37andSes=2andLanguage=E.

Parliament of Canada, House of Commons, Standing Committee on Environment and Sustainable Development. "Evidence – Dr. C. Scott Findlay." 4 May 2010. http://www.ourcommons.ca/DocumentViewer/en/40-3/ENVI/meeting-14/evidence.

– "Evidence – Dr. Michael Pearson." 4 May 2010. http://www.ourcommons.ca/DocumentViewer/en/40-3/ENVI/meeting-14/evidence.

Partners in Flight. *North American Landbird Conservation Plan*. Part 1, *The Continental Plan*. 2004. https://iwjv.org/sites/default/files/pif2_part1_0.pdf.

Patterson, Brent. "Health Canada Fails to Protect Bees from Deadly Insecticide." Council of Canadians, 20 May 2014. http://canadians.org/blog/health-canada-fails-protect-bees-deadly-insecticide.

Payton, Laura. "Parks Canada Hit by Latest Federal Job Cuts." CBC News, 30 April 2012.
    http://www.cbc.ca/news/politics/parks-canada-hit-by-latest-federal-job-cuts-1.1127446.
Peek, James, John Beecham, David Garshelis, François Messier, Sterling Miller, and
    Dale Strickland. Management of Grizzly Bears in British Columbia: A Review by
    an Independent Scientific Panel. BC Minister of Water, Land and Air Protection,
    6 March 2003. http://www.env.gov.bc.ca/wld/documents/gbear_finalspr.pdf.
Peter Yodzis Colloquium in Fundamental Ecology. "Sustainability, Socio-Ecological
    Complexity and Adaptive Management: Opportunities and Challenges."
    University of Guelph, 7–8 June 2012. https://peteryodziscolloquium.wordpress.
    com/2012-colloquium.
Petersen, David. Heartsblood: Hunting, Spirituality, and Wildness in America.
    Washington, DC: Island, 2000.
Phelps, Norm. The Longest Struggle: Animal Advocacy from Pythagoras to PETA.
    New York: Lantern Books, 2007.
Porphyry. On Abstinence from Animal Food. Bk 1. Trans. Thomas Taylor. 1823. http://
    www.ccel.org/ccel/pearse/morefathers/files/porphyry_abstinence_01_book1.htm.
– "The Rationality of Animals." In On Abstinence from Animal Food. Trans. Thomas
    Taylor. 1823. http://www.animal-rights-library.com/texts-c/porphyry01.pdf.
Preece, Rod. Animals and Nature: Cultural Myths, Cultural Realities. Vancouver:
    UBC Press, 1998.
– Brute Souls, Happy Beasts, and Evolution: Historical Status of Animals. Vancouver:
    UBC Press, 2005.
– "The Role of Evolutionary Thought in Animal Ethics." In Critical Animal Studies:
    Thinking the Unthinkable, ed. John Sorenson, 67–78. Toronto: Canadian Scholars'
    Press, 2014.
Project Coyote. "Nature Saskatchewan Passes Resolution Condemning Coyote
    Bounties." Press release, 14 October 2010. http://www.projectcoyote.org/
    newsreleases/saskatchewan.html.
Pursell, Allen, Troy Weldy, and Mark White. "Too Many Deer: A Bigger Threat to
    Eastern Forests Than Climate Change?" Cool Green Science, 22 August 2013. http://
    blog.nature.org/science/2013/08/22/too-many-deer/#sthash.uYS5iASx.dpuf.
Pynn, Larry. "B.C. Conservation Officers Criticized for 'Cavalier' Killing of Predators."
    Vancouver Sun, 13 July 2013. http://www.vancouversun.com/technology/conservation+
    officers+criticized+cavalier+killing+predators/11209072/story.html.
– "B.C. Wolf Management Plan Criticized as Veiled Attack on the Species."
    Vancouver Sun, 16 November 2012. http://www.vancouversun.com/technology/
    wolf+management+plan+criticized+veiled+attack+species/7562497/story.html.
– "Contest Offers Cash Prizes for Wolf Kills in Northeastern B.C." Vancouver
    Sun, 19 November 2012. http://www.vancouversun.com/technology/
    Contest+offers+cash+prizes+wolf+kills+northeastern/7572936/story.html.
– "Controversial 'Wolf Kill' Contest Has Not Resulted in Mass Slaughter, Sponsor Says."

Vancouver Sun, 20 March 2013. http://www.vancouversun.com/Controversial+
wolf+kill+contest+resulted+mass+slaughter+sponsor+says/8128659/story.html.

– "Permit Not Needed for Wolf-Kill Contest Because Event Is 'Skill-Based':
B.C. Gaming Branch." *Vancouver Sun*, 21 November 2012. http://www.
vancouversun.com/technology/Permit+needed+wolf+kill+contest+because+
event+skill+based+gaming+branch/7591981/story.html.

Raincoast Conservation Foundation. "Re: Comments on the Proposed Down-Listing
of the North Pacific Humpback Whale." Letter to SARA Directorate, 17 May 2014.
http://raincoast.org/wp-content/uploads/2014/06/humpback-de-listing-comments-
RCF-to-SARA.pdf.

Rainer, R., B. Bennett, S. Blaney, A. Enns, P. Henry, E. Lofroth, and J. Mackenzie. *On
Guard for Them: Species of Global Conservation Concern in Canada*. NatureServe
Canada, 2017. http://www.natureserve.org/sites/default/files/publications/files/
on_guard_for_them_natureserve_canada_2017_2.pdf.

Rambeau, Andrea Louise. "Determining Abundance and Stock Structure for a
Widespread Migratory Animal: The Case of Humpback Whales (*Megaptera
novaeangliae*) in British Columbia, Canada." Master's thesis, University of British
Columbia, 2008. https://open.library.ubc.ca/cIRcle/collections/ubctheses/24/
items/1.0066809.

RealAgriculture. "Standing on Principle, Neonic Court Battle Will Continue,
Says GFO Chair." 11 November 2015. https://www.realagriculture.com/2015/11/
standing-principle-neonic-court-battle-will-continue-says-gfo-chair.

Reeves, Andrew. "Controversial Spring Bear Hunt Returns to Ontario." *Alternatives
Journal*, 29 May 2014. http://www.alternativesjournal.ca/community/blogs/
current-events/controversial-spring-bear-hunt-returns-ontario.

Regan, Tom. *The Case for Animal Rights*. Berkeley: University of California Press, 1983.

Regehr, Eric V., Christine M. Hunter, Hal Caswell, Steven C. Amstrup, and Ian Stirling.
"Survival and Breeding of Polar Bears in the Southern Beaufort Sea in Relation to
Sea Ice." *Journal of Animal Ecology* 79, no. 1 (2010): 117–27.

Reichel, Justina. "Animal Rights Groups Slam Seal Hunt Bill." *Epoch Times*,
12 March 2014. http://www.theepochtimes.com/n3/558081-animal-rights-groups-
slam-seal-hunt-bill.

Reid, Edward. "Personal Expression as Exemplified by Hunting: One Man's View."
In *The Culture of Hunting in Canada*, ed. Jean L. Manore and Dale G. Miner,
205–10. Vancouver: UBC Press, 2007.

Reid, Roisin. "The Canadian Boreal Forest Agreement: Unlikely Allies Pursuing
Conservation and Sustainable Development in Canada's Boreal Regions."
Philanthropist 26, no. 1 (2014): 65–71.

Reidner, Heidi. "Bear Wise Program Cuts Worry Georgina." *Georgina Advocate*,
26 June 2012. http://www.yorkregion.com/news-story/1470417-bear-wise-
program-cuts-worry-georgina.

Reiss, Diana, and Lori Marino. "Mirror Self-Recognition in the Bottlenose Dolphin: A Case of Cognitive Convergence." *Proceedings of the National Academy of Sciences of the United States of America* 98, no. 10 (2001): 5937–42.

Richards, Arlene. "This Is How Polar Bears Deal with Climate Change." *Epoch Times*, 5 September 2015. http://www.theepochtimes.com/ n3/1745045-this-is-how-polar-bears-deal-with-climate-change.

Richardson, Lesley, and John Loomis. "The Total Economic Value of Threatened, Endangered and Rare Species: An Updated Meta-Analysis." *Ecological Economics* 68, no. 5 (2009): 1535–48.

Rickaby, Joseph, trans. *Of God and His Creatures: An Annotated Translation of the Summa Contra Gentiles of St Thomas Aquinas*. Catholic Primer, 2005. https://www. basilica.ca/documents/2016/10/St.%20Thomas%20Aquinas-The%20Summa%20 Contra%20Gentiles.pdf.

Riley, Shawn J., and Daniel J. Decker. "Risk Perception as a Factor in Wildlife Stakeholder Acceptance Capacity for Cougars in Montana." *Human Dimensions of Wildlife* 5, no. 3 (2000): 50–62.

Rist, Lucy A., L.A. Felton, L. Samuelsson, C. Sandström, and O. Rosvall. "A New Paradigm for Adaptive Management." *Ecology and Society* 18, no. 4 (2013). https://www.ecologyandsociety.org/vol18/iss4/art63.

Robb, Trevor. "Park Development Proposal Going Ahead without Hotel." *Edmonton Sun*, 25 July 2014. http://www.edmontonsun.com/2014/07/25/park-development- proposal-going-ahead-without-hotel.

Robinson, Barry. "Re: Maligne Tours Ltd. Conceptual Proposal." Letter from Ecojustice to Greg Fenton, superintendent, Jasper National Park, 9 December 2013. http://cpaws.org/uploads/JEA_and_CPAWS_submission_re_Maligne_Tours_ Conceptual_Proposal_9_Dec_2013.pdf.

– "Why We're Asking the Supreme Court to Weigh in on the Northern Gateway Decision." *Ecojustice Blog*, 28 September 2016. https://www.ecojustice.ca/faq- supreme-court-appeal.

Rollin, Bernard E. "Animal Mind: Science, Philosophy and Ethics." *Journal of Ethics* 11, no. 3 (2007): 253–74.

Romanes, George. *Mental Evolution in Animals*. New York: D. Appleton, 1884.

Roosevelt, Theodore. "Nature Fakers." In *Roosevelt's Writings: Selections from the Writings of Theodore Roosevelt*, ed. Maurice Garland Fulton, 258–67. New York: Macmillan, 1920. http://www.theodore roosevelt.com/images/research/speeches/ naturefakers.pdf.

– *Outdoor Pastimes of an American Hunter*. Mechanicsburg, PA: Stackpole Books, 1893.

Rosen, Ralph M. "Homer and Hesiod." In *A New Companion to Homer*, ed. Barry Powell and Ian Morris, 463–88. New York: Brill, 1997.

Ross, Monique M. *Legal and Institutional Responses to Conflicts Involving the Oil and Gas and Forestry Sectors*. Canadian Institute of Resources Law, January 2002.

https://dspace.ucalgary.ca/bitstream/1880/47199/1/OP10Conflicts.pdf.

Ross, P. Ian, and Martin G. Jalkotzy. "Characteristics of a Hunted Population of Cougars in Southwestern Alberta." *Journal of Wildlife Management* 56, no. 3 (1992): 417–26.

Ross, P. Ian, Martin G. Jalkotzy, and John R. Gunson. "The Quota System of Cougar Harvest Management in Alberta." *Wildlife Society Bulletin* 24, no. 3 (1996): 490–4.

Rousseau, Jean-Jacques. *What Is the Origin of Inequality among Men, and Is It Authorised by Natural Law?* Trans. G.D.H. Cole. Constitution Society, 1998. http://www.constitution.org/jjr/ineq.htm.

Rowlands, Mark. *The Philosopher and the Wolf: Lessons from the Wild in Love, Death and Happiness.* London: Granta, 2008.

Royal Commission on Seals and the Sealing Industry in Canada. *Seals and Sealing in Canada.* Vol. 1. Minister of Supply and Service Canada, 1986. http://www.thesealfishery.com/files/malouf_v1.pdf.

Royal Society of Canada Expert Panel. *Sustaining Canada's Marine Biodiversity: Responding to the Challenges Posed by Climate Change, Fisheries, and Aquaculture.* February 2012. https://rsc-src.ca/sites/default/files/pdf/RSCMarineBiodiversity2012_ENFINAL.pdf.

Rubec, Clayton, and Dale Stover. *A New Listing of Alberta Hunting, Resource Development and WISE Foundation Revenue Stamps, and Stampless Licence, Authorization and Special Quota Licence Stamps and Cards, 1964 to 1997.* January 2014. http://www.bnaps.org/ore/RubecStover-AlbertaHuntingStamps/RubecStover-NewCatNoListingAlbertaHuntingStamps-V2-Jan2014.pdf.

Rudd, Murray A. "National Values for Regional Aquatic Species at Risk in Canada." *Endangered Species Research* 6 (2009): 239–49.

Runge, Michael C. "An Introduction to Adaptive Management for Threatened and Endangered Species." *Journal of Fish and Wildlife Management* 2, no. 2 (2011): 220–33.

Russell, Charlie, and Maureen Enns. *Grizzly Seasons: Life with the Brown Bears of Kamchatka.* Toronto: Random House Canada, 2003.

Russell, Charlie, and Maureen Enns, with Fred Stenson. *Grizzly Heart: Living without Fear among the Brown Bears of Kamchatka.* Toronto: Random House Canada, 2002.

Russell, Don. *A Review of Wolf Management Programs in Alaska, Yukon, British Columbia, Alberta and Northwest Territories.* Yukon Wolf Conservation and Management Plan Review Committee, 6 November 2010. http://www.yfwcm.ca/YukonWolfPlanReview/going/documents/Wolfmgmtprogramreview Nov62010.pdf.

Ryder, Richard D. *Animal Revolution: Changing Attitudes towards Speciesism.* Cambridge, MA: Basil Blackwell, 1989.

– "Primatt, Humphry (bap. 1735, d. 1776/7)." *Oxford Dictionary of National Biography.* http://www.oxforddnb.com/index/47/101047020.

Salisbury, Joyce E. *The Beast Within: Animals in the Middle Ages.* New York: Routledge, 1994.

Salt, Henry S. *Animals' Rights: Considered in Relation to Social Progress*. New York: Macmillan, 1894. http://www.animal-rights-library.com/texts-c/salt01.htm.

Sandlos, John. *Hunters at the Margins: Native People and Wildlife Conservation in the Northwest Territories*. Vancouver: UBC Press, 2007.

– "Nature's Nations: The Shared Conservation History of Canada and the USA." *International Journal of Environmental Studies* 70, no. 3 (2013): 358–71.

Sanvido, Olivier, Andreas Bachmann, Jörg Romeis, Klaus Peter Rippe, and Franz Bigler. *Valuating Environmental Impacts of Genetically Modified Crops – Ecological and Ethical Criteria for Regulatory Decision-Making*. Zurich: vdf Hochschulverlag, 2012. https://vdf.ch/valuating-environmental-impacts-of-genetically-modified-crops-ecological-and-ethical-criteria-for-regulatory-decision-making-verdi-1617459707.html.

Sapontzis, Steve F. "The Evolution of Animals in Moral Philosophy." *Between the Species* 3, no. 2 (1987): 61–74.

Sax, Boria. "The Magic of Animals: English Witch Trials in the Perspective of Folklore." *Anthrozoös: A Multidisciplinary Journal of the Interactions of People and Animals* 22, no. 4 (2009): 317–32.

– *The Mythical Zoo: An Encyclopedia of Animals in World Myth, Legend, and Literature*. Santa Barbara, CA: ABC-CLIO, 2001.

Scarce, Rik. "What Do Wolves Mean? Conflicting Social Constructions of *Cams lupus* in 'Bordertown.'" *Human Dimensions of Wildlife* 3, no. 3 (1998): 26–45.

Schaefer, James A., and Paul Beier. "Going Public: Scientific Advocacy and North American Wildlife Conservation." *International Journal of Environmental Studies* 70, no. 3 (2013): 429–37.

Schaff, Philip, ed. "Of the Nature of the Human Soul Created in the Image of God." In *A Select Library of the Nicene and Post-Nicene Fathers of the Christian Church*, vol. 2, *St. Augustine's City of God and Christian Doctrine*, bk 12, ch. 23. Buffalo, NY: Christian Literature Co., 1887. http://oll.libertyfund.org/titles/schaff-a-select-library-of-the-nicene-and-post-nicene-fathers-of-the-christian-church-vol-2.

– ed. "That Christians Have No Authority for Committing Suicide in Any Circumstances Whatsoever." In *A Select Library of the Nicene and Post-Nicene Fathers of the Christian Church*, vol. 2, *St. Augustine's City of God and Christian Doctrine*, bk l, ch. 20, Buffalo, NY: Christian Literature Co., 1887. http://oll.libertyfund.org/titles/schaff-a-select-library-of-the-nicene-and-post-nicene-fathers-of-the-christian-church-vol-2.

Scheffer, Martin, Steve Carpenter, Jonathan A. Foley, Carl Folke, and Brian Walkerk. "Catastrophic Shifts in Ecosystems." *Nature* 413 (2001): 591–6.

Schmidt, Doug. "For Sale: One 'Almost Caribbean' Island." *National Post*, 6 August 2011. http://news.nationalpost.com/news/for-sale-one-almost-caribbean-island.

Schmiegelow, Fiona K.A., and Mikko Monkkonen. "Habitat Loss and Fragmentation in Dynamic Landscapes: Avian Perspectives from the Boreal Forest." *Ecological Applications* 12, no. 2 (2002): 375–89.

Schmunk, Rhianna. "Mother and Trio of Cougar Cubs Put Down in Penticton, B.C." *CBC News*, 17 January 2017. http://www.cbc.ca/news/canada/british-columbia/cougars-penticton-killed-1.3940195.

Schroeder, Susan A., David C. Fulton, Jeffrey S. Lawrence, and Steven D. Cordts. "Legitimization of Regulatory Norms: Waterfowl Hunter Acceptance of Changing Duck Bag Limits." *Human Dimensions of Wildlife* 19, no. 3 (2014): 234–52.

Scully, Matthew. *Dominion: The Power of Man, the Suffering of Animals, and the Call to Mercy*. New York: St Martin's Press, 2002.

Second Vatican Council. "The Human Community." In *Gaudium et Spes: Pastoral Constitution on the Church in the Modern World*, ch. 2. 1965. https://www.cctwincities.org/wp-content/uploads/2015/10/Gaudium-et-Spes-Pastoral-Constitution-on-the-Church-in-the-Modern-World.pdf.

Senate of Canada, Standing Senate Committee on Fisheries and Oceans. *The Sustainable Management of Grey Seal Populations: A Path Toward the Recovery of Cod and Other Groundfish Stocks*. October 2012. https://sencanada.ca/content/sen/Committee/411/pofo/rep/rep07oct12-e.pdf.

Serpell, James. *In the Company of Animals: A Study of Human-Animal Relationships*. Cambridge, UK: Cambridge University Press, 1996.

Shochat, Eyal, Susannah B. Lerman, John M. Anderies, Paige S. Warren, Stanley H. Faeth, and Charles H. Nilon. "Invasion, Competition, and Biodiversity Loss in Urban Ecosystems." *BioScience* 60, no. 3 (2010): 199–208.

Siemer, William F., P. Sol Hart, Daniel J. Decker, and James E. Shanahan. "Factors That Influence Concern about Human–Black Bear Interactions in Residential Settings." *Human Dimensions of Wildlife* 14, no. 3 (2009): 185–97.

Simard, M. Anouk, Christian Dussault, Jean Huot, and Steve D. Cote. "Is Hunting an Effective Tool to Control Overabundant Deer? A Test Using an Experimental Approach." *Journal of Wildlife Management* 77, no. 2 (2013): 254–9.

Singer, Peter. *Animal Liberation*. New York: Random House, 1975.

– *The Expanding Circle: Ethics, Evolution and Moral Progress*. Princeton, NJ: Princeton University Press, 1981.

Slagle, Kristina. "Building Tolerance for Bears: A Communications Experiment." *Journal of Wildlife Management* 77, no. 4 (2013): 863–9.

Slagle, Kristina, Jeremy T. Bruskotter, and Robyn S. Wilson. "The Role of Affect in Public Support and Opposition to Wolf Management." *Human Dimensions of Wildlife* 17, no. 1 (2012): 44–57.

Smallwood, Kate. *A Guide to Canada's Species at Risk Act*. Sierra Legal Defence Fund, May 2003. www.sfu.ca/~amooers/scientists4species/SARA_Guide_May2003.pdf.

Smith, Bruce. *Improving Humane Practice in the Canadian Harp Seal Hunt: A Report of the Independent Veterinarians' Working Group on the Canadian Harp Seal Hunt*. August 2005. http://www.cwhc-rcsf.ca/docs/technical_reports/IVWG_Report_EN.pdf.

Smith, C.U.M. "Homo Sapiens and Human Being." *Journal of Social and Evolutionary Systems* 17, no. 4 (1999): 413–34.

Smith, Rick. "Canada's Incredible, Invisible Endangered Species." *The Hill Times*, 5 July 2004. http://www.hilltimes.com/opinion-piece/opinion/2004/07/05/canadas-incredible-invisible-endangered-species/13810.

Sorabji, Richard. *Animal Minds and Animal Morals: The Origins of the Western Debate.* Ithaca, NY: Cornell University Press, 1993.

Sorenson, John, ed. *Critical Animal Studies: Thinking the Unthinkable.* Toronto: Canadian Scholars' Press, 2014.

Soulé, Michael. "What Is Conservation Biology?" *BioScience* 35, no. 11 (1985): 727–34. http://www.uvm.edu/rsenr/wfb224/whatisconservationbiology.pdf.

Soulé, Michael, and Reed Noss. "Rewilding and Biodiversity: Complementary Goals for Continental Conservation." *Wild Earth* 8, no. 3 (1998): 19–28. http://rewilding.org/rewildit/images/RewildingBiod.pdf.

St-Laurent, Martin-Hugues, Jean Ferron, Samuel Hache, and Rejean Gagnon. "Planning Timber Harvest of Residual Forest Stands without Compromising Bird and Small Mammal Communities in Boreal Landscapes." *Forest Ecology and Management* 254, no. 2 (2008): 261–75.

Stark, John D., and John E. Banks. "Population-Level Effects of Pesticides and Other Toxicants on Arthropods." *Annual Review of Entomology* 48, no. 1 (2003): 505–19.

Statistics Canada. *Human Activity and the Environment.* 2011. http://www.statcan.gc.ca/pub/16-201-x/16-201-x2011000-eng.pdf.

– "Table 6: Pesticide Use on Canadian Crop Farms – Provinces and Region." In *Farm Environmental Management Survey.* 2011. http://www.statcan.gc.ca/pub/21-023-x/2013001/t006-eng.htm.

Steel, Karl. *How to Make a Human: Animals and Violence in the Middle Ages.* Columbus: Ohio State University Press, 2011.

Steiner, Gary. *Anthropocentrism and Its Discontents: The Moral Status of Animals in the History of Western Philosophy.* Pittsburgh, PA: University of Pittsburgh Press, 2005.

Stewart, Frances E.C., Nicole A. Heim, Anthony P. Clevenger, John Paczkowski, John P. Volpe, and Jason T. Fisher. "Wolverine Behavior Varies Spatially with Anthropogenic Footprint: Implications for Conservation and Inferences about Declines." *Ecology and Evolution* 6, no. 5 (2016): 1493–1503. http://onlinelibrary.wiley.com/doi/10.1002/ece3.1921/full.

Stibbe, Arran. "Counter-Discourses and the Relationship between Humans and Other Animals." *Anthrozoös: A Multidisciplinary Journal of the Interactions of People and Animals* 18, no. 1 (2005): 3–17.

Stockwell, Craig A., Andrew P. Hendry, and Michael T. Kinnison. "Contemporary Evolution Meets Conservation Biology." *Trends in Ecology and Evolution* 18, no. 2 (2003): 94–101.

Stutchbury, Bridget. "Boreal Songbird Declines: Breeding and Wintering Ground Threats." Canadian Polar Commission, *Meridian*, Spring-Summer 2010, 1–5. http://www.polarcom.gc.ca/uploads/Publications/Meridian%20Newsletter/meri%20%20 10%20spring%20en.pdf.

Strategic Relations Inc. *Alberta's Feral Horses: Managing Populations.* Alberta Environment and Sustainable Resource Development, 26 April 2013. http://aep.alberta.ca/land/land-management/feral-horses/documents/FeralHorses-ManagingPopulations-2013.pdf.

Sumner, David Thomas. "'That Could Happen': Nature Writing, the Nature Fakers, and a Rhetoric of Assent." *Interdisciplinary Studies in Literature and Environment* 12, no. 2 (2005): 31–53.

Suzuki, David. "Beyond the Species at Risk Act: Recognizing the Sacred." *Journal of Environmental Law and Practice* 22, no. 3 (2011): 239–53.

Svenning, Jens-Christian, Pil B.M. Pedersen, C. Josh Donlan, Rasmus Ejrnæs, Søren Faurby, Mauro Galetti, Dennis M. Hansen, Brody Sandel, Christopher J. Sandom, John W. Terborgh, and Frans W.M. Vera. "Science for a Wilder Anthropocene: Synthesis and Future Directions for Trophic Rewilding Research." *Proceedings of the National Academy of Sciences* 113, no. 4 (2016): 898–906.

Sykes, Katie. "Human Drama, Animal Trials: What the Mediaeval Animal Trials Can Teach Us about Justice for Animals." *Animal Law* 17, no. 2 (2011): 273–312.

Taber, Richard D., and Neil F. Payne. *Wildlife Conservation and Human Welfare: United States and Canadian Perspectives.* Malabar, FL: Krieger, 2003.

Taylor, Brenda, Laurie Kremsater, and Rick Ellis. *Adaptive Management of Forests in British Columbia.* BC Ministry of Forests, 1997. https://www.for.gov.bc.ca/hfd/pubs/docs/Sil/sil426-1.pdf.

Taylor, Darren. "Shooting Back at Bear Hunt Critics." *SooToday*, 23 April 2014. http://www.sootoday.com/content/news/details.asp?c=71992.

Taylor, Paul W. "The Ethics of Respect for Nature." *Environmental Ethics* 3, no. 3 (1981): 197–218. http://www.wildsreprisal.com/PDF's/Defiance%20Enthroned/The%20 Ethics%20of%20Respect%20for%20Nature.pdf.

Theberge, John, and Mary Theberge. "Opinion: Ecologists Oppose B.C. Wolf Kill." *Vancouver Sun*, 19 February 2015. http://www.vancouversun.com/technology/Opinion+Ecologists+oppose+wolf+kill/10827496/story.html.

Theberge, John, Mary Theberge, John Vucetich, and Paul Paquet. "Pitfalls of Applying Adaptive Management to a Wolf Population in Algonquin Provincial Park, Ontario." *Environmental Management* 37, no. 4 (2006): 451–60.

Thomas, Chad R., Christopher Carr, and Cynthia Keller. "Animal-Totemic Clans of Ohio Hopewellian Peoples." In *Gathering Hopewell: Society, Ritual and Ritual Interaction*, ed. Christopher Carr and D. Troy Case, 339–85. New York: Kluwer Academic and Plenum, 2004.

Thomas, Roger K. "Lloyd Morgan's Canon." In *Comparative Psychology: A Handbook*, ed. Gary Greenberg and Maury M. Haraway, 156–63. New York and London: Garland, 1998.

Thompson, Ian D., James A. Baker, Susan J. Hannon, Robert S. Rempel, and Kandyd J. Szuba. "Forest Birds and Forest Management in Ontario: Status, Management, and Policy." *Forestry Chronicle* 85, no. 2 (2009): 245–57.

Thompson, John N. "Rapid Evolution as an Ecological Process." *Trends in Ecology and Evolution* 13, no. 8 (1998): 329–32.

Thompson, Nicholas S. "The Many Perils of Ejective Anthropomorphism." *Behavior and Philosophy* 22, no. 2 (1994): 59–70.

Thornton, Clarisse, and Michael S. Quinn. "Risk Perceptions and Attitudes toward Cougars in the Southern Foothills of Alberta." *Human Dimensions of Wildlife* 15, no. 5 (2010): 359–72.

Tocker, Robyn. "Fewer Hunting Licences, Shorter Season as Deer Populations Decline." *Western Producer*, 16 October 2014. http://www.producer.com/2014/10/fewer-hunting-licences-shorter-season-as-deer-populations-decline.

Ton That, Corinne. "Cull or Harvest? Conservationists Struggle with the Deer Explosion on Sensitive Lands." *CTV News*, 23 November 2013. http://www.ctvnews.ca/canada/cull-or-harvest-conservationists-struggle-with-the-deer-explosion-on-sensitive-lands-1.1557053#ixzz3LKNLvDud.

Treves, Adrian. "Hunting for Large Carnivore Conservation." *Journal of Applied Ecology* 46 (2009): 1350–6.

Trites, Andrew. "Attacks on Whale Science Send Shameful Message." *Huffington Post*, 24 June 2014. http://www.huffingtonpost.ca/andrew-trites/canada-humpback-whales-scientists_b_5527041.html.

Tryon, Thomas, *The Country-Man's Companion, or A New Method of Ordering Horses and Sheep*. 1684. Reprint, Ann Arbour, MI: Text Creation Partnership, 2003–07. https://quod.lib.umich.edu/e/eebo/A63788.0001.001?view=toc.

United Nations. *Convention on Biological Diversity*. 1992. https://www.cbd.int/convention/text.

United Nations Educational, Scientific and Cultural Organization. *Ramsar Convention on Wetlands of International Importance Especially as Waterfowl Habitat*. 1975. http://www.ramsar.org/sites/default/files/documents/library/current_convention_text_e.pdf.

University of Guelph. "Bee Flower Choices Altered by Exposure to Pesticides: Study." Press release, 14 March 2016. http://news.uoguelph.ca/2016/03/bee-flower-choices-altered-by-exposure-to-pesticides-study.

Urbanek, Rachel E., Clayton K. Nielsen, Mae A. Davenport, and Brad D. Woodson. "Acceptability and Conflict Regarding Suburban Deer Management Methods." *Human Dimensions of Wildlife* 17, no. 6 (2012): 389–403.

VanderZwaag, David L., Maria Cecilia Engler-Palma, and Jeffrey A. Hutchings. "Canada's *Species at Risk Act* and Atlantic Salmon: Cascade of Promises, Trickles of

Protection, Sea of Challenges." *Journal of Environmental Law and Practice* 22, no. 3 (2011): 267–307. https://papers.ssrn.com/sol3/papers.cfm?abstract_id=2126177.

van Maanen, Erwin, and Ian Convery. "Rewilding: The Realisation and Reality of a New Challenge for Nature in the Twenty-First Century." In *Changing Perceptions of Nature*, ed. Ian Convery and Peter Davis, 303–19. Woodbridge, UK: Boydell, 2016. https://www.econatura.nl/wp-content/uploads/2016/01/129CPerceptionsCh29PP.pdf.

Vaske, Jerry J., and Jennifer M. Roemer. "Differences in Overall Satisfaction by Consumptive and Nonconsumptive Recreationists: A Comparative Analysis of Three Decades of Research." *Human Dimensions of Wildlife* 18, no. 3 (2013): 159–80.

Vaughan, Andrew. "Seal Product Ban in Europe 'Justifiable,' Says WTO as Canada Plans Appeal." *Financial Post*, 25 November 2013. http://business.financialpost.com/2013/11/25/seal-ban-eu-canada-ruling.

Veerman, Nicole. "Judge Dismisses Maligne Court Battle in Jasper Park." *Jasper Fitzhugh*, 12 February 2016. http://www.fitzhugh.ca/judge-dismisses-maligne-court-battle.

Venter, Oscar, Nathalie N. Brodeur, Leah Nemiroff, Brenna Belland, Ivan J. Dolinsek, and James W.A. Grant. "Threats to Endangered Species in Canada." *BioScience* 56, no. 11 (2006): 903–10.

VerCauteren, Kert. "The Deer Boom: Discussions on Population Growth and Range Expansion of the White-Tailed Deer." *USDA National Wildlife Research Center – Staff Publications*, no. 281 (August 2003). http://digitalcommons.unl.edu/cgi/viewcontent.cgi?article=1276&context=icwdm_usdanwrc.

Vickerman, Sara, and James S. Kagan. "Assessing Ecological Integrity across Jurisdictions and Scales." Paper prepared in a workshop series hosted by the Institute for Natural Resources – Oregon Biodiversity Information Center, US Geological Survey, Defenders of Wildlife, and NatureServe, December 2014. https://www.defenders.org/sites/default/files/publications/assessing-ecological-integrity-across-jurisdictions-and-scales.pdf.

Vongraven, Dag. "IUCN/SSC Polar Bear Specialist Group Comments on Request for an Increase in the Foxe Basin Total Allowable Harvest by Qikiqtaaluk Wildlife Board." IUCN/SSC Polar Bear Specialist Group, 4 October 2013. http://pbsg.npolar.no/export/sites/pbsg/en/docs/PBSG-response-FB-NWMB-Oct2013-ENG.pdf.

– "Re: Written Hearing of the Nunavut Wildlife Management Board to Consider Proposed Modification to the 2012–2013 Level of Total Allowable Harvest for the Western Hudson Bay Polar Bear Subpopulation in the Nunavut Settlement Area." IUCN/SSC Polar Bear Specialist Group, July 2012. http://pbsg.npolar.no/export/sites/pbsg/en/docs/PBSG-response-NWMB-July2012-ENG-s.pdf.

Vongraven, Dag, and Elizabeth Peacock. *Development of the Pan-Arctic Plan for Polar Bears: Background Paper*. Akureyri, Iceland: Circumpolar Biodiversity Monitoring Program, CAFF International Secretariat, 2011. https://www.caff.is/monitoring-series/22-development-of-a-pan-arctic-monitoring-plan-for-polar-bears-background-paper.

Waithaka, John. "Policy on Management of Hyperabundant Wildlife Populations in Canada's National Parks." Paper presented at the Parks for Tomorrow Conference, Calgary, 8–11 May 2008. http://prism.ucalgary.ca/bitstream/1880/46916/3/Waithaka.pdf.

Waldick, Ruth. "Noteworthy – Legislation, Jurisdiction, and the Species at Risk Act." Interview with Ken Harris, chief of habitat conservation, Canadian Wildlife Service. Policy Horizons Canada, March 2004. http://www.horizons.gc.ca/eng/content/noteworthy-legislation-jurisdiction-and-species-risk-act.

Waller, Donald M., and William S. Alverson. "The White-Tailed Deer: A Keystone Herbivore." *Wildlife Society Bulletin* 25, no. 2 (1997): 217–26.

Walters, Carl. *Adaptive Management of Renewable Resources.* New York: Macmillan, 1986.

– "Challenges in Adaptive Management of Riparian and Coastal Ecosystems." *Conservation Ecology* 1, no. 2 (1997). http://www.consecol.org/vol1/iss2/art1.

Waters, Megan, Naomi Rose, and Paul Todd. *The Economics of Polar Bear Hunting in Canada.* International Fund for Animal Welfare and Humane Society International, December 2009. http://www.ifaw.org/sites/default/files/Polar%20Bear%20Hunt%20Economic%20Study.pdf.

Weber, Bob. "Scientists Criticize Alberta Wolf Bounties." *Global News*, 12 February 2014. http://globalnews.ca/news/1142366/scientists-criticize-alberta-wolf-bounties.

Wells, Jeff, Susan Casey-Lefkowitz, Gabriela Chavarria, and Simon Dyer. *Danger in the Nursery: Impact on Birds of Tar Sands Oil Development in Canada's Boreal Forest.* Natural Resources Defense Council, December 2008. https://www.nrdc.org/wildlife/borealbirds.pdf.

Wenzel, George. *Animal Rights, Human Rights: Ecology, Economy, and Ideology in the Canadian Arctic.* London: Belhaven, 1991.

– "Inuit and Polar Bears: Cultural Observations from a Hunt Near Resolute Bay, N.W.T." *Arctic* 36, no. 1 (1983): 90–4.

– *Sometimes Hunting Can Seem Like Business: Polar Bear Sport Hunting in Nunavut.* Edmonton: Canadian Circumpolar Institute Press, 2008.

Wesserberg, Gideon, Erik E. Osnas, Robert E. Rolley, and Michael D. Samuel. "Host Culling as an Adaptive Management Tool for Chronic Wasting Disease in White-Tailed Deer: A Modelling Study." *Journal of Applied Ecology* 46, no. 2 (2009): 457–66.

West Coast Environmental Law. "Fisheries Act Amendments Brought into Force Despite Widespread Opposition." 24 November 2013. https://www.wcel.org/media-release/fisheries-act-amendments-brought-force-despite-widespread-opposition.

Western Sportsman. "Hunting Forecast 2014: Ontario." http://www.westernsportsman.com/?s=hunting+forecast&x=0&y=0.

Wetherell, Donald G. *Wildlife, Land and People: A Century of Change in Prairie Canada.* Montreal and Kingston: McGill-Queen's University Press, 2016.

Whitaker, D.M., P.D. Taylor, and I.G. Warkentin. "Survival of Adult Songbirds in Boreal Forest Landscapes Fragmented by Clearcuts and Natural Openings." *Avian Conservation and Ecology* 3, no. 1 (2008). http://www.ace-eco.org/vol3/iss1/art5.

White, Lynn, Jr. "The Historical Roots of Our Ecological Crisis." *Science*, 10 March 1967. http://www.uvm.edu/~gflomenh/ENV-NGO-PA395/articles/Lynn-White.pdf.

Whitehead, Hal, Sara Iverson, Boris Worm, and Heike Lotze. "Independent Marine Scientists Respond to Senate Fisheries Committee Report 'The Sustainable Management of Grey Seal Populations: A Path toward the Recovery of Cod and Other Groundfish Stocks.'" *Marketwired*, 6 November 2012. http://www.marketwired.com/press-release/independent-marine-scientists-respond-senate-fisheries-committee-report-the-sustainable-1722244.htm.

Wielgus, Robert S., Hugh S. Robinson, and Hilary S. Cooley. "Effects of White-Tailed Deer Expansion and Cougar Hunting on Cougar, Deer and Human Interactions." *Transactions of the 72nd North American Wildlife and Natural Resources Conference* (2014): 211–16. https://wildlifemanagement.institute/sites/default/files/2016-09/4-Effects_of_White-Tailed.pdf.

Wiersma, Yolanda F., Thomas D. Nudds, and Donald H. Rivard. "Models to Distinguish Effects of Landscape Patterns and Human Population Pressures Associated with Species Loss in Canadian National Parks." *Landscape Ecology* 19, no. 7 (2004): 773–86.

Wiig, Øystein, Jon Aars, and Erik W. Born. "Effects of Climate Change on Polar Bears." *Science Progress* 91, no. 2 (2008): 151–73. https://www.researchgate.net/profile/Jon_Aars/publication/23184499_Effects_of_climate_change_on_polar_bears/links/02e7e5375c680c84cf000000/Effects-of-climate-change-on-polar-bears.pdf.

Wiken, Ed, W.G.B. Smith, Jean Cinq-Mars, C. Latsch, and David Gauthier. "Habitat Integrity in Canada: Wildlife Conservation at the Crossroads." Background paper for the National Conference on Guidelines and Tools for the Evaluation of Natura 2000 Sites in France, Montpellier, France, 3–5 March 2003. http://ccea.org/Downloads/en_relatedpublications_habitatintegrity.pdf.

Wilderness Committee. "Canada's Boreal Region." n.d. https://www.wilderness committee.org/manitoba/what_we_do/protecting_wild_lands/boreal_forest.

– "End Logging in Ontario and Manitoba Parks." 4 June 2015. https://www.wildernesscommittee.org/publication/end_logging_ontario_and_manitoba_parks.

Wildgen, Gabriel. "Canada's Government Needs to Stop Providing Subsidies for Fur." *Huffington Post*, 9 January 2015. http://www.huffingtonpost.ca/gabriel-wildgen/fur-farming_b_6437000.html.

Wildlife Trusts. "Bovine TB: Pilot Culls Ineffective." News brief, March 2014. http://www.dorsetwildlifetrust.org.uk/hres/bTB-pilot-culls-ineffective-UPDATED-March-2014.pdf.

Williamson, Douglas F. *In the Black: Status, Management, and Trade of the American Black Bear (Ursus americanus) in North America*. World Wildlife Fund, April 2002. http://www.njfishandwildlife.com/pdf/bear/policy_lit/williamson_traffic.pdf.

Wilson, Edward O. "Biophilia and the Conservation Ethic." In *Environment*, vol. 1, *Thinking and Knowing about the Environment and Nature*, ed. Jules Pretty, 23–9. London: Sage, 2006.

– *In Search of Nature*. Washington, DC: Island, 1996.

Wilson, Jeremy. "Green Lobbies, Pressure Groups and Environmental Policies." In *Canadian Environmental Policy: Ecosystems, Politics and Process*, ed. Robert Boardman, 109–25. Toronto: Oxford University Press, 1992.

Wilson, Steven F. *Recommendations for Predator-Prey Management to Benefit the Recovery of Mountain Caribou in British Columbia*. BC Ministry of Environment, 31 March 2009. http://www.env.gov.bc.ca/wld/speciesconservation/mc/files/Recommendations_Predator-Prey_Management_Final.pdf.

Wilson, Steven F., and D.M. Shackleton. *Backcountry Research and Mountain Goats: A Proposed Research and Management Plan*. BC Ministry of Environment, Lands and Parks, March 2001. http://www.env.gov.bc.ca/wld/documents/techpub/b103.pdf.

Winter, Jim. "Sealing: A Rightful Occupation." *Fishing News International*, 1 March 2007. http://freenewfoundlandlabrador.blogspot.mx/2007/03/sealing-is-rightful-occupation.html.

Wires, Linda R. *The Double-Crested Cormorant: Plight of a Feathered Pariah*. New Haven, CT: Yale University Press, 2014.

Wires, Linda R., and Francesca J. Cuthbert. "Historic Populations of the Double-Crested Cormorant (*Phalacrocorax auritus*): Implications for Conservation and Management in the 21st Century." *Waterbirds* 29, no. 1 (2006): 9–37.

Wise, Steven M. "Animal Rights, One Step at a Time." In *Animal Rights: Current Debates and New Directions*, ed. Cass R. Sunstein and Martha C. Nussbaum, 19–50. Oxford: Oxford University Press, 2004.

Wittmann, Karen, Jerry J. Vaske, Michael Manfredo, and Harry C. Zinn. "Standards for Lethal Response to Problem Urban Wildlife." *Human Dimensions of Wildlife* 3, no. 4 (1998): 29–48.

Wojciechowski, Stéphane, Christopher Brassard, Stewart Elgie, C. Scott Findlay, and Sue Mckee. "SARA's Safety Net Provisions and the Effectiveness of Species at Risk Protection on Non-Federal Lands." *Journal of Environmental Law and Practice* 22, no. 3 (2011): 203–22.

Wolf Awareness. "Wolf-Caribou Conservation Dilemma." n.d. http://wolfawarenessinc.org/predator-prey-relationships.

Wood, Forrest, Jr. *The Delights and Dilemmas of Hunting: The Hunting Versus Anti-Hunting Debate*. Lanham, MD: University Press of America, 1997.

Woodley, Stephen. *Engaging Visitors in Ecological Integrity*. Parks Canada, n.d. http://www.umanitoba.ca/outreach/pparfm/presentations/woodley.pdf.

– "Planning and Managing for Ecological Integrity in Canada's National Parks." In *Parks and Protected Areas in Canada: Planning and Management*, ed. Philip Dearden and Rick Rollins, 111–32. Don Mills, ON: Oxford University Press, 2009.

World Commission on Environment and Development. *Our Common Future*. United Nations, 1987. http://www.exteriores.gob.es/Portal/es/PoliticaExteriorCooperacion/Desarrollosostenible/Documents/Informe%20Brundtland%20(En%20ingl%C3%A9s).pdf.

World Wildlife Fund. "Dramatic Polar Bear Population Decline Needs Action: WWF." 17 November 2014. http://www.wwf.ca/newsroom/?16381/ Dramatic-polar-bear-population-decline-needs-action-WWF.

– *Living Planet Report 2016: Risk and Resilience in a New Era.* World Wildlife Fund International, 2016. http://awsassets.panda.org/downloads/lpr_living_planet_report_2016.pdf.

– "Record Low Sea Ice Underscores Need for Marine Protections." 24 March 2017. http://www.wwf.ca/newsroom/?24521/Record-low-sea-ice-underscores-need-for-marine-protections.

– "WWF-Canada Statement on the Clyde River Federal Court of Appeal Ruling." 20 August 2015. http://www.wwf.ca/newsroom/?18201/WWF-Canada-statement-on-the-Clyde-River-Federal-Court-of-Appeal-ruling.

Wristen, Karen. "Letter from the Executive Director." Living Oceans Society, *Rising Tide*, Spring 2014. http://www.livingoceans.org/sites/default/files/e-rising-tide-spring2014.pdf.

Wynne, Clive D.L. "The Emperor's New Anthropomorphism." *Behavior Analyst Today* 6, no. 3 (2005): 151–4.

Zoocheck Canada. "Spring Bear Hunt May Be Reintroduced in Ontario – Please Act Now!" 13 November 2013. https://www.facebook.com/canadazoocheck/posts/10151998374869588.

Index